FIGHTING AUSCHWITZ

FIGHTING AUSCHWITZ

THE RESISTANCE MOVEMENT
IN THE CONCENTRATION CAMP

Józef Garliński

Orbis Books (London) Ltd
London 1994

By the same author:

Poland, SOE and the Allies
    (English edition of Politycy i żolnierze)   1969
Resistance in Europe (co-author)   1973
Fighting Auschwitz   1975
Hitler's Last Weapons   1977
Intercept, Secrets of the Enigma War   1979
The Swiss Corridor   1981
1939: A Retrospect Forty Years After (co-author)   1983
Poland in the Second World War   1985
The Survival of Love   1991
The Reconstuction of Poland, 1914–1923 (co-author)   1992

A Polish edition of Fighting Auschwitz was published in 1974 by
Odnova Ltd (London). That edition includes more detailed bio-
graphical information and lists of the names of all participants in
the resistance movement in the camp.

The Author and the Publishers are grateful to
Colonel Jan Sochacki and Miss Wanda Jagoda for their
generous grants which made this edition possible.

First published in 1975 by
Julian Friedmann Publishers Ltd

This edition published in 1994 by
Orbis Books (London) Ltd
66 Kenway Road, London SW5 0RD

ISBN 0–901149–35–7

Printed and bound in Great Britain by
Biddles Ltd, Guildford and King's Lynn

To my wife

AUTHOR'S NOTE

In English the name Pilecki is pronounced 'Piletski'.

Union of Military Organisation is a literal translation of the Polish *Związek Organizacji Wojskowej.* In Polish this is grammatically incorrect, but it was the name as Pilecki wrote it.

The portrait of the author was taken when he was twenty years old in the uniform of a Polish Cavalry Cadet. The same picture was later used to make forged documents by friends of his, in Warsaw in 1944, who were trying to help him escape from Wittenberge, a small sub-camp of Neuengamme, where the author was sent after being deported from Auschwitz in August 1943. The courier bringing the documents to Wittenberge never arrived and the escape plan fell through. On the 4th May, 1945, the author was freed by the Seventh Armoured Division of the American Army.

vi

CONTENTS

ILLUSTRATIONS AND MAPS

The photographs used in this book are from the International Tracing Service in Arolsen, from the European Color Productions Ltd. and from private sources.

The portraits of resistance workers are in the order in which they appear in the text. The majority of the photographs are from what remains of the camp archives (Political Department).

ABBREVIATIONS

ACPW	*Akcja Cywilna Pomocy Więźniom* (Civil action for Help to Prisoners)
AK	*Armia Krajowa* (Home Army)
BIP	*Biuro Informacji i Propagandy* (Bureau of Information and Propaganda)
DAW	*Deutsche Ausrüstungswerke* (German Munitions Factory)
Gestapo	*Geheime Staatspolizei* (Secret State Police)
GOPR	*Górskie Ochotnicze Pogotowie Ratunkowe* (Mountain Rescue Organization)
HWL	*Hauptwirtschaftslager* (Main Industrial Camp)
Kedyw	*Komenda Dywersji* (Diversionary Command)
Kripo	*Kriminalpolizei* (Criminal Police)
NKVD	*Narodnyi Komissariat Vnutrennich Dyel* (People's Commissariat of Internal Affairs)
NN	*Nacht und Nebel* (Night and Fog)
ONR	*Obóz Narodowo-Radykalny* (National-Radical Camp)
PKP	*Polityczny Komitet Porozumiewawczy* (Political Advisory Council)
PPR	*Polska Partia Robotnicza* (Polish Workers' Party)
PPS	*Polska Partia Socjalistycza* (Polish Socialist Party)
PWOK	*Pomoc Więźniom Obozów Koncentracyjnych* (Help for the Prisoners of Concentration Camps)
RGO	*Rada Główna Opiekuńcza* (Chief Welfare Board)
RSHA	*Reichssicherheitshauptamt* (Chief Security Office)
SD	*Sicherheitsdienst* (Security Service)
SL	*Stronnictwo Ludowe* (Peasant Party)
SN	*Stronnictwo Narodowe* (National Party)
SOE	Special Operations Executive
SS	*Schutzstaffel* (Security Corps)
SZP	*Służba Zwycięstwu Polski* (In the Service of Poland's Victory)
TAP	*Tajna Armia Polska* (Secret Polish Army)
Wici	The youth organization of the Peasant Party
WVHA	*Wirtschafts- und Verwaltungshauptamt* (Economic and Administrative Head Office)
ZOW	*Związek Organizacji Wojskowej* (Union of Military Organization)
ZWZ	*Związek Walki Zbrojnej* (Union for Armed Struggle)

FOREWORD

If ever war was justified – and this 'if' is a big one – it was the war against German nazism that raged from 1939 to 1945. All its damage, death, and suffering were worthwhile, to get rid of the nazi system; and in particular of the system's concentration camps, which became an indispensable feature of it.

Of these camps, none were less than appalling. Among them the Auschwitz-Birkenau complex has a serious claim to be considered the worst; not only because it was much the largest. In all the records of what men have done to other men, there is no other place where so many people have been put to death so fast: over three million souls, in an area of fifteen square miles, in less than five years.

There are already a great many books on Auschwitz; a full list of books and articles on it would run to over seven thousand items. Why add another? Because it deals systematically for the first time with an element in the life of the camp that does extraordinary credit to its prisoners: the resistance movement that was created inside it and that, even in those conditions, the SS could never destroy. The author was for a short time a forced inmate himself, which gives him a special claim to touch the subject. Before he went there, he had been in resistance outside, as an officer of the Armia Krajowa, the Polish Home Army that was later decimated in the Warsaw rising. He had the good fortune to survive his months in Auschwitz. Looking back on them from a different circle of the SS inferno – Neuengamme, his next camp – he had insight enough to perceive traces of resistance activity in the place he had left: and could appreciate that he had had no chance to participate directly himself, because clandestine security in Auschwitz had to be so tight.

No one could pass through those camps without bringing searing memories away from them. Yet, thirty years on, Józef Garliński is able to master his emotions, and to compose as dispassionate, as impartial, and as comprehensive an account as the state of the surviving evidence he has seen allows. He lives in political exile, in west London; but has shown the tenacity and ingenuity to be expected of an old resister, in penetrating sources in contemporary Poland. Exile has provided one more barrier to be overcome, but no insuperable obstacle. He is as fair to the communist resisters as he is to their strongest Polish opponents; he is even as fair as he can be to the SS. He has simply followed his judgement and his sources, with what meticulous accuracy his footnotes testify; as does the award to him, for an earlier version of this book, of a doctorate by the University of London. Yet this is a great deal more than a refurbished thesis. It is a memorial to some of the bravest of those millions of brave women and men who struggled, in the teeth of the evidence, in spite of ordinary 'commonsensical' prudence, to resist the apparently irresistible juggernaut of nazism. The Poles, defeated in the first three weeks of war – occupied by both their secular enemies in combination, then fought over by them, and wholly occupied by each in turn – had an infinitely tougher war than the unbombed Americans, the unoccupied English, or even the comparatively gently-handled French. Nevertheless they had an exceptional record, even among the nazi-occupied countries, for reluctance to accept the new ordering of Europe; and some of them did astounding things.

Think for a moment of what Witold Pilecki, one of this book's central figures, did: he let himself be arrested by the Germans, in the deliberate hope that he would be sent to Auschwitz; succeeded in this aim; and then succeeded in two more, even more daunting. He set up the nucleus of an anti-nazi organization in the camp; and then escaped from it, to pass out word of what was happening inside. (Escape from Auschwitz was more common than from camps that were within German-speaking territory; over six hundred escapers are recorded, of whom about a third got away.) This is the sort of man with whom the following pages deal. They provide a clear, unadorned record of a story that needs no adornment: the tale of what people can do, at their last gasp from every normal point of view – military, medical, social – to show what strength and toughness and dignity and compassion lie in mankind.

                                                        M. R. D. Foot

INTRODUCTION

During my imprisonment in Auschwitz in 1943 I did not have any direct contact with the underground movement. I was in the Penal Company, in a block isolated from the rest of the camp.* Several dozen prisoners from my transport were sent there, probably on the instruction of the *Gestapo* in Warsaw, where we had come from. Before my arrest, I had belonged to the Polish underground military organization, the Home Army, and in the camp I noticed several signs that there was an underground prisoners' organization.

At that time, struggling for survival, I did not consider the matter too seriously, but, in the same year, I was taken off to another camp at Neuengamme near Hamburg, where, living in better conditions than in Auschwitz, I found out very much more about the underground camp organization. After the war I often thought about it, but only a few years ago was I able to study it seriously. I was encouraged, in fact almost forced to do so, by the memoirs of a former Auschwitz inmate, Witold Pilecki, who went voluntarily to the camp in order to build up an underground military resistance movement. These memoirs, in the form of a concise military report, which is to be found in the *Polish Underground Movement (1939–1945) Study Trust* in London, made a great impression on me. I realized that it was a very significant historical document, dealing with completely unknown details of certain underground activities during the last war. These activities testify to the great reserves of courage, determination and self-sacrifice which reveal themselves at times when the struggle for human dignity and freedom must be undertaken.

When deciding to write on this subject I was aware that one of the greatest difficulties would be the lack of German documents relating to the whole question. They would have been in the files of the Auschwitz Political Department (camp *Gestapo*), which contained reports submitted by responsible *SS*-men, testimonies of prisoners accused of underground activity, reports by camp informers, details of

---

* Prisoners were sent to the Penal Company for various offences in the camp. Sometimes they went there on the recommendation of the local *Gestapo* responsible for their deportation. As well as the twenty-five strokes, which every prisoner received on entering the Penal Company, there was cruel discipline, work after the evening roll-call, being driven on with sticks, and so on. The men's Penal Company was situated in Birkenau, the women's in the sub-camp of Budy.

escapes, and correspondence with the authorities in Oranienburg and Berlin. The possession of such material would have made my task very much easier, and would have provided some indication as to how far the *SS* were aware of this undercover work. It would also have been possible to compare such information with the testimony of the underground workers themselves.

Unfortunately these documents no longer exist. For several months before the evacuation of the camp, the authorities had begun to destroy all the documents concerning mass-killings, followed by all the administrative files, among which, of course, were those of the Political Department. Auschwitz, where so many people were put to death during the last war, was given special attention by the *SS* when it came to concealing traces of these crimes. The destruction of the camp's *Gestapo* files was not peculiar to Auschwitz. The archives of Buchenwald are today to be found at the *International Tracing Service* at Arolsen in West Germany, but with one important omission: there are no documents relating to the Political Department.

As a result of this, in studying the question of the Auschwitz underground it has been necessary to concentrate on Polish documents which survived the last war. Undercover communications with the camp were solely in Polish hands. Orders and reports, both Polish and international, originating from the camp underground were sent to the Polish resistance forces in occupied Poland, who forwarded them to the Polish Government and General Staff in London. All documents relating to the occupation of Poland during the last war were sent, after it was over, by the political and military authorities to the *Polish Underground Movement (1939–1945) Study Trust*, and it was of these archives that I made the greatest use. Another extensive source of material consists of the archives and publications of the *State Museum of Auschwitz*. My status as a political refugee has not allowed me to visit Poland, but a great number of personal contacts, dating from the war years and from my own imprisonment in Auschwitz, have enabled me to obtain almost everything I required. I felt that those who gave me help did so in the belief that the resulting work would give a true picture of what had taken place.

In addition to these two essential Polish sources, it has been necessary to consult the archives of the *International Tracing Service* in West Germany, which include the surviving dossiers of all the German concentration camps. This evidence has been supplemented by thousands of additional documents, based on personal accounts, publications and research. I spent many very busy days at the *International Tracing Service* offices, and I have been in constant contact with it since then.

I have also used the collections of the *Wiener Library* in London, the *Netherlands State Institute for War Documentation* in Amsterdam, the *Yad Vashem* in Jerusalem and the *BBC Written Archives Centre* in Reading.

However, access to the archives and collections of the above institutions provided only incomplete results, and had they been the sole sources of information, the detailed work on Auschwitz's underground movement could not have been possible. It has been necessary to delve into a far wider selection of publications, which have appeared in many languages and which deal with, or contain information on, the Auschwitz underground. Some works are devoted exclusively to this subject. It is significant that not a single one of these has appeared in West Germany. It must be stressed that some of these publications are suspect: political considerations have obliterated or falsified the record of events.

But it is not documents or publications which are the basis of my work. I have relied on unpublished, personal statements. I have had to seek out former Auschwitz inmates living in Poland and elsewhere in order to gain facts and information, often in the strictest confidence. I have had to arrange personal meetings, use questionnaires and correspondence extensively, in order to achieve the necessary results. Every fact has had to be re-checked, every answer weighed in the light of the informant's character. Some of my letters were never answered, and many of my informants, especially those in Poland, whom I managed to convince of the importance of cooperation, have asked for their confidence to be respected. The subject, as I have said, has been exploited and distorted for political reasons. Very often I was able to gain necessary information thanks to the fact, which inspired trust, that I myself had been a prisoner in Auschwitz.

Naturally a considerable part of my work has been based on the memoirs of Witold Pilecki, whom I mentioned earlier. A close examination of his character, of his past and of his idealist convictions, leads me to believe that his narrative is true and that its facts are correct. I have of course checked them and have compared them with other sources.

I have presented the underground movement chronologically as it developed over the years, interweaving it with the story of the camp itself. Changes in and around the camp affected underground work, and I have also dealt with the most important sub-camp, Birkenau, and the women's camp there; I have mentioned other sub-camps, such as Monowice, only superficially, since there are very few facts to go on, and their distance from Auschwitz meant that their underground efforts were really quite separate.

Extensive efforts have been made to supply prisoners' camp

numbers and they appear in the index. If the number is missing, this means that it is not recorded in the archives of the *Auschwitz Museum*, the *International Tracing Service* or the many publications and other accounts. Knowledge of the prisoner's number is very important, since it allows an accurate assessment of his date of arrival in the camp. This is possible thanks to the excellent work done by Danuta Czech in her *Calendar of events in the concentration camp of Auschwitz-Birkenau.*

I have adopted the principle of approaching each source critically, in order to check each fact. I have accorded greater significance to some writers, having arrived at the conclusion that they are objective and less likely to indulge their fancies. Sometimes one source alone was adequate for substantiating a fact.

In this work, which is documentary in character, I have tried to avoid too frequent analysis and interpretation, believing that facts speak for themselves. Sometimes, when it has been impossible to ascertain all the facts, I have had to resort to inference. In doing this I have attempted to present the truth and not defend any point of view or attitude.

I am well aware that amongst the prisoners in Auschwitz and its sub-camps there took place secret religious services, cultural activities, lectures and various attempts at teaching and learning. I have had to omit them from this account, since they were not organized on any permanent basis and do not constitute an underground movement in the full sense of the word. They were, of course, a demonstration of protest at the iron ring which the *SS* had tightened around the prisoners; they were a sign of rebellion against the system whose aim was to stupefy and destroy. My work, bounded as it is by well-defined limits, cannot include them, although they had great significance for the operation of the underground movement.

All forenames, surnames and place-names are written in their native spelling. For some widely known place-names, such as Warsaw and Cracow, the English forms have been used. The SEER system of transliteration has been used for Russian names. *SS* ranks and functions, as well as expressions commonly used in the camp, have all been translated into English. A list of the *SS* ranks and their British equivalents is included in the appendices.

This book would have appeared much later and with more imperfections had it not been for the professional advice and assistance of Professor Michael Foot, Professor James Joll and Dr. Antony Polonsky, to all of whom I am deeply indebted. I owe a similar debt to my friend from Auschwitz, Jerzy Budkiewicz, who is at present a full-time employee of the *International Tracing Service* in Arolsen. I have relied on his assistance for some years and his replies to dozens of questions and letters. I have also received help from the historical institutes mentioned earlier.

I must express my special gratitude to all those men and women, ex-prisoners of Auschwitz, who, by letter or conversation, recounted to me their experiences and details of the underground movement in the camp. It is impossible to mention them all here by name, and in any case many wish to remain anonymous. I want to assure them that I have done my utmost to ensure that the information received from them has contributed to the creation of an objective picture of the underground movement in Auschwitz. It is one of the least known secrets of the Second World War.

London, June 1974.

Józef Garliński

Part One

CHAPTER 1

Voluntarily to Auschwitz; the camp and its organization

1

It was the early morning of September 1940, when a man came out of a small building in a residential district of northern Warsaw and briskly set out towards the centre of the city. The pavements were still wet with dew. Trams clanged, lorries rattled by, and trucks, packed with German soldiers, rushed along, noisily overtaking all other vehicles. Men and women, silent and withdrawn, began to crowd the pavements, moving towards the main roads. Bundled-up country women with cans on their backs went from house to house, bringing milk to the capital from the nearby villages.

The man, now in the midst of a crowd of pedestrians, made his way through them decisively. Of medium height, well-built, about forty years old, with a quiet, resolute expression on his face, he walked like someone who had a more important object in view than getting on to a tram.

Suddenly the peaceful scene of people going to their work was disturbed. A tramcar drew up, and before it came to a stop men were jumping off and, shoving and pushing, running into the side streets.

'Go back, go back. German trucks, a round-up!'

Within a few seconds the street was deserted. On it remained alone the one man, who still went on his way with the same decided step. Now, round the corner, could be seen police trucks and figures crouched against the walls. Green uniforms appeared as if from out of the ground.

'*Halt, halt.* Hands up!'

2

In the covered riding-school of the 1st Regiment of Lancers over a thousand men lay side by side on the sawdust. Faces down and hands stretched out in front of them, they looked like rag dolls. But they were alive for they fidgeted, coughed, shifted in their positions. Several *SS*-men, with whips in their hands, moved around between the thronged bodies, treading on feet and heads, dealing out blows, kicking and swearing. In the galleries that ran round the riding-school stood machine-guns, aimed at the men lying below; beside them were more men in green uniforms.[1]

This scene was the result of the third round-up in Warsaw. This time the Germans did not hunt the people on the streets, but surrounded several districts, chiefly inhabited by professional classes, and led out all the men from their houses. The round-ups had two targets: to terrorize the nation and to catch a certain number of underground workers by throwing out a large net at random.

The man who had deliberately marched towards the *SS*-men and had allowed himself to be caught now lay among a heap of bodies. He did not fidget nor utter a sound, and thus had so far avoided the whips and boots of the *SS* guards. Lying there quietly, he could collect his thoughts and consider the situation.

His name was Witold Pilecki; he was an officer of the 13th regiment of Uhlans. In his pocket he had a skilfully forged identity card in the name of Tomasz Serafiński; it had been made for a reserve officer who had escaped capture after the capitulation of Warsaw and who for some time had hidden in the flat which Pilecki sub-

German soldiers arresting Polish civilians.

sequently lived in. Serafiński had left an insurance card behind him and the new lodger began to use it. Later other papers were forged to match it.[2]

The mere fact that Pilecki was illegally walking about free was quite enough, if he were picked up, to send him to prison. In December 1939 the German authorities ordered all officers, regular and reserve, to come forward of their own accord and go to POW camps, and on December 14th they specified the place of assembly. Those who did not do so were threatened with death. Out of about 20,000 officers who were hiding in Warsaw at that time, 400 are said to have come forward.

Pilecki, of course, did not obey the German order and began to play one of the leading parts in the Secret Polish Army, one of the numerous underground organizations. It later merged with the official secret forces, called the Home Army. This activity, in the eyes of the occupying forces, would have qualified him for the death sentence. But it was nothing, however, compared to what he was shortly to attempt. Pilecki had proposed to his commander that he should be assigned to a new task. In Warsaw there were plenty of other men who could carry out his functions. But a couple of months earlier the Nazis had opened a concentration camp at Auschwitz. Pilecki wanted to go there in order to organize the prisoners, look for means of resistance and mutual assistance, and send reports to Warsaw. Some form of contact with the outside world had to be found. The problem was how to get into Auschwitz? Pilecki was ready to let himself be arrested in a round-up.[3]

The idea was so daring that it was hard to accept at first. It was only after much insistence on Pilecki's part, when it was evident that he was really prepared to carry through his plan, that his commander accepted the proposal. All the details were discussed and the elements of liaison settled.

Now, when the first part of the plan had been realized, when he lay, stiffening in discomfort on the wet sawdust, he could once again reflect on his intentions and think over the whole enterprise. He was still in Warsaw, only yards away from friends and freedom, but the heavy hand of the occupiers, which he had himself sought, pinned him to the ground. He no longer had any choice; already around him panted and groaned the men who would shortly become his fellow camp-mates and would, in all probability, leave their bones there. Had he done the right thing; would he have the strength of body and mind to survive; would he have the energy to fulfil his task?

Two days later, after a few men had been released, the remainder were taken to Auschwitz.

3

In the office of *SS* General Eric von dem Bach-Zelewski in the police building in Wrocław, a conference took place. Present at it were *SS* Colonel Richard Glücks, Inspector of Concentration Camps, *SS* Colonel Arpad Wiegand, von dem Bach's right-hand man, and several other *SS* officers. Outside there were 30° Centigrade of frost, but in the well-heated office it was so hot that some of those present discreetly undid their uniform collars.

A German propaganda poster in Poland after the Polish-German campaign in 1939, intended to demoralize the Poles, showing a wounded Polish soldier telling Chamberlain: 'England, you have done this!'

It was the beginning of 1940, a few months after Germany attacked Poland in September 1939 and the partition of Poland between Germany and Soviet Russia. The *SS*-men discussed the plan of a new concentration camp. Up to this time six of these camps existed in the Great German *Reich*: Dachau, founded in the Spring of 1933, less than two months after Hitler's assumption of power, Sachsen-hausen, Buchenwald, Flossenbürg, Mauthausen and the women's camp at Ravensbrück. The camp at Oranienburg, founded in 1933, was closed down a year later. Just before the war there were alto-gether about 25,000 prisoners in these camps. Now, although the western lands of Poland had already been officially integrated into the German state, the Polish underground resistance had started to grow and the *SS* officers, planning mass arrests, directed their gaze towards Silesia, seeing there the place for the next camp. Their thoughts were of the future. They wished to create a camp for Polish prisoners and also find a site centrally placed in relation to all the territories which had not yet been conquered but which, in the course of the next few years, the *SS* believed would come under Nazi control. The chosen site would require convenient railway

Arrested Polish peasants and workers before deportation.

access and should be somewhat distant from larger centres of population. After discussion and examination of a map, the assembled officers accepted Arpad Wiegand's advice and their choice fell on Auschwitz.[4]

Before the war this was a small town in Polish Silesia, at the confluence of the Vistula and Soła rivers. It had a population of about 12,000, and was an unhealthy, malaria-ridden, poorly industrialized, ugly town, situated right on the edge of the Polish state. The choice was made and Glücks sent a report to the Head of the SS, Heinrich Himmler. As a result of this, on February 1st, 1940, a Commission went to Auschwitz. Though the Commissioners gave a negative opinion, a second Commission was sent in April under SS Major Rudolf Höss. They also came to the conclusion that the site was unsuitable for a camp designed to hold many thousands of prisoners. These people would have to live and work there for some time, so at least water and the most primitive sanitary facilities would be required. The site did not possess these two basic requisites. The water was foul, marshy and poisonous, and there was nowhere for impurities to be drained off. Despite this conclusion, Höss prepared a report in which he suggested that use could be made of the selected site. Himmler gave Höss his support and on April 27th an order was issued from his office that a concentration camp was to be constructed there. Two days later Glücks appointed Höss as Commandant.[5]

4

The site, which was soon to become the greatest cemetery in the history of the world, was at first of modest appearance. There were some old Austrian artillery barracks consisting of 20 brick buildings, mainly single-storied, dilapidated and filthy. They stood on the left bank of the river Soła in a suburb called Zasole. Next to the barracks stood several buildings belonging to the Polish Tobacco Monopoly, which were also within the perimeter of the proposed camp.

Höss chose five SS-men and arrived in Auschwitz on April 29th. On May 20th, SS NCO Gerhard Palitzsch brought thirty Germans from Sachsenhausen, almost all of them criminals. These were the first 'trusties' of the new camp, and they were given numbers from 1 to 30. In charge of them was No. 1, Bruno Brodniewicz, a German with a Polish surname, who became the camp's Senior Prisoner. The second newcomer to attain equal rank (an exceptional arrangement) was another German with the Polish surname, Leo Wieczorek, No. 30. Palitzsch was appointed *Rapportführer*, responsible for

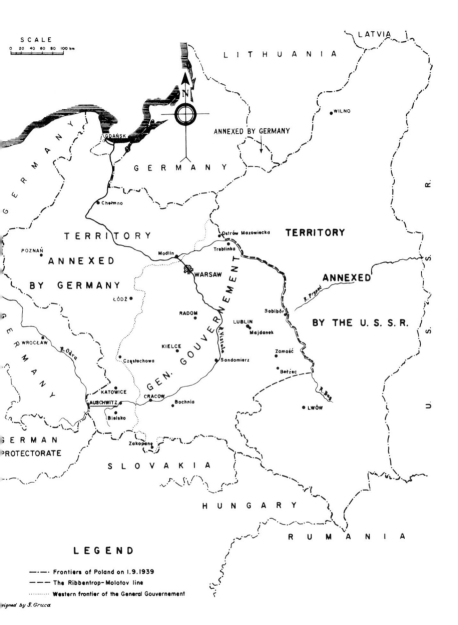

Map of Poland 14.6.1940, divided between Germany and Soviet Russia with the General Gouvernement in the centre.

discipline.[6] These three names have gone down in the history of Auschwitz.

The Town Council drafted 300 local Jews to the camp, and the cleaning-up of the neglected buildings began. They were guarded by fifteen *SS* cavalry-men, sent from Cracow. Even the most elementary tasks had not been completed when an inquiry came from the Department of Police and Security in Wrocław as to how soon the camp would be ready to receive the first consignments of prisoners. Before a reply had been sent, a train (for once a passenger train) arrived at the station in Auschwitz. It brought 728 Poles, all of them political prisoners, from a prison in Tarnów. They were mainly young men, caught on the frontier as they were attempting to reach Hungary *en route* to France, where the Polish Army was re-forming (and they were, therefore, called 'tourists' in the camp). In addition there were a number of priests and school-teachers, and several dozen Jews. The members of this transport were given numbers from 31 to 758 and they were put into quarantine in a building which had belonged to the Tobacco Monopoly.[7]

This first transport arrived in Auschwitz on June 14th, 1940, and this date is accepted as the official beginning of the camp. It occurred at the very moment when the Nazi *Reich* achieved one of the high points of its hitherto unchecked, conquering progress. During their journey through Cracow, while the train was standing at the station, the prisoners had heard a bulletin in which the German announcer, choking with emotion, reported the fall of Paris.

People who have survived Soviet camps know that the worst months were those during which they had to build their own prison from nothing. Prisoners were brought to the snow-covered, frozen Siberian wasteland and were ordered to set up camp there, to surround the place with wire, to dig plots, and later to erect huts, build kitchens, dig down for water and construct latrines. The climate was killing them, and yet they had to work beyond endurance, receiving even less food than prison regulations required.

It did not fall to the lot of the first prisoners of Auschwitz to experience such conditions, since they arrived in summer and were hustled into stone buildings, with an already operational kitchen, some plumbing and water. They were, however, to endure perhaps worse suffering by being guinea pigs for new experiments. This was the first camp for Poles and the first to be built on territory not inhabited by Germans, although it had been recently invaded and integrated into the *Reich*. The Poles took second place on Hitler's list, immediately following the Jews[8], so for them there had to be prepared a camp far more destructive than anything previously tried at Dachau, Sachsenhausen or Buchenwald. Experiments were performed, new forms of terror and torture were devised, more and more refined ways of maltreating prisoners were developed. For the first few days they were not sent to work, and instead had to undergo several hours of physical exercise which even the youngest of them could not take. They were kept standing at roll-call for hours on end, everything had to be done at the double, visits to the latrine were timed in seconds and they had to queue for their soup on their knees and eat it sitting on their haunches. The continual hurry, the continual running was enforced with sticks, without which the *SS*-men and trusties never appeared. At night, packed together on the straw, the prisoners were unable even to turn over. Nourishment consisted of about three slices of very heavy German bread, a scrape of margarine and less than a pint of watery soup. There was no hospital, and when work began on a caricature of a sick-bay, no doctors were allowed to work there.

This preliminary period, which caused a great many deaths, also provoked the complaints of the camp Commandant, Höss. As an expert on concentration camps (Dachau, Sachsenhausen), he could not tolerate the primitive state of the security arrangements, the small number of *SS* guards and the attitude of the villages surrounding his empire. In Germany he had dealt with a terrorized or indifferent population, while here, on land formerly Polish, he felt an atmosphere around the camp of hate, resistance and revenge, together with a readiness to help the ill-treated prisoners. He repeatedly sent reports to his superiors demanding wider powers, but they usually evoked no reply. It required the first escape to produce a reaction.

On July 6th a young Pole, with the symbolic name of Wiejowski (in Polish, a man on the run), disappeared from the camp. He was sought for three days and nights. For the whole of this time a cordon of *SS*-men encircled the camp and the prisoners' punishment roll-call lasted for 20 hours without a break.[9]

Höss at once profited from the occasion. When von dem Bach came on a tour of inspection on July 18th, Höss outlined the camp's position very clearly, and before the end of the month he received the go-ahead for the speedy eviction of the local population. First of all the area of Zasole, in which the camp was situated, was cleared of Poles, followed closely by several villages. An area of about 20 square miles was cleared and was recognized as coming under the camp's jurisdiction. From north to south the site measured 6 miles, from east to west more than two.[10]

On August 15th the first transport of prisoners from Warsaw arrived. In it were 513 political prisoners from the *Pawiak* jail and 1153 men caught on the streets and sent off to the camp without

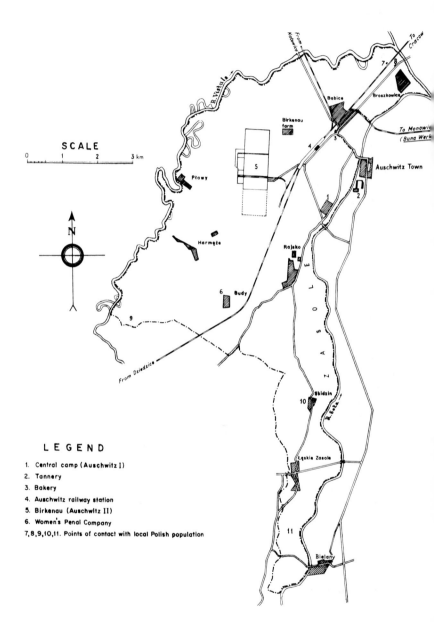

Map of the area under the camp's jurisdiction.

even having been interrogated by the *Gestapo*.

On December 31st a Pole, brought to the camp from Katowice, was given the number 7879. This did not mean that the camp actually contained that many inmates. There were in fact far fewer. A very small number had been released; many had been killed. On December 19th the Archbishop of Cracow, Prince Adam Sapieha, through the Parochial Office in Auschwitz, sent a letter to the camp Commandant, asking for permission to conduct religious services for Roman Catholic prisoners at Christmas. This request was declined but he was allowed to supply the prisoners with about 6,000 parcels of about two pounds each[11] – an indication that, except for the few released, about 1,800 prisoners had died or been murdered. The 6,000 remaining men could all be accommodated in the original camp. This was not long to be the case.

The huge area taken away from the local population awaited its new destiny.

5

The first winter of the war had been exceptionally long and cold; the second turned out to be even worse. In Warsaw the first snow fell on October 11th, while in the southern part of the country, nearer the mountains, the temperature remained constantly below zero.

By now the camp in Auschwitz was already four months old, yet the living quarters had not been prepared for winter, nor was there any winter clothing. In many barracks there were neither stoves nor windows, the prisoners went barefoot, without caps, sweaters or gloves, with ragged and dirty *Wehrmacht* uniforms thrown over their shoulders. Every day frozen men, who could no longer stand up, were carried back from work; hundreds went down with chills and lung diseases that killed them within days. With the exception of the trusties and the lucky ones who worked indoors, everyone was ill. The marshy, poisonous mists that did not lift until late in the day crept in everywhere and finished off those who might still have survived in a better climate.

Then came the terrible day of October 28th, 1940. At the time of the noon roll-call one prisoner was found to be missing, so the camp command ordered a penal stand-at-attention. It lasted from 12 noon to 9 p.m. The wintry autumn weather, much worse than a dry frost, reached the height of its bitterness. One of the prisoner-doctors recalls this day in his report:

. . . From dawn heavy rain or sleet had been driving down and a strong north-east wind was blowing. From noon onwards frozen men began to be carried or brought in on barrows, first one by one, later whole groups, and finally *en masse*. It was terrible to see these men, comatose, half-conscious, crawling, reeling like drunks, babbling incoherently and with difficulty, covered with spittle and foaming at the mouth, dying, gasping out their last breath. All day and all night our whole personnel never ceased in their efforts to save them. Above all they were given hot coffee and soup to drink. At that time we had no or practically no medicaments. The rooms had no stoves and often no windows. A few hundred people were saved thanks to the efforts of almost all the hospital personnel. 200 (two hundred) died all the same . . .[12]

On this day Pilecki, who had already been in the camp over a month under the name of Tomasz Serafiński, number 4859, experienced his first crisis. The arrival in Auschwitz, after a journey of many hours, had been a great shock – his imagination, though prepared for the worst, had still fallen short of the real thing. He thus relates the march from the railway station to the camp:

On the way one of us was ordered to run to a post a little off the road and immediately after him went a round from a machine-gun. He was killed. Ten of his casual comrades were pulled out of the ranks and shot on the march with pistols on the ground of 'collective responsibility' for the 'escape', arranged by the *SS*-men themselves. The eleven were dragged along by straps tied to one leg. The dogs were teased with the bloody corpses and set on to them. All this to the accompaniment of laughter and jokes.[13]

During his first days, however, Pilecki was lucky, for he was put on Barrack-room Service and worked in Block No. 17b. It was true that the Block Chief was 'Bloody Alojs', one of the worst German trusties, but it was indoor work with the privilege of extra food. Unfortunately it did not last long. Alojs demanded not only work but also severity and after a few days threw Pilecki out into the camp together with several others who did not want to wield sticks. It was already October and the prisoners were beginning to be overcome by the damp wind and cold from foggy marsh air. Pilecki survived the murderous roll-call, but was so exhausted that only the speedy help of a friend, a doctor working as a male nurse in the temporary hospital, allowed him to recoup his strength and get through the next days without breaking down.

One of the 'streets' in Auschwitz.

He survived, made himself a vest out of a cement-sack, although he risked being beaten for doing so, and, assisted by an extra bowl of soup from the hospital, went back to building up the network which in a few months was to cover the most important nerve-centres of the camp.

6

Auschwitz was built from the very beginning on principles already practised for seven years in other German concentration camps. At the head stood a Commandant, who was responsible for everything, and to whom, directly or indirectly, every *SS*-man and every prisoner was subordinate. Beside his own Commandant's Office, with an adjutant and the censorship of mail, he controlled four operational instruments: the camp itself with all the prisoners and the *SS*-men employed there, the Political Department, the Administrative Department and the garrison that guarded the camp. The *SS* doctors belonged to the latter.

These departments could be described in the above sequence, but it will be more logical to deal with them in the order in which they developed as the camp expanded. The camp Commandant requires no separate attention, since his activities are obvious. It seems therefore best to start with the camp itself, its prisoners and the *SS*-men employed there.

Directly in charge of the camp was an *SS* officer with the rank corresponding to Captain, whose deputy, responsible for discipline, was a *Rapportführer*, an NCO. Under him were *SS* privates, each of whom superintended one of the barracks where the prisoners lived. The organization and assignment of labour was carried out by another *SS* officer; under him were the *SS*-men who went out with the *Kommandos* (prisoner working-parties). This was all concentrated in a separate office.

The Guard Garrison was under its own Commander and only when on duty was it subordinate to the Commandant of the entire complex. It manned all the watch-towers around the camp; it formed a great chain of guards embracing the whole large area in which the prisoners worked, it provided *SS*-men to guard prisoners who were sent to work outside the chain of guards; and to it belonged the company of specialist dog-handlers. The soldiers of the Guard Garrison had no right to interfere with the administration of the camp, for the inmates' discipline was none of their business and in principle they were not concerned with how the prisoners worked. Their main task was to guard, to see that nobody escaped from the camp and that any attempted rebellion or attack from outside was immediately dealt with. Every meeting with an *SS*-man was a possible risk for a prisoner, but the soldiers from the garrison were less dangerous in this respect, unless it was a question of an escape.

The *SS* doctors belonged formally to the garrison and must be mentioned here, though only from the organizational point of view. Their role will be described more fully in the context of the health service and prisoners' Hospital. The Senior Medical Officer was the *SS* doctor for the whole garrison, normally with rank corresponding to Colonel. Subordinate to him were the *SS* Chemist, the Disinfection Department, the Dental Unit, the *SS-Hygiene Institut*, *SS* doctors for the troops and *SS* camp doctors. The Senior Medical Officer was responsible to the camp Commandant. No *SS*-men, regardless of rank, were allowed to interfere with the doctors; the Hospital was, as it were, independent.

The next operational instrument was the Camp Administration. Its head was responsible for billeting and the supply of food and clothing, both for the *SS* garrison and all the prisoners. The organizing of the German camps was riddled with cynicism and disregard for their own regulations, but this was perhaps most glaringly evident in the Administration, which, although it did not give any opportunity for refined brutality, yet hung over the prisoners as a constant, inexorable, slow sentence of death.

The rations officially laid down for the prisoners were only 2,150 calories for those doing hard labour, and 1,738 calories for the rest, whereas the indispensable norm for the former should have been 4,800 and for the latter 3,600 calories. The camp Commandant and the head of the Administrative Department knew this and yet, instead of trying to ensure that the prisoners got at least these starvation rations, both, fully aware of what they were doing, robbed the helpless wretches. In Auschwitz, twice a week, a huge lorry drove up to the prisoners' store-rooms and tons of food supplies were unloaded from it and carried to the *SS* kitchen. Every soldier in the garrison knew that still more food was stolen by the many trusties. As a result, even if extra punishment or the guard's stick did not knock his bowl out of his hand, a prisoner got a maximum of 1,744 calories daily and the worst-treated had to be content with only 1,302 calories.[14] It was not strange that in the daily, secret report made to the Commandant, the list of those who had died 'from natural causes' contained, more than any others, names of people who had starved to death. Hunger was the most frightful, the most hateful incubus, hanging over the prisoners. Neither. Palitzsch nor the Political Department, nor the most terrible of the trusties ever managed to destroy so many human beings as did this merciless enemy of life. Only the gas chambers were more effective.

And yet Rudolf Höss in his memoirs, describing the work of his administrator, could say:

> He should pay special attention to the billeting, clothing and above all the feeding of the prisoners. By means of constant control he should personally superintend the cooking of the food. Prisoners should be fed well and to repletion.[15]

After this astonishing statement, musing further on the duties of the administration, Höss wrote:

> The keeper of the prisoners' deposits must see that any insurance policies or cards in his keeping do not lapse. Premiums for social insurance should be paid by the administration, private insurance by the prisoner himself.[16]

So wrote the Commandant of the camp, in which the *SS* officer, directly in charge of the prisoners, greeted each new transport with the words:

> If there are any Jews in the transport, they cannot live more than two weeks, if there are priests, they may live one month, the rest three months.*

The Commandant's last instrument for keeping prisoners under control was the Political Department. The importance of this institution in the system of Hitler's camps was so great that it ought to be given priority, if it were not for the fact that chronologically it came to the camp last. First the *SS* garrison had to be brought in, later the barracks had to be built and surrounded by barbed wire, then the prisoners were herded into them, and only then could the *Gestapo* start its work.

To understand the basis of the system of concentration camps one has to remember that in principle the Nazis did not consider them as places where a man served his sentence. Occasionally, as the result of a special order, a man came straight to a camp with definite sentence of a certain number of years, but the general rule was different: a camp was a dumping-ground to relieve pressure on the prisons at the disposal of the *Gestapo* or *Kripo*.† These were usually crowded, particularly during the war, and men were sent to camps in order to make room for the recently arrested. The criminal prisoners, who had fixed sentences, cursed this system bitterly, for the time spent in a camp was not counted towards their sentence. In theory, after spending a certain number of years in a camp, in much worse conditions than in prison, they were to return to their cells after the war to finish their sentence. Recidivists were never intended to be released. Political prisoners were in a different situation. They were generally interrogated with refined brutality, but normally were neither tried nor sentenced. They were to stay in the camp until the end of the war at least; sometimes the *Gestapo* sent a directive that they were to be liquidated there, either at once or after some time. So they were also put, so to speak, into storage. Those who were brought to the camp as the result of a round-up were also not serving any sentence, for nothing had been proved against them and they had not stood trial. They were the harvest of the total terror, which was intended to frighten the whole nation and deprive it of the will and courage to resist.

---

* A tablet with this speech hangs in the Auschwitz Museum.

† *Kriminalpolizei.*

Remembering this general principle, it is easier to understand the role of the Political Department in a concentration camp. First of all it was an agency of the security forces of the great area over which Hitler's *Reich* ruled. A file on each prisoner, unless he had been caught in a round-up, was sent to the camp with a copy of the papers on his case. The Political Department acted as the long arm of the local *Gestapo* and 'looked after' the arrested man. It has been mentioned above that the order for liquidation could come to the camp after the prisoner. Sometimes it was carried out years later. Inexperienced men, who had just arrived in the camp constantly hoped for a miracle, hoped to be set free. Each morning at roll-call they expected their numbers to be read out and that that would mean freedom. After a few months they changed their minds and, like the rest of the camp, quaked when an *SS*-man, with a list in his hand, appeared before the rows of men standing at attention. They knew by then that this man was the harbinger of death, that those whose numbers were read out would go to Block No. 11 and, perhaps that very morning, would find themselves against the black wall.

In the central camp executions were carried out in Block No. 11, generally by a shot in the back of the head from a small-calibre gun. The naked prisoner stood against a black wooden board on the wall. The camp prison, called 'the bunker', was also in the basement of this block.

Sometimes a number read out in the morning meant that the *Gestapo*, for one reason or another, had decided to re-open the interrogation. The prisoner might be questioned on the spot or he might be returned under escort to his original prison and fall into the hands of the same official who had tortured him before. Thus, being taken to a concentration camp did not mean that contact with the *Gestapo* had at last been ended.

The second task of the Political Department was to look after internal camp security, to keep a file on every prisoner, to interrogate them in cases of violation of the camp rules, to pursue them outside the camp in case of escape (by sending out police notices) and to ensure in general that discipline in the camp was kept at a high level. It also carried out the formalities connected with releases. In this respect it was not overworked.

It is hard to know whose way it was best to keep out of in Auschwitz: *Rapportführer* Palitzsch or the head of the Political Department, Second Lieutenant Maximilian Grabner, and his assistant, Wilhelm Boger. Palitzsch personally performed many thousands of executions (he himself admitted the killing by his own hand of 25,000 prisoners)[17], by shooting with a small-calibre gun;

on his own initiative he tortured prisoners and frequently sought the opportunity to do so – thus he was generally regarded as the most dangerous man in the camp. However, a cold appraisal of the facts leads to the conclusion that the decisions of the Political Department, with Grabner at its head, claimed more victims. Even if one discounts the sentences that only passed through the hands of this Department, since they had been forwarded by *Gestapo* officials elsewhere, it imposed thousands itself. Palitzsch carried them out and thus he was pointed at from all sides as a murderer; but he was, after all, Grabner's tool. In many towns the cellars of the *Gestapo* earned themselves ill fame as places of torture, but very few of them reached the level of the Political Department in Auschwitz and in very few places were such subtle means of torture thought up.

7

These five operational instruments in the hands of the Commandant of Auschwitz were terrible weapons, but the picture would not be complete if one were to omit an extension of the iron grasp of the *SS* – the trusties.

In all Hitler's concentration camps, beginning with Dachau, the principle of using prisoners in the administration was widely employed. This was not only because it stemmed from an old tradition. The camps swelled in numbers, and during the war exceeded all expected dimensions. Everywhere there was a lack of men, the *SS* were needed at the front, and more assistance had to be found. So a great network of trusties was built up, which duplicated the work of the *SS* at almost every level.

The highest in the camp hierarchy was the Camp Senior Prisoner. In Auschwitz, quite exceptionally, this function was divided at first between two criminal prisoners whom Palitzsch brought in May 1940 from Sachsenhausen. By a subtle irony of fate both were Germanized Poles. The first was Bruno Brodniewicz, the second Leo Wieczorek.

Below the Camp Senior Prisoner the functions divided into two separate branches: labour and living quarters. The labour was superimposed by *Capos*,* at the head of individual *Kommandos*, under whom were Foremen. Several *Kommandos* might come under

---

* The expression *Capo* came from the Italian meaning 'chief', literally 'head'. It was used by Italian workmen making roads in southern Germany. It first caught on in Dachau and from there went to the other German camps. It was spelled with a 'C', as in the original Italian.

one trusty, who then wore the arm-band of an *Obercapo*. All the *Capos* and Foremen in Auschwitz wore yellow arm-bands.

At the head of each Block was a Block Chief, who was responsible for discipline, order and handing out rations. Under him was Barrack-Room Service, which cleaned out an apportioned part of the barracks and brandished sticks. The trusties on the Blocks in Auschwitz wore dark-red arm-bands.

Besides these two main branches of the hierarchy there were trusties in every corner of the camp. They were in the Stores, the Kitchens, the Work-Shops, the Building-Sites; they even managed to get into the Political Department. Formally they were not superior to the other prisoners, but in many cases they were more influential and had more power than *Capos* and Block Chiefs, although, as a rule, they carried no sticks.

The first trusties were recruited solely among criminal prisoners. The *SS*, which treated political opponents with the greatest brutality, were less strict towards pickpockets and burglars. These, anyway, had had experience of prisons and knew how to set about things; thus they were given all the appropriate jobs.[18]

The reign of criminal prisoners was the most terrible period in the German camps. The *SS*-men, although trained in brutality as part of the camp system, were after all on duty, and when it was over they went into the town or returned to barracks. Only the exceptionally sadistic types stayed on in the camp to torment the prisoners. But with the trusties it was different. They had nowhere to go, so for twenty-four hours a day they reigned over their fellow-prisoners. They knew all their secrets, their relationships and weaknesses. The *SS*-men conformed to certain rules; there was a distance between them and the prisoners. They might even be afraid of informers. Where the trusties were concerned, none of this obtained. The necessity of keeping alive forced solidarity upon them: their criminal past had taught them to be crafty, there were no standards by which their attitudes to fellow-prisoners was regulated, and ideas of ethical behaviour were seldom known to them, They wanted to live, so they kept alive at the cost of others. They stole food by lessening the helpings doled out; they drove others to work with sticks to avoid it themselves; they spied to earn privileges and save themselves from informers. With very few exceptions they were zealous executors of the system of oppression and terror.

The *SS* command approved these conditions, for they provided a guarantee that the great mass of prisoners would never escape control and that, hating the thousands of trusties as they did, they were unlikely to form a united front with them. By this method another very important aim was achieved: the internal urge to rebel, which every prisoner was bound to feel, was not always directed against the *SS*. The criminal parasites were so vexatious that frequently their robbed and maltreated victims blamed them for almost all the crimes committed.

This state of affairs did, however, change as years passed. The camps got bigger, especially during the war, and absorbed hundreds of thousands of new prisoners, almost exclusively political. Nobody wanted to die without a fight, so there began a struggle for power. The political prisoners began to fight for the privileged positions so far occupied by criminals.

The 'green triangles'* began to close their ranks, and the camp command supported them; but the political prisoners' attack was so strong that the safe-breakers and pickpockets occasionally had to sound the retreat. It was not an easy struggle, for it was fought for the right to live, and was carried on in conditions beyond the wildest imaginings, and there was no room for fair play.

The first breach in the criminals' line of defences brought with it further losses. Those political prisoners who managed to get jobs in the camp gave a hand to their fellow-politicals. Sometimes they were held together by ties of nationality, very often by common political views, almost always by the ideas that had made them oppose Hitler and had led them to the camp.

All jobs depended on the *SS*-men, so it would seem that theirs would have been the sole decision on the choice of trusties and the colour of their triangles. That was so, but only at the beginning of the Nazi camp era. Later, with the mass influx of prisoners and the speedy build-up of all the camp apparatus, the problem became too big for the *SS*-men and the criminal trusties. They had been first to rule inside the camps because, when these camps were built, they arrived from local prisons first. They had to be used, because only they had experience. The colossal growth of the camps and the increase in the numbers of political prisoners completely changed the situation. The criminals were not clever enough to organize huge camps, with thousands of prisoners and many complicated problems. Life proved stronger than intentions. The camp command had to accept political prisoners as trusties, for it realized that they were better able to cope with such problems as administration, rationing of food, organization of labour and supplies. After all, what did it matter if the reds began to push out the greens? They were all going

---

* In the German concentration camps every criminal prisoner wore a green triangle on his blouse and trousers, while political prisoners wore a red one. Jehovah's Witnesses wore violet triangles, homosexuals pink and 'antisocials' black.

The main gate at Auschwitz with the slogan 'Freedom through work'.

to die in the camp eventually.

The taking over of the internal centres of power by political prisoners, mainly Communists, brought about new cliques, gave further opportunites for abuses, and sometimes meant discrimination against those of different political conviction. But on the whole it made the terror less and brought some relief to the great mass of the prisoners.

By the time war broke out, the red-triangle prisoners had most influence in the majority of the camps on German soil. But Auschwitz was a new camp. There, in 1940, German criminal prisoners ruled, and it was a long time before this state of affairs was to change.

8

In the early spring, on March 1st, 1941, Heinrich Himmler came to Auschwitz for the first time.[19] Before this visit, in January of the same year, the great chemical concern, *I. G. Farbenindustrie*, had proposed that a huge synthetic-rubber plant, *Buna-Werke*, should be constructed next to the camp. Marshal Göring, who was responsible for the *Reich's* economy, accepted this plan and issued an order to the effect that Auschwitz prisoners should be seconded to the corporation as slave-labour. The *SS* would receive payment for this work.[20]

Himmler entered the camp, but he did not even see the prisoners, since they had been locked into their barracks for fear of an attempt on his life. He made a thorough inspection of the preliminary work of the *I.G. Farben* concern, which was explained by its chief executives, and he then went round the whole area, including the deserted villages from which the Polish inhabitants had been expelled. He stood for a time on the bridge over the railway-lines, with a good view over the dismal emptiness of the flat landscape. He remained there in silence, while behind him his suite stood stiffly and respectfully at attention. In the afternoon, after lunch in the *SS* Hospital canteen, a conference took place.[21]

The *Reichsführer SS* presented his plans and gave his orders sharply, positively and with a coldness which paralysed subordinates and terrified listeners. On the site of the village of Birkenau, at a distance of two miles from the camp, there was to be built a new camp for 100,000 people. It was to be for prisoners of war. The main Auschwitz camp was to be expanded to take 30,000, and 10,000 prisoners were to be sent to the *Buna-Werke*.[22]

The Sheriff of Silesia, Fritz Bracht, leapt from his chair and began to argue loudly that the plan was quite impracticable. There was no drinking-water on the site; the marshes had not been drained; there were not enough bricks, cement, wire or wood. Himmler stopped him with a decisive movement of his hand:

> Gentlemen, it will be built. My reasons for constructing it are far more important than your objections.[23]

Work got under way on the gigantic scheme. Teams of prisoners were moved into the area to demolish the empty houses and prepare the ground for the new huts. *SS*-men fanned out among the surrounding towns and villages with orders to collect anything which could come in useful for the construction work.

Day after day new transports arrived at the unloading ramp of Auschwitz and deposited new victims in the hostile environment. For the first year they were exclusively Poles except for some Germans, the earliest trusties. However, the principle that the camp

Selection taking place on the ramp at Auschwitz.

was to be used for the terrorizing and extermination of Poles only
was soon abandoned. On June 6th, 1941, a transport of Czech
political prisoners arrived from Brno. The first one to enter the camp
gate was given the number 17,045.[24] After the decision to build the
Buna-Werke and Himmler's March orders, this was the second
crucial date in the camp's history, but not the most important.

Several weeks passed and an urgent message was received from
the Head of the *SS* by the camp Commandant, who was to report
immediately to Berlin.* Himmler received him with his usual dryness
and briefness, ordered his adjutants to leave the room and said:

> The *Führer* has ordered that the Jewish question be solved once
> and for all and that we, the *SS*, are to implement that order.
> The existing extermination centres in the east are not in a

---

* The precise date is unknown, nor is it given by R. Höss in his memoirs, which
say only 'in summer 1941'. Robert M. W. Kempner in his book *Eichmann un
Komplizen*, p. 101, says that Eichmann arrived at Auschwitz in late summer 1941
to discuss with Höss the execution of Himmler's order, and Höss notes in his
memoirs that Eichmann arrived very soon after Himmler's order. So it appears
that Höss was called to Berlin about August 1941.

position to carry out the large actions which are anticipated.* I have therefore earmarked Auschwitz for this purpose, both because the area can easily be isolated and camouflaged. At first I thought of calling in a senior *SS* officer for this job, but I changed my mind in order to avoid difficulties concerning terms of reference. I have now decided to entrust this task to you. It is difficult and onerous and calls for complete devotion notwithstanding any difficulties that may arise. You will learn further details from *Sturmbannführer* Eichmann of the *Reich* Security Head Office, who will call on you in the immediate future.

The departments concerned will be notified by me in due course. You will treat this order as absolutely secret, even from your superiors. After your talk with Eichmann you will immediately forward to me the plans of the projected installations.

The Jews are the sworn enemies of the German people and must be eradicated. Every Jew that we can lay our hands on is to be destroyed now during the war, without exception. If we cannot now obliterate the biological basis of Jewry, the Jews will one day destroy the German people.[25]

Höss stood still straighter, tried to say something, but Himmler stopped him with an icy look and dismissed him with a wave of the hand.

The Commandant returned immediately to the camp, failing to give the usual report to his direct superiors in Oranienburg, and without the slightest delay set about executing the order. Soon afterward Adolf Eichmann arrived and together they went round the area and chose a site for the construction of a gas-chamber. This was a deserted farm in the north-west corner of Section B III of the future camp in Birkenau. It was called Bunker No. 1.

The clouds which drifted ceaselessly over Auschwitz – clouds impregnated with blood, suffering, cruelty and violence – thickened and darkened. In their midst grew a thunder-bolt, the greatest and

---

* When Himmler mentioned the problem of liquidation centres in the East, he could not have been thinking of Chełmno, Sobibór, Bełżec, Treblinka or Majdanek, since they were all built later. He must have been thinking of the *ad hoc* sites, which were organized by the *Einsatzgruppen*, special units, responsible to the chief of police and security. They moved into occupied territory close behind the combat troops with the object of combating all anti-German and anti-*Reich* elements behind the front. Their efforts were directed above all against Jews, Communist Party members and partisans.

most dreadful crime in history; it was soon to strike and shake the world.

But then the world did not want to hear it . . .

CHAPTER 2

The build-up of underground work in the camp.

1

Outwardly it might seem that Auschwitz was the least ideal place to start an underground organization. All reasonable arguments and calculations spoke against any hope of successful underground work; yet, as it turned out, the situation was favourable. Clandestine action is usually taken and is usually successful when all other forms of action have failed, when desperate people must seek secret ties to help each other, to fight an enemy who is too strong for open struggle.

This was how things stood in Auschwitz. It would have been impossible to create worse conditions, a more perverse and brutal system, a more complete lawlessness; and therefore the normal human reaction was bound to be resistance. Its first manifestation was the whisper to the neighbouring prisoner during the hours-long roll-call: 'Hang on, don't let yourself be killed.' Only the very weakest, the least resistant, died from hopelessness, accepting the role of cattle led to the slaughter.

Pilecki had gone to the camp with a prepared plan of action and a vision of what he wished to achieve there. His first experiences in the camp led him to change some of the ideas which had seemed good in Warsaw but which were, in fact, unrealistic. However, his basic plan remained unchanged. In his report Pilecki formulated it as follows:

To establish here a military organization with the following aims:
Keeping up fellow-prisoners' spirits by supplying and spreading news from outside.

Organizing, as far as possible, extra food and dividing clothing among those in the organization.

Sending reports outside and, above all, preparing one's own units to take over the camp, if the moment should come, in the form of an order to drop either weapons or parachutists on the camp.[1]

In a place as well guarded as Auschwitz, among terrified and terrorized men, with the knowledge that spying eyes were everywhere, the underground movement had to be built up on very much more precise foundations than that which already existed in occupied

Poland. Pilecki decided to begin by forming the first group of five men, confidentially initiated, who would not know each other, in this role at least, and who would be united only through the person of the leader. This group of five, called the 'upper' and under Pilecki himself, must on no account have any direct contact with the next 'upper' five to be formed. These first groups were to form the highest level of the network. The lower levels were to consist of further 'fives', subordinated to those that had been formed earlier. Each mobilized prisoner was to have a code-name and take an oath in the form prescribed by the authorities of the clandestine Polish army fighting in the underground. Pilecki had gone to Auschwitz as a soldier and so the network he built up was called 'The Union of Military Organization'.[2]

At this period there were only Poles in the camp, so the organization was purely Polish. The cautious enrolment of members had at that time no political overtones. Any Polish prisoner, as long as he was trustworthy, could become a member. In this first phase of the war, after the shock of the September tragedy, the whole nation, with few exceptions, was united by one common idea: not to be crushed by the occupiers. There were two of them – Germany and the Soviet Union – and the same feelings applied to them both. There were, naturally, differences of opinion among the Polish parties and political movements, but not in their attitude towards the invaders. It was only later, when the Soviet Union became a member of the anti-Nazi coalition, that complications arose.

After a few weeks in the camp Pilecki saw plainly that it would be impossible to enlist every trustworthy prisoner into the secret network. Even the best of men, if he belonged to an ordinary working group and worked with the shovel out of doors, was not worth much, for he himself needed help first of all. Pilecki would have to look for contacts among those who worked indoors and had some position in the camp. His first thought was of the Hospital, which, although still very primitive, afforded shelter from the cold, extra food and opportunities for helping others. The second place to be considered was the Labour Assignment Office, and also the Building Office, filled with colleagues from earlier transports.

Pilecki was a good judge of men and possessed an instinct which rarely failed him, but he thought long about his first step before he took it. In the beginning he adopted the principle that he would build up his contacts among men whom he found had been in the military underground movement before their arrest, above all in the Polish Secret Army. He realised, however, that it would be better to choose men who could get lost in the crowd and who had no past history that was likely to be known to the Political Department. For this reason he rejected, at least at the beginning, higher-ranking officers who were in the camp under their own names. If the *SS*-men were to smell a rat, suspicion would immediately fall on them.

He thought things over, weighed the chances, took every possibility into consideration and, as often happens, made his first advances to a man who did not fulfil the conditions laid down. The first man he swore in, to whom he entrusted the leadership of the first 'upper' five, was Colonel Władysław Surmacki.[3]

2

At the same time as Pilecki went voluntarily to Auschwitz, a great air battle was taking place over the British Isles. This was a last desperate attempt by the British to hold back Hitler's victorious armies, which, having conquered Belgium, Holland and France, and forced the British Expeditionary Force into the sea, were now standing by the English Channel, waiting for the signal to embark. The air battle, in which 100 Polish pilots took part, did not go according to Hermann Göring's wishes and the Germans at last met with their first defeat. But this was a feeble, hardly noticeable glimmer of hope. Black night covered Europe when, in a remote corner of the old continent, in boggy, wired-in compounds, among curses, blows, death and madness, a few brave men had begun to weave a secret network of underground resistance. Hitler had reduced concrete defences to rubble, destroyed tanks, trodden the heaviest guns into the mud. In Auschwitz these men were taking him on with their bare hands. What hope could they have?

Colonel Surmacki was a man already over fifty, a geodesist, who spoke perfect German, since he had finished his university studies in Germany before the First World War. He had arrived in the camp with the first transport from Warsaw, on August 15th, 1940. He had settled in fairly well, for, thanks to a fortunate acquaintance he was employed in the Building Office and worked indoors in the warmth. This not only enabled him to survive the worst period but also gave him important opportunities. With the greatest caution he began to make up his 'five'.

The first candidate, Dr. Władysław Dering, was recommended to him by Pilecki as someone the latter had known in Warsaw, where they had both belonged to the Secret Polish Army. Dering had come from the capital in the same transport as Surmacki. Doctors were not yet assigned to the camp Hospital,[4] which was not really operational, so Dering found himself in a casual *Kommando* that was building a road. He very soon began to fail in health and caught dysentery.

Emaciated and near to death, he was taken into the Hospital by two other Polish doctors, Marian Dupont and Edward Nowak, who were already working there as male nurses. After he had recovered, but while he was still too weak to walk, he aroused the interest of the head doctor of Auschwitz, *SS* Major Max Popiersch, a Silesian who spoke good Polish and who was a decent man. Dr. Leon Głogowski brought him to Dering's bunk and told him who the sick man was.[5] Popiersch, aware of the frightful plight of the prisoners and wanting to help them, asked about Dering's medical experience and gave him the job of organizing a casualty ward in the Hospital. The formalities connected with taking him into the Hospital had to be completed by Hans Bock, the head of the Hospital barracks. Bock was a German criminal prisoner who was in charge of the Auschwitz Hospital from the beginning and ruled it like a dictator, almost independently of the Senior Prisoner of the camp. Bock turned out, in fact, to be a good, honest man, and in a great measure it was thanks to him that it was possible to build up the camp Hospital.[6]

Dr. Dering's work in the Hospital began as a result of Popiersch's decision, and Pilecki's organization thus took its first step on that terrain. It was a significant step. The Hospital shortly became one of the two pillars on which the slowly constructed clandestine network was to be based.

The next to be enrolled was Jerzy de Virion, a cavalry captain, who had also belonged to the Polish Secret Army in Warsaw and of whom Pilecki had a high opinion. In the camp he was known as Jerzy Hlebowicz.* The fourth member of the first 'five' was Alfred Stössel, a young Second Lieutenant from the first transport, caught by the Germans while trying to cross into Hungary *en route* to France. He had a fairly strong position in the camp, for he was a Block Chief of the Hospital barracks in which infectious patients were kept.

One final contact was made and the first 'upper' five was thus complete. All its members were sworn in by Pilecki. It is not known who the fifth member was. One can only assume that he came to the camp from Warsaw. These first camp contacts depended as a rule on personal acquaintance, a common background of previous resistance, group or party attachments, sometimes prison friendship.

As soon as the first 'upper' five was complete, it was confronted with the problem of establishing contact with Warsaw. An initial report had to be sent to confirm that the plan for underground work in the camp had begun. Pilecki started to look round for an oppor-

---

* As to how this name was established and other difficulties in Pilecki's report, see Appendix II, item 2.

tunity. There were contacts with Polish civilian workmen who worked in or near the camp. But Pilecki had to be very careful, for after the first escape from the camp the civilians were suspect and were the objects of ceaseless control and repression.

Fortune is said to favour the bold, and so it was this time. Pilecki, beginning to widen his contacts swore in a fellow-prisoner to whom he gives the number 6 in his report. This man had a stroke of amazing luck. From the Gestapo central office in Warsaw came the order for his release.*

These were the early days of the camp, and when anyone was released, which happened very rarely, there was no quarantine. The prisoner, as long as he looked reasonably healthy, was called out from his barracks at the morning roll-call, sent first to the Political Department, and then to the Stores where personal effects were kept. He changed and cleaned himself up and was taken to a small wooden hut near the camp gate. There the duty *SS*-man gave him his instructions, reminding him that everything he had seen in the camp was secret, and let him go free. Luckily Pilecki, who had contacts in the central camp office, had known earlier that the release papers had arrived and he was able to contact the man briefly. The released man had not only to be told how to make contact in Warsaw, the password and counter-sign, but had also to learn by heart the most important elements of an oral report. The risk of writing anything down at this early stage of the camp and the underground was too great to be taken.

It was thus in November 1940 that the first report reached Warsaw about the camp and the military underground network formed there.[7]

3

At this time underground activity was growing in Poland. The military had been the first to act, since on September 27th, 1939, one day before the capitulation, the organization In the Service of Poland's Victory (*SZP*) had been formed in Warsaw. Later its name was changed to the Union for Armed Struggle (*ZWZ*) and finally, in February 1942, changed again to the Home Army (*AK*). Soon after the military, the politicians became active, and the leadership

---

* Very occasionally, when a prisoner was sent to the camp only as the result of a round-up, he might be released by means of great efforts on the part of his family. It has been impossible to decipher the name of the man who was Pilecki's first messenger to Warsaw.

of the political parties was re-organized. Three of them, the Peasant Party (*SL*), the National Party (*SN*) and the Polish Socialist Party (*PPS*), the strongest and the most dynamic, created a Political Advisory Council (*PKP*) alongside the commander of the underground army.[8]

These were not the only groups which worked covertly at that time. The whole country, from the first days of the occupation, was covered by an invisible network of secret activity. People refused to accept defeat; the behaviour of both occupying powers was cruel and brutal, and anybody who could possibly do so joined an underground movement. About 100 groups of a military type were active; political, cultural, scouting and self-education groups had sprung up; secret printing presses had been set up in cellars dug out under the foundations of houses. Warsaw capitulated on September 28th, and already on October 10th the first issue of a clandestine weekly, *Poland Lives*, appeared there.[9]

The mass underground activity did not at this time include the Communists. Under the Soviet occupation they did not need to hide, for the opinions voiced by Russia were their opinions, so they could operate openly. On the German side it was different, but it was hard for them to begin anti-German underground activities when Stalin had signed a pact with Hitler, had helped him to start the war, and was supporting him with large supplies before the attack on the West. It is true Stalin was somewhat alarmed by the collapse of the front there, and by France's defeat, but he did not cease to send supplies to the Nazis. Communists, not only in Poland, but all over the world, were disorientated, and although they did not dare to criticize, they did not seem to know what to do. In any case the German police in Poland left them alone at this time. So they waited for further developments.[10]

Life in the camp was tightly cut off from the outside world, and yet the barbed wire, watch-towers, chains of *SS* guards, machine-guns and searchlights could not isolate Auschwitz from the growing underground activity. Almost every day new prisoners were brought to the camp, many of them dragged away from underground work, and from them news reached other inmates. It was not by chance that the underground in the camp began to resemble the set-up which already existed in occupied Poland.

By the same transport which brought Pilecki from Warsaw there came to the camp a young member of the Polish Socialist Party, Stanisław Dubois, who was arrested with forged papers as Stanisław Dębski and whose real identity was still not known to the *Gestapo*. In the capital, immediately after the surrender, he had immersed himself in underground work. He was one of the founders of the

Fighting Organization of the Polish Socialist Party (*PPS*), and had worked in propaganda where he had issued anti-German manifestos and leaflets.[11]

In Auschwitz there were already a number of members of the *PPS* and among them thirty young sportsmen from the Warsaw workers' club *Skra*, who as the result of a denunciation had fallen victims of an unexpected attack. On the night of July 2nd, 1940, the *Gestapo*, in possession of an almost full list of members and activists, had arrested these men and taken them to their headquarters and then to the main prison in Warsaw, the *Pawiak* prison.[12] After interrogation they were sent to Auschwitz with the first transport from Warsaw, on August 15th, 1940. Dubois had known many of them when they were free, and so had no trouble with the first contacts. He also easily picked out Konstanty Jagiełło, a member of the *PPS* and the Socialist scouts, who arrived with the second Warsaw transport on September 21st, 1940. In October a new underground organization began to take shape. The conspirators had no idea that right alongside them someone had already started up a similar 'military' organization. They acted spontaneously, as had happened elsewhere in occupied Poland.

On January 7th, 1941, Norbert Barlicki, a long-standing and experienced member of the *PPS*, a former Minister of the Interior and Mayor of Łódź, was brought to the camp. Dubois at once reached out a helping hand to him, for the old man would have died within a few days in an ordinary *Kommando*, and told him about the secret work that had already begun. From this moment the build-up of the underground network took on greater impetus. Dubois thought that they ought to carry on inside the camp what had been begun in Warsaw. Barlicki supported this idea and so the new clandestine cadre was given the name the Fighting Organization of the *PPS*.[13] It was built up on a system of 'three',[14] based on the same principles as those Pilecki had used when forming his 'upper' fives.

On January 1st, 1941, only a few months after Pilecki and Dubois had come to the camp, a young right-wing activist, Jan Mosdorf, one of the leaders of the National Radical Camp (*ONR*) was brought from Warsaw. He soon sought out comrades whom he had known when he was free. They also began cautiously to organize a new network based on the principle of 'sixes'.[15] There is no evidence to show exactly when this was, but circumstances suggest an early date, about the beginning of spring 1941. Young, energetic men, accustomed to an active life, could not remain passive, seeing what was happening around them. Some witnesses and historians[16] have linked Mosdorf's network with Professor Roman Rybarski, a

Witold Pilecki   Władysław Surmacki   Władysław Dering

Jerzy de Virion   Stanisław Dubois   Konstanty Jagiełło

Norbert Barlicki   Jan Mosdorf   Roman Rybarski

Kazimierz Rawicz   Henryk Bartosiewicz   Bernard Świerczyna

Leading men in the resistance movement.

prominent member of the National Party, with whom he is said to have co-operated closely. It would seem, however, that this co-operation took place after Mosdorf had commenced his underground work in the camp, for Rybarski came to Auschwitz only on July 24th, 1941, more than six months after Mosdorf, in a transport from Warsaw. It should also be remembered that the National Radical Camp before the war had had an ideological dispute with the more conservative National Party, and co-operation between Mosdorf and Rybarski would not have come about automatically.

As well as these earlier and more developed underground groupings, there were other attempts at organizing prisoners to give them a better chance of survival and self-defence. One of these was started up by Colonel Kazimierz Rawicz, who came to the camp under his assumed name of Jan Hilkner and was never identified by the *SS*. At Easter (1941) he started to set up a military underground network under the name of the Union of Armed Struggle (*ZWZ*),[17] a camp continuation of the *ZWZ* already mentioned. One of his earliest and best co-workers was Henryk Bartosiewicz, entered in the camp files as Bartoszewicz, arrested in Łódź for belonging to *ZWZ* and taken to the camp on January 11th, 1941. The organization set itself two tasks: offensive intelligence work, which collected information about the behaviour of the German authorities in the camp, and defensive work, which sought out spies.[18] Offensive intelligence was carried out by Lieutenant Bernard Świerczyna, a Silesian brought to the camp from Cracow on July 18th, 1940. He became *Untercapo* and later *Capo* of the Clothing Store, where he was very useful. A few months later the *ZWZ* group was joined by Wing Commander Teofil Dziama.

A little later, in May 1941, Colonel Aleksander Stawarz, who arrived on April 5th, 1941, in a transport composed of 933 prisoners from Cracow and Tarnów, started to set up a similar group. At the same time Lt. Colonel Karol Kumuniecki, brought from Warsaw on January 7th, 1941, was building up his network.[19] There were also other attempts, generally initiated by military men, which soon joined other groups or else ceased to exist. Almost no information about them has been preserved.

CHAPTER 3

The underground organization in the neighbourhood
of the camp; secret work in the Hospital; the first
report to London; the organization of labour and
underground workers in important positions; the
German-Russian war.

1

The terrain destined for the camp was cleared of its population in
1940 and a large area under the camp's jurisdiction was created, but
although Silesia had been incorporated into Hitler's *Reich*, the
Germans did not order a mass exodus of Poles, other than farmers.
The reason was that a large percentage of them had been miners for
years and coal was very necessary to the German war economy. The
Poles could have been evicted, but other skilled men could not have
been found to replace them. Sometimes exceptional situations arose:
at the request of the mining authorities the Germans allowed evicted
families to return to their homes.[1]

These circumstances proved very favourable to the inmates of
Auschwitz. The camp was cut off, surrounded by barbed wire and
guarded by watch towers, chains of guards and patrols. But with the
large number of inmates increasing every day, and with working
parties who went outside the camp, as there was work for them everywhere, it was impossible for the Germans to prevent contact with the
local population, who were almost exclusively Polish.

The first contacts came about very early, while the camp was being
set-up and built. The huge barracks-town did not yet possess its own
specialists in every branch of trade and craftsmanship and the choice
of prisoners rounded-up and driven there was fortuitous. The rapid
build-up required the help of labourers and craftsmen from outside.
They were recruited from the neighbouring towns and villages and so
every day outsiders came into the camp, almost always Poles, who
worked together with the prisoners. The camp command forbade all
talking with the outsiders and threatened the most stringent punishments, but human instincts proved stronger than orders. The first
escape from the camp, in July 1940, succeeded thanks to the help of
Polish civilian electricians. They were arrested and subjected to cruel
interrogation. Indeed von dem Bach finally sentenced them to

death.* But even this fearful example did not put a stop to further contacts.

Prisoners at work.

The earliest links between the camp and the outside world did not have the character of organized activity. The neighbouring population, seeing the wretches working nearby, building roads, digging trenches, cutting down trees, while constantly under blows of the whip, pitied and tried to help them. Sometimes the *Kommandos* came so close to Polish homesteads from which inhabitants had not yet been evicted that it was possible to exchange glances and even a few words. Once a prisoner from the sub-camp in Budy, Stanisław Furdyna, sneaked into a Polish cottage and asked for food. Sometimes food was left in hiding-places, mostly in empty houses, not yet demolished, or under trees; medicines and dressings were similarly hidden. Some SS-men did show a little humanity and closed their eyes to the prisoners getting food from the local population; others indicated

---

* Himmler changed this sentence. They received three floggings of twenty-five lashes and were sent for five years to a third-degree concentration camp. The SS divided concentration camps into three categories: the best (Dachau, Buchenwald), second (Sachsenhausen), and the worst (Auschwitz, Mauthausen).

that they could be bribed and, in return for a good meal, allowed the prisoners to be given food.

It was true that this was only the beginning of the war, but the Germans had imposed a rigorously controlled system of ration-cards, which limited the possibility of free buying to such an extent that those who started to organize help for the prisoners of their own accord were obliged to bring their neighbours into the plot so as to get food from them. Even bread was in short supply, for the Germans controlled the mills and sealed up the primitive private grindstones. Uncontrolled milling was regarded as a crime and the baking of bread an illegal activity. These regulations were not generally observed by the Poles, mostly families of miners, who were hard and determined people. By not obeying orders they were killing two birds with one stone: showing their disregard of German regulations and helping the prisoners. The seals were broken at night and grinding and baking were carried out.

During these first months of unorganized, spontaneous help, two miners' wives, Helena Płotnicka, mother of five children, and Władysława Kożusznikowa, showed particular sympathy towards the prisoners. The Zdrowak family in Budy was very active, as were Janina Kajtoch in Babice, Zofia Szczerbowska in Stare Stawy and two land-surveyors, Antoni Mitoraj and Karol Petkowski of the Water Conservation Board in Bielsko. Since these men had the appropriate papers, they could move freely about the area near the camp.

The initiative was taken up by many others and the circle of those in the secret kept growing and their activity began to take the form of a clandestine society. In a short time it became a directed organization with more extensive backing, for the need of the prisoners was growing and from the camp came requests for aid which showed signs of organized collective activity behind the barbed-wire.

The first *Kommando* and that which had the best chance of establishing permanent contact with the outside world, was the group of surveyors. It was set up very early, for measurements were essential to the construction of the camp. Several young people from the first transport were amongst the surveyors as well as an older colleague, engineer-surveyor Kazimierz Jarzębowski. This working group went outside the camp every day and moved fairly freely, although it was accompanied by SS-men. The surveyors sometimes had to enter villages that were still inhabited, while the carts of peasants under contract, carrying building materials, went from place to place throughout the area. Naturally contact with them brought the threat of severe punishment, and the outsiders could at any moment find themselves imprisoned in the camp, but there was frequently occasion for secret contact. There were many convenient ditches, trees, old sheds and houses. Besides, specialists such as surveyors, always enjoyed greater freedom within the area of the camp.[2]

Pilecki, through Colonel Surmacki, had a strong foothold in the Building Office and through it had made contact with the surveyors. This too was done by Surmacki, as Pilecki, being at that time still a newcomer, was limited in his movements. A young boy, who already worked in the Building Office, and who was in touch with Surmacki, approached Jarzębowski and so a further underground soldier was recruited. Jarzębowski enjoyed great popularity among his young colleagues and had no difficulty in enrolling some of them into the underground ranks. The first of these were Janusz Skrzetuski (real name Pogonowski), Leon Rajzer and Bogusław Ohrt. In this very early phase there was no question of setting up escape routes or getting in touch with partisans, of whom there were none at that time, nor of establishing liaison with Warsaw, for Pilecki was doing that in another way. The main object of the contacts was to get food and medicines into the camp and to exchange information.

Jarzębowski, in the course of his work as a prisoner-surveyor, several times met another surveyor, Romanowski, who was from the coal-mine at Brzeszcze (prisoners later worked in this mine). He managed to establish regular and secret contact with Romanowski, and through this channel much information was transmitted in both directions.

During the second half of 1940, with the support from the Auschwitz District of *ZWZ*, there came into being an organization called the Civil Action for Help to Prisoners. Its task was to collect food, medicines and clothing and get them into the camp. Through the same contacts messages were passed in and out.[3]

A little later, in the spring of 1941, Colonel Rawicz set up another means of liaison. One of his men, Major Zygmunt Pawłowicz, became a cart-driver and used to go outside the camp with his *SS* guard. At the railway station he managed to approach Polish engine-drivers and through them send news to Cracow of his whereabouts and possibilities of action.[4] A fragile, but permanent thread of liaison existed between the camp and the intelligence branch of the Cracow District of *ZWZ*. In the latter months of 1941 a special cell for liaison with the camp at Auschwitz was set up at the H.Q. of the Cracow District.

Also in the spring of 1941 the Socialists (*PPS*) established their liaison. This was undertaken by Dubois, again with the help of the surveyors. Jarzębowski was the middle-man in the correspondence carried out between the camp and a Socialist activist in Brzeszcze, Jan Nosal. Later some civilians who worked inside the camp were mobilized for this secret activity. They took letters from the prisoners to people outside the camp, mostly to Nosal. The latter had already been in contact with Wojciech Jekiełek, an activist in *Wici* (the youth organization of the *SL*) and the Peasants' Battalions.* From supporters of the *SL* in the neighbourhood of Auschwitz, he had set up a group to keep in touch with the prisoners and give them assistance.[5]

Pilecki sent his reports to Warsaw, to the H.Q. of the underground army, and at the same time by local channels news was sent to nearby Cracow. A tiny percentage of the prisoners began to profit by the help sent from outside. Although this amounted to very little, the hope and optimism it aroused was enormous.

·2

The bitterly cold second winter of the war drastically thinned out the ranks of the prisoners in the camp. On February 1st, 1941, a new transport arrived from Warsaw; its members were given numbers above 10,000, but there were no more than 7,000 prisoners in the camp at that time; the rest had either died or been murdered.[6]

Pilecki at this time survived a second crisis. He was suddenly ill, with a very high temperature, almost 40°C. Although it was winter, de-lousing had just been ordered in the camp. The prisoners, stood naked for hours in the open air, while their Blocks and clothing were disinfected. Fear of the risk of typhus and selections in the Hospital kept Pilecki working up to the last moment, but when he was almost unconscious he had to give in. He was taken to Block 15, and put on the floor, on the remains of a palliasse in room 7, just below an open window. He was given one blanket. Lice attacked him so fiercely that, although almost delirious from fever, with his remaining consciousness he joined battle with them. He shook them off his neck ceaselessly, and used a piece of wood to obstruct the fresh columns of insects which climbed onto the blanket. He enlisted the aid of his right-hand neighbour who also did not want to give in.

After three days and three sleepless nights, however, he had to seek further help. Through a male nurse, Tadeusz Burski, he sent a note to Dr. Dering, who came quickly with another doctor, examined the patient, diagnosed inflammation of the left lung and had him taken to Block 20. After a bath and an injection Pilecki found himself in a clean bed and could sleep at last. There, due to strict cleanliness and isolation, there were no lice and no danger of typhus. After ten days the illness passed its crisis and he was able to get up, although still very weak. He was kept on as a male nurse.[7]

---

* The military organ of the *SL*. They merged with the Home Army in summer 1943. In the meantime they co-operated.

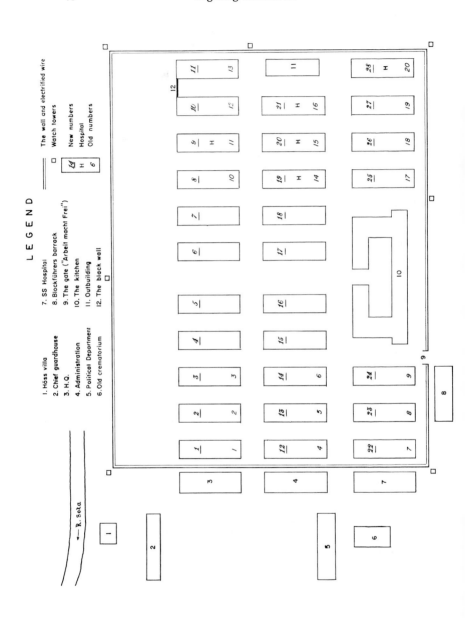

Map of the central camp.

It was then, during the month he worked in the Hospital, that he was able to see for himself the effectiveness of the Hospital as one of the two main branches of the resistance organization he had created. The initial difficulties had been overcome and out of the primitive sick-bay, almost without drugs and with casual labourers as doctors (for the latter were at this time employed only as cleaners or nurses) a Hospital had been formed. It was directed by a German criminal prisoner, Hans Bock, as mentioned before. Bock was proof of the fact that one should not generalize. He had never studied medicine, but he was kind-hearted, was courageous in the face of *SS* brutality and felt for the plight of his fellow-prisoners. By obstinacy and persuasion, and making use of the privileges he received as a *Reichsdeutsche*, he saw to it that doctors were moved to the Hospital and gradually got them appointed to positions appropriate to their qualifications. In addition, the modest Hospital dispensary increased in size.

At first the *Häftlingsrevier* (prisoners' Hospital) occupied Block 16; a little later it also took over Block 15 and by the end of 1940, Block 20.* Bock, backed up by the Polish doctors (at that time there were no others in the camp) and in agreement with Dr. Popiersch, on whose ambitions he played cleverly, fought for and obtained important privileges for the Hospital. It was a separate administrative unit within the camp and no one was allowed to enter it without the permission of the *SS* camp doctor. The restriction applied not only to prisoners, but also to *SS*-men. There were cases known of conflicts between the *SS* doctors and the Political Department, who considered that the whole camp came under their jurisdiction. Once granted, privileges were upheld and the camp Commandant took the side of the Hospital. There were striking examples of this. At the time that the camp doctor was *SS* Captain Friedrich Entress, the Political Department sent an informer, a Russian named Zolotov, to the Hospital to become a nurse and spy on the doctors. The underground movement had been keeping tabs on informers and Zolotov had been uncovered earlier. Entress was informed by

---

* The name *Häftlingsrevier* was later changed to *Häftlingskrankenbau – HKB*. In the summer of 1941, when the camp was being built up and eight new Blocks were constructed on the roll-call ground, all the numbers were changed (see plan on page 48).

The Hospital Blocks were then given new numbers:
Block 15 (Schonungsblock)   new No. 20.
Block 16   ,,   ,, 21.
Block 20   ,,   ,, 28.

From Władysław Fejkiel (No. 5647). 'Medycyna za drutami' ('Medicine behind barbed-wire'), *Doctors' Memoirs*, Warsaw 1965, pp. 457–465.

a Polish doctor that a prisoner had arrived who, although there was no vacancy, was demanding to be taken in as a nurse and was sure he would be, because the Political Department wanted it. Entress reacted by kicking the spy out and going immediately to the camp Commandant. He came back with the statement that the authority of the Hospital had been confirmed and that nobody except the Senior Medical Officer and himself had any right to meddle in its affairs.[8] This did not save the Hospital from later selections for the gas chambers and from other crimes committed there, but these were carried out by doctors in *SS* uniforms. Cases which could be laid to the account of the prisoner personnel of the hospital were exceedingly rare.

Dr. Dering, a noisy, brusque, difficult man, but a good doctor, had gained a strong position in the Hospital. But he was not the first there. The earliest was Dr. Stefan Pizło[9] from the first transport, and soon after him came others.* The first Hospital clerk was Kazimierz Szczerbowski; the first pharmacist was Włodzimierz Lachowicz, who was assisted by Marian Toliński. When Lachowicz died of typhus in 1942 Toliński took over his function. A laboratory was established beside the Hospital and was directed until the last days of the camp by Witold Kosztowny. Dr. Głogowski worked there for a few weeks before he was accepted into the Hospital. For a short time too, Professor Antoni Jakubski was employed there. (He was probably the oldest prisoner to survive the camp from the very beginning to the end. When he was brought there in the first transport, he was already 62.)

Out in the camp terror raged. Men died of hunger and cold; they died of wounds caused by sticks; they drowned in the latrines, or threw themselves on the electrified wire fences (a well-known form of suicide in the camp). But in the Hospital it was quiet. There was a pallet to lie on; there was even an extra spoonful of soup. The Hospital personnel did not have to attend roll-call, where the prisoners frequently stood for hours on end. It was not surprising that practically every prisoner tried to get there either as a patient, or, the dream of thousands, as a member of the staff. Almost all medically qualified prisoners ended up working in the privileged conditions of the Hospital within a few months.

However, where male nurses were concerned things were different. Qualifications played a minor role, for changing dressings was

---

* The names of the doctors who worked in the Hospital during its early phase are in Appendix III, item 1.

something easily learnt and no special knowledge was required for the ordinary care of patients. These positions were frequently gained by craftiness and the ability to push oneself forward. The first male nurses were recruited from the earliest transports. They were young men who did not always understand that the privilege of a favoured position carried with it the duty of doing the job conscientiously. There were among them, of course, some first-class men and these were kept on. But when the Polish doctors took over under the sympathetic care of Hans Bock, some of the less conscientious were thrown out into the camp. Room was made for the older prisoners, the physically weak, men of merit and also those who were already connected with the camp underground movement.[10]

A prisoner who committed suicide by throwing himself onto the electrified fence.

In addition, therefore, to helping the most needy and one's friends, the Hospital offered widespread opportunities for underground work which reached all over Auschwitz. But a man who was accepted into the Hospital on the recommendation of Pilecki's organization had to take upon himself the risk of secret contacts. If these were exposed it would almost certainly lead to cruel interrogation in the Political Department and execution against the 'black wall' of Block No. 11. Thus work in the Hospital was far from being safe.

The list of male nurses and other personnel of the Auschwitz Hospital is long and it is impossible to re-create it in its entirety. One can only enumerate some who were definitely there in the early phase.*

The Hospital also afforded many opportunities to save prisoners from the trusties and sometimes even from the SS. The life of Dr. Głogowski, mentioned above, was saved in this way.† Later on, when selection for the gas-chambers began, this became of greater importance. The same applied to transports to other camps, which some prisoners preferred to avoid. The case was hopeless when the Political Department wanted a prisoner, but even they were several times outwitted. In February 1941 a Polish seaman from Silesia, Kurt Machel, who ran the camp Canteen for prisoners‡ was thrown into the bunker. He was sentenced to death and was awaiting execution. From time to time one of the prisoner-doctors was taken to the bunker to examine the seriously ill, or to see if there was any infectious illness among the confined men. Machel was a member of the underground and it was decided to save him.

Dr. Dering, during a short visit to the bunker, whispered to him how to simulate acute appendicitis. Although Machel was awaiting execution, his 'appendicitis' resulted in his being sent to have an operation. This was a typical example of the principles on which the Germans based their conduct. On the one hand the decision to torture to the point of death or disablement and to execute; on the other, determination to heal the men who had no right to live. Even when, during interrogation, all the necessary information had been extracted and only the sentence remained to be carried out, the victim's life was sometimes saved and expensive medicaments were used so that he should not die too soon and Nazi justice could be

---

* The names of the male nurses who worked in the Hospital during this period are in Appendix III, item 2.

† See Appendix II, item 1.

‡ The prisoners' families were allowed to send them first 30 and later 40 marks a month. In the canteen they could buy cigarettes, saccharine, mustard, and sometimes salad made with vinegar (all products harmful to the body, especially in the camp).

satisfied by an execution. Kazimierz Szczerbowski, in his memoirs on the earliest days of Auschwitz,[11] cites a bizarre example of this logic: prisoners were ordered to carry bricks up a temporary staircase to the first floor and to come down by jumping out of the window. Many of them, especially the old and enfeebled, broke arms and legs. They were loaded into ambulances and taken to the hospital in Gross Strehlitz to be treated.

Machel was taken to the hospital where the medically unnecessary, but under the circumstances indispensable, operation was performed. He stayed in the Hospital as a convalescent and in the meantime his family, informed by underground liaison, quickly made efforts to save him. By his agreeing to sign the *Volksliste* and to join the *Wehrmacht*,[12] Machel's sentence was repealed and he was released from the camp.*

The Hospital also afforded opportunities of another kind. The whole camp was permeated by spies from the Political Department who, in exchange for minor privileges such as an extra bowl of soup or a better *Kommando*, recruited numerous candidates to this work. Irrespective of nationality, there was no group that could say there were no traitors amongst them. The terrible conditions of life in the camp broke men. The underground movement knew about the spying and warned people against it, but this was no guarantee of security and was not enough of a 'threat' to deter others. Secret sentences were passed, and these were usually carried out in the Hospital. Many an informer of the Political Department died in the cellars there.

Later, when in 1942 typhus was rife, the menace of an underground sentence even extended to *SS*-men. The Hospital laboratory was from the very beginning run by Witold Kosztowny, an early member of the underground, sworn in by Pilecki in the autumn of 1940. Very secretly Kosztowny started to breed lice infected with typhus. The *SS* could not easily discover this. Who, after all, would see the difference between a normal louse and one infected with typhus? Kosztowny's experiments were a guarded secret, known only to a very few of the most trustworthy prisoners. Later these lice were thrown onto the most hated members of the guards, or handed to them in

---

* This example is given as proof of what the camp Hospital could do and not as an example of how a prisoner should have behaved. Thousands of prisoners could have got out of the camp if they had been willing to sign the *Volksliste* and enlist in the *Wehrmacht*. The men in Auschwitz, especially the members 'of the camp underground, knew that this was not the way to freedom. Signing the *Volksliste* meant that the person involved accepted that he ceased to be a Pole and became a German. Many Poles, especially from Silesia, were sent to Auschwitz for the very reason that they had refused to sign the *Volksliste*.

sweaters to which they had taken a fancy. In this way the Senior Medical Officer, Siegfried Schwella, who died of typhus on May 10th 1942, was liquidated.[13] Attempts were also made to kill the head of the Political Department, Maximilian Grabner, and, above all, the *Rapportführer*, Gerhard Palitzsch. He did not catch typhus, but his wife died of it and this changed the pattern of life of the cruel *SS*-man and ultimately decided his fate.*

The Hospital's opportunities reached further. Under the pressure of the later events of the war, in the second part of 1942, the Germans began to retreat not only on the battlefields but in many other sectors of the struggle. Not humanitarianism, but necessity had caused them to begin to regard the prisoners as creatures resembling men. They had hands, after all, and these were becoming more and more valuable. At first a good prisoner was a dead or dying one; later a good prisoner was one who lived and worked. The Auschwitz Hospital increased in size and began to extend to the numerous sub-camps. Local Hospitals were set up and doctors and assistant personnel sent there, while the sick were brought to the central Hospital for operations and dental treatment. This was an ideal situation for the underground workers, who needed to make contact with all their posts. In this way threads ran out from the Auschwitz underground movement to the women's camp later set up in Birkenau, to the factory *Buna-Werke* and to many other sub-camps, crowded with men in striped garments.[14]

Of the medical personnel, at that time exclusively Polish, almost all joined Pilecki's organization or were connected with it through the secret political groups. It is impossible to be sure of every name. From among the extensive and very mobile group of male nurses and other Hospital workers it is still more difficult to single out the soldiers of the camp underground at that time.†

While Pilecki, as a male nurse, was spending a month in Hospital, his organization grew very quickly. Under various pretexts he was able to move round the camp and make new contacts. His men were also working and building up further 'lower' fives.

3

Pilecki's first report, transmitted to Warsaw orally in November 1940 by means of a released prisoner, was immediately made use of.

---

*See page 217.

†The names of the doctors and male nurses who belonged to the underground are to be found in Appendix III, item 3.

The contents were included in the secret mail, sent by courier from the Commandant of the *ZWZ*, which arrived in London via Stockholm in March 1941. This was consignment No. 3 containing *inter alia*, a report of the internal situation in Poland up to January 30th 1941 and, in Par. III, 'The Camp at Auschwitz'. The courier took this mail to the base *Anna* in Stockholm, whence it was sent to London on March 2nd, 1941. In London the VIth Bureau (liaison with Poland) of the Polish General Staff collected it on March 18th and filed it as No. 874/41. This was not a precise staff report treating the subject with faultless accuracy, but the information, on life in the camp, the treatment of the prisoners, the work they were forced to do, their clothing, food and punishments, was in all respects exact.[15] The Polish Government in London made use of this information as propaganda addressed to the Western world, including the United States which was friendly but still neutral. Warsaw, for its replies to the camp, used the same method but in reverse. Through prisoners arriving from the *Pawiak* prison, among whom were some initiated into the secret affairs of the camp, Pilecki received confirmation that his report had been received and encouragement to build up the organization he had begun.

In this preliminary period, when the underground was taking its first steps almost in the dark, sending reports via released prisoners was found to be the most practical method. Releases were very rare, but they did happen from time to time. It all depended on whether the released man was already a member of the secret camp organization. The risk of sending anything by someone who was not completely trustworthy was unacceptable for the underground and for Warsaw, as both sides would have had to reveal their secret contact.

While in Hospital Pilecki had sworn in a male nurse, Tadeusz Burski, a young boy picked up in a Warsaw round-up. Suddenly an order for his release arrived, thanks to the efforts of his sisters, and so, at the beginning of February 1941, a new report went to Warsaw. A month passed and another chance cropped up: again the release of a man from a Warsaw round-up, Władysław Szpakowski, who was already a member of the camp underground. His wife had managed to obtain his release through the Swedish Consulate. Szpakowski left the camp on March 7th, 1941, and took with him the fullest possible picture of everything that was happening there. Through him Pilecki was able to forward more details of his own organization.[16] These were general details; neither the names or numbers of the prisoners, nor the *Kommandos* or Blocks in which they worked and slept were included. Warsaw did not need these details and it might have meant the end of everything if the *Gestapo* had discovered the secret and detained Szpakowski. The latter, since he was carrying a written report, was not given further information on the underground network and knew no names. In underground work the less one knew the better. Nobody could depend on a man being able to withstand interrogation and torture.

4

When, in May 1940, Gerhard Palitzsch brought from Sachsenhausen thirty Germans, most of them criminal prisoners who were given all the most important functions in the new camp, they were regarded as bandits, often worse than the most dangerous SS-men. This first judgement, based on the terrible experiences of the early weeks of camp life, was, however, unfair. The thirty trusties, armed with sticks and shouting in guttural German, were hardened over the years to camp life and its special discipline. Led by Brodniewicz and Wieczorek, they caused general consternation; but there were in fact some decent men among them. The example of Hans Bock had proved that one should not generalize, and others, too, showed themselves worthy of respect and honour. One German prisoner whose memory stirs a sympathetic feeling in the hearts of those who managed to survive Auschwitz was Otto Küsel, who worked in the camp Labour Assignment Office.

It has been mentioned earlier that the camp underground movement was based above all on two foundations: the Hospital and the office which organized labour. The achievements of the Hospital were the most important, for it helped thousands, being a haven which, even though for a short time, gave shelter from the ill-treatment of the camp; it was also the place where the invisible threads of the underground network crossed. The Labour Assignment Office could not come near to competing with the far-reaching and, very often, rapid achievements of the Hospital, but it was also of great importance. The Germans created it in order to get every prisoner into the grip of the daily toil and to squeeze from them every last ounce of energy. Only at the very beginning, when it had not yet been decided what to do with the prisoners and when they were tormented above all by physical exercises, was it possible to transfer from one *Kommando* to another, for later each had its own central register.

There were good and there were very bad *Kommandos*. Work out of doors, with a few exceptions, was reckoned as bad, and in winter was equal to a death sentence. The man who decided the distribution of labour was a power in the camp, and this man was Otto Küsel.

Of medium height, slim, about thirty years old, with a kind, friendly smile, he never raised his voice and never even spoke a harsh word to the most miserable of his fellow-prisoners. Naturally he had SS-men over him, but this was a purely formal control. He was more intelligent than they were, so that in practice the organization of labour throughout the camp, which grew with every day, depended wholly on him and the prisoners working under him.

Prisoners at work.

Anyone who spent a long time in Auschwitz knew that Otto Küsel wrangled with the SS-men to get the brutal severity of the *Kommandos* lightened, that he attempted to limit the hours of hard labour, and that he tried to bring prisoners back from work when there was a very severe frost. He was checked, he was threatened with punishments, he often lost the struggle; but many prisoners owe their survival to him.[17]

Since for the first year the camp was purely Polish, Poles worked in the Labour Assignment Office. Küsel liked his assistants, was sympathetic to their national feelings and co-operated with them. In this early phase of the camp underground it was difficult to ask Germans to join, but in practice the result was almost the same as if he had. Pilecki brought into his organization some young people who worked together with Küsel and through them was able to influence Küsel and get his own men into *Kommandos* important to the organization. This applied especially to all groups of craftsmen. It is difficult to establish exactly when Pilecki got his men into the Assignment Office. From data in statements supplied by others it appears to have been by the beginning of 1941. The earliest contact was Jerzy Pozimski (known in the camp as Jork); Pilecki himself writes in his report that in the latter half of 1941 he recruited Mieczysław Januszewski, a young Pole, a 'tourist', who a few months later, at the turn of 1941/42 entered the Labour Assignment Office. He stood by Küsel's side and began to be of great service to the underground organization.[18]

After the initial confusion about who worked where, a plan for work in the camp was quickly prepared and numerous *Kommandos* were formed. The construction of the camp required specialists such as carpenters, locksmiths, electricians, stonemasons, sewage-workers and gardeners. They began to be sorted out and formed into *Kommandos*. Their work was often indoors and did not require great physical effort, such as dragging a roller, carrying bricks on the run or digging ditches in the rain and mud. Every prisoner tried to get into these better *Kommandos*, and if he was clever and had some natural ability he managed to hide there for a while. But in the end only really skilled men remained in them, or else those who had the backing of the Labour Assignment Office. Every *Capo* and foreman, even if he was a decent man, looked after his own interests and avoided unskilled men, who might easily make a mess of a job and expose him, as supervisor, to the risk of being given twenty-five strokes and transferred to a bad *Kommando*. It was different if he had orders from Küsel to retain a certain prisoner.

Not quite a mile away from the main camp, to the north-east, there was a Tannery. The *SS* command took it over, surrounded it by a fence, set up watch-towers at each of the four corners and turned it into a centre for craftsmen. As well as the tanners, *Kommandos* of locksmiths, blacksmiths, cobblers, tailors, painters, upholsterers, leather workers and wood-carvers worked there. The carpenters had two workshops in other places. Some of them worked in a small workshop in Block 9 (old numeration), some in a large one on the *Industriehof I* (building site).

The area of the Tannery became, beside the Hospital, the second reservoir in which the underground workers began to gather. Pilecki looked for contacts there and, through the men he had recruited early, brought new members into the organization. Thanks to his influence with the men surrounding Küsel, by careful allotment of work he got some of his best men into the various

Kommandos there. In this manner he carried out his basic plan of action, which required that all the most important *Kommandos* should be controlled. After a few months, numerous threads of the underground network came together in the Tannery. Apart from the strong position established here, a second aim was achieved. The craftsmen moved round the camp very freely, as they were often called to do various jobs. Because of this they were also able to help with internal liaison for the camp organization.[19]

A very important unit was the group of electricians, for in the workshop where the radios of the *SS* were repaired, war news was listened to and *Polskie Radio* (Polish Radio) from London was received. After the fall of France, when the Polish Government and the Polish Armed Forces found themselves in Great Britain, an agreement was reached between the Polish authorities and the BBC. Certain times were reserved for Polish speakers and leaders to speak to Poland, giving political and military news, informing listeners of developments in the international situation and encouraging them to hold out. By radio, too, went coded information concerning air operations, after the drops of equipment and trained parachutists from Great Britain to Poland had begun.[20] Each broadcast was always preceded by the announcement: 'This is Polish Radio Warsaw, Łódź, Cracow, Lwów, Wilno, Poznań, Katowice and Toruń speaking on the London wavelength.'* Among the prisoners working in the electrical workshop were engineer Jan Pilecki (no relation of Witold); a highly skilled specialist, engineer Eugeniusz Tołłoczko; Zygmunt Kędziora and Franciszek Roman, all of them sworn in. Unfortunately in May 1941 the *SS*-men caught them and all four were sent to the Penal Company. Tołłoczko died in the camp (shot as the result of this); the others survived the war.[21]

Witold Pilecki had to leave the Hospital after a month and, thanks to his contacts, got into the big carpenter's workshop on the building site. The *Obercapo* there was a German criminal, Arthur Balke, one of the first thirty trusties. He was another *Reichsdeutsche*, and is remembered with favour in the history of the camp. He never struck anyone, he looked after his *Kommando*, created better conditions for it, endeavoured to get extra rations and shielded his workmen when, as the camp grew in size, he was ordered to send them to much worse labour. Pilecki already had some experience of carpentry, as he had worked for a time in the small workshop. In his new work he met a number of young men who made a very good impression on him. In a short time, after they had withstood his critical

---

*These were the Polish towns, which had had radio stations before the war.

observation, he decided to form his second 'upper' five there. It was organized in March 1941 and was made up of the foreman of the workshop, Władysław Kupiec, his brother Bolesław (six brothers were in the camp), Major Antoni Trojnicki, Tadeusz Słowiaczek and Tadeusz Pietrzykowski (known in the camp as *Teddy*).[22] Władysław Kupiec was sworn in personally by Pilecki. The five other Kupiec brothers, Bolesław, Karol, Józef, Jan and Antoni, joined Pilecki's organization. Only Władysław, Jan and Antoni survived the war.[23] Bolesław, a very skilful wood-carver, made several small figures in which secret letters, as well as some of Pilecki's reports, were smuggled out.* A little later these men were joined by other prisoners, among them a young boy, Edward Ciesielski, sworn in by Major Trojnicki, and Stanisław Jaster. Both became part of the history of the camp. The big Carpenter's Shop employed numerous prisoners and, with a man as good as Balke at its head, became one of the stronger points of the camp underground.

Beside the Tannery and the Carpenter's Shop there were other important places to which attention had to be paid, where Pilecki also managed to make contacts. In the Clothing Store the *Capo's* deputy was a Silesian, Bernard Świerczyna, who was already in secret touch with Colonel Rawicz. Pilecki took over this contact and gained an excellent and very courageous co-worker.[24] In the store with Świerczyna worked other prisoners who belonged to the underground; they would probably not have been kept there if they had not been useful.

The prisoners' clothing deposits were stored in the *Effektenkammer*. Jerzy Janicki, Adam Stapf and Roman Taul worked there; all three were members of the underground. It was a key position as every released prisoner had to go to the store where there would be the chance of a last meeting with him. In the stables of *Industriehof I* worked Karol Świętorzecki, who was released on May 15th, 1941,

---

* A very moving scene took place on November 20th, 1971, at Wieliczka, in the Parish Hall of Father Władysław Grohs, a former Auschwitz prisoner. Present were Karol Świętorzecki and Władysław Kupiec, also former prisoners of the camp, as well as representatives of the Auschwitz Museum and Polish Television. Father Grohs had in his possession a wooden statute of the Virgin, carved in the camp at Auschwitz. The visitors thought that there might be a secret receptacle in it, so far unopened. Władysław Kupiec recognised the work of his brother Bolesław, found the camouflaged opening and brought out a piece of paper hidden inside. He was too moved to read it. Others present did so and found that it was not a report but a letter to the underground organization outside the camp from the Kupiec brothers, asking for their parents in Poronin to be looked after. (Ludwik Kubik, 'A secret letter from Auschwitz', *Tygodnik Powszechny*, Cracow, 2.1.1972.)

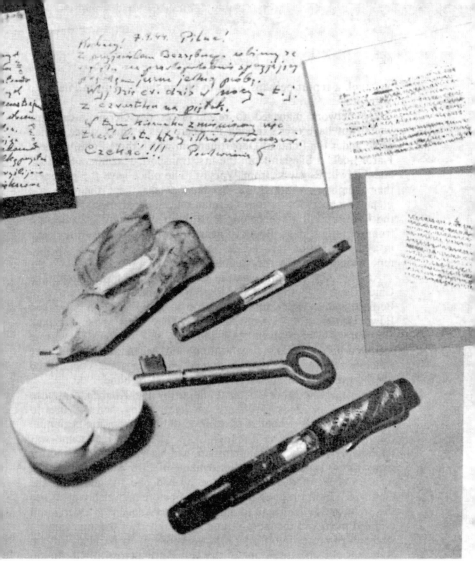

Hiding places for secret letters. The two letters on the right are in code. The one at the top was sent into the camp from those outside helping with escapes: '7.9.44 Urgent! Dear, After the arrival of "Toothless", because of probably favourable weather, we will organize one more try. You will get out tonight – that is *Thursday-Friday*.

In this sense *we are changing* the contents of the letter which is being sent at the same time. Wait!!! Yours.'

("Toothless" is a nickname for a member of the underground outside the camp; the letter referred to is probably one sent to someone outside the camp who was to help the escapees.)

and took a report perhaps given to him in the store from Pilecki to Warsaw.[25]

The network managed to reach places the Germans certainly would not have ever expected it. There was a small office, which came under the Political Department, in which three Poles worked: Karol Bock, a Silesian from the first transport, Kazimierz Smoleń* and Ludwik Rajewski from Warsaw. The office gave the prisoners their numbers, wrote down personal details, kept the files and prepared papers for various German official departments, including the RSHA.† All three belonged to the underground organization from its earliest days. Being so near to the camp *Gestapo* they were in a good position to overhear some of the Germans' secrets and report them to the underground leaders.

Another key position was the Central Office of the camp. The Chief Clerk was Erwin Olszówka, who came to the camp with Bernard Świerczyna from Sosnowiec in June 1940. With him worked Edwin Kufel, a Pole from Gdańsk. They both spoke excellent German and were given their jobs for this reason. They were recruited into Pilecki's organization and began at once to give valuable service. All German orders, including some confidential ones, were communicated quickly to the underground.

The Vegetable Store, in the building by the Kitchen, was also fairly important. The work there was light, giving men a chance to sit down and to get hold of extra food. Almost from the beginning the man in charge was Tadeusz Lisowski, whose real name was Paolone. His family, of Italian origin, had been settled in Poland for many years. He used the assumed name of Lisowski because, as a regular officer of the Polish Army, he had had to hide from the Germans. He was a good man and even before he was brought into the organization he began to gather into his *Kommando* elderly and crippled men, and the more prominent members of the intelligentsia who needed protection. Under him worked Norbert Barlicki, Roman Rybarski, Stefan Jaracz, one of the best Polish actors, the theatrical producer Leon Schiller and many others.[26] Jaracz and Schiller, who were later released, started to organize secret declamations and one-man theatrical performances. This had a remarkable influence on the morale of the prisoners who had the privilege to attend them. Later on, when Lisowski joined Pilecki's organization in the second half of 1941, his help became even more productive. As the *Capo* of the Vegetable Store he was accepted as a senior trusty by the Germans,

---

* Now director of the Auschwitz Museum.

† *Reichssicherheitshauptamt* (Chief State Security Department).

and could accomplish much.

The organization was also established in certain Blocks. From the evidence preserved it is known that the Block Chiefs of No. 3a and No. 5, Stanisław Koprowiak and Baltosiński, belonged to it at that time. In the Hospital, at the head of the Infection Block (No. 20, later No. 28) was Alfred Stössel; in Block No. 25 (new numbering) the Block Chief was a Silesian, Alfred Włodarczyk, and his deputy was Edward Kulik. All were underground members.

To the list of Pilecki's contacts must be added the nucleus of a 'postal service', which came about thanks to the ingenuity of one of the first members of the underground organization, a reserve officer named Franciszek Targosz. He spoke German perfectly (during the First World War he had served in the Austrian Army) and also knew the German mentality, so without anyone's help he succeeded in making for himself an excellent camp 'job'. He managed to convince the SS-men that in a camp such as Auschwitz a museum was necessary. He got accommodation in Block No. 24 (new numbering), gathering round him a number of painters, sculptors, jewellers and watch-makers and formed an excellent *Kommando*. The museum, besides the exhibits which formed the basis of its existence, also produced various pretty and valuable articles, such as cigarette cases, small boxes and brooches. Targosz got some of the SS-men from the camp Censor's Office interested in his products, came to a secret agreement with them and illegal exchanges began. In return· for a beautiful present the censors agreed to stamp blank letter forms with the word '*geprüft*' (passed by censor), with the addition of a special mark in coloured pencil. These marks and colours were constantly changed and were even more important than the stamp. A blank letter-form marked in this way went out without further control and anyone could write what they wished on it. Many of Targosz's fellow-prisoners benefited from his help, as well as the underground network. Pilecki sent reports by this means and sometimes even received answers, for Targosz sometimes worked in the Censor's Office and had access to the mail coming into the camp, so he could take out letters addressed to men known to him. As a rule the names were of prisoners who were already dead, so nothing could have been discovered even if the Political Department had got on to this correspondence. The work was precise and delicate; it was never uncovered and went on for years.[27]

The widely spreading underground network did not contravene Pilecki's basic principle that it should be founded on a system of fives. He himself organized only the 'upper' fives, and they branched out downwards and sideways. Pilecki alone took the risk of knowing, at least by name, most of those recruited. This knowledge on his part was contrary to the rules of underground work, but in camp conditions this extra control proved to be a necessity.

The organization of the 'upper' fives, the most important and the most trusted groups, was carried out slowly. It was confined to men in whom Pilecki had complete trust, who in his opinion would not break down even under the cruellest interrogation, and who had the opportunities and the ability to recruit further members of the underground. Thus, after the first 'upper' five, which was formed in the autumn of 1940, the second came into being only in March 1941, when Pilecki was working in the main Carpenter's Shop. The third he managed to form in May of the same year owing to the fact that in the spring there arrived large transports from Warsaw, in which were colleagues of his from the Secret Polish Army. In one transport, in April, came Lt. Stefan Bielecki, Pilecki's second-in-command in underground work in Warsaw. He was accompanied by Włodzimierz Makoliński, a Captain of the 13th Uhlans, and Stanisław Maringe; they were later joined by Dr. Jerzy Poraziński, and Szczepan Rzeczkowski. These men formed the third 'upper' five. They could hardly be pleased at being arrested, but their arrival allowed Pilecki to take a new, big step forwards. Bielecki and Makoliński especially turned out to be quite indispensable to the underground work.[28]

5

Twelve months after the camp at Auschwitz was set up, the fortunes of war were still favourable to the Germans. Great Britain had repelled the attacks of the German bombers and saved herself from invasion, but she had still not the strength to attack in Europe. Operations had been conducted in North Africa with some success, but these had no immediate significance for the outcome of the war. Greece and Yugoslavia had resisted Axis pressure, but German tanks had broken this resistance and Hitler had subjugated both countries. The British Expeditionary Corps in Greece, the last Western formation on the continent of Europe, had been thrown back to Crete, and it had to withdraw from there after a great German parachute operation. The United States was friendly but still neutral and Soviet Russia, bound to the Nazi *Reich* by the Ribbentrop–Molotov Pact, not only did not fight Hitler, but assisted him with enormous amounts of supplies.

In Auschwitz by the spring of 1941 the fresh Nazi successes had increased the terror and raised the level of *SS* brutality. The *SS* were annoyed that the prisoners fought for their lives, that they tried to escape and in every way to evade the draconian rules. *Capos* were instructed that during working hours more of the weak prisoners should be murdered, even if they had to be finished off by sticks. Many *SS*-men helped in this. Prisoners were drowned in the latrines, smothered in the mud, driven on to the electric wires. The roll-calls were especially prolonged to increase the number of deaths. But since the physical and mental pressures so far employed were not apparently sufficient, more refined methods were to be used.

At the beginning of January 1941 the Commandant had decided that a prisoners' orchestra should start rehearsing.[29] He formed and built it from a group of good musicians, who became a special tool in his hands. They were ordered to play when missions from outside came to inspect the camp, as a proof of the exceptionally good treatment the prisoners were receiving. The orchestra was also used for another purpose. Every day, very early in the morning, it played gay marches by the gate as the *Kommandos* went out to work. It played again late in the evening, equally gaily, as they returned to the camp, dragging the corpses of their dead or murdered comrades, driven on by sticks, surrounded by a gang of yelling trusties and laughing *SS*-men. Many a prisoner, hanging on to the last remnants of his strength and nerves, broke down during such a return.

From the very beginning collective responsibility had been imposed; now it was stepped up. Several times, in retaliation for the escape of individual prisoners, the camp Commandant or another *SS* officer picked a number of prisoners out of the Block in which the escapee had lived and sent them to the bunker, where they were left without food and water to die of starvation.

The first such selection, which took place on April 23rd, 1941, on Block No. 2, went down in camp history for another reason. When 10 prisoners had been chosen, Marian Batko, a physics master from the Grammar School at Chorzów, stepped out of the ranks and asked that he should be taken in the place of one of his former pupils. He died in the bunker on April 27th.[30]

There was a second such case in the history of Auschwitz. At the end of July 1941, under the same circumstances but in Block No. 14, Father Maksymilian Maria Kolbe, a Franciscan from Niepokalanów, voluntarily offered his life. The selector at that time was the *SS* officer in charge of the camp, Karl Fritzsch. In this way Kolbe saved the life of the father of a family, Franciszek Gajowniczek, who survived the war and now lives in Poland. It is significant that, contrary to their common practice, the *SS* left Gajowniczek alone, and enabled him to survive. Father Kolbe died in the bunker on

Father Maksymilian Maria Kolbe, who sacrificed himself to save Franciszek Gajowniczek.

August 14th, 1941*; he was finished off by an injection given by Hans Bock, Senior Prisoner of the Hospital.[31]

This barbaric manner of deterring men from escaping, reinforced by the threat that in place of the escapee his parents, wife, or brothers and sisters might be arrested and brought to the camp, caused Pilecki's organization to abandon escapes as a way of regaining freedom.[32] He himself wrote in his report as follows:

> At that time we, as an organization, took up a definitely negative attitude to escapes. We did not organize any escapes and we condemned any step in this direction as a sign of extreme selfishness, until the position altered fundamentally in this respect. For the time being all escapes were 'wild-cat' affairs and had nothing to do with our organization.[33]

The fact that Pilecki and his closest co-workers had the authority to stop the underground soldiers arranging escapes proves that the organization was influential by that time, and that their contacts with the prisoners, scattered through the barracks, were good.

The terror in the camp grew greater, the death-toll increased, while almost every day there came transports of new prisoners from many parts of Poland. The newcomers brought word that all over the country there were large numbers of troops, that the Germans were wrought up and that arrests and round-ups on the streets had of late greatly increased. There was a feeling of nervous tension which suggested that some new, important event was approaching.

---

* After many years of collecting evidence, the Vatican beatified Father Kolbe on October 17th, 1971.

Because the electricians had been caught and four active underground soldiers sent to the Penal Company, Pilecki had lost one method of listening in to the radio news, but there was a radio in the Hospital. Jan Pilecki, before being sent to the Penal Company, had supplied Dr. Dering with a small radio set. The Hospital was at that time being rebuilt and put in order, and so in Block No. 21, where the surgery and the *SS* doctor were located, the radio was hidden under the floor of his office and covered with linoleum and carpet. The aerial was joined to the telephone wires connecting Block No. 21 with Block No. 28. The German doctor was very proud of his office and several times praised the prisoners who had managed to make it so comfortable. His face would have been worth seeing if he had ever known what lay under his feet. At night, after the *SS*-men had left the camp, communiqués were listened to from the distant fronts.[34]

On one such night, June 22nd, 1941, just before reveille, the listeners caught the news that the German armies had crossed the demarcation line and penetrated deep into Soviet-occupied territory on a huge front reaching from the Baltic to the Black Sea.

Part Two

CHAPTER **4**

The uniting of the military organizations; agreement
between the military and political groups; the
building of Birkenau and other sub-camps;
the extermination of Jews.

1

The news of the German attack on Russia went round the camp
like lightning and caused great jubilation. The camp was still predominantly Polish, and the Poles knew from history that every
Russo-German agreement boded ill for them, and every war between
these two powerful neighbours might benefit their country.

The general rejoicing also reflected the hatred that the Nazis had
aroused against themselves in all the occupied countries. This hatred
was probably at its peak in Auschwitz, and at this time it eclipsed

Nazi rally.

the age-old grudges and grievances against Russia, as well as every political calculation. Everyone wished for Russian successes and prayed for a Nazi defeat. The camp – always ready for any optimistic rumours, which were known as *paroles* – vibrated with such stories during the first days of the Nazi-Soviet war.

The monitoring service in the hospital worked efficiently and Pilecki, with his nearest co-workers, received the latest radio news every day.[1] The bulletins were so extraordinary that the underground did not know what to make of them. The Western stations lost themselves in generalities, Polish Radio from London gave no better information and the German announcers fairly choked with enthusiasm as they shouted of stupendous victories. Apparently the Panzer troops were advancing as fast as supplies of fuel would allow, Nazi planes had almost complete mastery of the air, several important towns had been taken, whole Russian armies had surrendered.

All this sounded unlikely, but after a few days it was impossible to believe that these communiqués were just Goebbels' propaganda. The Western stations began to confirm the German reports, which were also corroborated by the behaviour of the SS-men. The first day they had gone quietly about the camp without shouting and one could feel reserve, even fear. They were not pleased by the opening of a new front, fearing its implications and realizing that it would prolong the war. Russia was a huge country of nearly 200,000,000 inhabitants and possessed of boundless natural resources. Even uncritical belief in the *Führer* could not hide these facts and gave no guarantee that the new attack would be crowned by success. This mood changed radically, however, after a few days. The German armies' victorious advance, confirmed from various sources, was an undeniable fact. The SS-men's disquiet changed into noisy joy. Their self-confidence was doubled, and the prisoners at once became aware of this to their cost. For a long time there had not been so many soldiers in the camp. Laughing and joking, they hit men at every opportunity, ordered them to do everything at the double, shouting that the end of war was round the corner and that all of them would be dead in a couple of weeks.

Just as the first news of the war had aroused rejoicing among the prisoners, so now, when the optimistic forecasts had turned out to be wrong, the whole camp fell into a state of depression. Was there no force which could withstand Hitler, would no help come from anywhere?

In July the camp had direct evidence of what was happening on the front. Several hundred Soviet prisoners-of-war were brought to the camp and set to the hardest work, digging out sand. Within a few days they had been murdered with iron bars, spades and pistols.[2]

A little later, on July 28th, a transport of 575 sick prisoners, almost all Poles, left the camp, having been told that they were going to a sanatorium in Dresden. They were taken to Sonnestein and killed in the baths by carbon monoxide. This was the first selection in Auschwitz for the gas-chambers.[3] It is true that the murder was committed outside the camp, but these two facts, the killing of the first group of Russians, who were after all prisoners-of-war, and the first selection for gassing, were a dreadful portent of what was to happen in the near future.

In September the new horrors brought about by the German victories were again exemplified. On the third of the month, by orders of the Senior Medical Officer, Siegfried Schwella, 250 consumptives were taken from the Hospital Blocks to Block No. 11 together with 600 Soviet prisoners-of-war. These were officers and political commissars chosen from prisoner-of-war camps on the basis of a special order No. 8 issued by Reinhard Heydrich on July 17th, 1941. They were all driven into the bunker, the cellar windows were covered with earth and made air-tight and crystals containing the gas *Cyklon B* were thrown in. This was the first time this gas was used for the mass murder of human beings. The officer responsible in the absence of Höss, was his deputy *SS* Captain Karl Fritzsch.[4]

2

The news from the front was bad, and life in the camp became harder and harder, but for this very reason it was necessary to increase and strengthen the underground organization.

Pilecki was now well settled in the Carpenter's Shop, where he had recruited every one he could, and he looked round for chances of expansion. Next to the Carpenter's Shop under the same *Obercapo* Balke, was the Wood-carving Shop. Pilecki had some friends there who got him into this *Kommando* on November 1st, 1941. The foreman of the Wood-carving Shop was a well-known skier from Zakopane, Tadeusz Myszkowski, from the first transport. Around him he collected other men from Zakopane and the mountains, who were excellent wood-carvers and painters on glass. Among these artists were Bronisław Czech, many times ski-champion of Poland and a great sportsman, Izydor Łuszczek, another outstanding ski-jumper, and Władysław Kupiec's brothers Antoni and Bolesław, who also came from the main Carpenter's Shop. These were all fine young men and Pilecki had no difficulty in bringing them into his underground work.

In November *Obercapo* Balke left the Carpenter's Shop and handed over his duties to another German, Konrad Lang. This decent and

Teofil Dziama   Aleksander Stawarz   Karol Kumuniecki

Janusz Pogonowski   Tadeusz Paczuła   Władysław Fejkiel

Marian Toliński   Mieczysław Januszewski   Jan Pilecki

Edward Ciesielski   Stanisław Jaster   Karol Świętorzecki

Leading men in the resistance movement.

gentle man, who loved art and the craft of wood-carving, moved some of the best carpenters to the carving *Kommando* and obtained permission from the camp authorities to separate it from the Carpenter's Shop and transfer it to the area of the Tannery. This suited Pilecki very well. He found himself together with almost all the top *Kommandos*, the camp aristocracy. After the Hospital, the best opportunities for underground work lay there, in this group of prisoners who had got themselves into key positions. Pilecki took advantage of this to widen further the net of his organization, first of all among the wood-carvers. A new cell was formed consisting of some young prisoners, among them the famous sculptor Xawery Dunikowski.

At this time the camp administration began to reorganize the camp and to put the *Kommandos* into common residential blocks. The Tannery was given Block No. 25, and Pilecki was transferred there with a number of the men with whom he worked and who were also members of the camp underground organization. He was put into room No. 7 where Henryk Bartosiewicz was in charge. He was a powerfully built man, broad-shouldered and ever-smiling. At that time he was also working in the Tannery area and very soon he and Pilecki became close friends.

It was only now, towards the end of 1941, in spite of the great increase in numbers of the underground organization, that Pilecki formed his fourth 'upper' five, including Henryk Bartosiewicz, Capt. Stanisław Kazuba and Konstanty Piekarski. Pilecki did not write down the names of the other two. A transport had recently come from Lublin and in it was the Head of the Cavalry Department, Colonel Jan Karcz. Pilecki, himself a cavalryman, had known Karcz before the war and trusted him. For the second time he waived his principle of not accepting high-ranking officers (the first exception was Col. Surmacki) and brought Karcz into his organization. The Colonel got work in the Tannery area, so he was fairly well-off from the point of view of living conditions. For the time being, however, his usefulness to the underground was small.

The principle of not accepting high-ranking officers who were in the camp under their own names, though correct in itself, gave ground for an attack on Pilecki which caused him to alter his attitude. His colleagues in the underground suggested that it was only a pretext to allow him, a mere captain, to remain at the head of what was by now an established military organization. This accusation coincided with a decision to start talks with the other military groups, of whose existence Pilecki was naturally aware.

The formation of the fourth 'upper' five turned out to be a good move, for its members had excellent contacts in the camp.

Pilecki's new friend, Henryk Bartosiewicz, had already been a member of the camp underground, for he had belonged to the *ZWZ* group, organized by Col. Rawicz. And it was Bartosiewicz who made a useful suggestion that appealed to Pilecki. Col. Rawicz was a high-ranking officer, as the prisoners organized in his secret network realized, but he had come to the camp as a civilian, Jan Hilkner, and was known as such to the Political Department.[5] Pilecki wanted to link Rawicz's group to his own extensive network, but realized that the colonel would not serve under a captain. Hence Bartosiewicz's proposal: why not hand over the military command to Rawicz? The *SS*-men believed him to be a civilian, so there was no danger of their watching him particularly carefully. By handing over the command to Rawicz three problems would be settled in one stroke: the two strongest military organizations would be united, a high-ranking officer would be at the head, and all the requirements for underground security would be preserved. Pilecki's role would now be a different, but by no means a lesser one. He would be the organizing head of the whole system; he would go on building up the secret, military network, and all the invisible threads would still be joined in his hands.

Col. Rawicz at that time worked in the Vegetable Store, so contact was easy and Bartosiewicz was the go-between.[6] Pilecki told Rawicz what he had so far achieved and his ideas for the future. The Colonel recognized the value of these achievements, agreed to Pilecki's plan and took over formal command of the whole organization (*ZOW*). Together with him, Col. Dziama and several other officers joined Pilecki. The two underground networks did not merge immediately, for that was impossible; but they were connected by the persons of their leaders.

This was a great step forward, with important consequences. In spite of the enthusiasm and optimism of the underground fighters in the camp, their forces were small and their potential minimal. They could get their colleagues into better *Kommandos*; they had contacts in the Hospital, in the Labour Assignment Office, in the Central Office of the camp, in the Tannery and in the Building Office; they sent reports outside the camp; they passed on radio news to the other prisoners; they received help in the form of medicines and food from the outside organization and were in constant touch with it; but all this gave them no chance whatsoever if an order should come to raze the camp to the ground and kill all the prisoners. Now, with this first step towards uniting all the underground camp activities, organized self-defence became a real possibility. At that time it was not as clear as at the end of war that the liquidation of all prisoners and erasing the traces of the crimes was being seriously considered by Heinrich Himmler; but the men, organized secretly not only in Auschwitz, but in other German concentration camps, had this in mind.

After this first success in integrating the military underground groups, Pilecki turned his sights on to the politicians.[7] He knew, of course, that they were organized in the camp; he realized their importance and knew some of them personally and was thus able to start talks. These took place in the Hospital, late at night, when the *SS*-men had left the camp after the evening roll-call.

3

The Fighting Organization of the *PPS* (Polish Socialist Party) had existed in the camp since the autumn of 1940, when it was established by its first leader, Stanisław Dubois, and since then it had grown considerably. Its members were by now placed in many important parts of the camp, and it was in liaison with the outside world. The same was true of the right-wing front, built up by Jan Mosdorf together with some young activists of the National-Radical Camp (*ONR*) supported by the authority of the eminent representative of the National Party (*SN*), Prof. Roman Rybarski. The Peasant Party (*SL*), strong and numerous as it was in Poland,was not represented by an organized network within the camp, but was active in the surrounding countryside and afforded the prisoners help. The political affiliations of the people who organized this help were known to the leaders in the camp.[8]

Pilecki, in his preliminary talks, aimed not at uniting the existing networks but at reaching agreement amongst their leaders on the establishment of a political committee, which would give support to the military cadres and become a symbol of underground unity in the camp. There is no evidence which makes it possible to state with whom he began his discussions, but from his report it appears that coming to an agreement was not easy and that the talks went on for some months. In this respect he was in the same situation as the Polish leaders in Warsaw and elsewhere during the first phase of the occupation, when they had to build up an underground army out of nothing and at the same time rebuild the political parties and get them to work together. This took time, but it was finally achieved. Immediately after the lost campaign against Germany in 1939 a military underground organization arose (in the first phase *SZP*, later *ZWZ*); then the political parties were formed and gave it support. In Warsaw, from the end of February 1940, there existed a Political Advisory Council comprising the Peasant Party, the National Party and the Polish Socialist Party. At Auschwitz, it was no coincidence that a balance between left and right was sought in such an agreement. There were probably some Polish Communists in the camp at that time, but it was difficult for them to organize, as the Polish Communist Party had been illegal before the war and the Polish Workers' Party (*PPR*) was not founded till January 1942.[9] Many Polish Communists found themselves, as might be expected, on the Russian side of the dividing line between Germany and Russia in 1939, and moved further eastwards as the Germans advanced in 1941.

Pilecki himself does not state precisely in which month political agreement between the upper ranks was achieved, but from his report and the evidence of other members of his network it seems that this took place at the beginning of December 1941. In his report he devotes little space to it, barely a few sentences, but they are very expressive:

> At last I lived to see the moment of which once I had dreamed hopelessly – we had organized a political cell of our organization, where colleagues worked together in harmony, who in the outside world had fought venomously in Parliament.
>
> . . . It was necessary, in fact, to show Poles daily a mountain of Polish corpses before they could be brought to agree together and to realize that, above all their differences and hostile attitudes towards one another in the outside world, there was a more important cause to be served, namely that of a common front against the common enemy.[10]

From the Polish Socialist Party, Stanisław Dubois and Adam Kuryłowicz and lawyer Wacław Szumański came into this common political body. Norbert Barlicki had died on September 27th, 1941. From the right-wing came Roman Rybarski, Jan Mosdorf, Stefan Niebudek (a lawyer), Piotr Kownacki and others.[11] Lack of data makes it impossible to cite all the names.

On Christmas Eve 1941, on the Poles' greatest holy day, celebrated also in Germany and therefore honoured even by the *SS*-men, late in the evening, when the camp had quietened down and the soldiers had left it, when the door of the barracks had been slammed shut, a very unusual ceremony took place in Block No. 25. Everywhere the prisoners had tried to arrange some sort of celebration and even the most embittered hearts beat a little more warmly, but on Block No. 25 where Pilecki and many of his closest colleagues lived, this Christmas Eve took on a very special character. Room No. 7, where Bartosiewicz was in charge, was strongly guarded. It was beautifully decorated, and a Christmas tree had been set up with the Polish eagle, cut out of a turnip, at the top. The Block Chief, the Silesian Alfred Włodarczyk – a member of the underground network, as was his deputy, Edward

Kulik – allowed several colleagues from other blocks to be invited. Nobody said it aloud, but the small circle who were in the secret knew that the top representatives of the underground organization, military and political, would be coming. Pilecki was anxious to see them together, to unite them and cement their co-operation. It was a risky step and against all the principles of underground work, but the conspirators decided that with great care it could succeed and that it would pay off.

The hosts, the Block Chief and his deputy spoke first, calling for solidarity and expressing the prisoners' longing for their homes;[12] then the doyen of the assembled underground workers addressed the gathering. Norbert Barlicki having died, this role fell to Professor Rybarski. Surely never during his long career as a politician and parliamentarian had his speech struck a more profound note, and never had he been listened to with such attention. He spoke optimistically, as though freedom were close at hand. The Socialist Dubois spoke in reply and shook the professor's hand warmly. Differences of ideology had been blotted out, political barriers had ceased to exist. The two men were surrounded by a circle of soldiers of the camp underground, including Witold Pilecki, Col. Kazimierz Rawicz, Col. Jan Karcz, Lt. Col. Teofil Dziama, Henryk Bartosiewicz, Capt. Stanisław Kazuba, Bernard Świerczyna, Dr. Władysław Dering, Dr. Rudolf Diem, Capt. Tadeusz Lisowski, Włodzimierz Makoliński, Stefan Bielecki and others.

The great risk of the Christmas Eve meeting paid off a hundredfold in increased solidarity, and there were no disastrous consequences.[13]

4

The end of 1941 marked the beginning of a great build-up of the Auschwitz camp. Himmler was interested in this, for a death-factory was being created there which was to lead to the 'final solution' of the Jewish question. In addition a huge industrial complex was being created, to serve the needs of war and at the same time to bring enormous financial gains to the *SS*. Hermann Göring, responsible for the economic planning of the Third *Reich*, was thus also interested in the camp.

In October 1941 engineer Hans Kammler, head of department C of the *SS* Chief Economic and Administrative Office (WVHA), visited the camp and brought with him the decision that at Birkenau a prisoner-of-war camp was to be made ready, not for 100,000 but for 200,000 inmates. Special *Kommandos* were immediately formed,

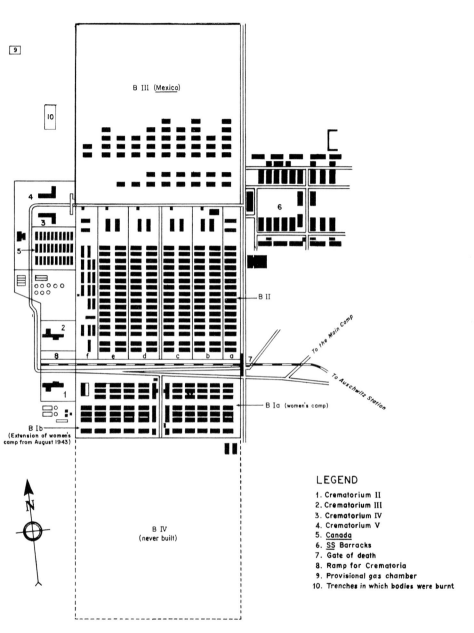

Map of Birkenau.

comprising thousands of prisoners. In 1942 there were about 8,000 in the *Kommandos*.[14] Every day they covered an area of several miles and on the sites of the depopulated villages demolished the remaining houses, levelled the ground, filled in the marsh, constructed a primitive sewage system and marked out the camp roads and the fields where the barracks were to stand.

Two plans were made for the camp in Birkenau. The first, drawn up by one of the prisoners in the Building Office and approved by the camp authorities on October 15th, 1941,[15] envisaged living space for 100,000 (Himmler's order of March 1st, 1941), in a rectangle 2,300 feet long and 400 feet wide. To the left of the road and the railway siding was to be the quarantine camp where the newcomers were to be housed for the first weeks; to the right two ordinary camps. Work had already begun when Kammler brought the order that the building was to be doubled in size. The work begun on the quarantine camp was continued and in this way there arose Section B I (*Bauabschnitt I*), divided into two fields: *a* and *b*. It was to accommodate 20,000 prisoners. On field *a*, brick barracks were built. The walls were thin, of one brick only; there were no ceilings or floors; the small windows let in very little light. The prisoners were to sleep on 'bunks', in vertical tiers of three. The 'bunks' were about six feet wide, the height between one level and another was thirty inches. A barracks contained 62 three-tiered 'bunks'. There were to be four men to a 'bunk' so the whole would contain 744 prisoners. In practice six or more prisoners were put into one 'bunk'. In the Penal Company there were sometimes fourteen, and the prisoners had to sleep in a sitting position, unable even to straighten their backs.[16] On field *b*, beside the Kitchen and the Washroom, only one barracks was of brick. Accommodated in it was the men's Penal Company transferred on May 9th, 1942, from Block No. 11 in the central camp. The small yard was surrounded by a high wall, for the Penal Company had to be isolated from the camp. The large number of the remaining barracks in Birkenau were wooden stables (each for 52 horses) without ceilings, floors or windows; they were draughty, for there was a wide space between the roof and the walls. The three-tiered 'bunks' were to take about 1,000 prisoners in each barracks.

On March 1st, 1942, the part of the central camp set aside for Soviet prisoners-of-war was emptied and those who were still alive were transferred to section B I *b* of the still uncompleted Birkenau. On the same day that this sub-camp was included in the central one, a common register was introduced and a common roll-call ordered. Two weeks later, on March 13th, a selection was made in the central camp: 1,200 sick and convalescent men were chosen and transferred to the same section (B I *b*), to Block No. 4 (later No. 7), the so-called

Isolierstation. These men were doomed to die. Anyone who was not killed on the spot or did not die during the endless standing at atten-

The inside of a barracks at Birkenau.

tion, inspections and 'sport', was destined to end up in the gas chamber.[17]

In the second plan, drawn up on August 15th, 1942, the section B I, already built, was preserved, but the rest was altered, as the camp had to accommodate 200,000 prisoners. To the right of the road and the railway ramp, section B II was planned; further on, beside it, section B III, and to the left of section B I, section B IV. Each of them was to accommodate 60,000 and was to be built in wooden barracks of the stable type. The whole formed a colossal rectangle 7,800 feet long by 2,400 feet wide, surrounded by wire and watch-towers. Inside the rectangle there were to be twenty separate camps, cut off from each other but forming one great whole.

Besides B I only section B II was completed in full. It was divided into 6 fields: *a*, *b*, *c*, *d*, *e* and *f*. Field *a* was the men's quarantine, field *b* was for Jewish families brought from Theresienstadt, field *c* for workshops, field *d* for the men's camp with the Penal Company, field *e* the camp for gypsy families, field *f* the Hospital. All this was carried out in 1943. The first transport from Theresienstadt arrived on January 21st, 1943; the first gypsy transport on February 26th; the men were transferred from section B I *b* in the summer. Section B III, known in the camp as *Mexico*, was only started later and was never finished; section B IV remained on the drawing-board.[18]

A composite photograph showing the size of Birkenau.

The building of Birkenau is a particularly tragic chapter in the history of Auschwitz. The inhabitants of the villages were turned out of their homes, the houses demolished, and the poor-yielding fields were dug up. But all around lay the marshes which it was almost impossible to cross during the autumn and spring rains. Even under normal, civilized conditions work in this area was reckoned to be very heavy, and under camp conditions it was a method of extermination. Saturation bombing, Stalingrad, and the turning-point of the war had not yet come and the prisoners' lives counted for nothing, for industry was not yet crying out for them. The buildings had to be put up as quickly as possible; the means of doing so were primitive and all technical deficiencies had to be made up by the prisoners with their bodies, sweat and blood. The newly-created *Kommandos* were mostly made up of prisoners from the later transports, for the earlier prisoners, already established, did everything possible to keep out of them. Poorly dressed starving men, not yet hardened to camp life, floundered through snow, rain and mud, driven on by shouts and blows with sticks. They fell beside the road leading from the central camp, broke arms and legs under the heavy beams and iron rails, drowned in the boggy soil. When later, in 1943, other prisoners dug sewage trenches on the terrain of Birkenau, the spades and picks brought to light boots, the remains of striped clothing, spectacles, wheels with broken spokes, bones of horses and men.[19] Thousands died before the camp was set up, and this was only the beginning of the worst era in the history of Auschwitz.

The fate of the Soviet prisoners-of-war at Auschwitz is closely connected with the first months of its largest sub-camp. This was only a fragment of the gigantic tragedy, involving many millions of lives, which was played out on the lands occupied by the Germans, but it is such an appalling episode that it cannot be passed over.

After the first two transports of July and September 1941, the men in which were murdered at once without even being given numbers, the Auschwitz authorities were told that bigger transports would be arriving from the POW camp in Łambinowice (Lamsdorf), having been designated by Himmler for work on the building of Birkenau. In September 1941, 9 Blocks (Nos. 1, 2, 3, 12, 13, 14, 22, 23 and 24) of the central camp were assigned to these men. The Blocks were surrounded by electrified barbed wire and over the gate was a sign: *Russisches Kriegsgefangenen Arbeitslager* (Russian POW labour camp). On October 7th a transport of 2,014 soldiers arrived. At short intervals during October and November further transports arrived, and the number of prisoners-of-war brought to Auschwitz reached 11,975.[20]

According to Höss's memoirs, the men who accompanied these prisoners said they had been selected from a much larger number and that the strongest and healthiest had been chosen. In fact they were a poor lot of men, almost starved, barely able to stand and unfit for any work. It might seem that since they had been brought to build Birkenau on the orders of the *Reichsführer SS* they should have been given care, medical attention and extra food, and only then put to work, which in late autumn, in the marshes, was bound to be especially heavy. Höss attempts to make out that this was so, but the facts refute this absolutely. The prisoners went on getting insufficient food, less even than the rest of the camp, and were treated so brutally that they were bound to die in a short time. For several days they were given neither blankets nor underclothing, they were kept naked in the frost for hours on end and were hosed down with water, while during working hours the *Capos* had special orders to murder them on the slightest pretext. Every day, when the *Kommandos* returned from Birkenau, carts loaded with corpses followed behind them. The mortality was so high that when the prisoners were transferred to Birkenau on March 1st, 1942, to the barracks on section B I *b*, barely 945 of them were alive.[21]

Birkenau was built, it was constantly asserted, to be a large POW camp. In practice it was never a POW camp for a single day, and the fact that Soviet prisoners-of-war worked and died to help build it in no way modifies this fact.

5

Auschwitz was above all a death camp, but the needs of war and the business interests of the *SS* were a reminder that the prisoners could

A factory built inside the area under the camp's jurisdiction.

be used in industry and that every ounce of energy should be got out of them to the advantage of the Third *Reich*. Already in January 1941 Dr. Otto Ambros, a director of the great consortium *I. G. Farben*, had come to Katowice, and after inspecting the terrain had decided that Auschwitz would be an excellent place in which to build a synthetic rubber factory, *Buna-Werke*.[22] In February an order was issued by Marshal Göring, head of war production, that all Jews were to be evicted from Auschwitz, as their homes would be needed for the workmen building *Buna*. Jews were sent to the ghetto at Sosnowiec. Himmler, when he inspected Auschwitz in March 1941, confirmed this decision. The camp was to supply *I. G. Farben* with 10,000 prisoners. Naturally this slave labour was to bring the *SS* enormous profits. *I. G. Farben* paid six marks a day for a skilled workman and four marks a day for an unskilled man. Some demands for payment, issued by the camp, have been preserved, from which it appears that for a seven-month period of work by male prisoners and a nine-month period of work by female prisoners various firms paid 12,753,526 marks.[23]

In April 1941 the first prisoners began to walk to a place called Dwory, situated four miles east of the camp. There *Buna-Werke* had already been built. The number of prisoners increased nearly every day. The work was very heavy and the day was made longer by the wearisome march there and back. Later the prisoners were taken by train. On May 31st, 1942, they were put into a sub-camp in Monowice, near Dwory. This sub-camp, built by *I. G. Farben*, constantly grew in size.

After Monowice came Jawiszowice, situated several miles south of the camp. On August 15th, 1942, a sub-camp was opened there, built half-way between the coal-mines in Jawiszowice and Brzeszcze. The building of this sub-camp was financed by the firm *Hermann Göring Werke*, and in the beginning 150 Jews were put into it; later their number rose to 2,500. This was the first time in Germany that prisoners had been employed in mining underground.[24]

Also in August 1942 a further sub-camp was opened in Goleszów, situated more than six miles from the central camp, to the south west. Here the *SS* had their own cement factory. At first there were 300 prisoners there, later their number rose to 1,000.

Close to the central camp there were three sub-camps; these, like Birkenau, were reckoned as part of the central camp, the numbers from their roll-calls being sent there every time and added up as a whole.

The sub-camp at Harmęże, situated two miles to the west of the central camp, was the first to be set up, on December 8th, 1941. It was then inhabited by fifty prisoners, who since April 1941 had formed a *Kommando* employed in breeding fish and conducting experiments. From June 1942 a group of fifty women prisoners was also located there, looking after fowl and rabbits.[25]

A little further south, at the same distance from the main camp, was the sub-camp Rajsko, with its horticultural experiments. This was set up in the spring of 1941, after Himmler's visit in March, for he, as an agriculturist, was very interested in plant growing. At first there was no sub-camp and a *Kommando* of about 150 men from the main camp went there to work every day. From the spring of 1942 about 300 women prisoners started to go there also. The sub-camp was finally set up on June 12th, 1943, after which only the women lived there and the men continued to come from the central camp.[26]

Finally, about less then a mile to the west of Birkenau lay the sub-camp Pławy, also set up in 1943. Both men and women prisoners lived there, employed in cattle-breeding and cultivation of the soil.

These three sub-camps, situated so close to the central camp and Birkenau, played their part in the underground activities. Firstly, through them there was contact with the civilian population, as some specialist workers came every day or others brought in cattle feed, seeds and implements. It was also easier to escape from these sub-camps and the underground used this route several times.

As the war dragged on, the need for cheap slave-labour grew. Between 1942 and 1944 the authorities of Auschwitz built many more sub-camps, bringing their number up to 39. The farthest away was at Brno in Czechoslovakia. Of these 31 worked for factories and industrial plants.[27]

6

When Himmler gave Höss the secret order to prepare Auschwitz for the 'final solution' of the Jewish question, he said that further details would be furnished by Adolf Eichmann. Towards the end of August, or perhaps the beginning of September 1941 (the exact date is not known), *SS* Major Eichmann, head of the Jewish Department (IV B 4) in *RSHA*, came to the camp and acquainted Höss with the whole plan. First the eastern part of Upper Silesia and the south of the *General-Gouvernement* (central Poland designated by Hitler for Poles) was to be cleared of Jews; later, transports from Germany, Czechoslovakia, finally from France, Belgium and Holland, were to be expected. Together the *SS*-men deliberated professionally on how to carry out this colossal task, which, even in the first phase, would involve over a million people. They decided that the killing would have to be done by gas, for shooting women and children daily in such numbers would be too much even for *SS*-men. They also rejected the method used by the *Einsatzgruppen*, whereby engine exhaust fumes were pumped into chambers built on lorries, as being too inefficient.[28]

They had to look for a place for a sheltered gas chamber. Höss took his guest round the whole camp, and in the north-west corner of what was later section B III in Birkenau pointed out a deserted smallholding which might fulfil the conditions provisionally. It was out of the way, hidden by a wood yet not too far from the railway. After the building had been made air-tight it would be possible to gas up to 800 people at a time. They did not then think of crematoria; the bodies were to be buried in a neighbouring meadow. When this gas chamber came into use it was called Bunker No. 1. The means of killing did not have to be sought, for Karl Fritzsch had just completed his experiments and *Cyklon B* used hitherto for destroying vermin, was at their disposal.

While Auschwitz was being provisionally prepared for the extermination process, Eichmann was working on the problem in other sections. On January 20th, 1942, an inter-Ministerial conference was held at Wannsee to co-ordinate the great, State-wide operation. There, among other things, the difficulties of rail transport were discussed. Many high-ranking German officials learnt then of the plans for the 'final solution'.[29]

On March 26th, 1942, the first *Transport-Juden* arrived at Ausch-·witz, sent by Eichmann's Jewish Department of the *RSHA*. These were the 999 Jewesses from Slovakia. As the priority in which Jews from different countries were to be murdered had already been fixed, Höss let this transport into the part of the camp set aside for women, and for clothing gave them the uniforms of murdered Soviet prisoners-of-war. Several further transports from Slovakia and France during the next few months were also brought into the camp, but the fate of these people was terrible. They were murdered in such cruel ways that the plight of the other prisoners in the camp might even appear bearable by comparison. They were simply beaten to death, trodden into the mud. Out of 973 Jews brought from Slovakia on April 17th, 1942, only 88 were alive 17 weeks later (i.e. 91 % had died); of 464 Jews brought from Slovakia on April 19th 1942, only 10 were alive 16 weeks later (i.e. 98 % had died).[30]

On May 12th, 1942, for the first time a transport reached the camp and was sent straight from the railway ramp to the gas chamber in Bunker No. 1. It consisted of 1,500 Jewish men, women and children from Sosnowiec.[31]

This was a turning-point in the history of Auschwitz. From the very beginning, to be there had been almost the same as being under a death sentence. Tens of thousands of prisoners had already died there. Groups of prisoners had gone almost straight from the railway-trucks to their death by shooting or beating. Tests had been made with gas. But up to then it had not been an extermination camp in the full sense of the word. From May 12th, 1942, the name *Vernichtungslager* (death camp) hung like an ominous cloud over the fenced-in marshes where a colony of human ants sought vainly for help.

The transports from the *RSHA* became more and more frequent; before each one a statement was sent to the camp's command, saying: 'the transport conforms to the directions given and is to be included in the special operation'. As Bunker No. 1 could no longer cope with the increased workload, on June 30th, 1942, a second temporary gas chamber was put into operation, in another house in a clearing in the wood to the west of section B III at Birkenau. Near both the chambers, barracks had been built in which the victims undressed. At the same time the *SS* authorities asked two German firms (*Hoch und Tiefbau – A.G.* and *Schlesischer Industriebau Lenz und Co. – A.G.*) for estimates to build crematoria in the camp. Burying the corpses in trenches was too primitive and quite impracticable when it was intended to murder millions of people.

In accordance with Himmler's orders all Jews sent to Auschwitz in *RSHA* transports* were to be murdered, and this order was scrupulously carried out, although these transports did not go straight to the gas chambers. Only regard for previously settled priorities held them up. Before the death machine was perfected and gathered momentum, however, an order came from Berlin in the middle of 1942 that selections were to be made and those fit for work kept in the camp. German industry was crying out ever more insistently for labour. Eichmann and the whole department of the *RSHA* was demanding the speediest extermination, but another department, the *WVHA*, represented by Oswald Pohl, responsible for the business side of the *SS*, wanted munition workers. The needs of war won. On July 11th a transport of Jews sent by the *RSHA* from Slovakia was the first from among whom selections were made. 182 men (numbers from 46463 to 46644) and 148 women (numbers from

The railway line leading up to 'the gate of death', as the main entrance of Birkenau was known. ▷

---

* A small number of Jews reached Auschwitz in other transports (sometimes among other nationalities), and these had a greater chance of survival. Jews who fell into German hands as soldiers had some legal protection, but only to a certain degree. In Auschwitz, as a prisoner, was an English army doctor, Dr. Sperber (No. 85512), taken out of a POW camp (J. Sehn, *Obóz* . . ., p. 119).

8576 to 8723) were chosen and brought into the camp, while the rest went to their death.

The scenes which took place during the selections and in front of the gas chambers are almost beyond description.* The condemned, of course, were told that they had come to a labour camp and that they were only to have a bath and be disinfected, but the atmosphere of the transport and their reception in the camp had aroused their worst fears. Women gathered up their children and clasped them to themselves, they tried to hide them among their clothing, sometimes even pushed them to one side, so that they should not appear to belong together. A few summoned up great courage and, with deadly fear in their eyes, joked with the children, gave them toys and laughed, trying to make them feel at ease and be unaware of the spectre of death.[32] Sometimes, while they were undressing in front of the gas chambers, people uttered horrible shrieks and went into a frenzy of fear. These were at once taken behind the building and killed by a shot from small-bore weapons. The SS-men, even though they had been trained with special discipline and had an implicit belief in the rightness of orders from above, had to be given vodka and extra rations.

The whole frightful procedure was to be kept secret and the SS-men who took part in it signed a special declaration,† but, as usual, not everyone obeyed this strict order, and in any case the massacres were too great to be hidden. The camp underground organization sent reports outside, which got to Warsaw and thence to London, but

---

* On August 30th, 1942 a doctor of medicine and philosophy, Professor extraordinary of Anatomy at the University of Münster, SS-*Obersturmführer* Johann Kremer, took up the position of SS doctor in the camp. His office required his presence at the selections and the gassings. Kremer kept a diary. Here are some entries:

'2.9.42. At 3 a.m. I was present for the first time at a "special operation". In comparison with it Dante's inferno seems to me to be almost a comedy.

18.10.42. In cold and rainy weather I was present to-day, Sunday morning, at the eleventh special operation. Terrible scenes with three women who begged for their lives.

8.11.42. This afternoon yet another special operation, the fourteenth, at which I have been present. In the evening a very pleasant gathering in the *Führersheim* ... Bulgarian red wine and Croatian slivovitz were served.' (*Auschwitz note-books*, No. 13, 1971, pp. 40, 48, 52).

† '1. I know and I learned to-day that I will be punished by death if I lay my hands on Jewish belongings.

2. About all the actions, necessary in the evacuation of Jews, I must keep absolutely silent even among my comrades.

3. I undertake to carry out these actions efficiently with my whole person and all my strength.'

even if there had been no organization, the secret could still not have been kept. In the summer of 1942, when the numbers murdered were growing fast, the Germans stopped burying the corpses and began to burn them in trenches and on pyres. The remains of those already buried were also dug up and thrown into the fire. The stench spread far and wide and the entire local population began to talk of the burning of Jews. The bodies were burnt day and night to keep up with the frequent transports; the flames leapt up high and were so visible that the anti-aircraft units began to complain, but no notice was taken of them.[33] The murder lust, backed up by Himmler's orders, was stronger than logic and all humane instincts.

A crematorium being built in Birkenau.

In the countries from which Jews were sent to Auschwitz they were told that they were going to labour camps in the East and should therefore take as many of their valuables as they could carry. Doctors should take their instruments with them, dentists their chairs, musicians their violins. In Greece people even signed contracts with the German authorities for the purchase of lots and shops in the Ukraine. The wealthy Jewish families of Western and Southern Europe sold shops, houses, flats and factories and bought up jewellery,

A gas chamber.

gold, diamonds, dollars, and the best clothing as they prepared for
the forced journey. The transport in crowded cattle-trucks served to
damp their hopes of a decent future, but arrival at the camp really
opened their eyes. When the train stopped at the ramp and the shout
of *Alles raus*! ('get out') rang out, the travel-weary people came face
to face with a reality which they had not foreseen. Driven from the
trucks, they were allowed to take with them only what they had on
them or in their pockets. They were told that all their possessions
would be returned to them, but although the *SS*-men had instructions
to behave correctly, their faces caused fear. The people went straight
to the gas chamber or to undergo selection, and thousands of trunks,
suitcases, bags and packages were loaded into vans and taken to the
barracks, known in camp jargon as *Canada*. These were built between
the Munitions Stores and the Railway Station. Not only the things
brought from the ramp were taken there, but also everything stripped
from the people who went naked to the gas-chambers. Very soon the
capacity of the barracks proved insufficient, so *Canada II* was built
in the western corner of the section B II in Birkenau. 30 huge barracks

were put up there, which were soon overflowing. The articles began to be laid out between the barracks, and the huge piles soon reached the height of the roofs. The whole procedure of collecting, sorting and despatching the effects of the murdered Jews was named 'Operation Reinhard' in honour of the head of the *RSHA*, Reinhard Heydrich. The following figures will give some idea of its scale and the amount of goods taken in this way. In January 1945, just before the camp was evacuated, the *SS*-men set fire to the *Canada* barracks and only six of them were not destroyed. After the Germans had gone the following were found in them: 348,820 complete men's outfits, 836,255 complete women's outfits, 5525 pairs of women's shoes, 38,000 pairs of men's shoes, 13,964 carpets and innumerable sets of false teeth, spectacles, shaving brushes, etc.[34]

Shoes in *Canada* from those killed in the gas chambers.

The arrival of Jewish transports and all the surrounding circumstances basically changed the character of the Auschwitz camp. Not only did it become a place for mass murder, but at the same time an area of the most striking contrasts. The Jews' effects were segregated in *Canada* and, although this was punishable by death,[35] they were smuggled into the camp and also outside it. The *Capos* and Block Chiefs began to wear the finest silk underwear, shaved with the most expensive soap, trampled in the mud with the most fashionable shoes. Margarine, salami and bread ceased to be their basic diet. From *Canada* there came into the camp tins of sardines, Dutch cheeses, the most expensive French wines and cognac. The Block Chief of the Penal Company, a power in the camp, invited criminal prisoners to a birthday party with champagne and roast goose, smuggled from outside the camp for dollars.[36] For a small onion one could buy a gold watch; for a bit of butter from a parcel sent by relations, a diamond of several carats. The treasures of *Canada* reached even the poorest *Muzelmen*,* for food taken from Jewish transports was sent to the kitchen and thrown into the pots. The camp soups became thicker, but one had to look out, for sometimes a razor blade, an old button, or a gold five-dollar piece might be found in the bowl.[37]

The *SS*-men were infected by the frenzy for loot and easy riches. Everything taken from the Jews was supposed to go to Berlin and sorted out there. Watches were sent to front-line *SS* units, clothes to the bombed towns, ingots of gold from the victims' teeth to the *Reich* bank, jewellery to the Swiss market. Even the hair cut off the corpses was sent to a factory in Bavaria.[38] For an *SS*-man to appropriate anything at all from Jewish effects meant disgrace and the death sentence, but greed for possession was stronger than any threats. Partnerships were formed between prisoners and *SS*-men: the former carried out valuables from *Canada*, the latter guarded him and shared the loot. The soldiers were free to go where they wanted, so they carried their share outside the camp and gave it to trusted people, sometimes their families, in the hope that after the war they would be able to enjoy their wealth. After the war the terrain where the camp had stood became a place where a special type of 'geologist' found what he was looking for. During its existence the camp became a huge black market, perhaps the biggest in Europe at that time, with a constant exchange of goods with the outside world. Railway-men, civilian workers and, above all, the soldiers from the *SS* garrison were the go-betweens. Discipline weakened, as was inevitable, since even the Commandant himself, Rudolf Höss, was unable to control his lust for possessions. He

---

* Camp jargon for a prisoner completely broken down (mainly from hunger) physically and mentally.

several times visited the Tannery and from its *Obercapo* received a number of valuable objects removed from *Canada*.[39]

Yet Auschwitz had changed its basic character. From the very beginning it had been terrible; now it became even more ghastly, but in a different way.

CHAPTER 5

The underground network in Birkenau; Pilecki's
contact with the Czechs; the transmitting station;
the first escapes; revolt in the Penal Companies;
further unification of the military groups.

1

The turn of the year 1941–42, the building of Birkenau and other
sub-camps, and the transformation of Auschwitz into an extermination camp, all had a great influence on the camp underground
movement, which was now faced with new tasks. Pilecki, in his
report, writes:

> Thus began the year 1942 – as regards the camp in Auschwitz
> the most terrible, as regards the work of our organization in the
> camp the most interesting, the year in which we attained our
> highest achievements.[1]

The main task for the immediate future was to set up an underground post in Birkenau. Formally it was only a sub-camp, but it
was growing very fast in size and importance. New sectors and areas
were being developed and on them hundreds of barracks were being
constructed, two temporary gas chambers were in action and Jews
were being massacred; nearby was situated the barracks called
Canada, overflowing with riches.

The underground needed a way of gathering information quickly
and efficiently, and of communicating it to the central camp. From
there it went to Warsaw. The West had to be told of the crimes
committed against Jews, the murdering of prisoners-of-war and the
new methods of liquidation. From August 1941 they were even
being killed by injections, for which the weakest prisoners, already
unable to work, were selected. These selections were made from
among all the prisoners, not only Jews. At first hydrogen peroxide,
benzine, evipan and phenol were injected, later phenol only, straight
into the heart.[2]

In March 1942 the few remaining Soviet prisoners-of-war were
moved to Birkenau and after them, a couple of weeks later, a
certain number of other prisoners, mainly Poles. These were sick
and convalescent, numbering 1,200, taken from the Hospital and
destined to be exterminated in Birkenau. They were put into the

Izolierstation. In addition there were a certain number of healthy prisoners, who were to work in the administration and on the further enlargement of the camp. Pilecki had some of his men among these. This was useful, but in his opinion none of them was capable of taking over the role of leader for the whole of Birkenau.

Just then, when it was becoming necessary to consider nominating someone for this position from among his colleagues in the central camp and trying to get him sent to Birkenau to a good *Kommando*, which could have been arranged through Otto Küsel, the *SS*-men themselves settled the matter. Col. Karcz was already a member of the organization, but he worked in the area of the Tannery and was wasted from the point of view of underground work, as there was nothing for him to do there. Suddenly, on April 2nd, 1942, the Political Department sent for him and after interrogation he was put, that same day, into the bunker. Every day he was taken for further interrogation, accompanied by beating. Pilecki was informed of this at once. It was impossible to get near Karcz, but it had to

Birkenau

be presumed that the *SS*-men were asking him about the camp underground movement, of which they must have been aware. Pilecki regretted that sentiment had caused him to depart from the principle of keeping out of the underground senior officers imprisoned under their own names. After nine days Karcz, pale and barely able to stand, came out of the bunker; that same evening he saw Pilecki and Bartosiewicz and said:

> Well, congratulate me – they let me out. They asked if there was any organization in the camp. Don't be afraid, I didn't tell them anything. I'll tell you about it to-morrow . . .[3]

But this meeting never took place, for the next morning Karcz was moved to Birkenau, perhaps because the *SS*-men still suspected him of having secret connections and wished to make them more difficult. Pilecki waited for a few days and then made contact with him through Bartosiewicz, who was at that time working in the sewage *Kommando* which used to go to Birkenau. Karcz was asked to take over the leadership of the underground there and after short consideration he agreed. This took place towards the end of April 1942.[4]

It would have been hard to find a better candidate. Karcz's basic disadvantage was that he was in the camp under his own name and, as a high-ranking officer, had already aroused the interest of the Political Department; but he had come out of the bunker alive, and under severe interrogation he had not broken down nor given anything away. In this he had given proof of the toughness necessary under difficult conditions, and it could be expected that when faced by a new test of strength he would again not break down. He had, however, to reckon with the possibility of further interrogation and strict observation. This hampered his movements, necessitated extra caution and was a hindrance in carrying out his tasks, but otherwise he was an ideal choice. He was a man in the prime of life, able to undertake any work; his fellow-prisoners liked and trusted him; he knew how to cope with difficult men: the trusties, even the criminals, showed him a certain respect.

This derived from the peculiar atmosphere of concentration camps. A policeman, judge or public prosecutor would be killed once the criminal prisoners discovered who he was; priests also had a hard time, although they were protected by some of the political prisoners; soldiers, on the other hand, were badly treated by the *SS*-men but not by their fellow-prisoners. When a senior officer found himself in the camp, if he was spared by the Political Department and if he proved tough and adaptable, most prisoners accepted his authority and accorded him respect and even obedience. The criminals, especially the 'high-class' ones, burglars and safe-breakers with big-time or international reputations, felt a certain satisfaction that they could live together as comrades. They felt the same way towards eminent intellectuals, provided the latter showed endurance. This was the basic condition, proving that the prisoner was really a man. Automatically this comradely attitude of the *prominents** was a safeguard against chicanery on the part of the lesser criminal trusties, recruited from thieves, pick-pockets and ponces.

In this respect the German concentration camps were bound by the traditions brought from the prisons. Safe-breakers and high-class burglars belonged to the highest category in the criminal world and it rarely happened that they were petty-minded. They did not torment their fellow-prisoners, they did not disgrace themselves by beating weaker men or stealing from comrades. They treated the small-time thieves, fences and ponces with disdain and hardly talked to them. They looked for the company of intellectuals, scientists and senior officers, considering them their equals.[5]

Col. Karcz quickly made himself at home at Birkenau for, thanks to Pilecki's contacts, he had the support of the Labour Assignment Office, which had an independent section in the sub-camp. From March of 1942, Józef Mikusz, a Silesian, had been working in this section and he kept the files of prisoners' trades. He had been in Pilecki's organization while still in the central camp, and now, through him, the more important prisoners belonging to the underground, (Karcz included) were put into good *Kommandos* and good Blocks in Birkenau. In the group of electricians, which had considerable freedom of movement, was Henryk Porębski, through whom Mikusz had been recruited to Pilecki's organization. He made out the lists of prisoners sent to the gas chambers from Birkenau and also the lists of transports sent to other camps. These lists were sent secretly to the central camp. The *Capo* of the *Kommando* in the roofing-felt factory was Edward Jasiński. Because this *Kommando* went far beyond the camp every day, he was a vital liaison with the outside world, smuggling out letters which were sent through his contacts with civilians.

Karcz gathered many men in and bound them together by secret ties; but he also had to build up around him the apparatus to direct the underground work in the extensive camp. Some of these men were placed in the Jewish blocks in order to try and alleviate the suffering of the human mass crowded into them. Liaison with the Soviet prisoners was carried out by Bogdan Gliński. Contact with the central camp, with Pilecki and the underground hierarchy there, was established through Bartosiewicz, who, as already mentioned,

---

* *Prominent* – slang for a prisoner in a good position in the camp.

went to Birkenau almost every day. Apart from information, which was collected and sent to the central camp, the chief task of the underground in the huge sub-camp was the assistance given to fellow-prisoners, especially those who had joined the secret network and rendered service to it.[6]

2

On June 6th, 1941, almost exactly twelve months from the formation of Auschwitz, the first transport of Czechs arrived. There were sixty of them and they were given the numbers from 17045 to 17104. From then onwards the camp began to take on an international character, although to the end Poles predominated. At first the flow of other nationalities was minimal. On July 18th, among a transport of forty-five men, two Spanish political prisoners were sent from Germany; on September 28th, twenty-two Yugoslavs from Veldes, also political, and the same day eight Austrians from Klagenfurt. Later, little by little, more Czechs and Yugoslavs arrived, but only the influx of Soviet prisoners-of-war made it evident that not only Polish and German were spoken in the camp.

Pilecki realized that the camp underground could not close its eyes to the inflow of representatives of the other nations, and that it must look for contacts among them. But the problem was difficult and had to be approached cautiously. Even the recruiting of newly-arrived Poles depended to a great extent on pre-war acquaintanceship and former underground, political or other affinities. Bringing into the underground someone completely unknown was always done with the greatest of care. How could one decide whether to trust strangers? Hatred of the Germans alone was not sufficient; one had to look for men one already knew belonged to a definite ideological group, were genuine believers of a known religion, or belonged to an acceptable political movement.

Of the other nationalities in the camp the most numerous at that time were Russians, but they were being murdered wholesale and contact was difficult. As long as they were in the central camp they were kept in blocks wired off from the rest of the prisoners, driven to work in their own *Kommandos* and isolated from the camp. Finally, and not surprisingly, their education and upbringing, combined with their treatment in the camp, caused them to behave with the utmost reserve. They had their own leaders, mainly officers who concealed their rank. One could sometimes help them with an extra loaf of bread or a cauldron of soup, but it was still too soon for any real contact.

Pilecki considered the Czechs, observed them, looked out for any chance acquaintances, but it was only the 7th transport that enabled him to take a more serious step. On January 15th, 1942, 135 men arrived from Prague and were given numbers from 25551 to 25685. From the central camp office, where the organization had its men, came the information that the Czech transport was entirely composed of intelligentsia, almost all members of the *Sokół* organization. By a coincidence they were put into room 7 in Block No. 25, where Pilecki lived together with many of his underground colleagues from the *Kommandos* working in the Tannery.

The Czechs made an excellent impression, and their *Sokół* membership made it likely that they would be trustworthy. *Sokół* was also known in Poland and played a serious educational role among tough and patriotic young people. Sport was their main interest, but they also practised drill and learnt order, discipline and comradeship. The organization had spread among many of the Poles who had emigrated to the United States, and the *Sokóls* had furnished many volunteers for the Polish Army in France during the First World War.

The group of prisoners living in room 7 were so close together that they were able to welcome their Czech brothers suitably. Pilecki, of course, could not appear personally, but through one of his friends he arranged everything with the Block Orderly, a young Pole Stanisław Kożuch. After the evening roll-call and after the bread had been given out, when the prisoners were getting ready to lie down, Kożuch, in the name of the Poles living in the room, greeted the Czechs cordially and promised them help. He urged them to keep together and show endurance, explaining that among the camp adherents of the fist and the stick they would also meet Poles, but that their behaviour was not a measure of the sentiments of the Polish nation. The Czechs were moved; Jan Stranski, a lawyer from Prague who spoke good Polish, stepped forward and thanked the Poles cordially. Later the whole transport joined in the well-known Czech song: 'There under the dark, green sycamore . . .'

Pilecki waited a little longer and then contacted Stranski secretly.[7] This was the first attempt, and a successful one, at establishing underground organizational co-operation with a representative of another nationality in the Auschwitz camp. The leader of the Czech group trusted the Poles and they did not let him down. Thanks to their help he obtained a good position in the central office and, largely thanks to this, survived the camp. Certain instructions must have come with the Czech transport, for the SS-men employed a series of ingenious petty cruelties towards the prisoners from it. The Czechs were tough, were not afraid of work and normally did not give in easily; yet, in spite of the help of the Poles, after a few winter months less than twenty remained out of the 135. Fate smiled on these, for suddenly, on May 12th, 1942, they were set free.[8] It is difficult to establish whether those released were all from this same transport. The death of so many Czechs and the release of several others did not prevent further underground contacts, for new men were constantly arriving, the transports mostly coming from Brno and Prague. The Czechs were usually kept in the central camp, but they were sometimes sent to Birkenau and other sub-camps.

3

The growth of the camp and of the underground movement made it necessary for contacts with the outside world to be widened and accelerated. The system employed so far, with reports being sent to Warsaw through released prisoners and occasional contacts with civilian workers, was now inadequate and Pilecki was privately thinking of starting up his own radio-station in the camp. The plan, outwardly unrealistic against the background of camp life and the terror reigning there, was yet not devoid of all chance of success. The camp had grown so large that there were hopes of finding a good hiding-place, and such details as the dates and hours of the call signs and the wavelength could be passed to the outside world fairly easily. The problem was how to get hold of the parts, especially valves. As often happens, a coincidence again turned out to be helpful, in addition to the organization's own valuable contacts.

In the spring of 1942 Mieczysław Januszewski from the Labour Assignment Office came one evening to Pilecki's block and told him in great secrecy that the *SS*-men were looking for two cartographers for the *Funkstelle*, the radio-telegraph centre attached to the Auschwitz *SS* Command. Pilecki had been waiting for news of this kind, for the necessary parts could be obtained there. A decision was taken quickly and Januszewski put forward the numbers of Pilecki and Konstanty Piekarski, from the fourth 'upper' five. They were not specialists, but with ingenuity and a passable knowledge of maps they could hold their own in the *Funkstelle*. During a few weeks, with the help of Lt. Rosa, already a member of the underground, they managed to obtain all the necessary parts and get them into Block No. 20, which belonged to the Hospital and where Alfred Stössel, a member of the first 'upper' five, ruled as the Block Chief.[9] There, in the cellar, underground electricians set up a transmitting station. It was an excellent place, for typhus was rife in the camp and the *SS*-men were very unwilling to enter the infected area: Block No. 20 was specially set aside for infectious illness. Through

contacts, established earlier for sending reports and secret correspondence, the Silesia District of the Home Army was informed of
the wavelengths on which they would broadcast. Reception was
organized as near as possible to the camp. For seven months Stössel
transmitted from the secret radio-station. Transmissions were
infrequent, at various times; the bulletins concerned new transports,
the death rate in the camp and general living conditions. Unfortunately no details concerning reception have been preserved; none
of the people near the camp, who organized the monitoring of the
secret station and forwarded the news, survived the war.

The SS-men soon got to know that the transmitter was working
and looked for it furiously. They pulled up floors in the workshops
and stores, tapped the walls, questioned informers. It was a painful
time for the whole SS garrison, as it undermined their prestige and
made fools of them in the eyes of the prisoners. The search for the
transmitter was carried on outside the camp as well, in areas adjoining it. The SS-men never found it, but in the autumn of 1942 it was
thought necessary to dismantle the set and stop transmitting. Too
many prisoners knew about it and not all would be able to keep
silent.[10]

Some informants state that the organization had a second crystal
set at this time, but Pilecki's report does not confirm this.

4

During the first months of 1942 the camp authorities were informed
by Berlin that they were no longer to apply the principle of collective
responsibility for escapes, which had till then been carried out mainly
by keeping the prisoners standing for hours at roll-calls. The new
regulation was issued only because too many prisoners died or fell
sick at these roll-calls, and they were needed for work important to
German war production. On receiving this information the Union
of Military Organization (*ZOW*) changed its mind about opposing
escapes and Pilecki decided to use this method as one of the ways of
sending reports to Warsaw. It also represented a last chance for
those who had been in trouble with the *Gestapo* before their arrival
in the camp. Sentences of death were frequently sent on to the SS
in the camp in cases such as these, to be carried out after a certain
time.

The first choice fell on an excellent soldier of the underground
and close co-worker of Pilecki's, Stefan Bielecki. Wincenty Gawron
decided to escape with him. They had both been sent to prison and
to the camp on a charge of possessing arms; any day they might be

summoned to Block 11, to the 'wall of death'. The secret contacts in the Labour Assignment Office helped them to be transferred to the sub-camp Harmęże, from where escape was easier. On May 16th, 1942, they disappeared under darkness and managed to cross the terrain under the camp's jurisdiction. Gawron decided to hide in a village not very far from the camp; Bielecki headed in the direction of Warsaw with Pilecki's report. Soon it was in the hands of the Home Army Commander.[11] At that time contact between the military underground organization in the camp and the H.Q. of the Home Army in Warsaw was regular and well-established. Pilecki was also in touch with the District Commanders of the Home Army at Cracow and Silesia. The plans for a fight for the camp were to be synchronised with the plans for a general uprising in Poland.

This first trial run of escapes, which started a further series some of which were organized by the camp underground, was only the prelude to a daring achievement which took place a month later and which became part of the history, not only of Auschwitz, but of all the German concentration camps.

On June 20th, 1942, in the afternoon, a private car, a Steyr 220, drove up to the barrier which separated the camp zone from the rest of the country. In it were two officers and two NCOs of the *SS*, armed with pistols and rifles and wearing helmets. The *SS*-man on guard at the barrier, who was ordered to check all passes, seeing the officers' uniforms, omitted the formality and quickly lifted the pole, saluting and shouting *Heil Hitler*. The Steyr drove quickly through the streets of the town of Auschwitz, crossed the bridge over the Soła and turned north. Twice the car met groups of working prisoners with *SS*-men guarding them; several times it had to turn back, for the driver had mistaken the road.[12]

The evening roll-call in the central camp was the occasion of a terrific scene. It turned out that four prisoners were missing, as was the Steyr car of the head of the *HWL* (the central industrial camp), *SS* Captain Kreuzman, in charge of the motor Workshops and Garages. Höss's deputy, *SS* Captain Hans Aumeier, who had just ridden in from *Buna* in time for the roll-call, screamed in rage that he had passed the Steyr on the way and returned the salute of the officers in it.[13] The *SS*-man who had let the car through was brought from the guard-house, and the numbers of the prisoners working in the *HWL* were checked. It was soon established who was missing: Eugeniusz Bendera, Stanisław Gustaw Jaster, Jósef Lempart and Kazimierz Piechowski.[14] A chase was ordered and all the neighbouring police and gendarmes were alerted, but in vain.

The daring escape was prepared in classic style by four prisoners. Firstly they made keys to the Uniform and Arms Stores, taking impressions in bread and making replicas at the locksmith's. When this had been done, they obtained the necessary personal documents and passes and copied them, adding the secret marks, which were changed every week, sometimes every day. They had to expect a proper check at the gates. Prepared for everything, they had the nerve to pass the guards and working parties in full daylight. It created a great stir in the camp. Thousands of prisoners passed on the details by word of mouth, camp gossip multiplied the number of escapees and the quantity of arms taken, and the helplessness of the *SS* was laughed at. These four brave men never realised how they had raised the spirits of their fellow-prisoners, how much optimism they had aroused. Only a few of the inner circle of the underground knew that one of the escapees, 2nd-Lt. Stanisław G. Jaster, was a member of the camp underground organization and Pilecki's courier, and that he had taken the latest report to the H.Q. of the Home Army.[15] So, when the four men reached the neighbourhood of Stary Sacz and changed their uniforms for civilian clothes, Jaster took leave of his companions and set off for Warsaw.*

The first two escapes, either organized or made use of by the Union of Military Organization, were the beginning of a long series of similar attempts. Some were successful, some ended tragically. There were many cases when the escapees were re-captured. As a rule they were publicly hanged and the whole camp had to be present, but before this they had to undergo cruel interrogation in the Political Department. *SS*-men always suspected that other prisoners had helped in the escapes and tried to get the full details of the plot and the names of the people involved. The re-captured needed heroic strength to keep silent. Their deaths were always cruel. Comically dressed up, they had to march round the camp beating a drum and wearing a placard on their breasts with the words: 'Hurrah, I am back'. In spite of such tragic failures, throughout the period of the camp underground, this method was used to send out reports and men on special assignments.[16]

5

Pilecki, in his preliminary plans, when he went voluntarily to the camp and operated there during the first months, had dreamt of staging a fight with the *SS* garrison and freeing the prisoners. The unreality of these ideas at the beginning was very obvious, and later, in spite of the creation of the camp underground and contacts with

---

* For Jaster's subsequent fate see Appendix II, item 3.

the partisans, the possibilities of such action were not greatly improved. In 1942 there were still minimal chances of a revolt, and yet attempts at a fight and mass escape were made twice on a limited scale. Both attempts concerned the Penal Companies.

On May 27th, 1942, in the yard of Block No. 11, 168 prisoners who had been brought from Cracow on April 24th and 25th were shot against the 'wall of death'. On the same day about 400 prisoners brought from Warsaw and Cracow during 1940–1941 were sent to the Penal Company, which from May 9th, 1942, had been in Birkenau in Block No. 1, Sector B I *b*.[17] There every prisoner had a black patch in the shape of a circle sewn on his blouse and trousers, while the newcomers had to sew on an extra red circle. This meant that the Political Department regarded them as particularly dangerous and that they were to be treated in a special way. The men were all very uneasy, as the transfer to the Penal Company was bound up with the shooting of 168 colleagues. Zenon Różański, who was at that time a prisoner there, describes the development of events:

> A week later 8 men with red circles were called out after the morning roll-call, sent to the central camp and shot there in Block No. 11. Two days later another 10 'red circles' were called out after the morning roll-call, and again came the news that they had all been shot. When for the third time prisoners from this group were summoned to the central camp, it became clear that the wearers of the 'red circles' had been sentenced to death . . .
>
> The atmosphere in the company became heavy. The 'red circles' began to keep apart from the others. Every free moment one saw them gathered together and breaking off the conversation if anyone else approached them. During work periods they worked twice as hard.[18]

The news from the central camp about the shootings reached the Penal Company through the underground, for Pilecki's network had several men there: cadet-officer Stanisław Maringe, Henryk Lachowicz, Jerzy Poraziński, Zenon Różański, Capt. Chruścicki and his son Tadeusz.[19] Pilecki was informed of the situation. From his contacts in the Political Department he knew that all the 'red circles' were doomed, so he had to give thought to an attempt to save his colleagues who were sentenced to death.

The whole of the Penal Company went to work near the river Vistula, where they were building a canal called *Königsgraben*. The *SS*-man in charge at that time was *SS* Sergeant Otto Moll[20], assisted by a number of trusties, almost all German criminals. The circumstances of working not far from the river and outside the camp laid the way open for some chance of escape. This was taken advantage of, and, through the underground's communication channels, men outside the camp were told to prepare help for escaping prisoners on the far side of the Vistula. Henryk Lachowicz took on himself the role of organizer and leader of the main group of 'red circles'. On the appointed day, at the moment when Moll's whistle to cease work sounded, the group was to jump the *SS*-men, disarm them and run for the embankment by the Vistula. This action, lasting a few seconds, would be the signal for the other groups of 'red circles' and for the rest of the prisoners, for the escape was to include everyone. Each group would have to force the Vistula embankment independently and swim across the river. The contacts alerted on the far side would arrange their further escape; much would depend on individual courage, enterprise and luck. Naturally, heavy losses were to be expected, perhaps even 200 prisoners would fall to bullets or be caught and murdered, perhaps more would die and only 50 be saved; but how much better that would be than to wait passively for certain death.

It was decided that the attempt to escape would take place on June 10th. On the 9th Pilecki received a note from Poraziński: 'to-morrow during working hours'.[21] It was a beautiful, sunny day, with no suggestion of a change of weather. Suddenly, at about four o'clock, clouds appeared in the sky and rain began to fall; some minutes later this turned into a downpour. In the torrents of rain it was almost impossible to see. Those in the know were not upset by this, as it could only facilitate their plans for work would go on to the end of the day; it never stopped for bad weather. But this time they were mistaken. Unexpectedly Otto Moll came out of his hut, looked around and with one long, shrill whistle gave the signal to knock off work. It was only half-past four. The following moments are described by Różański, who was also ready to escape:

I turned my head to where Lachowicz was working with his group. They were by themselves, about 300 metres from the next group. What now? What would Lachowicz decide? Could the whole, carefully prepared operation be carried out now? I could feel cold shivers running down my spine, I stood motionless, as if hypnotised. Suddenly I heard a shout from the embankment. Several prisoners are rushing it. The figure of the guard disappears and soon after I see him on the ground. The escapees are running past him. The distance between me and where they are is a good 200 metres. A few metres from me Moll is standing, completely taken by surprise. If I move, I thought quickly, he will put a bullet into my head. The prisoners are running wildly from every side. The guards are throwing down their rifles and chasing along the embankment. I can see plainly figures running across the wall and disappearing on the other side. Suddenly on the embankment appears *Capo* Karl 'Dachdecker'[22] with other *Capos*. He is holding an axe in his hand and shrieking savagely. A few metres from him the prisoner Pajączkowski runs on to the wall. Karl threw himself on him. For a moment they struggled. In the end Pajączkowski fell to the ground beneath Karl's blows. This was the turning-point. The other prisoners running towards the embankment suddenly stopped and *Kommandoführer* Moll remembered that he had a pistol . . . Bullets began to whistle round the ears of the escapees. The order came: lie down.[23]

Unfortunately the unexpectedly early signal to knock off work upset the conspirators' plans. It is possible that at the last moment they lost courage anyway; only fifty prisoners with 'red circles' under Lachowicz's leadership disarmed the nearest *SS*-men and tried to get away. Thirteen fell to the hail of bullets,* a number turned back and only nine reached the Vistula and freedom.†

The camp authorities, applying the principle of collective responsibility despite the general order from Berlin, took bloody retaliation for the attempt at a mass escape. Danuta Czech in her Calendar of camp events describes it thus:

On June 11th after the morning roll-call there remained about 320 prisoners wearing red circles. Over 100 prisoners wearing black circles, and between ten and twenty with red ones, were led out under a strong escort of *SS*-men to work in the *Königsgraben*. About 10 a.m. *Lagerführer*‡ Aumeier arrived with some *SS*-men and demanded of the 320 prisoners that they surrender the organizers of the revolt. As he got no reply he called out 20 prisoners from the ranks. 17 he shot personally; 3 were shot by *SS Hauptscharführer*§ Hössler. In the afternoon a number of prisoners of the Penal Company from the camp hospital were added to the remainder. The clothes and boots were dragged off the condemned men. Their hands were tied behind their backs with barbed wire. The whole column of about 320 prisoners was

---

* Their names are in Appendix III, item 4.

† Their names are in Appendix III, item 5.

‡ *SS* Officer directly in charge of the camp.

§ Warrant Officer.

led to the Bunker in Birkenau, where they were gassed. Altogether on that day 20 prisoners of the Penal Company were shot and 320 gassed.[24]

The epilogue to the whole incident took place on July 8th, 1942. On this day two members of the Penal Company, who had taken part in the escape and been recaptured in the area of the camp, were hanged publicly. They were Tadeusz Pejsik and Henryk Pajączkowski.

In the light of present knowledge of all the decisions and events of that time, it could be argued that the first attempt at an organized, open revolt and escape partly by the use of force (disarming the guards), with the support of the underground military organization, was worthwhile. The 'red circles' were already doomed and none of them would have left the camp alive. Seven were saved by the escape, and there would have been more if work had not stopped early, something which could not have been foreseen. The fidelity of the German trusties had also been under-estimated; they stood by the side of the SS-men and showed more determination and experience in preventing the escape than the latter.

It was a different matter when a similar attempt was made in the women's Penal Company. At the beginning of June 1942, in the sub-camp at Budy, situated several miles to the south-west of the central camp, a women's Penal Company was formed, to which were sent 400 women. There were 200 Polish women, political prisoners, brought in transports from Cracow on April 27th and May 28th, 1942, and a certain number of Germans and Jewesses from Slovakia and France.[25] The company worked under the very worst conditions, building an embankment along the Vistula and deepening ponds. The SS-women and the trusties tormented the prisoners and murdered them on any pretext. In the summer of that year, late at night, the French Jewesses started an attempt at revolt, trying to frighten the trusties with stones and sticks. The attempt did not succeed, and none escaped.

The Commandant of Auschwitz, Rudolf Höss, saw the situation as follows:

After I received the news I went to the camp at once and found that the Frenchwomen had been killed by sticks and axes, some had had their heads torn off, others were killed by being thrown out of a window from the upper floor. The trusties, professional criminals, had come out of the fight victorious. They were all Germans. Some of them wounded ... During the investigation it was established that the guards had thrown their sticks over

The 'gate of death' – the entrance to Birkenau.

the wire to the trusties, professional criminals. The French prisoners who survived explained that they had revolted from despair, since the *Capos* ill-treated and tormented them.[26]

About ninety Jewesses from France died at that time, and nobody got away. On August 16th, 1942, the women's camp was moved to Birkenau, and on that same day the Penal Company was also transferred there and put in Block No. 2. Of the 400 women prisoners sent to Budy in June, only 137 remained.[27]

This attempt at an open revolt, the second in Auschwitz, was probably unconnected with the camp underground. The women had been in Auschwitz only from March 1942; they were held in the isolated Blocks although in the men's camp, and the first contacts with the men were just beginning. Besides, it is hard to imagine that the Union of Military Organization, led by Pilecki, or any of the political groups, could have urged them to an action of this kind. In the final analysis there is no evidence that the attempt to fight by the women's Penal Company was any more than a spontaneous gesture of despair.

6

Pilecki continued to work at uniting all the camp underground movements, especially the military ones, into one big network, and attained further success. With Bartosiewicz's help he brought into his organization Col. Stawarz and Lt. Col. Kumuniecki. Long talks and much persuasion were necessary to induce them to this; in the end the conditions of camp life overcame considerations of prestige. This was another exception to the principle that senior officers were to be avoided; but there was no way round if all the underground forces were to be joined in a single movement. Both colonels had their contacts, which strengthened the ranks of the camp underground army. The cadre was further strengthened by other officers, for on April 18th, 1942 a new transport of 461 prisoners came from Warsaw. Among them were Maj. Zygmunt Bohdanowski, who was in the camp under the name of Bończa, and Lt. Col. Kazimierz Stamirowski, who had lost his right hand following an attempt at suicide in the *Pawiak*. Bończa was known to Pilecki from Warsaw, where at the beginning of the occupation they had built up the Secret Polish Army (*TAP*), together, so he joined the camp underground at once, bringing Stamirowski with him. Thanks to the underground they both got into good *Kommandos*.

This further strengthening of the underground network, supported by the political agreement already reached, the setting up of the first cadres in Birkenau, and the co-operation established with the Czechs, allowed Pilecki to move on to much more difficult tasks and plans. Up to now the underground had been employed in self-help, getting colleagues into good *Kommandos* and important positions, collecting information and sending it to Warsaw, making contact with the outside world near the camp, strengthening the underground network and spreading news. It had also begun to organize escapes and had set up a radio station. Now Pilecki could think of preparations for eventual self-defence. The camp was swelling with the thousands of newly-brought prisoners. Terror was increasing; the weaker prisoners were being killed off by phenol injections; the equipment for mass murder was being constructed at great speed; every day new transports of Jews were arriving and being sent straight to the gas chambers – who could foresee what orders might come from Berlin concerning all the prisoners of Auschwitz? If the order was for mass liquidation they would either have to fight or die passively.

Pilecki had envisaged an armed struggle taking place on orders from outside, and with outside help in the form of a parachute drop of men and equipment. It was still much too early for such orders and such help, but the underground organization was now strong enough to think of preparing for defence, to prevent the mass of prisoners from being murdered without any resistance. There are no exact data from which to estimate how many soldiers were in the underground network at that time, but it is very probable that in the central camp and Birkenau there were well over a thousand of them. Pilecki, with reference to the period of March 1942, says in his report that he recruited over 100 co-workers,[28] but they were only those known to him personally, whom he himself had brought into the organization. The initial system of 'fives' had already grown enormously; new members were recruited outside it; the organization's contacts reached far and wide, and without undue exaggeration it can be accepted that Pilecki's cadre alone numbered about 500 prisoners, while each of his direct contacts had further connections. To this total must be added those recruited by Col. Rawicz, Col. Stawarz and Lt. Col. Kumuniecki. There were also the underground forces of the Socialists and Nationalists. Occasionally the same person was to be found in more than one group, as happens in clandestine organizations, but this does not alter the general calculation. After about a year and a half's work and a steady increase in strength, the core of the underground cadre was bound to be strong. Besides Birkenau, the movement also had contacts in other sub-camps, especially in Monowice near *Buna-Werke*.[29]

Col. Rawicz was the formal head of the whole military enterprise, but for this very reason he could not be reckoned as a fighting commander, being absorbed by matters of organization. Pilecki considered that the best person for the command was Maj. Bończa-Bohdanowski, an officer in the prime of life who also knew the terrain well, for before the war he had commanded a battery of the 5th *DAK* (Squadron of Horse Artillery) stationed in this district. Pilecki put forward his name and Rawicz agreed without reservation. Maj. Bończa took the code-name *Bohdan*.[30] After his appointment a plan of action and military preparations had to be decided upon. Pilecki notes in his report:

I decided then, and Col. Rawicz agreed, that a plan for eventual action should be worked out, depending on the tasks to be performed, which we reckoned basically to be four.[31]

This was because the plan for taking over the camp, for which, as the end of our work here, we wished to prepare organized units, had to be worked out in two forms. Differently for a working-day, differently for night-time or a holiday, when we were in the blocks. The reason was that at that time *Kommandos*

Józef Kupiec

Bolesław Kupiec

Władysław Kupiec

Karol Kupiec

Jan Kupiec

Antoni Kupiec

Kazimierz Smoleń

Ludwik Rajewski

Stanisław Kazuba

Jan Karcz

Wacław Szumański

Piotr Kownacki

Leading men in the resistance movement.

were not quartered together. So there would be different contacts, liaison and commanders during working-hours, and different ones in the blocks. A separate plan of action had to be worked out in each case.[32]

In fact the camp was still being re-organized. Some *Kommandos* had been put together in the same Blocks (for instance Block No. 25, where tannery specialists lived) and so they were together day and night, which facilitated underground planning. But the great majority dispersed after work and were scattered among the various Blocks. This was why Pilecki found it necessary to foresee four separate tasks, with four commanders for four separate posts. After discussion with Rawicz and Bończa, Pilecki proposed that they should be held by Capt. Stanisław Kazuba, Capt. Tadeusz Lisowski (*Capo* of the Vegetable Store) and two other officers, a Lieutanant and a Captain, whose names it has not been possible to establish. A chaplain was also appointed, Father Zygmunt Ruszczak.[33] In this phase military preparations involved only the central camp. Birkenau was still being built and underground work had only just begun there; the other sub-groups were too far away or had insufficient forces. This nomination of Commanders, the first attempt at preparing Auschwitz for a fight, was based on the assumption that, besides the underground cadre, thousands of unorganized prisoners would take part in self-defence. According to Pilecki's report the nomination took place before Easter 1942.[34]

The inclusion in Pilecki's organization of Colonels Stawarz and Kumuniecki, and before them Karcz, meant finally abandoning the principle of avoiding known senior officers. Once again reality proved stronger than abstract rules. It would have been better to have less conspicuous men in the organization, but then it would have been impossible to make plans for integration of the different military organizations. It was also perhaps a lesser evil to take the risk of sending to the bunker and severe interrogation a senior officer in whom the Political Department might be interested, as Col. Karcz's example had proved that these officers were of stout fibre and the risk was therefore more acceptable.

But even the worst hardships of camp life could not cure deep-rooted psychological tendencies, and Pilecki was suddenly faced by difficulties which, himself a modest man, he had not in the least foreseen. Jealousy broke out among the senior officers whom he had brought into the unified military organization. This did not apply to Lt. Col. Surmacki, who, quite unexpectedly, at the very end of 1941, was released from the camp and went to Warsaw, carrying Pilecki's latest report. His release was brought about by a

German, a former fellow-student in Germany before the First
World War, now a senior officer in the *Wehrmacht*, the German
army.* The emotions of envy and rivalry did not affect Col. Karcz
either, for he was at the head of the organization in Birkenau. This
huge sub-camp, which was shortly to be built up enormously and
to outgrow the central camp, afforded far-reaching and independent
opportunities. The difficulties might have been smoothed over but
for the fact that Col. Stawarz, a man of brusque manners, ranked
senior to Col. Rawicz and so considered that he ought to have
command of the whole enterprise.[35] Rawicz was very hurt and, when
mediation proved fruitless, decided it would be better for him to
step aside. A large transport was about to leave for Mauthausen,
and he managed to get himself included in it. Before the transport
left, he suggested to Pilecki that, in his place as the head of the whole
organization he should appoint Group-Captain Juliusz Gilewicz, an
elderly man, who was very popular with the other prisoners.
Gilewicz accepted the proposal,[36] joined Pilecki's organization and
worked for it loyally, while Rawicz, on June 9th, 1942, left for
Mauthausen. He intended to try to escape on the way, but
circumstances did not permit it.†

A few days after Rawicz's departure, on June 15th, the Political
Department suddenly summoned Col. Stawarz to the bunker. Even
the best informed underground workers were astonished: there was
no reason at all for this action. Stawarz was not interrogated, no one
else was involved in the case, and there were no further arrests. He
was shot the same day at the 'wall of death'.[37] Perhaps it was the
carrying-out of a sentence sent after him by the local *Gestapo*.
Perhaps it was because he was a high-ranking officer in the camp
under his own name.

Two months later the underground network sustained a second,
perhaps even more painful, loss. It was accidental and completely
unnecessary. Someone who knew that Stanisław Dubois was in
Auschwitz sent him a parcel from abroad. As at that time parcels
were not allowed in the camp, this caused the Political Department
to suspect that he had some secret contacts with the outside world.
The parcel was delivered to Dubois on August 19th; two days later
the head of the camp *Gestapo*, Maximilian Grabner, came to the
Cement Works where Dubois worked and took the prisoner to
Block No. 11. That same day he was shot against the 'wall of death'.[38]

---

* For the further fortunes of Surmacki see Appendix I.

† For the further fortunes of Col. Rawicz see Appendix I.

CHAPTER 6

The women's camp; the Hospital; liquidation
of spies; re-allocation of military cadres;
Himmler's second visit.

1

When on March 26th, 1942, the first transport of women from
Ravensbrück, 999 in all, was brought to Auschwitz, it caused surprise
among prisoners and trouble for the Command. Blocks 1–10
inclusive in the central camp had been assigned to them and separated
from the men by a high fence. There is no exact evidence concerning
the composition of the transport, but it is known that there were
only German women in it, mostly criminals, who took over the
positions of trusties, possibly some Jewesses and possibly some
Frenchwomen.[1] Two hours later another transport arrived also
numbering 999 and entirely composed of Jewesses from Slovakia.
Later further transports arrived more and more frequently.

The SS-men showed no consideration for women in the camp.
From the initial humiliation, when they were ordered to strip in the
presence of soldiers and were shaved on the head and body by men,
they went through every form of ill-treatment. They were put to
work at making roads, levelling the ground, cleaning out ponds
(this was done by the women's Penal Company); they had to live
in the crowded barracks with the three-tiered bunks, unable to wash
or get sufficient rest at night. They died of hunger and fell beneath
the blows of the SS-men's sticks, just as did the men. A pitiful
sight was the marching of the women's working groups to the hard
physical labour outside the camp, when with the greatest difficulty
they dragged their legs out of the heavy mud. They were herded by
well-fed SS-men, often on horseback, with leather whips in their
hands, while barking Alsatians ran round the staggering group as if
it were a flock of sheep.

This, however, was not the worst. Amongst the men homosexuality
was spreading, practised mainly by German criminal prisoners, who
had been there for many years. They would entice or force young
boys to spend time with them. These were nevertheless isolated
incidents. The women's situation was somewhat different. There
were amongst them many young, attractive girls who had not yet
lost their looks in the camp, and there were also older women who
were attractive to men. The guards could of course go into town

after duty and find female company, or they could meet *SS*-women; but the easiest conquests were to be found within the camp. It was true that there were very severe punishments for contacts with prisoners, but in Auschwitz, where the *SS* guard was already fairly corrupted by the treasures of *Canada*, the threat of punishment frightened few. There, for a piece of bread, or under the threat of beating, selection for the gas chamber or denunciation, women could easily be obtained, for what means of defence had they? Some little place could always be found, whether in the room of the Block Chief Woman, or in one of the storerooms, or during work. Some of the influential trusties, who at times were more dangerous than the *SS*-men, behaved likewise.

This pressure of sexually-starved, brutal, aggressive men, demanding unconditional acceptance, deepened and degraded to the utmost limits the women's misery. Who could protect them, if the camp Commandant himself, Rudolf Höss, living with his wife and children in a villa right next to the central camp, was having an affair with a prisoner, Eleonora Hodys (known in the camp as Nora), whom he accommodated in the *SS* Prison, in the basement of the central Administration Block, and whom he visited there?[2] In such a situation he was not inclined to punish other *SS*-men for similar breaches of discipline.

Yet the anguish of the women did not end there. Many of them had been arrested together with their families. It happened that in the same camp, not very far from each other, were a mother and her young son, or a wife and her husband. The terrible fear for one's dearest, who were dying nearby, the fear for one's children, whom no-one could help, drove people mad, and destroyed every moment of rest.

Yet the worst fate was that of those women who were arrested and sent to the camp with small children, or who arrived at the camp pregnant, and gave birth there. Only at the very end of the war was it permitted to save babies; during the first years they had to die, often before their mothers' eyes. In Auschwitz women trusties, German criminals, simply drowned them in buckets of water.[3] Witnesses will never forget the desperate scenes which took place in the autumn of 1943 in the women's camp in Birkenau. As the Eastern Front moved west, there began to arrive transports with Soviet women, many of whom had small children with them. After a few days came the order: the children must be taken from their mothers. It was widely known that they would go to the gas chambers. The mothers decided to resist. Armed *SS*-men threw themselves on them, beat them and tore the children bodily away. Terrible, heart-rending screams of the frenzied mothers carried through the camp and drove the men prisoners to the limits of their endurance. Yet they were quite helpless.

Nevertheless contact between men and women in Auschwitz did not only have a negative, humiliating and tragic side. Any contact between men and women was punishable, but in practice it was difficult to keep them apart. Various specialists such as electricians, locksmiths, carpenters and sewage workers had to go into the women's Blocks, and furthermore these Blocks were served by the same Kitchen as the men's Blocks. The doctors and male nurses also came into contact with the women. Many prisoners made every effort to get into the women's camp. In some cases they had mothers, wives, daughters or sisters there. Often there was also the understandable male desire to help a woman. These contacts, at first irregular, began with time to take on a more permanent character. The camp was enormous, there were plenty of places where two people could hide for an hour or two and men in good camp jobs organized secret meetings with women in the same position. Sexual relationships were more frequent than might have been supposed. These secret contacts very often led to friendship and much deeper feelings, which, against the terrible background of camp life, developed sometimes into love. Promises were exchanged, bonds were forged with the most fervent words of trust, which were usually brutally broken by the evil genius of war or by the violence of the *SS*. Yet there were those who managed to survive and meet after the war. A few, extremely successful marriages resulted.[4]

The first two transports of women did not provide a basis for underground work in their camp, since conditions were not favourable. The composition of the first transport was too random, and the large number of German criminals made any clandestine confidences difficult; the second, sent to the camp by the Jewish department of the Chief Security Office of the *Reich*, the *RSHA* (VI B4), was destined for extermination, and within a very short time met its doom.

A month later, on April 27th, a transport of 127 Polish women arrived at the camp from Cracow.[5] As political prisoners they had already had some secret contacts and experience of underground work, but by themselves they could start nothing. Luckily, just beyond the barbed wire, lay the men's camp, in which the prisoners, mostly Poles, were already organized, occupying key positions and controlling the Hospital.

Among the women from Cracow were a certain number whose relatives, husbands, brothers, fathers and sons were already in Auschwitz, and they were the first to make contact with the men's camp.[6] Two prisoners, Konstanty Jagiełło and Henryk Bartosiewicz, both members of the military underground, were particularly active in this respect. Both managed to change their *Kommandos* in order to enter the women's camp.

Their reports, as well as those of other prisoners who came into contact with the women, convinced Pilecki and his co-workers that at this stage of the camp's existence nothing could be expected of the women and that it would be a mistake to draw them into the military underground movement, with all its dangers. Most of the women were already skeletons; many were sick and what they needed most was speedy relief in the form of food, medicaments and the assistance of people with knowledge of medicine. This became the task of the men's camp underground movement.

Besides the Kitchen, where the underground had some influence, thanks mainly to Lisowski as *Capo* of the Vegetable Store (so that extra soup could always be smuggled in to the women), the main burden of help had to fall on the Hospital staff. The work of the prisoner-doctors and their strong position there, added to the fact that almost all of them were soldiers of the underground, afforded great possibilities. Medicines were already available, smuggled in from outside the camp or stolen from the *SS* Dispensary, so there was something to share. The chief suppliers of medicines to the women's Blocks were Jagiełło and Bartosiewicz.[7]

Such was the picture as regards underground work in the earliest phase of the women's camp at Auschwitz. Perhaps some women had secret ties. It was only possible to encourage them to try for jobs in which it would be easier to survive and to help fellow-prisoners. It is interesting that very few memoirs and statements have been preserved about this earliest period, when the women were kept in walled-off Blocks within the area of the men's camp. One can only conclude that it was difficult to set up anything at that time, and that the women who survived this period have little to relate other than the difficulty of keeping alive. Also there are very few surviving witnesses from the men's camp who had contact with them.

The situation changed only when, on August 16th, 1942, the women were moved to Birkenau and put into Section B I *a*.[8] Living conditions there were dreadful. The women were driven into barracks, partly brick, partly wooden, which had been inhabited previously by Soviet prisoners-of-war, now almost totally liquidated.

We had already been dirty, lice-ridden, flea-ridden in the former camp, but what we found in the brick stables exceeds every idea of dirt and insects. Huge, hungry lice crawl over the palliasses, like ants out of a disturbed ant-heap. We had already spent four months in two-storeyed, brick blocks, which in comparison with

Barracks in Birkenau (wooden barracks had no windows).

barracks remained in our memory as quite bearable. Here everything was damp, the earth floor gave way under our boots, the
palliasses stank of mould and human sweat. On rainy days water
dropped on our heads through the leaky roof. The period in the
camp after we were taken to Birkenau was the most dreadful of a
dreadful time, it was the nadir of dirt and misery . . . To have
lice breeding on one's own skin was nothing, but to go into a nest
of other people's hungry insects, thirsty for human blood, was a
nightmarish experience, impossible to describe.[9]

This description shows that the move to Birkenau in no way improved the women's lot, especially as there was no change in their
working conditions. On the contrary, they worsened, for the bog
surrounding their new camp made conditions much more unpleasant.
However, contact with the women in Birkenau was easier than in the
walled-off Blocks in the central camp, and clandestine links began
to be formed between them and the camp underground.

The chief reason for the greater ease of contact was the primitive
state of the sub-camp. It had been inhabited by prisoners, but it
still lacked drainage, water, roads, a hospital and many other

amenities which are necessary if living, even at the meanest level, is to be possible. Every day specialists went there from the central camp. After they had gone through the gate no-one took very much notice of them; they had only to watch out for *SS*-women, German trusties and prying informers.

The most important persons who visited the women's camp as part of their duties as prisoner-employees were the doctors and male nurses from the central camp.* They were delegated from the Hospital Blocks Nos. 21 and 28, and every morning after roll-call they marched in the company of the Senior Prisoner of the Hospital, Hans Bock, and an NCO of the *SS* health service, to Birkenau, returning for the evening roll-call.[10] They were led to Block Nos. 22, 23, 24, 25 and 26, in which were the beginnings of the women's Hospital. In charge of it as Senior Prisoner was a German, Orli Reichert, an idealistic Communist, kind to her fellow-prisoners; she was assisted by a German midwife, Sister Klara, and a Slovak Jewess, Dr. Ena Weiss. To help them they had a certain number of prisoners, mostly criminals. The Senior Prisoner of the whole women's camp was a pretty young Polish girl, Stanisława Starostka, known as *Stenia*, and famed for brutality. Shouting and swearing, she beat and kicked other women, driving them to work without a moment's respite. But, occasionally, when she came across one of her fellow-prisoners from the jail in Cracow, she helped them.

In this preliminary phase of the women's camp in Birkenau, as two years earlier in the men's camp, doctors were not allowed to practise their profession in the Hospital[11], probably because they were all Polish or Jewish. Some of them did work there as nurses and it was due to these that the five crowded Blocks did not become the ante-room to death. The men who came in every day were at first shocked although they were already experienced prisoners; but they at once set to work to save the thousands of dying women. These had been struck down by various illnesses, but above all by typhus, which was raging at that time all over Auschwitz. There were pratically no medicaments on the spot, so at once, at the very beginning of this work, the underground movement, already strengthened by Pilecki and firmly based in the central camp, joined in. The doctors working for it – Dering, Diem, Fejkiel, assisted by others – began secretly to prepare packets which their colleagues took with them to Birkenau. Marian Toliński, the camp dispenser and a member of Pilecki's organization, distinguished himself at that time; a little later he was supported by Jan Sikorski

---

* The list of doctors and male nurses and laboratory assistants is in the Appendix III, item 6.

from the *SS* Hospital dispensary. The supply-line of medicines to the women's camp very soon got involved in a mass of private affairs. Every evening the group which went to Birkenau was beseeched by hundreds of near relations of this or that woman prisoner. Everyone wished to send something: a last piece of bread, a letter, an article of underclothing. The enormous needs of the women's camp in the way of medical help could not be satisfied by a few doctors and male nurses, so the underground began to look for additional middle-men. As well as Jagiełło and Bartosiewicz, other prisoners who used to go into the women's camp were drawn into this dangerous work.* Helena Matheisel, a young Polish woman working at that time as a clerk in the hospital, says that some packets of medicines, sent to her by Marian Toliński, were carried by *SS*-men. Unfortunately their names have slipped her memory. Every and any way was used: medicines were smuggled in oxygen bottles, in double-bottomed cases, in tool-bags. Women who went to the central Hospital once a week for treatment, or to the dentist, carried medicines in their underwear.

The continuous deterioration of the women's health and the necessity of some sort of care for them forced the *SS*-men to make two decisions. The first was made more or less four weeks after the time when the male medical group was formed to go to the women's camp every day. The doctors, Bolesław Zbozień, Janusz Mąkowski and Nicet Włodarski, and the male nurses, Stefan Czubak, Wiesław Kielar, Julian Kiwała, Zenon Ławski, Stanisław Paduch and Jan Wolny, were picked out and transferred permanently to Birkenau, to Section B I *b*.[12] They lived in Block No. 12, where there was already a Hospital, set up in April 1942 by Dr. Głogowski. Section B I *b* was inhabited at that time by men; it was handed over to the women only in the summer of 1943. These doctors and male nurses merely slept in Block No. 12 and spent the whole day in the women's camp, separated only by the road and two rows of barbed-wire. Dr. Zbozień became the head doctor of the women's Hospital, Ławski took over Block No. 22, Wolny No. 23, Kiwała No. 24 and Włodarski No. 25.[13] Dr. Głogowski and some of his male nurses helped them as far as they were able.

The second decision concerned women doctors, who so far had had to work in various *Kommandos* or hide in the Hospital as cleaners and nurses. In November 1942 they were allowed to go to the Hospital Blocks and practise their profession openly.[14] It was then that the great organizational and professional qualities, as well as

---

* Their names are in the Appendix III, item **7**.

the great hearts, of several women doctors and nurses were revealed.* These were mainly Polish, for at this time they were the most numerous nationality at Birkenau. Aided by the afore-mentioned doctors and male nurses they carried on a stubborn, determined, never-failing fight for the lives of their fellow-prisoners, regardless of their origin, political opinions or nationality. Besides their daily service of medical assistance and care, these people, at the risk of their own lives, broke the *SS* rules and regulations, hiding patients due to be selected for the gas-chambers, changing their medical cards and keeping them for long weeks in the Hospital Blocks. And this at a time when the *SS* showed no mercy.

> The principle of the women doctors and assistant personnel was above all and in any way to save human lives, threatened every moment by the administration of the German doctors . . . To-day I have a scale of comparison for the work of the doctors and nursing staff in the camp and after liberation. I can appreciate to the full, with acquired experience, the enormous efforts they made and their utterly devoted and disinterested work. This was an overt resistance movement, without any struggle for power and without any political aspects.[15]

This statement by a former prisoner of Birkenau, now practising as a doctor in Poland, contains a great truth and perhaps comes the nearest to describing the state of underground activity at that time in the women's camp. In the men's camp there was some possibility of preparing for armed self-defence, even for a fight to take over the camp with help from outside; there were signs, sometimes even glaring ones, of a fight for influence and privilege, which in the post-war period was fully evidenced in regard to certain persons, especially in Poland. The crowd of emaciated women were in no state to even think of armed struggle; among them there were no glaring examples of contention between groups divided by ideology or interest. In the face of death all the women prisoners were equal, and they were treated as such by the medical and nursing staff.

The above description differs sharply from some accounts, published especially in the immediate post-war years. In these there are too many suggestions that only groups of a certain political hue were active in organizing the camp resistance movement and helping others. To-day, from the perspective of years, another picture is emerging more and more clearly: those that joined together in the underground and helped others were above all people of strong

---

* The names of the women working in the Hospital at that time are in Appendix III, item 8.

character, able to bear their own burdens and sympathetic to the sufferings of others. Naturally people's origins, nationality, language, religion, political opinions, past acquaintanceship, etc., formed a basis for mutual trust and facilitated the first contacts, but later, when they got to know each other, the strength of underground activity and help to others perforce depended on qualities of character and heart, regardless of nationality, religion, education or political opinions. This was very distinctly expressed by Ella Lingens, an Austrian, who recalled the problems of Auschwitz many years after the war:

> Six of us women doctors (four Polish, one a Jewess from Prague, in Czechoslovakia and I) lived as friends in one room. We supplemented the prison food by sharing our parcels. We discussed difficult cases, consulted each other on them and deliberated on what the patients needed and how best to cure them. There were no problems of nationality among us.[16]

It is difficult to-day, in a list of nearly a hundred names, to distinguish the women doctors and nurses who were consciously recruited into the camp underground movement from those who acted in a corresponding way of their own accord, or carried out the recommendations of the organization without asking or knowing who gave them. A number of sources agree in naming some who definitely joined the underground movements, having been contacted in one way or another.*

In the later phase of Birkenau, towards the end of 1943 and in 1944, these women doctors, who belonged to the camp underground (*ZOW*) were joined by others.†

In the late autumn of 1943, when the Germans had to retreat from Russia, they evacuated their camps there and many of the women prisoners, especially Russians, Ukrainians and Byelorussians, found themselves in Birkenau. Women doctors were taken into the Hospital and joined in the fight for the lives of sick women. The same was true of the nurses, of whom a large number were recruited from among the women brought from Russia.[17]

Medicines could be smuggled in from the central camp and the men from the underground risked their lives to this end, but it was still not enough to keep the sick women alive. They also needed food, and this could not be smuggled from the central camp in sufficient quantities to be any use. It had to be 'organized'‡ from

---

* Their names are in Appendix III, item 9.

† Their names are in Appendix III, item 10.

‡ Camp slang for stealing from Stores, Kitchen etc.

the women's own Kitchen. However, there were prisoners there who knew what had to be done and, defying danger and punishment, they supplied the Hospital with extra cauldrons of soup, potatoes and boiled water flavoured with herbs. This last was absolutely priceless, for drinking the muddy fluid which dripped from the few taps brought on dysentery and other illnesses. The patients, especially those with typhus, begged for water and only the Kitchen could supply it. Several women worked there and helped the Hospital: among them was Celina Mikołajczyk, the wife of Stanisław Mikołajczyk, who in July 1943, after the tragic death of General Sikorski, became Prime Minister of the Polish Government in London.* This assistance increased still more when Zofia Hubert, a soldier of the camp military underground, became *Capo* in the Kitchen.

Although saving the women's lives was the prime object, the underground also needed to establish contacts among them. Reports were necessary on their situation, on the movements of transports, on selection for the gas chambers. Also some preparations, however rudimentary, had to be made in case of an intended liquidation of the camp and an attempt by the *SS* to murder all the prisoners. It was important to communicate news from the outside world, which had a considerable effect in keeping up the spirits of the thousands of dying women. The women's camp on December 1st, 1942, numbered 8,232 prisoners.

The first contacts with the women's camp were made by Henryk Bartosiewicz and Konstanty Jagiełło.[18] This began in the Blocks detached from the men's camp, and took place on a larger scale in Birkenau. Through one channel went help for the women's Hospital, and although any smuggling was done at the risk of death or long interrogation in the bunker, it was the less dangerous channel, for it was no proof of an organized underground. One could always say that one had acted of one's own accord to convey medicines to one's mother, wife or sister. The second channel, much better camouflaged, concerned contacts that were absolutely clandestine. As well as Bartosiewicz and Jagiełło, who, with their low camp-numbers and belonging to the right *Kommandos*, could get into Birkenau without difficulty, doctors and Hospital workers played the role of liaison officers.† There were others, some of whom were mentioned above in connection with carrying help to the Hospital.

These liaison officers were recruited from among those *Kommandos* that went to work in Birkenau daily (hospital workers, sewage

---

* The names of women active in the Kitchen are in Appendix III, item 11.

† Their names are in Appendix III, item 12.

workers, electricians, locksmiths, tilers etc.). Among electricians this contact was maintained by Henryk Porębski, imprisoned in the men's part of Birkenau. The contacts on the women's side were Wiktoria Klimaszewska, Antonina Piąkowska, Dr. Janina Węgierska, Helena Matheisel and Stefania Hercok.[19] During the first months the women were in Birkenau these contacts were occasional only. The men brought radio news, monitored in secret, from their camp to the women, who passed it on to all the blocks through trustworthy liaison girls, not necessarily members of the camp underground. Returning to the central camp, the men took with them reports of selections, transports and mortality among the women. They also advised the women on how to fulfil the most important camp functions.

In the spring of 1943 these contacts took on a more concrete form. From the central camp they were maintained by the *Capo* of the Vegetable Store, Capt. Tadeusz Lisowski (Paolone), already for some time a member of the Union of Military Organization. In Block No. 4, half of which served as an office for the women's camp, where Narcyza Kielan was active, and half as a dormitory for women prisoners employed in the various camp offices, a secret 'post-box' for the military organization was created. In underground language this meant a place to which messages were delivered and from which they were collected. This was in mid-1943. Through this now came orders from the central camp, news and reports. On the same Block was set up the first women's 'five', which consisted of Zofia Bratro and Stanisława Rachwałowa, both from the excellent *Kommando* where new arrivals were registered; Helena Hoffman from the neighbouring, small sub-camp Rajsko; and Wiktoria Klimaszewska and Antonina Piątkowska, working as Barrack-room Service on Block No. 4.

As soon as the first 'five' had been formed, Lisowski sent instructions concerning the main types of activity to be undertaken:
   —to find light work for the weaker prisoners;
   —to pass on by word of mouth news from the radio and press, supplied by *Kommandos* which were in touch with civilians at work;
   —to contact and co-operate with prisoners of other nationalities, e.g. Yugoslav, Czech etc.;
   —to keep in contact with the military organization in the men's camp;
   —to pass on, whenever possible, information about life in the camp to the civilian population outside the camp through trustworthy prisoners;
   —to make every effort to keep young women and girls alive.[20]

Maria Elżbieta Jezierska

Janina Kowalczykowa

Barbara Stefańska

Maria Żelińska

Ella Lingens

Katarzyna Łaniewska

Alina Przerwa-Tetmajer

Krystyna Cyankiewicz

Antonina Piątkowska

Leading women in the resistance movement.

These instructions did not exceed what was possible and did not demand any aggressive activity on the part of the women. They did not even refer to preparations for resistance in case of an order to liquidate all the women prisoners.

Besides the Hospital and Kitchen, the women's underground organization, as in the men's camp, began to get into other positions which influenced the fate of the imprisoned. In the Labour Assignment Office there worked Wanda Marossányi, a young Polish girl whose ancestors had come from Hungary many years before, and who came to the camp with her mother. She proved to be invaluable, although, according to her own statement, she never belonged to the camp underground officially.[21] She managed to arrange good jobs for people who needed them, and to see that mothers with daughters and sisters were put into the same *Kommandos* and the same sub-camps. From her father, who worked in the Labour Assignment Office in the men's part of Birkenau, she would receive messages, sent by fathers, husbands and brothers, and these she conveyed as far as she was able.

Some women who joined the underground worked in the Clothing Store, and they were able to do a lot of good, supplying others with extra underclothes, sweaters and blankets. In the Sewing-Rooms, on the side, old sheets were made into underclothes for children, who had been brought to the camp with their mothers or born there, and who were not murdered during the last months at Birkenau.

A group of prisoners was secretly engaged in knitting ear-muffs, sweaters and gloves for partisan units of the Home Army in the neighbourhood of Auschwitz. These objects were later carried out of camp by prisoners who worked in the fields or went to work in the nearby sub-camps. This very moving co-operation between the camp and the resistance soldiers fighting Germans was very important to the morale of the women involved in it. Although deprived of their freedom, they had at least the satisfaction of doing their bit in the struggle against the enemy.

A secret letter sent by Krystyna Cyankiewicz, a woman prisoner in Auschwitz, to her mother in Cracow. The letter, sent via the underground, begins:

1 (Wednesday) September 1943

My darling little Mother!

My intuition was right. At last the so impatiently awaited lengthy letters have arrived. One dated 18.VI, the other 4.VII. Both so wonderful, so dear to me. I cannot express how much happiness they have given me. When I read them, for a moment it seemed to me that I was at home with you all, in that home of which we dream at night, for which we long the whole time. The knowledge that, there at home and free, are those dearest to us, who love us so and await our return with unwavering faith, is a comfort to us and gives us strength and patience, to hope that one day we will regain our freedom. Mother dear, I am writing this letter although I don't know if it will reach your beloved hands. I am so happy when I can talk to you – writing down my thoughts. It seems to me that I am at home. . . .

There were also some women in the Bread Stores who belonged to the underground. They helped their fellow-prisoners with extra loaves.

This extra bread was earmarked for the weakest and most famished and – I swear – was distributed without any distinction of nationality, simply where the need was greatest, simply to save a woman from death by starvation.[22]

There was also a Parcels Office, situated in Block No. 5, from the summer of 1943, when the women's camps grew larger and took in section B I *b*. The woman in charge there was Maria Kozakiewicz, under whom worked about thirty women of various nationalities. They worked in two shifts, day and night. All parcels had to be searched in the presence of an *SS*-woman, who allowed only food for immediate consumption; letters, photographs and medicines were confiscated. Kozakiewicz, however, often managed to keep back these articles and give them to the addressee. Often, too, parcels addressed to deceased persons were handed over to the Hospital instead of being sent to the main stores. The Parcels Office was also responsible for deliveries to the sub-camps, like Rajsko, Harmęże etc., and this made possible clandestine contacts with the women there. Through Marian Szajer from the men's camp, Kozakiewicz had contacts with the partisans. He finally escaped from the camp and was able to join them.[23]

Other contacts with the men took place through Walentyna Konopska and Danuta Mosiewicz, who worked as office clerks in the Political Department near the men's camp. Konopska was secretly in touch with Henryk Bartosiewicz.[24]

Further opportunities were afforded by the Building Office. Several women worked there, and some of them belonged to the underground. They helped to pass on many reports from the women's camp to the central one.

In this Building Office also worked two Czech women, engineer architect Vera Foltýnová and Valedia Valová. One of the important achievements of the underground movement in the women's camp was connected with this office. In the middle of 1944, when the Eastern Front was already on Polish territory, a rumour went round the camp that the *SS*-men were intending to destroy the crematoria and wipe out all traces of them. It was then that Vera Foltýnová with the help of her compatriot copied the plans of the four great crematoria and the gas chambers and handed them over to Krystyna Horczak. The latter took them to Piątkowska for temporary concealment. Sealed in jars they were hidden under the cement in the wash-room on Block No. 4, together with the lists of 9,000 dead Polish women, drawn up by Monika Galica. In October of that year the jars were dug up and the papers sewn into a belt, which Piątkowska wore for a time while waiting for an opportunity to send them outside. This was done by Zofia Gawron, who was at that time working on the building of a breakwater on the Vistula and was in contact with the civilian foreman in charge of this work, Franciszek Zabuga. He undertook to hand it over to her family in Brzeszcze. The operation was successful and the plans of the crematoria reached Cracow, where they were given to the District Commander of the Home Army. They were used as evidence at the trial of Rudolf Höss, the camp Commandant.[25]

As the Birkenau camp grew in size, so also the number of women there increased and they began to arrive from all over occupied Europe. Besides Polish, Jewish and German women there came others from France, Belgium, Holland, Czechoslovakia, Russia, Yugoslavia and Hungary. The earliest underground work was begun among Polish women, who were recruited by emissaries from the men's camp belonging to the military organization set up by Pilecki, or to the political groups that co-operated with the military one. Up to the first weeks of 1943 there were no signs of any other such enterprise. It was only when a transport of 230 French women, political prisoners (given the numbers from 31625 to 31854), arrived from Romainville on January 27th that the situation changed.

In this transport were several Communists from the French resistance movement: Danielle Casanova, Maie Politzner, Helene Salmon-Langevin, Ivonne Blech, Henriette Schmidt, and Raymonde Salez. Under the leadership of Casanova, who on May 10th of that same year died of typhus, they started the nucleus of a Communist group,[26] which was enlarged by the German Communists, Orli Reichert, Gerda Schneider and Anna Blumeier. The Czechs, Anne Binder and Dr. Zdena Nedvedová, and a Polish woman, Joanna Szabłowska, are also said to have belonged to it.[27] When the women took over Section B I *b.* in the summer of 1943, an underground group was set up there too, led by an Austrian woman, Herta Soswinsky. To this group belonged the Russians, Irina Ivannikova, Zhenia Sarycheva and Viktoria Nikitina, all of whom worked as nurses in the hospital; the Czechs, Vera Foltýnová and Vlasta Kladivová; the Poles, Wanda Jakubowska and Pelagia Lewińska; the Austrian Judith Dürmeyer and the Belgian Jewess, Malla Zimetbaum. Much later, in the middle of 1944, they were joined by the French woman, Odette Elina. Jakubowska is said to have been the liaison officer between the women and the men's underground movement in the central camp.[28]

It is hard to establish when serious underground work was started among the Soviet women. There were certainly individuals sent to

Stanisława Rachwałowa

Wanda Marossányi

Maria Maniakówna

Halina Czarnocka

Leading women in the resistance movement.

the camp earlier on, who occasionally joined in the underground activities of Polish or Jewish women, but it must be accepted that the more serious and closer contacts were only established in the second half of 1943, when numerous transports of women from camps in Russia began to arrive at Birkenau. It is also certain that the Russian women, like the men from Soviet Russia, kept themselves to themselves and that their underground organization contacted other national groups only at the top level, through their leaders. Direct contact between fellow-prisoners in the knowledge that both belonged to underground organizations was limited by Russian women to Communists. Their years of isolation from other countries, and their upbringing in a quite different political system created a barrier of distrust which only a few individuals managed to break down.

Nina Guseva, who came to Birkenau in October 1943, has given a few details of the underground activities of the Russian women and their contacts with the other nationalities.

I made friends with Nadia Kotenko, a school-mistress from Kharkov. From her I learnt of the existence in the camp of a secret organization. The members of this organization were people of various nationalities. I also joined their ranks in the group of Russian prisoners.

Nadia Kotenko introduced me to the Polish woman Wanda Jakubowska, to the Frenchwoman Maria Diamont, to Maria-Eliza, to the Czechs – the school-mistress Vlasta Beerová and Ružena Veissova, to the German Gerda Schneider, the Yugoslav Stefa Stibler and others. The well-known French social worker Marie-Claude Vaillant-Couturier also belonged to the organization.

At that time in our Russian group were: Nadia Kotenko, Lubov Sinitsina, Lena Fomina, Zhenia Kostenko, Zoya Taralina, Klava Stolarova, Anya Kuznietsova, Halina Kontsevaya, Nina Orlovska, Sonia Milakovska, Zhenia Tsyplakova.

. . . We got a lot of help from the secret organization in the men's camp. Through comrades Piotr Mishin, Nikolay Raisky and Vassili (I don't remember his surname) we got from there medicines, sometimes bread, clothes. This help was organized by Aleksander Fyodorivich Lebedev and other comrades. The Frenchwoman Marie-Claude organized medicines through French doctors.[29]

The lot of Jewish women in Birkenau was very hard, for they had usually got there as the result of selection from the transports designated for the gas chambers. They had lived through dramatic and painful separation from their relatives, they were alive almost by a miracle and every day, every hour, they were threatened with the same end. Under these circumstances it was difficult for them to maintain close contact with non-Jewish women or set up any serious underground organization of their own. All the same many of them, thanks to their adroitness and knowledge of languages, managed within a short time to get themselves into good positions, such as Block Chiefs and Barrack-room Service. They worked in the Hospital as doctors and nurses, worked in the separate Political Department for the women's camp, were employed in the various offices, in the Kitchen, in the Parcels Office.[30]

Their occupancy of important functions gave them great opportunities, which they used to help other prisoners, mainly Jewesses from various countries, which was quite understandable. These opportunities may also have been used for the purpose of setting up an underground network. The beginnings must have been the same as among the Polish women. First their dying fellow-prisoners had to be looked after and this was usually spontaneous work;

later clandestine contacts aimed at collecting information, liaison with the men's camp, and other tasks could be thought of. A certain number of Jewesses from various countries were in contact with the Communist group, which started up in 1943.

The underground links among Jewesses in Birkenau and their secret liaison with the men's camp on Section B II came to light in connection with the revolt in the *Sonderkommando** on October 7th, 1944. The revolt was not successful and two days later three Jewesses were arrested: Ella Gartner, Toszka and Regina (surnames unknown), who worked in the Ammunition Factory, *Union-Werke*, in the camp grounds. They were accused of carrying explosives out of the factory and handing them over to the *Sonderkommando*. Several days later another four Jewesses were arrested, among them Róża Robota, working in the prisoners' Deposit Store next to the crematorium No. IV. On January 6th, 1945, several days before the evacuation of the whole camp of Auschwitz, Ella Gartner, Róża

Experimental Block No. 10.

---

* The very large *Kommando* of prisoners working at the gas chambers and crematoria. See Chapter 11.

Robota, Toska and Regina were hanged in the women's camp.[31]

In Birkenau there was a relatively large number of women from Yugoslavia (Serbs, Croats and Slovenes), who were chiefly imprisoned because of their activities with the partisans. Those who had been with Gen. Michailović's partisans were called 'royalists'. Among them was the General's wife, who died of typhus in 1943. It is hard to establish which were the more numerous: 'royalists' or 'reds' from among Tito's partisans. The secret military 'five' and its further connections maintained contact with the 'royalist' Yugoslavs,[32] while later the Communist underground was in contact with the 'reds'. One of them was Stefania Stibler. Lack of data makes it impossible to give any other names with certainty.

The above data must be complemented by the underground connections in the experimental Block No. 10, although this was in the central camp, inhabited otherwise solely by men at this time. On May 30th, 1942, Professor Carl Clauberg wrote to Himmler suggesting sterilization experiments on the women prisoners in Auschwitz; on July 7th he received the latter's permission and in the autumn of that year he began these experiments, chiefly by subjecting the women to X-rays. In Block No. 10 there were always several hundred young women, mostly Jewesses, and a couple of dozen medical personnel, doctors and nurses, recruited from among the women prisoners. A Slovak woman doctor Slava Klein organized and underground information group, which sent out news of the experiments to the men. A Polish Communist, Dr. Dorota Lorska, also belonged to this group.[33]

It must be accepted that in the area of the women's camp in Birkenau there were more underground links among national and international groups which cannot be reconstructed. Such links also existed among the women in the various sub-camps, like Rajsko, Harmęże, Budy and others, though there is not enough firm evidence to permit a detailed account of them. Generally speaking, any underground activity among the women could be only of a limited character, as among the men. The large numbers of men and women in the underground movements arose only after the war and chiefly in the imagination of persons who used them as a stepping-stone to a career. The women's activities were very dependent on what was happening in the central camp and the male part of Birkenau. The nucleus of the whole activity was formed by the initiative of the military men, who after some time came to agreement with the political groups that existed alongside them. When the men's underground movement took on an international character, this had its influence on the women's camp too. The chief area of activity was the Hospital, and next to it the Labour Assignment Office, and

Kommandos afforded the best opportunities. A lot of activity consisted of spontaneous mutual aid, which is very often classed under the general heading of the resistance movement.[34]

2

The summer of 1942 was the peak period of the typhus epidemic. This terrible disease first appeared in the camp in April 1941, when a transport arrived from Lublin. In it there were several men ill with typhus and many more infected.[35] The Germans were afraid of all infectious illnesses, but they were slow in starting to fight the typhus in Auschwitz, either thinking that it would die out quickly, or regarding it as an ally which would help in exterminating the prisoners more rapidly. It was only when the disease had spread right through the camp and reached the *SS*-men's barracks that the command took fright and begun to use preventive methods, but in a manner so typical of them as to produce the opposite effect. Instead of

Lists of prisoners (numbers only) killed by phenol injections. These lists were made by the resistance movement and smuggled out of the camp.

raising the hygienic standard of the camp, isolating the Blocks and feeding the prisoners better so that they might be more resistant to the disease, the *SS*-men began to organize selections to the gas chambers, taking the sick and convalescent from the Hospital and also killing them *en masse* by injections of phenol.

The Hospital Blocks, which so far had been the dream of nearly all the prisoners, now became death Blocks to be avoided. Prisoners who fell ill of typhus hid in the latrines, on the Blocks, in their *Kommandos*, incurred the blows of the trusties, tried to 'walk off' the illness, fainted at roll-calls, anything rather than go to the Hospital and risk selection for the gas chambers or an injection of poison. The terrible disease raged throughout the camp. It was intensified by the transports of Russians, bringing a new species of Siberian lice and a new variety of typhus, and when Birkenau was set up and thousands of men and women were herded there to exist in the most frightfu' unhygienic conditions, it reached its peak. Almost entire *Kommandos* died; rooms in the Blocks were emptied, though filled again and again to overflowing. At that time an average of 73 prisoners died daily from typhus in the central camp alone.[36]

The epidemic was bound to take its toll of the cadre of the camp underground. A number of soldiers from Pilecki's organization died; at the beginning of September Pilecki himself had to go into Hospital.

The Hospital in the central camp was at that time already organized and working flat out, both at saving the lives of the sick and in underground activity. It occupied the following Blocks: No. 28 (Administration and Admission Centre, Casualty, Internal Illnesses, Observation Wards); No. 21 (Surgical Department with an operating theatre on the ground floor, a Septic Department with 160 beds and the Department for Suppurating Wounds with 500 places to lie down); No. 20 (Infectious Department); No. 19 (Department for Dysentery and Internal Illnesses and Department of Surgery on Suppurating Wounds), as well as No. 9 (Convalescents). In these there worked about 60 doctors and over 300 male nurses, for 2,500 patients. Among the male nurses there were about 200 Poles, several Germans and Czechs, a fair number of Jews from various countries, and others.[37] The head of all this was still Hans Bock, with another German criminal, Peter Welsch, as second in command, but the doctors had firm control of all medical matters and, in effect, almost everything that happened there. As the camp gradually acquired an international character, so there were increasingly representatives of other nationalities among the doctors and male nurses; but the chief medical positions still remained in the hands of Poles.*

---

* The list of doctors of various nationalities is in Appendix III, item 13.

At the head were Dr. Rudolf Diem, Dr. Władysław Dering and Dr. Władysław Fejkiel,[38] all three working for the camp underground (*ZOW*), but the number of clandestine workers in the Hospital was increased by the new doctors, constantly arriving in the camp.* The greatest self-sacrifice was shown by the young and energetic Stanisław Kłodziński, a third-year medical student who was taken into the Hospital as a doctor. He was enlisted into the military underground in the autumn of 1941 and became a priceless asset, especially by receiving medicines smuggled in from outside the camp or from the *SS* Dispensary. Pilecki, who relied on the Hospital for a considerable part of his underground work and knew the area well, wrote of him:

> He worked to the utmost in a position which favoured his activity so well that there was no need to tie up any loose ends or change anything. I only knew that I could count on him absolutely.[39]

It was this doctor who tended Pilecki with the greatest care and pulled him through the dreaded illness.

The list in Appendix III, item 13, of doctors who got into the central Hospital does not include all the names, but it can be seen that there were among them representatives of various nationalities. It is hard to imagine, however, that any of these were drawn into the underground as early as 1942. The work was too important and too dangerous for completely unknown men to be brought into it on the spur of the moment. In any case there are no data on this. But in all probability the doctors' help was used without all of them being told the details of the clandestine set-up. This was necessary because saving the sick and convalescent from selection for the gas chambers, the illegal acquisition and distribution of food and medicines and other similar activities required the co-operation of almost the entire personnel. It is notable that in the hospital there was not one German prisoner doctor. Not because the *SS*-men did not want them there, but simply because there were no doctors among the German prisoners in Auschwitz, as most of them were criminals.[40]

As has been said, the above data refer exclusively to the central Hospital. There is very little information on the underground work in the Hospitals of the sub-camps, with the exception of the women's camp at Birkenau. In the men's camp there, Dr. Leon Głogowski had been active from April 1942 and had set up the Hospital.

The lack of exact personal data in respect of underground work in the sub-camp Hospitals does not alter the fact that they were an important element in the secret liaison with the main camp, where the

---

* Their names are in Appendix III, item 14.

camouflaged leadership of the whole underground movement was situated. The central Hospital had an operating theatre, a Dental Surgery, a Laboratory, a Dispensary and other facilities, of which the prisoners from sub-camps could sometimes make use.[41] Naturally this gave many opportunities for secret contacts.

It should be noted that on August 20th, 1942, a small transport from Dachau, seventeen prisoners in all, arrived at the camp. These were exclusively Germans and Austrians, political prisoners with much experience of camp life. Among them were two German Communists, Karl Lill from the Sudetenland and Ludwig Wörl, and an Austrian Communist from Vienna, Hermann Langbein. They were supposed to be specialists at fighting typhus and were assigned to the central Hospital either as male nurses or as clerks. Langbein found himself on Block No. 21 as a night clerk with the task of making out the lists of dead. Spending all his time in the Hospital, he was isolated from the rest of the camp and knew very little of the local conditions, so different from Dachau.

About a fortnight later, on September 6th, SS Major Dr. Eduard Wirths arrived from Dachau and took over the position of the Senior Medical Officer. He had known and liked Langbein in Dachau and at once made him his secretary.[42] A prisoner in this position had great opportunities. Wirths looked round the camp, saw what were its most pressing needs and decided that fighting typhus was the most urgent task and that this must be done at once. He did not have to start at the beginning for, just before his arrival, on August 29th, a general de-lousing had been ordered. After that, taking advantage of the large-scale movement of prisoners, the camp authorities decided that members of the individual *Kommandos* should live together in the same Blocks. Besides fighting typhus Wirths had other plans which came to light later.

During his term of office, in the late autumn of 1942, medical experiments began being carried out on the prisoners. Block No. 10 in the central camp was separated off and several hundred women, nearly all Jewish, were put there and subjected to sterilization. Men were treated likewise. These experiments were carried out by Professor Carl Clauberg and Dr. Horst Schumann. They were a direct result of Nazi plans to change the map if not of the whole world, then at least of Europe. Some nations, such as the Jews, and later the Poles and other Slavs, were to be completely, or almost completely, eliminated; other nations were to be transported to new settlement areas. Sterilization experiments led to infertility and turned people into animal-like creatures, who would be adapted solely for work, of course under the control of, and for the benefit of, the Germans. By X-ray radiation of the reproductive organs of both men and women

efforts were made to lead to their infertility without affecting their
strength, so that they could continue to work. These experiments were
unsuccessful; gangrene set in, signs of mental disturbance appeared,
which, particularly in the women, often took on a more permanent
nature.[43] The decisions for those experiments were taken at a level
above Dr. Wirths and he was not responsible for them. Many
eye-witnesses agree that he was an upright man and that he tried to
alleviate the prisoners' suffering.[44]

The order to put prisoners into separate blocks according to which
Kommando they were in, and Dr. Wirths' arrival in the camp had
some influence on the further development of the camp underground.

3

In the preceding account of the part played by the Hospital in
bringing help to the prisoners and in underground activities, mention
has been made of the liquidation of informers, individuals suspected of
acting for the Political Department. There were large numbers of
them in the camp, and this is not astonishing. In such a brutal
struggle for life, with no quarter given, where for many any trick was
legitimate if it was to one's own advantage, the *average* level of hon-
esty and comradeship was bound to be low. The informers were
recruited from various nationalities; they were on every Block, almost
in every *Kommando*. A prisoner's social class, pre-war position, political opinion, religion – none of these were decisive in the camp, nor
were they a guarantee of how he would behave. Titles, honours,
hereditary privileges were all left outside the gate and a man entered
the camp stark naked, dressed only in his own dignity and his own
character, which made itself known in the hours of trial. How many
misunderstandings there were in this respect, how many surprises!

The informers represented various nationalities and generally
concentrated on the groups they knew best: Poles spied on Poles,
Germans on Germans, Jews on Jews. They were recruited in many
ways. Most often it happened during interrogation, when by means of
physical torture and the threat of it, as well as by mental pressure, the
prisoners were forced to co-operate and to inform on their fellows.
Once a man had broken down, there was no way back. The Political
Department kept a firm hold on the victim, on the one hand threaten-
ing fresh torture or even death, and on the other giving small privileges, like extra food and easier conditions of work, which in the
camp were of the utmost importance. These advantages, offering a
chance of prolonging one's existence, attracted many volunteers who
of their own accord sought secret contact with the *SS*-men. Matters

even reached the stage that in 1942 the authorities set up outside Block No. 15 a box into which prisoners were to put denunciations. This fact was publicised on all the Blocks and the prisoners were urged to write letters signed with their names or numbers, or else anonymous, chiefly concerning conversations among prisoners. Auschwitz would not have been Auschwitz if this box had remained empty. Every evening, at 10 p.m., *Rapportführer* Palitzsch came and took out a good-sized packet of scribbled notes. Neither he nor the informers knew that Pilecki, through one of his men, opened the box secretly. In the Locksmith's Shop a key was made, using an impression made in bread, and in the evening, when it was already dark, a crowd was created by the box. In the confusion one of the prisoners swiftly opened the box and took out the papers. They were quickly sorted in one of the Blocks and the most dangerous were taken; the rest were returned.[45] Those who in their zeal had gone so far as to give their number or sign their treacherous documents were put on to the camp underground black list.

The fight against informers, who sooner or later were bound to hit on some traces of the camp underground, was one of the movement's chief tasks. In addition to the method cited above, they were found out in various ways. The work of the Political Department, although so dangerous to the prisoners, was carried out in a blatant fashion and the *SS*-men, certain of their complete superiority, made little attempt at concealment. Their contacts with the informers were too open, too obvious. Besides, in the barracks of the camp *Gestapo*, situated just outside the wall and barbed wire of the central camp, prisoners worked as cleaners. The underground managed to bring some of them into its network. They observed comings and goings in the hated barracks, saw who went into it, listened to conversations and reported everything back to their superiors. A growing number of informers thus became known to the underground leaders.

The first task in the fight against spies was to warn the general run of prisoners whom to distrust. This was done discreetly through the far-reaching secret network, which by mid–1942 had its men in all the working-groups of any importance and in all the Blocks. The second and much more difficult task was to liquidate at least the most dangerous informers. Here again the Hospital played an important part, as it was the best place for this purpose.

Living conditions in the camp were primitive and brutal: the price of life was next to nothing, at all roll-calls the body of a dead prisoner was as good as the living man, each *SS*-man and trusty had almost a free hand to kill any prisoner. But for exactly these reasons the liquidation of spies was not carried out mechanically. The underground soldiers had the ambition to be better than their oppressors. Informers were not sentenced to death without due consideration of their case and proof of their treachery. Within the Union of Military Organization there was an underground court, composed of Dr. Rudolf Diem from the Hospital and two barristers, Stefan Niebudek and Józef Woźniakowski, as well as a man close to Pilecki, Henryk Bartosiewicz.[46] These were not trials in the strict sense, for there was no means of arranging them in the camp. It was impossible to bring the accused to defend himself, or to have anyone to represent him, but alleviating circumstances were taken into consideration, bearing in mind of course that all this was taking place in a concentration camp. After all, the prisoner who stole a piece of bread from his neighbour was very often lynched on the spot and only a saint would have tried to defend him. All the evidence was examined and sentence passed. When it was proved that someone had been spying, the only sentence was death. It was nearly always carried out in the Hospital.

The best-known *Gestapo* informer in the camp was Stefan Ołpiński (No. 67214), a Pole who before the war had moved to Germany and became a *Reichsdeutsche*, following a court case in Poland in which Ołpiński had received a prison sentence of some months. In the camp he organized a group of helpers who nosed round the whole place looking for traces of an organization or preparations for escape, this being one of the worst offences and involving death for those who attempted it or aided the attempt. Ołpiński worked almost openly: he was granted obvious privileges by the Political Department, lived in a separate room on Block No. 25, got his food from the *SS* Kitchen and so on. He was also supposed to receive medical treatment in his room and not in the Hospital.

Several instances of spying and denunciation were proved against him and the military organization sentenced him to death. The sentence was to be carried out in the Hospital. This was by no means easy, and it was not until the end of 1943 that someone whom Ołpiński trusted but who was a soldier of the underground managed to persuade him to accept a sweater containing typhus-infected lice. About a fortnight later the informer fell ill and in spite of his own and his protectors' protests he was taken to the Hospital, to Block No. 20. The Polish doctors, afraid of being held responsible by the Political Department, informed Dr. Wirths of Ołpiński's illness. Dr. Wirths, unexpectedly, took matters into his own hands and proceeded as if he also wished for the informer's death. Ołpiński had no chance at all. He died about a fortnight later.* This was in the first half of January 1944; the exact date is not known.[47]

---

* The names of some of the best-known informers are in Appendix III, item 15.

Pilecki in his report gives other methods by which some informers were liquidated. One had castor oil put into his soup, and when he got diarrhoea and went to the Hospital, men in Pilecki's confidence brought about his death in the same way. In the second case an agent of the *Gestapo* lying in the hospital had his lungs X-rayed, the wrong plates were substituted and, when *SS*-man Josef Klehr was going round the hospital looking for victims for his lethal injections, the prisoner was pointed out to him as tubercular. He took down the agent's number and the following day killed him with an injection of phenol into his heart. Another time a similar liquidation of an informer by the Germans themselves was to have been contrived, but that time there was a terrible scene, as Grabner, head of the Political Department, found out the truth and ordered Klehr in the future to submit to him beforehand every list of those to be injected.[48]

The activity of the underground in fighting their most dangerous enemies was not limited only to spies. In the Hospital Laboratory Witold Kosztowny bred typhus lice, which were thrown on to the coats of the most hated *SS*-men. Grabner, his right-hand man, Wilhelm Boger, *Rapportführer* Palitzsch and others were all hunted in this way, but unsuccessfully. Nevertheless, typhus did get into the *SS* barracks and caused serious losses there. The Senior Medical Officer, Siegfried Schwella, died of it. The sick soldiers were taken to Hospital in Katowice, where they generally died. A special order was issued on September 7th, 1942 by Hans Aumeier, by which the *SS* soldiers were confined to barracks and the whole camp was proclaimed a closed area.

The fight against informers and the attempts to infect *SS*-men with typhus are a graphic illustration of what Auschwitz was like and what methods were used there to win the battle for life and to combat the inhuman lawlessness of the *SS*-men. It is impossible for people living in safety today to judge, thirty years later, these desperate struggles. A former Auschwitz prisoner, Adeleide Hautval, expressed this very clearly:

> I don't think anybody in the world to-day has the right to judgement or decision as to what he himself would have done in those completely improbable conditions with which one stood face to face in places like Auschwitz.[49]

4

After the general delousing, which unfortunately consisted not only of poisoning the typhus-carrying insects but also of murdering

numbers of sick and weak prisoners, and after the *Kommandos* had
been quartered in groups in the same Blocks, a new situation was
created in the camp, which was taken advantage of by the camp
underground.

There was no longer any need for two plans in case of a fight to
free the camp. Previously, when the groups going out to work had
been formed from various Blocks, the prisoners were scattered
around during the day, formed different groups and thus separate
battle plans were needed during the day and the night. Now the same
prisoners were together during both day and night, and a single
mobilization plan was quite adequate. Pilecki accepted a proposal to
re-organize all the forces of the underground army in the central
camp and divide them into battalions. All the blocks were two-storied
with the ground-floor bearing the number of the block and the first
floor this same number with the addition of the letter *a*. Each storey
had its own Block Chief and was a separate unit in the organization
of the camp. Pilecki decided that each storey should be the equivalent
of a skeleton platoon, and the whole Block a two-platoon company
with a Commander at its head.

Naturally the strength of these platoons and companies would
depend on their power of attracting other prisoners in support at the
moment fighting broke out. A considerable number of unorganized
prisoners could certainly be expected to join the underground
soldiers, take their revenge on the *SS*-men and help in regaining freedom. Several blocks would make up a battalion. This plan was discussed with Col. Gilewicz and received his approval. According to
Pilecki the scheme appeared as follows:

I divided the whole into four battalions.

As commander of the whole – for the purpose of military action
– I proposed, as hitherto, Major Zygmunt Bończa-Bohdanowski.

As commander of the first battalion – Major Edward Gött-
Getyński. Blocks: 15, 17, 18.

As commander of the second battalion – Captain Stanisław
Kazuba. Blocks: 16, 22, 23, 24.

As commander of the third battalion – Captain Tadeusz Lisowski
(Paolone). Blocks: 19, 25, the kitchen and the hospital personnel
from blocks 20, 21, 28.

As commander of the fourth battalion – Captain Julian 'Trzęsimiech'. Blocks: 4, 5, 6, 7, 8, 9 and 10.

I did not organize the rest of the blocks for technical reasons, as
they were either only just brought into use, as 1 and 2, or used for
stores, as 3, 26 and 27, or just being built, as 12, 13, 14, or the
special block: 11.[50]

Doctors were also appointed to definite positions. Dr. Diem was to head the medical service of the underground army during the fighting, Dr. Czesław Jaworski was to be his deputy. They were both army doctors. Dr. Dering was to be the Commandant of the camp Hospital.[51]

The division into battalions also included their current tasks during the period before any outbreak.

The four battalions had duties divided among them in the following way: each battalion had a week of duty, i.e. it was responsible for action in the event of an air-raid or a drop of arms.[52]

These changes in the central camp took place at the beginning of October 1942 and constituted a fairly elaborate plan, which with help from outside had some chance of success. Thanks to couriers, using escapes and contacts with civilian workers and the local population, Pilecki was in constant touch both with the H.Q. of the Home Army in the capital and with the Commanders of the Districts in Cracow and Silesia. His great desire for action and fighting, linked with the terrible picture of the camp, the murdering of the prisoners and the operations of the gas chambers, caused his reports to be extremely aggressive and led him to present the camp underground's capabilities in a very optimistic light. The Home Army Command judged its chances differently; it knew that without a general uprising and the control of the area around the camp there was no chance of saving many thousands of prisoners, and thus it did not give Pilecki either the promise of support nor the authority to begin an independent fight.

The actual division into battalions was only the first step towards an eventual uprising. Some hope was offered by a camouflaged arms-store underneath the main barracks of the Building Office. A few pistols and some ammunition, which had been stolen from *SS*-men, were hidden there. Many young Poles, members of the *ZOW*, worked in this office and they prepared a hiding-place beneath it. Another factor which increased the chance of at least a temporary takeover of the camp was the making of secret keys to the *SS*-men's Arms Stores. Some soldiers of the garrison, sometimes former NCOs of the Polish Army who were now *Volksdeutschen*, got into contact with certain prisoners and let it be understood that if it came to fighting they would be on their side. The same soldiers supplied information of the Command's plans and the information, checked by other sources, was usually exact. This was not, of course, a mere matter of humanity: the underground soldiers knew well that the waverings of some *SS*-men were caused by defeats at the front, but in the balance this mood might be useful at the decisive moment.

Immediately after being cured of typhus, Pilecki, with Bartosiewicz's help, got into the *Kommando* of tanners. Here he worked side by side with Col. Gilewicz and they were in constant contact. In the Tannery area there were gathered together every day, in various *Kommandos*, about 500 efficient, strong and well-fed craftsmen. They were the nucleus of the underground camp army; the craftsmen and the Hospital personnel were most to be relied on.

During the time that the camp underground forces were being re-organized there twice occurred events which almost led to open revolt, which might easily have turned into a general fight. On October 28th, 1942, the *SS*-men during the morning roll-call read out the numbers of about 280 prisoners, mostly from Lublin and Radom, and drove them on to Block No. 3. When the *Kommandos* had gone to work and the camp was partially empty, the 280 men were taken to Block No. 11. They were mostly young, still in good physical condition. In the camp their fate was already known, and they too knew it. Only the memory of the threat, recently proclaimed, that for any attempt at escape or revolt the prisoner's families might be brought to the camp, kept them from snatching the weapons from the hands of the few *SS*-men escorting them. A few hours later in the Hospital area the numbers of a few Poles, members of the Hospital personnel, were read out and they were led to Block No. 11, to be added to the hundreds of condemned waiting there. Then five members of the military organization, among them Dr. Jan Suchnicki, Leon Kukiełka and Eugeniusz Obojski, led from the Hospital, tried to fight. They barricaded the doors of the Block and began to call on others to try to defend themselves and to rouse the whole camp to resistance. Before this could have any effect, one of the trusties informed the *SS*-men of what was happening. Palitzsch arrived with several soldiers and immediately shot the five who dared to fight. The rest shared their fate a few hours later. It is hard to know how things would have gone if all those condemned to death at that time had tried to fight. Many of the *Kommandos* were only waiting for the signal to take up their hidden arms.

The second case was different, but perhaps caused even more of an upheaval in the camp, which was still for the greater part Polish. In December of the same year, 1942, among the many articles brought from *Canada* to the Tannery there began to appear Polish country-style boots, peasant clothing, prayer-books and rosaries. Soon afterwards there came a secret report from Birkenau that these belonged to Polish peasant families, brought from Zamość province straight to the gas chambers.[53] This was the result of Himmler's decree of November 12th, 1942, to open up the first territory for German colonization in the *General Gouvernement* (central Poland).

Birkenau.

During a few months, from November 1942 to January 1943, over 100,000 Poles were displaced from Zamość province and some tens of thousands of Germans settled in their place. The Polish underground movement, with the Home Army at its head, undertook reprisal action, attacking the villages colonized by Germans and the German guard-posts. The settlement operation was partly prevented and partly much-delayed.[54]

At the same time over a hundred boys aged from ten to sixteen were brought to Birkenau, the children of families just murdered in the gas chambers. They were given numbers and dressed in striped clothes. The older prisoners immediately took them under their care, brought them food and gave them warm underclothing. The sight of the children amidst the terrible camp conditions was a reminder of home and freedom and awakened a desire to help. Hopes arose that the boys might be saved and might survive, when suddenly they were taken to the central Hospital in Block No. 20 and killed there by phenol injections. So many corpses were to be seen in the camp that

Heinrich Himmler

Reinhard Heydrich

Oswald Pohl

Adolf Eichmann

Rudolf Höss

Leading *SS* personalities.

the sight of them made no impression on the prisoners, but this pile of children's bodies aroused such passions that the news passed like lightning through all the Blocks and *Kommandos* and raised tempers to boiling-point.[55] The leaders had great difficulty in restraining their fellow-prisoners and underground soldiers from unco-ordinated reactions of rage and despair.

These were difficult decisions, but necessary. Any premature outburst would have meant the massacre of thousands of helpless prisoners. It was still necessary to wait for the right moment.

5

The middle of 1942 was also an important period because the head of the *SS* Heinrich Himmler then visited Auschwitz for the second time. His visit lasted two days, July 17th and 18th; he was accompanied by Fritz Bracht, the *Gauleiter** of Silesia, *SS* General Ernst Schmauser and *SS* Maj. General Heinz Kammler. Himmler made a thorough inspection of the camp and its amenities, was present at the 'selection' of a transport of Jews which had just arrived at Birkenau, saw them gassed in Bunker No. 2 (the four great gas chambers and crematoria were not yet ready), inspected the *Buna-Werke* and demanded a demonstration of punishment by flogging in the women's camp. At a final briefing in Höss's office he ordered the latter to liquidate all Jews unfit for work, to build up Birkenau as quickly as possible, to stop escapes by every available means and to give priority to enlarging the munitions industry. As a reward for services he made Höss an *SS* Lt. Colonel. During the inspection all the deficiencies of the camp came to light, such as the over-crowding, bad hygienic conditions, the terrible state of the prisoners, which was pointed out to Himmler by Bracht, Kammler and Höss. He brushed them aside with the stern statement: 'nothing is difficult for an officer of the *SS*'.[56] Not only did he not limit the transports arriving at the camp almost daily, but gave warning that their number would increase.

This inspection showed clearly that there would be no further changes to improve the prisoners' lot apart from the abolition of collective responsibility for escapes and apart from the policy of sending into the camp those Jews who were able to work, which saved them, at least for a time, from the gas chambers. These two alleviations – the abolition of the murderous, hours-long roll-calls by way of reprisal for an escape, and the prolonging of the lives of Jews fit for work – were not dictated by humanitarian considerations, but solely by the need for labour in the munition factories. For the same reason prisoners (except Jews) were allowed to receive food parcels from their families. Thousands of prisoners survived the camp thanks only to this regulation, which came into force at Christmas, 1942.[57]

---

* Sheriff.

CHAPTER 7

Losses among the underground soldiers; help from outside the camp; the partisan units; Pilecki's escape.

1

Himmler's visit also had some effect on the camp underground movement, for it increased the keenness of the SS-men and the Political Department. The secret organization had now reached such dimensions that a well-directed stroke by their persecutors was almost to be expected. The Germans, with the help of spies, had been nosing round for so long that they were bound to have some success.

In the autumn, when the potatoes were being clamped, even the Block Chiefs were put to work.[1] Among them was Alfred Stössel, from the first 'upper' five, who at that time controlled Hospital Block No. 28. Someone must have revealed that he belonged to the underground movement, for in his absence Gerhard Lachmann of the Political Department went to Stössel's room. Not finding him there, Lachmann went off in the direction of the gate. Stössel's Barrackroom Service colleagues realised the danger and at once got everything out of the room which might have implicated him. Lachmann came back, searched the room thoroughly and, although he found nothing, waited for Stössel to return from work and immediately took him to the bunker on Block No. 11. This was on October 29th, 1942.[2]

From the bunker Stössel was taken almost every day to the Political Department for interrogation; sometimes it was carried out on the spot. Pilecki was very uneasy, for Stössel knew a lot and it could be dangerous if he were forced to speak. Luckily when it came to the test he showed great endurance and strength of character. He said nothing, he betrayed nobody, not a single prisoner was taken for interrogation through him. The enquiries went no further. It is hard to say how things might have turned out if he had not had a spark of luck. He fell ill with typhus and was taken to the Infectious Block. Under normal conditions to go down with typhus would hardly be considered luck, but in Stössel's situation it was.

One would have to experience certain degrees of comparison oneself to understand, that, whereas for the prisoners in the camp, freedom was outside the barbed wire, for the men in the bunker freedom was the area of the camp. So that getting out of the bunker, even ill, on to the typhus block was for him a kind of freedom.[3]

His severe illness, partial loss of consciousness, the stay in the Hospital – all this held up the interrogation and allowed the underground workers to make contact with Stössel, although there was almost constantly an *SS*-man by his side, usually Lachmann. When the sick man began to recover, on February 19th, 1943, he was taken back to the bunker and the interrogations recommenced. Once again the prisoner proved to have enough endurance to give nobody away. However even his young body could not stand up to the physical and mental pressure after his severe illness. He died in the bunker during the night of March 3rd–4th, 1943.[4]

Six weeks after Stössel* had been uncovered a second blow fell on the military underground. On December 16th, 17th and 18th, 24 prisoners were taken from several Blocks and put into the bunker.† On one of them, Zdzisław Wróblewski, a cavalry officer, were found some notes considered as proof that he was in charge of an underground military group. At the same time arms were supposed to have been found in a shed beside the household stores of the *SS* garrison, and, in the attic of Block No. 17a, a revolver. Wróblewski and another of the arrested prisoners, Józef Krall, were tied up and subjected to a cruel interrogation. A speciality of the Political Department at Auschwitz was tying a prisoner's hands to his feet and hanging him from a metal bar between two tables. In this position he was swung to and fro and beaten with strips of metal, boiling water was poured into his nose and when he lost consciousness cold water was thrown over him. The others had also tasted these methods. Only two of them were set free again in the camp and one was transferred to the Penal Company at Birkenau; the rest, between frequent interrogations, awaited their fate in the bunker. With the one exception of a Jew, Manfred Bock, they were all Poles, mostly young men from good *Kommandos* (clothing stores, cleaners in the *SS* barracks, grooms).

As Pilecki did not mention this group in his report, it has to be presumed that the group was still independent or was connected with the Union of Military Organization through the group of Col. Rawicz, Col. Stawarz or Lt. Col. Kumuniecki. The last supposition is the most probable, as was borne out by events which took place a couple of weeks later.

On January 6th, 1943, when the working groups started to disperse after morning roll-call, prisoners working in the Clothing Stores,

---

* For opinions about Stössel, see Appendix II, item 4.

† Their names are in Appendix III, item 16.

Arthur Liebehenschel

Richard Baer

Hans Aumeier

Maximilian Grabner

Gerhard Palitzsch

Oswald Kaduk

Wilhelm Boger

Leading *SS* personalities.

Deposit Stores, Disinfection and a small office at the Political Department were ordered to remain on the spot. *SS* Captain Hans Aumeier, accompanied by the head of the camp *Gestapo*, Maximilian Grabner, *Rapportführer* Palitzsch and others came up to them. One of Grabner's men, Lachmann, who must have had some information, several times asked: 'Where is the colonel?', and when Lt. Col. Kumuniecki stepped forward, the prisoners were questioned as to their professions and divided into three groups. *Reichsdeutschen* and *Volksdeutschen* were sent to work, and Poles were divided into those who admitted to being educated or looked like intellectuals, and the rest, who were reckoned to be working-class. This last, fairly numerous group, was sent to the very hard labour of digging gravel (*Kiesgrube*). Among them were several intellectuals belonging to Pilecki's organization, including Maj. Bończa-Bohdanowski, who passed as a forester, and Kazimierz Radwański. The rest, fifteen in number, were led to the bunker.*

Pilecki's report suggests an explanation of these events.[5] On Christmas Eve, 1942, a gathering took place to celebrate the holy day in Block No. 27, where the uniform and linen stores were situated and where Bernard Świerczyna worked as a deputy *Capo*, with many Poles in his group. A great many prisoners arrived, Świerczyna recited a patriotic poem, the atmosphere was gay but rather too free and easy for the camp. An unwelcome guest may have been present and lodged information. If this was the explanation, however, Świerczyna would certainly have gone to the bunker first, and since this did not happen another alternative must be considered. The whole affair might have been caused by the picking up of Wróblewski and his friends, who probably belonged to Lt. Col. Kumuniecki's group which, although it had already joined the Union of Military Organization, still preserved its identity as a cadre. This would explain why Lachmann first of all looked for a colonel, who must have been given away by one of the tortured prisoners of Wróblewski's group. This also seems a probable theory since the *SS*-men attacked only a couple of weeks after the Christmas party, and the information, if it had been given, would have been lodged at once. The segregation of the prisoners into groups also proved that the *SS*-men were acting blindly, that the forced confession, if any, was in very general terms and chiefly concerned Lt. Col. Kumuniecki, and even then without his name.

There were now some tens of prisoners in the bunker, but the affair did not end there. During the following days the *SS*, chiefly the Political Department, sent another twenty-two men to the bunker from various Blocks.† They were still mostly young men, who might have been suspected of belonging to the military camp underground. Quite unexpectedly Col. Jan Karcz, commander of the Union of

---

* Their names are in Appendix III, item 17.

† Their names are in Appendix III, item 18.

Military Organization in Birkenau, found himself among them. In the middle of 1942 he had been sent to the Penal Company (the sentence was six months), but thanks to the help of underground colleagues, Władysław Ostrowski and Zenon Różański, he had got out of it and was living on Block No. 7 without the *SS* being aware of it.[6] In January 1943 his six-months' sentence ended and Karcz, tired of hiding in Block No. 7 and fearing that he would be found out, decided on a resolute step. He went himself to Hans Aumeier, reported that his sentence was over and asked to be moved to an ordinary block. This took place on January 23rd, 1943. Aumeier that same day ordered him to be shut up in the bunker, where he met the group of colleagues earlier incarcerated over the Wróblewski and Kumuniecki affairs. Aumeier must have known what he was doing and what Karcz's fate would be, for two days later there was a selection in the bunker; 51 prisoners were chosen, including many suspected of underground military activity (Karcz, Kumuniecki, Gött-Getyński and others), and shot against the black wall. Only two of Kumuniecki's group, Bronisław Motyka, the Chief of Block No. 7, and his clerk, Jan Wróblewski, escaped this fate and were let free into the camp. The rest, mainly connected with Zdzisław Wróblewski, were executed on February 4th, 13th and 16th.[7]

This was the first blow at the military underground in the camp which showed signs of being an organized action, directed against many of the soldiers enlisted by Pilecki or brought into the Union of Military Organization by him later. The victims included courageous Col. Karcz, the Commander of the underground in Birkenau, Lt. Col. Kumuniecki, who had great authority and had brought into the Union many prisoners, Maj. Gött-Getyński, Commander of one of the underground battalions, and many other brave officers and soldiers. They all belonged to the organization started by Pilecki and this blow shook him severely. It was true that the fortunes of war were already beginning to turn the other way and that it could already be seen that the Germans were not going to win.

At the beginning of February 1943 the great, months-long battle of Stalingrad, in which many thousands of Germans were taken into Soviet captivity, ended. This eventually became the turning-point of the Second World War. The aerial bombardment of the *Reich* was becoming ever heavier and its population, still far from the fronts, experienced for itself the meaning of total war, as begun by Hitler. This had its effect on the behaviour of the *SS*-men and lessened their keenness, but the dangers of camp life had not abated perceptibly. It was obvious that the Political Department already knew of the underground organization, which was now very extensive, that it was looking for clues, and that a further attack would be carried out on a wide front involving the central camp, Birkenau and perhaps also the outlying sub-camps.

2

As resistance spread over the whole country, its strength also increased in the neighbourhood of the camp. The number of people outside who helped to smuggle in food and medicines, or acted as intermediaries to pass on news and sometimes illegal correspondence, increased considerably. In addition to the organizations already mentioned, a new one was set up by the Socialists (*PPS*). In May 1943 a young Socialist, Edward Hałoń, from Brzeszcze, a small town in the neighbourhood of Auschwitz, came to Cracow to meet Adam Rysiewicz, the district secretary of the *PPS*.[8] This was not their first meeting, for they had been working together for some time, with the assistance of other socialists, in helping prisoners in the camp. The meeting took place in the apartment of Teresa Lasocka, who worked for the Chief Welfare Board (*RGO*). It was headed by Count Adam Ronikier and had been set up in 1940 with German consent as a strictly charitable organization. In 1943, after the war had reached its turning-point, the Germans tried to use it to make contact with the Polish people, without any success. Lasocka was in touch secretly with the Government Delegacy (*DR*), which represented the Polish Government (at that time in London) and was the highest underground political authority in the occupied country. In addition to the Government the Poles also had their own armed forces in the West: a land army, a navy and an air force, which fought openly against the Germans under British command. At the same time in Poland, under the occupation, secret political parties were operating, on which was based the Government Delegacy, and there also existed an underground army, called the Home Army (*AK*), which carried on the struggle with the occupiers by means of diversion, partisan warfare, sabotage and propaganda. This army was supplied by drops of personnel and equipment from Great Britain, and, beginning in 1944, from Italy.[9]

At this meeting it was decided to set up a committee called Help for the Prisoners of Concentration Camps (*PWOK*). Lasocka and Rysiewicz were to support it with their contacts in Cracow, while Edward Hałoń was to build up a network around Auschwitz. The committee's title spoke of 'camps' in the plural, but it was clear that it referred to the camp at Auschwitz. The task of the new organization was not only assistance in the form of food and medicines, but also to help in escapes and look after any prisoners who managed to get out of the hell of the camp. Therefore Hałoń was to organize an armed group, capable of fighting locally if necessary.

It is not unnatural that when discussing the problem of the help given to the camp at Auschwitz, one constantly comes across the same names in various accounts and memoirs. There were several groups active near the camp (*ZWZ* – later *AK*, the Socialists, the Peasants' Battalions) and there were different people at the head of each; but at the lower levels, the people close to the camp and in practical contact with it, the same names crop up again and again. It often happened that the same people belonged to two secret organizations with similar aims. This was especially so around the camp of Auschwitz, for only local people who had lived there for years or been resettled in the area could make contact with the prisoners working outside the barbed wire. Only they could find pretexts which would carry conviction to the *SS*-men. Therefore, having mentioned these various groups, it would be pointless to try to assign the active inhabitants of the towns and villages near Auschwitz to one or the other with any certainty. Later, in post-war conditions, the political character of certain actions was inflated and it was claimed that the political views of individuals decided their degree of self-sacrifice. Nothing is further from the truth. They were simply motivated by compassion for others and the pity aroused by their fate.[10]

Whole families, sometimes even teenagers, took part in this assistance for the camp and liaison with it. They were generally very poor families, some of whom had been turned out of their own homes and holdings, who took the food out of their own mouths in order to send it secretly to those yet more in need. They would watch where the *Kommandos* outside the camp worked, and leave food for them in various places. Sometimes they managed to exchange a few words with the prisoners.

The needs of the camp were, of course, endless, and so those who organized aid on a larger scale needed the help of many others, especially those Poles who still ran flour-mills, bakeries, grocery stores and chemists' shops. It was characteristic that amongst the people helping the camp, there were also *Volksdeutschen*, who, despite having opted in favour of German descent, still felt themselves to be Poles. This happened in Silesia, which like Alsace and Lorraine, was the frontier of German influence. As a result of years-long pressure many Polish families, with Polish names, were Germanized. This process was completed by Nazi terror. There were, however, families with pure German names, who, despite everything, retained a strong sentiment for Polish culture and considered themselves to be Poles. After the first shock, when the might of Hitler's Germany was displayed in 1939 and crushed Poland, many hearts quailed and many people, saving themselves first of all from deportation, accepted the *Volkslist*. With the developments of the war and not only just because the Germans were beginning to lose, but also because of what the Nazis were showing themselves to be, these people began to understand that they had been wrong and that they had nothing in common with the Germans. Now, when they could see what was happening in the camp at Auschwitz, and when there arose ways of helping the prisoners, they secretly volunteered for this. The list of those helping was long and embraced many names from various local towns and villages.

With the agreement of Polish shops, forged ration cards were put into circulation; without them it would have been difficult to do much. They were printed in Warsaw from specimens sent from Silesia. The plates were made in the secret works of the Home Army and sent to the printing presses of the Peasants' Battalions. Considerable sums of money were also sent by the Government Delegacy.[11]

The help sent in the form of medicines, especially anti-typhus serum in 1942, when tens of thousands of camp prisoners died needs separate consideration. Constant assistance came from Maria Bobrzecka (code-name *Marta*), the owner of a chemist's shop at Brzeszcze, who, in spite of German control, managed to stay on as manageress. Contacts with the camp reached as far as Cracow, 30 miles away, and found support there in Maria Hulewiczowa (code-name *Brzeska*) and Teresa Lasocka, already mentioned, who, apart from her many other activities related to liaison with the camp, supplied thousands of ampoules of serum. A large quantity of these was also supplied by Justyna Hałupka from Hecznarowice. The success of these operations is proved by a secret message from Janusz Pogonowski from the surveyors' *Kommando*, sent to the organization outside the camp on July 31st, 1942. 'I have received about 1000 ampoules of various medicines (coramine, aligipuratum etc.), they have all been sent to the sick-bay in the K.L. Auschwitz.'[12] Dr. Władysław Dziewoński of Kęty and Dr. Sierankiewicz of Brzeszcze also helped.

From the camp itself the most active contact with the outside world was maintained by the surveyors' *Kommando* with Kazimierz Jarzębowski and Janusz Pogonowski; but they were not the only people doing this. Contact was also maintained through the Building Office, where the *Capo* was Władysław Plaskura, a member of *ZOW*. He communicated with a civilian girl, Helena Szpak, who lived in the town of Auschwitz and came in to work each day at the Building Office. She was the secret liaison officer with the outside world.[13] Other contacts went through the gardening sub-camp at Rajsko, the fish-ponds in the sub-camp at Harmęże, the camp for free workers, also through the *Buna-Werke*, and through many more groups that went to

Zygmunt Janke   Jan Wawrzyczek   Helena Płotnicka

Władysława Kożusznikowa   Karol Petkowski   Jan Nosal

Wojciech Jekiełek   Adam Rysiewicz   Teresa Lasocka

Maria Bobrzecka   Maria Hulewiczowa

Poles outside the camp who helped the resistance movement.

work outside the camp. Pilecki himself was not in direct touch with the men who maintained liaison with the outside world, but used Dr. Dering where medical matters were concerned, and Lt. Col. Dziama and Henryk Bartosiewicz for the rest.[14]

This great amount of activity around the camp was bound to give rise to German retaliations, and many of the people involved in this work fell into the hands of the police and the *SS*. Some were sent to the camp to share the fate of those they had helped, and usually died there. Among those who thus gave their lives was Helena Płotnicka, the wife of a miner and the mother of five children, who devoted herself throughout the war to helping those in the camp. She was arrested on the 19th May, 1943, together with her thirteen-year-old daughter, Wanda, and was brought to the camp. The arrest was the result of her co-operation with the surveyors' *Kommando*, whose *Capo* was an informer of the Political Department, Stanisław Dorosiewicz. She was immediately taken to Block No. 11 and the camp *Gestapo* began its interrogation. She was beaten unconscious, hung up by her hands tied behind her back, red-hot oil was poured into her nose, her teeth were smashed out, her finger-nails were torn out, she was starved and not given water, in an attempt to force her to betray those with whom she had been co-operating outside the camp and to reveal with which prisoners she had been in contact. She was able to endure all this, and not a single name did she utter. A great help to her resisting the *Gestapo* was the contact which the camp underground made with her in the bunker. She was told that Dorosiewicz had informed on her, and that he did not know a great deal about her. This allowed her to avoid traps during her interrogation. Finally the *SS*-men themselves grew tired and they allowed her to move from the bunker into the women's camp in Birkenau. There her fellow-prisoners surrounded her with the most tender care; they got her into the hospital, saw to it that she had good food and medicine, and allowed her to regain her health. Unfortunately they could not save her life. On the 17th March, 1944, typhus killed her. After her death the prisoners wrapped her body in a clean sheet, which was a rare occurrence in the camp, and laid on it a few green spring branches, to honour her great sacrifice before her remains were engulfed in the fire of the crematorium. Her young daughter was released.[15]

In addition to Płotnicka many other local people also ended up in the camp and laid their bones to rest there. Only a very few managed to survive the war.*

---

* The names of the people who helped the underground and died in the camp are in Appendix III, item 19.

3

In addition to bringing material assistance to the camp and carrying information and secret correspondence, thought had also to be given to armed units in the immediate vicinity of Auschwitz. The idea of an attack on the *SS* garrison, constantly in Pilecki's mind, was also in the thoughts of those who operated outside the camp. Such an attack would be the crowning-stroke of their activities, but first they had to perform many immediate tasks, less daring, but also important. Plans had to be laid for the creation of partisan units.

At the very beginning of the camp's history, in mid-1940, this had been completely out of the question. Just after the September defeat, in the face of quite exceptional terror, against a background of deportations and the integration of Silesia into the *Reich*, it would have been difficult to find people who would have dared to undertake such a thing. A year passed and the Nazis themselves, as a direct result of their total and senseless reign of terror, produced a situation in which people began to think of armed resistance. Amongst them were above all those whom the police were seeking and hunting: people who had been officers in the Polish army, who had belonged before the war to patriotic organizations, who had not supplied food quotas, or had not volunteered for work in the *Reich*. Since such people could not live at home, as the police had their houses under observation, in despair they went off to the nearest woods and formed a small diversionary groups. Some were armed only with pistols, which had been buried after the September campaign; but they were already becoming an irritation to the German police and authorities. Here they attacked a village town-hall and burnt documents and ration cards, there they attacked a German shop and took all the goods, somewhere else they shot a well-known German informer. The fame of their minor successes spread rapidly through the population, and gossip increased the number of attacks and liquidated spies. From an original group of a few people a small partisan force began to develop.

In the autumn of 1941 a staff officer of *ZWZ* District Auschwitz, Lieutenant Jan Wawrzyczek, formed a small diversionary group, with the code-name *Marusza*. It was composed of a few men hiding from the Germans and operated in the region of Łęki, not more than about six miles south of the camp. Later its strength rose to twenty odd partisans with a few rifles, pistols and grenades at their disposal. These weapons had been buried by Polish units in September 1939, and were now dug up, cleaned and put into working order. The chief tasks of the small unit were liquidating spies, taking supplies from German food shops and destroying files in German Government offices.

In 1942 Wawrzyczek expanded his partisan activities to another two units, also small ones. In October the District suffered heavy losses as a result of arrests, and amongst others the Germans seized his superior officer. Wawrzyczek managed to avoid arrest and took over command of the District, continuing to command the partisan units. In the Spring of 1943 he managed to amalgamate three units into one larger one, which was given the code-name *Sosienki*. Its numbers never exceeded 80 partisans; they were armed with a dozen or so rifles, an equal number of pistols, several dozen grenades and 22 Sten guns dropped from the United Kingdom. Wawrzyczek saw the tasks of the new unit as follows:

- Organizing sabotage and diversionary operations near the barbed-wire enclosure to occupy the enemy's attention;
- Organizing contacts with the camp underground, exchange of mail;
- Disorganizing the enemy's economic life;
- Organizing the escape of political prisoners, help with individual escapes;
- Armed struggle in the Auschwitz district;
- Keeping up the spirit of Poles, fighting the enemy terror, reprisals.[16]

One of the most important points connected directly with the camp was co-operation with escapees and affording them help when they had got outside the barbed wire. Escapes became more numerous in 1943 and the partisan units played an important part, picking up many prisoners near the camp and taking them into their ranks. This will be discussed in later chapters in connection with co-operation with the underground in the camp. Here it need only be stressed that it was not until 1943 that outside organized assistance for escapes began to be really effective, for it was only then that the *AK* partisans near the camp were equipped for such tasks.

Sosienki was the only partisan unit in the near vicinity of Auschwitz. It is true that Edward Hałoń in 1943 began to form a fighting group of *PPS*, but it never had more then a dozen or so soldiers and in spite of the great assistance that it gave to escapees from the camp, it could not be called a partisan unit. The same applies to the Peasants' Battalions.[17]

To the north, in the vicinity of the camp, nothing much could be done for the area was thickly populated, flat and open; but to the south, no more than fifteen miles from Auschwitz, lay the Beskid hills, well-forested and suitable for partisan operations. There, in the second half of 1942, diversionary groups of the Home Army began to form. The Socialists also had people in the area. Later, in 1943, small partisan patrols grew out of these groups, whose strength increased on account of the numerous arrests. Threatened men fled to the forests. The code-names of these groups came from the names of the places near which they were formed, e.g. *Romanka, Malinka, Brenna, Ustroń, Czarne.* Wacław Zdyb, who had been Cavalry

Watchtowers at Birkenau.

Captain, was the commander of *Kedyw* (diversionary command) of the Silesian District of the Home Army. He united these groups at the turn of the year 1943–1944 and formed two partisan companies out of them. One was commanded by Lieut. Józef Barcikowski, who had escaped from Auschwitz on October 24th, 1944. The companies, using the code-name *Garbnik*, seldom operated as a complete unit, for it was hard to get provisions; moreover, circumstances at the time permitted of small operations only. It was commanded by Lieut. Czesław Świątecki. The men were poorly armed, but among them were a number of escapees from Auschwitz. In the autumn of 1944 there were twenty-one of them.[18]

Further to the north, near Sosnowiec, in the second half of 1943, out of two diversionary groups of *PPS* were formed two partisan companies of the Home Army, They usually had their headquarters and operated on the territory of the *General Gouvernement*, near Kielce and Cracow, for the territories incorporated into the *Reich* were too 'hot'. Together they formed the partisan unit *Surowiec*.[19]

As well as the above-mentioned units, which were of a skeleton character but could quickly increase their strength in case of need, the Silesian Legion existed not far away. This was composed of men who had left their homes in September 1939 and did not return to them when the campaign was over, but settled down in and near Cracow. Neither they nor their families could return, for they were former Silesian insurgents, who took part in the three uprisings against the Germans in 1919–1921. Political and social workers, officers and many others were in a similar position, with the local *Gestapo* eagerly waiting for their return. In autumn 1939 Major Marian Kilian began to organize them secretly. He first made contact with the *ZWZ* in Cracow and was later in touch with the District *AK* and its commandant Col. Józef Spychalski, a parachutist from Britain. Since the underground soldiers of the Legion lived in and near Cracow but were to fight in Silesia, the Districts Cracow and Silesia *AK* decided that they would be under Cracow as a garrison and under Silesia operationally. The Legion was a cadre unit which could easily increase its strength. In 1943 it numbered about 500 underground soldiers.

These partisan units and the Silesian Legion, plus smaller groups operating in the area – this was the strength which the Commandant of the Silesian District of the *AK* would have at his disposal if it were decided to attack the guards of the Auschwitz camp. They would be complemented by the camp underground and many other prisoners who would join in the fight. There were very few weapons, so it was hoped to get them from drops or capture them from the enemy.[20]

4.

For several reasons Pilecki, at the beginning of 1943, began seriously to consider the necessity of escape.[21] It was not of himself that he was thinking, for after all he had, of his own free will, allowed himself to be picked up in Warsaw and taken to Auschwitz. The motives behind this decision were wholly bound up with the organization he had founded.

There could be no doubt that the underground network, already in existence for over two years in such an exposed area as a concentration camp, was bound sooner or later to become the object of attack from the Political Department and to suffer losses. This Pilecki fully understood and therefore, although the executions of January and February 1943 shook him and deprived the underground of many valuable men, he did not despair or feel that the organization as a whole was threatened. How fortunate it was that the instigator and organizer was himself, an ordinary, inconspicuous prisoner, brought to the camp after a round-up, a man of whom the *Gestapo* had no record, who was not a senior officer or known to have a past which might single him out. In this respect the camp underground had passed the test, and so had the brave men who were thrown into the bunker and subjected to cruel interrogation. All the same, the fear of disclosure existed, for Pilecki's role of organizer was by now known to many underground soldiers. What would happen if, in the case of further arrests, one of them broke down under interrogation and gave him away? Pilecki himself was tough and self-confident, but could he guarantee to stand up to every kind of pressure?

The second reason for his decision was also connected with the *Gestapo* campaign against the underground. Through his contacts Pilecki had learnt from the Political Department that the command was planning a number of transports to other camps and in them, above all, were to be Poles with low numbers from good *Kommandos*. This was for the same reason that the Germans were organizing big round-ups in the towns and deporting men to camps. As well as by terror they fought the underground movement in this way, for among those picked up there were bound to be a certain number of resistance workers. This same device was now to be employed in Auschwitz. The *SS*-men knew that there was a resistance movement in the camp, that its leaders were Poles and that its members were chiefly young men. It was logical to suppose that the underground workers, especially the more important ones, would be working in the better positions in the camp.

This proved to be correct. During March 7th, 8th and 9th, 1943, about 6,000 numbers were read out, all Poles, representing the best element in the camp, from good *Kommandos* in the stores and work-shops. Pilecki was among them. They were taken to block Nos. 12 and 19 and kept under guard. A medical board began to sit. The underground immediately made efforts to recover many of its members under various pretexts. Pilecki got a rupture belt from the hospital and, wearing this, was rejected by the board. Only the healthy were chosen; a man with a rupture could perish in Auschwitz, but he was not supposed to be sent to work in a munitions factory. A number of other underground soldiers also managed to get them-selves rejected and the main organizational cadre remained. But four big transports, which on March 10th and 12th left for Buchenwald, Neuengamme, Flossenbürg and Gross-Rosen, carried away 4,000 of the best Polish element. A month later, on April 12th and 13th, two more transports left, this time for Mauthausen, taking a further 2,000 Poles. Pilecki realized that the Germans were transporting poten-tial soldiers who would certainly have joined in any fight for the camp even if they were not already connected with the underground. There was of course no lack of prisoners in the camp – others arrived to take the places of those transported – but they had to be organized afresh, again placed in good *Kommandos* and Pilecki ought no longer to do this for it would expose him dangerously. Besides he might be transported himself; a second time it might prove impossible to keep him back.

In addition to the activities of the Political Department and the threat of transports, another factor cropped up. On December 29th, 1942, four important trusties escaped from the camp: Otto Küsel, Józef Baraś, Mieczysław Januszewski (from the Labour Assignment Office) and Bolesław Kuczbara (who was in charge of the Dental Surgery).[22] Only Januszewski belonged to the military underground, but the other three knew a lot of the camp's secrets. The escape, during which Kuczbara wore *SS* uniform, was successful and he and Küsel headed for Warsaw while Baraś and Januszewski decided to go to Cracow. Suddenly, at the beginning of April 1943, alarming news came from the capital: Kuczbara had been caught and since March 20th had been in the *Pawiak* prison in Warsaw as Janusz Kapur, but his real identity was already known to the *Gestapo*.[23] This informa-tion was brought by a prisoner from the *Pawiak*, who before his arrest had been in the Secret Polish Army. In the camp he met and talked to one of his former comrades, now a member of the camp underground. In this way, through transports from Warsaw, the camp received a lot of news from the capital, for the prisoners in the *Pawiak* who belonged to the underground movement were in contact with their comrades through the prison intelligence service of the H.Q. of the Home Army. The Germans, who had occupied a

Mieczysław Januszewski, Józef Baraś, Otto Küsel, and Władysław Kuczbara, after their escape, together with the Poles who were hiding them.

considerable part of Europe, were, of course, short of men. There-fore former warders usually still worked in the prisons of the occupied countries. Although some Germans and Ukrainians were posted to the men's section of the *Pawiak*, several Polish guards remained, and, furthermore, the same Polish doctors, who came in from the town, were retained. Home Army intelligence entered into secret contact with them, and, by means of their help, secret correspon-dence began to be passed. Their task was only to bring messages into the prison; these then travelled through a network of trusties, of whom, as in the camp, there were many, and who enjoyed certain privileges. The Home Army intelligence net in the *Pawiak* was particularly strong and extensive.[24]

The news of Kuczbara's capture was bad. Although he had never been enrolled into Pilecki's organization, he knew a lot about it, for some of the lines of secret communication ran through the Dental

Surgery. He knew the names of the camp leaders, like Pilecki, Gilewicz, Bartosiewicz and others, and he was a very unstable and unpredictable person. Once, in the camp, he had drawn up two diplomas, one for Gilewicz and the other for Bartosiewicz, stating on them that they were awarded for 'independence work', and it was only with great difficulty that they had been taken away from him and destroyed before they fell into the wrong hands.[25] In the camp he had collected gold from *Canada*, belonging to the victims of the gas chambers, and the underground movement was opposed to prisoners who did this. There were unpleasant rumours about his past, and his dental qualifications were questionable. In order to save his life he might promise to work with the *Gestapo* and betray all he knew about the camp underground.*

But even this most serious threat was not the final reason that made Pilecki decide that, just as he had gone voluntarily to the camp in 1940, so now he must leave it. It had been easy to get into Auschwitz; to get out was immensely difficult. But Pilecki, deeply convinced that he had a mission to perform, believed that he would succeed. The argument that finally weighed with him was the necessity of reporting personally to the H.Q. of the Home Army and presenting the problems of Auschwitz as he saw them. Many reports had gone to Warsaw and Pilecki had many times reported that the camp was preparing to fight and could do so. These reports, however, aroused no echo. Warsaw was silent and sent no orders to authorize the planning of a fight, nor information concerning preparations for outside help. In the opinion of Pilecki and the officers of the Union of Military Organization such help would require not only an attack by the local partisan units, which would have to increase their strength quickly, but also a parachute drop and the bombing of the *SS* stores and barracks. Pilecki grew impatient and indignant; his nearest co-workers also grew impatient. Thus the founder of the camp underground organization came to the conclusion that it was time for him to go to Warsaw and personally explain the situation in Auschwitz to the Home Army Commander. At the time this was Gen. Stefan Rowecki, and Pilecki expected him to lend a favourable ear to his proposals.

On April 13th, 1943, when another large transport of Poles left for Mauthausen, Pilecki decided that he would have to escape in the very near future. The first and the most important problem was to turn over all his contacts and functions so as to leave the organization he had set up in the best possible state.

---

* For the further fortunes of four of the escapees and the connection of the Kuczbara case with Jaster (pp. 102–03), see Appendix II, items 3 and 5.

As already mentioned, the man nominated to take over the military command when fighting broke out was Major Zygmunt Bończa-Bohdanowski (code-name *Bohdan*), so Pilecki first of all informed him of his decision. 'I entrusted to him, *Bohdan*, responsibility for the whole organization in the event of action.'

After the conversation with Bończa there followed a second meeting.

> I went to my friend Henryk Bartosiewicz and entrusted to him the organizational side of the whole – with the help of brave, straightforward Col. Juliusz Gilewicz, who was the official leader of the whole set-up and a friend of Bartosiewicz.[26]

Pilecki for some time had had Bartosiewicz in mind as his successor, and now, in a long conversation, he told him all the secrets of his organizational contacts. They concerned above all the names of the more important persons, mostly known to Bartosiewicz, the secret channels of liaison inside the camp and between the nearer sub-camps, as well as with the outside. Since, in the period before his escape, Pilecki attached the greatest importance to matters concerned with the relief of the camp by armed action, these were also passed on to his successor.[27]

After these two conversations and a meeting with Col. Gilewicz and some of the key men, Pilecki started to make his preparations to leave the camp. He had already picked out two members of his secret organization, Edward Ciesielski and Jan Redzej (in the camp as Jan Retke), with whom he meant to escape.[28]

It was now necessary to decide on the exact means of getting away. Pilecki had for some time been considering the possibilities of escape, even when he had no intention of escaping. This was simply a contingency. He tried to see whether it was possible to sneak out through the sewers and several times he secretly went down into them. Each time he came back covered in filth, having found that the exits beyond the wire were too close to the watchtowers. He finally came to the conclusion that it would be easiest to escape from a group which was working outside the camp and which was guarded by only a few *SS*-men. But it was not only a question of choosing the best plan of escape, it was also a matter of organizing it so that fellow-prisoners from the same blocks and working groups would not suffer. So several prisoners, all of whom belonged to the military camp underground, had to be let into the secret.

It was decided that it would be easiest to escape from the bakery, which was situated outside the camp, about a mile and a half in the direction of the town. This was an outside *Kommando*, and in such groups only certain prisoners could work, and then with the consent of the Political Department. Therefore nominations for these jobs were given out and signed by the *SS*-man from the Labour Assignment Office, Warrant Officer Hessler. Jan Redzej was already working in the bakery and it was after a reconnaissance by him that this route was chosen. Now Pilecki and Ciesielski had to get sent there. There could be no question of using the normal procedure. Certainly neither Pilecki nor Ciesielski had as yet had any contact with the Political Department, but they could not risk any attention from it while they were preparing an escape. They had at all costs to acquire two blank forms already signed by Hessler, and forge them appropriately. Ciesielski arranged this through a prisoner working in the camp Office. The blanks were signed and stamped, but were already made out in other names and related to other working groups. They very carefully erased these details and wrote in the new names and new *Kommando* allocations.

It was thought that the best time for the escape would be during Easter, when discipline among the *SS*-men was slightly relaxed, and Easter Monday–Tuesday was chosen, the night of April 26th–27th, 1943. The bakers worked in two shifts, so it was necessary to get on to the night shift and, before that, on Block No. 15, where the bakers lived. This required taking a whole series of small, but, in the camp, difficult steps. Pilecki worked in the excellent *Kommando* in the Parcel Office and it would have looked far too suspicious to ask the *SS*-man in charge of it to agree to a transfer. So he pretended to be taken ill suddenly and on Easter Saturday Dr. Rudolf Diem took him into the Hospital and put him on the typhus Block No. 20, in the room run by an underground soldier. Pilecki's discharge from hospital at the right time was a matter for Dr. Władysław Fejkiel, who was in the secret.[29] Ciesielski was another matter. He was one of the permanent Hospital personnel, as a male nurse, and his transfer to another *Kommando* and another block required the consent of the Hospital Senior Prisoner. This function had just been taken over by a German political prisoner, Ludwig Wörl, from the previous head of the hospital, Hans Bock, who had been deprived of his function on April 3rd, 1943, for homosexuality and transferred as a Block Chief to the Hospital in the sub-camp of Monowice (*Buna-Werke*). He died later in the camp.[30] The card with Hessler's signature turned out to be very helpful. It was used at the last moment, on Easter Monday, April 26th, and although Wörl was very surprised at being deprived of a male nurse, who was not even a baker, he could not protest or check the card. It was Easter and Hessler had gone away on a few days' leave. Ciesielski went to Block No. 15 and there met Pilecki whom Dr. Fejkiel had just discharged from the hospital, stating that the diagnosis of typhus was wrong. Fejkiel risked a lot by this, as he might be suspected of having helped in the escape. The escapees had previously supplied themselves with all they needed. From Bernard Świerczyna in the Clothing Store they got civilian clothes and some hundreds of dollars; from another prisoner a key to the door of the bakery; from Witold Kosztowny a preparation to kill their scent so that the dogs could not pick it up; from Marian Toliński medicines and three capsules of cyanide potassium. They did not intend to fall into the hands of the SS alive. This was all hidden by Ciesielski in the hospital, where there were a lot of cubby-holes. Now they had a few hours in which to persuade the *Capo* of the baker's working-group, a Sudeten German who had only come to Auschwitz a month earlier, that on their first day they should go with the night shift. He was persuaded by a piece of a roast chicken smuggled in from outside the camp and presents from *Canada*. When he saw tins of sardines and chocolate he was quite speechless. In a camp, in the heart of Germany, one could only dream of such luxuries.

At 6 p.m. eight prisoners and six SS-men left the camp and marched towards the bakeries. Three prisoners and three SS-men went to the SS bakery; five prisoners, among them Pilecki and his friends, and three soldiers, went to the camp bakery. Pilecki and Ciesielski wore civilian clothes under their prison stripes; Redzej was already dressed in civilian clothes, except that red stripes were painted on the trousers and jacket and his camp number was sewn on. In Auschwitz, as in many other German concentration camps, for lack of striped suits the prisoners often wore civilian clothes taken from new arrivals, or old uniforms with oil-painted red stripes down the trousers and on the back. Normally groups working outside the camp had to wear prison stripes. Redzej was a deputy *Capo*, so he was allowed to wear a civilian suit. This made the escape easier. When they got to the forest he scraped off the red stripes with a knife. In the bakery, which was strongly secured, with all the windows barred and the doors reinforced with metal and fastened by an iron bar, they met the day shift just coming off and three civilian bakers, who joined the night shift. Altogether there were five prisoners, three of whom were in the plot, three civilians (Polish-speaking but to be treated with caution) and three SS-men.

The plan for the escape, thought out to the last detail, involved waiting until the early hours of morning, when the human body is at its lowest ebb and reactions are blunted; then they would cut the cables of the alarm system, open the reinforced door with the forged key, undo the screw holding the iron bar fastening the door, and dash out into the night, to the east, towards the Vistula. All this was not as easy as it may sound. Escape from the camp was regarded as the greatest of all crimes and so all the SS-men had special instructions; they were liable to severe punishment for negligence, but got special leave for thwarting an attempted breakout. For the prisoners it was either success or death.

Nobody got away from Auschwitz without a bit of luck, and in this case too, apart from the courage and skill of the escapees, luck played an important, perhaps decisive part. First began the heavy work, superintended by three civilian bakers, who at once realized that Pilecki and Ciesielski were in a bakery for the first time in their lives. But their surprise at this was kept quiet. It turned out that baking was exhausting, particularly as they were so inexperienced. After a few hours they were so tired that one of them pretended to be ill and, with the SS-man's assent, lay down for a while and the other hid while carrying coal to the ovens. In the bakery it was hot and this was made worse as they had civilian clothes on underneath their striped suits.

It was already quite dark and past midnight, but before they could get out of the building and begin the escape, they had to perform two tasks. Redzej had to unscrew the bar, which held the reinforced door, while Ciesielski had to cut the telephone wires. They had only a few minutes to do it in. Both operations were successful, but they were almost found out, since SS-men were continually prowling round inside. Then came two o'clock in the morning, time to escape, as many minutes had passed since the wire had been cut, and the SS-men rang the camp every hour saying that everything was in order. The three conspirators were on the point of rushing for the door, opening it with the home-made key and dashing out into the night, when suddenly, through the grated window of the bakery they saw on the other side an SS uniform. It had begun to rain and a soldier had taken shelter by the bakery with his girlfriend. Trembling with emotion, they had to return to work to avoid arousing suspicion.

Suddenly Pilecki, who had been watching the window, gave the signal that the loving couple had gone. They leapt for the reinforced door, unlocked it and pushed with all their might. But the door was stuck and refused to give. Redzej was a giant with broad shoulders, Pilecki and Ciesielski were no weaklings; several terrible seconds passed before the door suddenly and quietly opened. The damp spring air embraced them. They carefully closed the door behind them, and put wheelbarrows, planks and stones against it, to make it difficult for the SS to open it, and then they dashed off into the darkness. It was raining, in the distance the lights on the camp wire were twinkling, the darkness around them was complete.

The bad weather was extremely fortunate, yet at the same time it transformed the marshy area around the camp into a sea of mud. After running for several minutes the escaped prisoners had to slow down to a brisk walk. They reached the banks of the Soła river, swollen and icy-cold. They halted and threw off their prison uniforms, letting them drift down-stream. Redzej did the same with the camp numbers sewn on his trousers and jacket. At that moment they heard a short burst of machine-gun fire. It was the SS-men at the bakery informing the camp that they had discovered the escape. It was now necessary to cross the river immediately and move off quickly to the east, but the current was so strong that they could not risk swimming across. Suddenly they heard the sound of an approaching train. This told them where the railway bridge was. Once again fortune smiled at them; the bridge was guarded (they saw the sentry's hut) but no-one challenged them. Continuing eastwards, they reached Monowice, where the sub-camp for prisoners working at the *Buna-Werke* was situated. They circled the camp very cautiously, floundering through the mud and endless ditches, and finally they reached the Vistula. Only now did the nervous tension decrease somewhat and they felt a terrible hunger. Unfortunately they had provided themselves with everything except food. This had crossed their minds in the bakery, but at the last moment, in the heat of the dash for freedom, they had forgotten to grab a few loaves. They moved further east along the river, looking for a boat, for swimming across was beyond them. Redzej was a professional soldier, in the prime of life, Ciesielski was barely twenty, and Pilecki, although forty-five, was also in good physical condition. All three of them had had good camp jobs, but it seemed quite impossible to swim the icy river swollen with spring waters. Yet fate wanted the escape to succeed. They saw a small boat chained and padlocked to a post. They wrenched at the chain a couple of times, but it held firm. Redzej pulled out of his pocket the key which he had used to open the bakery door. By a miracle the key fitted, the padlock opened. Half a mile away, on the other side of the river, the black shape of a wood could be seen. They ran breathlessly up to it, went in and fell on the wet leaves. The first stage of the escape was over.

The whole of the following day they sat and slept in the wood on the wet undergrowth. They were tormented by hunger and thirst, and Pilecki was doubled up in pain, for the damp had caused inflammation of the sciatic nerve. He could barely move, when, at nightfall, they moved off to the east, but the walk warmed up the nerve which later began to feel better. They headed for the church in Poręba, whose parish priest was a relative of one of the prisoners in the camp underground, and who knew of their escape. They hoped that the priest would be able to help them cross the frontier to the *General Gouvernement.*

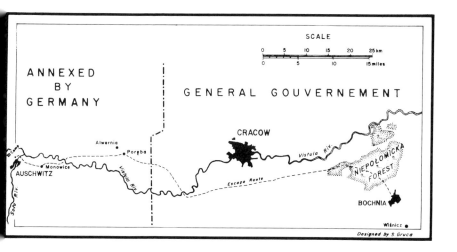

Map of Pilecki's escape route.

At daybreak they again slept for several hours in the wood and, when it was quite light, they saw on a hill the tall tower of a church. It had to be Poręba. Redzej looked the most presentable, since he was bald, and his closely cropped head did not look strange; he was thus delegated to go and talk to the priest. He entered the church and soon returned with a man in a cassock, who quickly told them that they had to crawl up to the monastery walls nearby, and that they must be extremely careful, since they were very near the frontier. He would soon bring them some food and try to find a guide. He also told them that they were not in Poręba, but in Alwernia, a few miles further north. He was not the priest they had been aiming for and who had been recommended to them, but he was a Pole and trusted them. They grasped his hands with emotion.[31]

The excellent food which the priest brought (it was after all Easter), rebuilt their strength. In the evening they left with a guide for the frontier and during the night they crossed it uneventfully. They found themselves on the territory of the *General Gouvernement,* where Hitler allowed Poles to live and from where there were no deportations.

Several times they knocked at the doors of village cottages and always got help, food and shelter for the night from complete strangers. Once again they had to cross the Vistula, by ferry. Nobody asked any questions and nobody accepted money. This was in the Cracow area, a province which had belonged to Poland for a thousand years, inhabited solely by Poles. They headed for Bochnia, about fifty miles to the east of the camp, right on the other side of Cracow, where there lived the family of another camp prisoner and member of the underground movement.

Once again, already to the east of Cracow, not far from Bochnia, they were threatened by danger, which almost ruined the escape. In the Niepołomicka Forest they came across a woodman's hut and were calmly passing it, when suddenly some German soldiers appeared, and shouted to them to 'Halt, Halt!'. They fled, followed by shots. The small group split up. Pilecki, lightly wounded in the shoulder, found Ciesielski; but Redzej had disappeared somewhere. Dispirited and tired they ran for a long time eastwards. It was the evening of May 2nd, when they finally reached Bochnia. Without any difficulty, asking children, they found the address to which they were going. In front of the house stood a middle-aged man, and when they said 'Good day' he immediately asked them inside, as if he had been waiting for them. This surprised the escapees, for he asked no questions, but just led the way through two rooms and pointed to a third. He himself discretely moved aside. Pilecki and Ciesielski looked around and saw a bed. On it, fast asleep, lay Jan Redzej.[32]

5

After a rest, Pilecki at once asked to be put in touch with the nearest Home Army unit and a few days later found himself in Wiśnicz. Here an extraordinary meeting took place. The Commandant of the underground unit was Tomasz Serafiński (codename *Lis*), the man whose papers Pilecki had used when taking his first steps in occupied Warsaw. It was under Serafiński's name that he had allowed himself to be caught in Warsaw and had lived through nearly three years in Auschwitz. A report was sent at once to the Home Army District in Cracow and at the same time Pilecki sent a letter to an underground address in Warsaw known to himself.

On June 1st Stefan Bielecki, who had escaped from Auschwitz on May 16th, 1942, and taken a report to the Home Army H.Q. arrived from the capital. He brought money and false papers and wished to take his friend and his companions to Warsaw, but

Pilecki at first refused. He wanted to find out for himself what were the chances of an attack on the camp from the outside, and of setting up a new partisan unit.

These were fruitless efforts, doomed to failure in that phase of the war, and the Home Army District in Cracow adopted a decidedly negative attitude. Pilecki, discouraged and annoyed, decided to go to Warsaw in order to persuade H.Q. to accept his plans. He also wanted to render a full report on the situation in the camp and the atrocities being committed there. His decision to go was precipitated by the news that on June 30th Gen. Stefan Rowecki, Commander of the Home Army, had been arrested. On August 25th Pilecki arrived in Warsaw.

He was received at the H.Q. and passed on to the officer concerned with Auschwitz.

In the autumn of 1943 I put my plan for an attack on Auschwitz to the Chief of Planning of *Kedyw*,* who told me: 'After the war I will show you a heap of files on the subject of Auschwitz, all your reports are there . . .'

I wrote my last report on the subject of Auschwitz on 20 pages of typescript and on the last page colleagues who had carried reports wrote in their own hand to whom and when they had handed these reports.

I collected eight such statements, as the others concerned were either dead or absent from Warsaw.

As well as working in a certain department of H.Q., I was occupied in looking after the families of prisoners in Auschwitz, either alive or dead.[33]

Neither Pilecki's final report† nor his personal intervention had any effect on the decision of H.Q. and the Commander of the Home Army. No action was taken to relieve Auschwitz and free the prisoners. The highest authorities of the underground army considered that the forces at their disposal were too few and too poorly armed, that the underground organization inside the camp was almost helpless and the *SS* garrison too numerous and well-equipped.

On August 22nd, 1944, the strength of the garrison of the central

---

* *Kedyw* (abbreviation of *Komenda Dywersji*) was an organization set up by the commander of the *AK* towards the end of 1942. Its aim was to carry out sabotage and diversion, to organize the nucleus of partisan units, to liquidate traitors, to carry out reprisals against the Germans and to organize self-defence among the population.

† It has been impossible to establish whether this report has been preserved.

camp, Birkenau and Monowice (*Buna-Werke*) was 3,250 soldiers of whom 120 were officers.[34] In 1943 it was at least about the same. Besides, if open fighting broke out, the *SS* could get assistance from the German units stationed not far from the camp. Even if a surprise attack were successful and the camp were opened up for a few hours, what would happen to the many thousands of prisoners freed for a short time? On April 25th, 1943, the men's camp with Birkenau and the nearby sub-camps, numbered 46,055 prisoners and about 10,000 women. [35] A large percentage of them were not only unable to walk far but in need of immediate medical and hospital treatment. An attack on the camp with any hope of success, i.e. rescue for prisoners, would only be possible within the framework of a country-wide rising, at the time when the Occupation began to disintegrate. This moment was still far off, and it was becoming more and more likely that it would never come.[36]

From the *Kedyw* officer with whom he was in official contact Pilecki learnt of the problems of parachute drops and supplies received from the West, the range of the flights and the possibilities of effective bombing. These were crucial factors without which no rising in Poland could have any chance of success, and on which the camp underground organization had reckoned so hopefully. It was only then that Pilecki understood why Warsaw had given them so little information on this subject and had not authorized preparations for open fighting. He realized that the optimism in the camp had no support in the reality outside. Dropping parachutists into the camp was technically impossible and dropping supplies very limited because of the distance. The same applied to bombing. Pilecki still did not know, for the H.Q. of the Home Army themselves had no idea that Poland had been excluded from the strategic plans of the Western Allies,[37] who could not be interested in a major air operation which would be required to support the capture of such a large complex as Auschwitz.

All this information was of the highest importance to the camp underground organization, and Pilecki sent it by a secret route and in an agreed code to Captain Stanisław Kazuba,[38] a Commander of one of the secret battalions.

After doing so Pilecki devoted himself to working in one of the departments of H.Q., but not for one moment did he cease to take an interest in Auschwitz. He was in uninterrupted secret contact with it until the outbreak of the Warsaw Rising on August 1st, 1944, in which he took an active part.*

---

* Of the two prisoners who escaped with Pilecki, Jan Redzej was killed during the fighting in Warsaw and Edward Ciesielski was badly wounded. Stefan Bielecki also fell during the Warsaw Rising.

Part Three

CHAPTER 8

Summary of the previous period; influx of
various nationalities; the Austrian group; the
French group; the Soviet group; other groups;
formation of the *Kampfgruppe Auschwitz*

1

With Pilecki's escape a crucial period of underground work in
Auschwitz ended. What was accomplished in this period took place
during the years in which Hitler's Germany, strengthened by the
pact with Soviet Russia, stood at the peak of its power and took no
account of anyone or anything. The first transport of prisoners
arrived at the camp on June 14th, 1940, on the very day that the
victorious Nazi troops entered Paris. Hitler might well have believed
that he had already won the war. At that time, therefore, he had no
need of the political prisoners who were later used to work in the
munitions factories. His attitude was to let them die in the camps,
the sooner the better. At no stage were they treated with greater
brutality than during the first years of the war. Added to the physical
suffering was the perhaps even more painful mental suffering. Not
only was there no sign of the end of the war, but not even the slightest
gleam of hope that the Nazis could lose it.

If the prisoners' existence in other camps was very hard, it was
even more so in Auschwitz, at that time inhabited almost exclusively
by Poles. It was a new camp and had not yet witnessed the struggle
of political prisoners against criminals for positions in the camp.
It was ruled, under the *SS*, by the German criminal prisoners, and
this fact made conditions still worse.

And yet, thanks to the courage and self-sacrifice of many of the
prisoners, a strong underground organization was formed and all the
most important camp functions taken over by it. It controlled the
Hospital, the Labour Assignment Office, it had its men in the
surveyors' *Kommando*, the Central Camp Office, the Tannery, the
Kitchen, the Food and Clothing Stores, the Building Office, in many
other *Kommandos* and in many Blocks, even in the Political Department. Naturally this involved ousting criminal prisoners from many
functions and replacing them by political prisoners. A certain

percentage of German criminals in key positions worked with the camp underground, without belonging to it formally.[1] A strong network was built up in the men's part of Birkenau; contact was made with the women's camp and underground work started there. The network reached to the sub-camp in Monowice (*Buna-Werke*). By various means, including for a time its own radio-transmitter, contact was maintained with the Home Army in Warsaw and Cracow. Already towards the end of 1940 the first report of what was happening at Auschwitz had been sent out and the world learned of this thanks to the information service of the Polish Government in London.

The camp had strong links with the underground groups of Poles operating in the vicinity, from whom the prisoners received aid. A number of escapes were organized and two-way contact was established with partisan units of the Home Army (*AK*) already operating round the camp, who found support in the activities of the Socialists (*PPS*) and the Peasant Battalions. During this period the first contacts were made with other nationals, as transports of them began to arrive. Pilecki started collaboration with the Czechs, Col. Karcz in Birkenau with the Russians. The most difficult thing of all was finally achieved: all the Polish military underground groups were combined together into one whole. The Union of Military Organization (*ZOW*), a name used first by Pilecki, now designated the whole Polish military underground in the territory of Auschwitz and the sub-camps. Thanks to this unification it was possible towards the end of 1942 to divide the now substantial forces of the central camp into battalions based on the locations of the prisoners in the various blocks. This strong military network was given political support, thanks again to the efforts of Pilecki, which brought about the harmonious co-operation of the Polish Left (*PPS*) with the Right (National Party and *ONR*).

These important achievements were made possible by the collaboration and understanding of a very large number of men and women prisoners, but above them all towered the personality of Witold Pilecki, for he was the only one who had come to the camp of his own free will. His extreme altruism and sense of mission put him in a quite exceptional position. He gave out an aura of strength which affected men quite unknown to him,[2] who did not even know his real name (he was known in the camp as Tomasz Serafiński) and who knew nothing of his past. Thanks to these qualities and his freedom from any prejudice of class, nationality, religion or political opinion, he was able not only to build up his own network but also to bring about unity with other military groups, who would otherwise probably have contended for influence and authority in the camp underground. The same applies to the political groups, who subordinated themselves to one military command and gave it ideological support. This was only possible because no group tried to force their ideas on others or to insist that their ideology was the right one. The struggle against brute force and Nazism bound them all together.

At the beginning of 1943 the strength of the camp underground might have been reckoned at a couple of thousand men. It was naturally weakened by the executions in 1942 and 1943; the loss of Stanisław Dubois and of Cols. Stawarz, Kumuniecki and Karcz was a great blow; but there was no faltering in either the attitude or the determination of the underground soldiers. The transports to other camps were very harmful, for they thinned out the organized ranks, but new men took the place of those transported.

After the first year or two, living conditions in the camp improved somewhat, while, on the other hand, Auschwitz–Birkenau literally became an extermination camp (*Vernichtungslager*) as a result of the mass murders of Jews and others in the gas chambers and by phenol injections. In the middle of 1942 collective responsibility for escapes was abolished, which meant that the hours-long, debilitating roll-calls no longer took place. Also in the middle of 1942, 'selections' began to be made among the Jewish transports brought to their death. This was some alleviation of a barbarous system, for a small percentage of young and healthy people got a chance to prolong and perhaps save their lives. At the end of 1942 permission was given for the prisoners to receive food parcels, except for Jews and Soviet prisoners, and orders came from Berlin that the flogging of prisoners was forbidden.[3] This last regulation was not observed but, generally speaking, existence in the camp became easier and prisoners who were not actually under sentence of death had a chance of survival.

These alleviations had nothing to do with the camp underground movement, which was powerless to affect the decisions of Berlin or of the camp command. At the most, this or that *SS*-man might be amenable to underground influence. The easing of conditions in the camps was brought about by one main cause: the Germans were beginning to experience defeats in the field; they needed every soldier there, and every man fit for work in the *Reich* and the occupied countries. All the new camp regulations sprang from these needs. Old people and the majority of women and children were still murdered, but able-bodied men were allowed to live in slightly better conditions so that they could be used in the hundreds of factories built within or near the concentration camps.

Pilecki's purpose in escaping from Auschwitz was not to save himself in the face of personal danger, for after all he had gone to the camp voluntarily, but to carry out a further stage of his mission. He knew that the strong military organization formed by him was losing strength through executions and mass transports to other camps; he had received no orders from the Home Army to begin the fight which he was convinced was a necessity. So he decided that he must himself report to Warsaw on the situation in the camp. He left behind him in Auschwitz a strong military cadre prepared for action, supported by vigorous political forces, in touch with the military underground outside the camp and having made the first approaches to the other national groups of prisoners. Once outside the barbed wire of Auschwitz he ceased to have any direct influence on what happened there, but he became the most fervent and best-informed spokesman on camp affairs in the H.Q. of the Home Army in Warsaw. If there had been any chance of fighting and bringing help to the camp from outside, it would have been Pilecki who had done most to bring it about.

2

After Pilecki's departure there were no great changes in the command of the Union of Military Organization. The Union was still commanded by Col. Juliusz Gilewicz, while Major Zygmunt Bończa-Bohdanowski was still the prospective commander if fighting should break out. The clandestine battalions continued to exist and all the important positions in the Hospital, the Tannery and other *Kommandos* remained in the hands of the same men. Key matters of the organization came into the hands of Henryk Bartosiewicz, who had been entrusted with them by Pilecki. He was a good choice, full of energy and optimism, yet cautious and also lucky. He worked in the Sewage *Kommando* and so was free to move around the central camp and Birkenau, both the men's and women's camps. His previous activity was a guarantee that he would be able to cope with his difficult task.

The execution of Col. Karcz had weakened the military underground in Birkenau, and the central camp underground gave the order to employ the greatest caution and wait for the bad period to pass. There was no man suitable to take over at once the functions of the murdered colonel, but from among his nearest co-workers Kazimierz Gosk,[4] in the good position of the clerk responsible for the roll-calls, began to come to the fore. Henryk Bartosiewicz went to Birkenau from the central camp almost every day, taking Gosk his orders and collecting the most important reports from him.

The political agreement between the Left and the Right, brought about with such difficulty by Pilecki, still existed and afforded support to the military cadres. After Dubois' death the Socialist leaders were Konstanty Jagiełło and Adam Kuryłowicz, joined two weeks later by Józef Cyrankiewicz, who was brought to the camp from Cracow on September 4th, 1942. He had been arrested in April 1941 in the secret office of the commander of the Cracow District *ZWZ*,[5] and spent the next year and a half in the Montelupi prison. Although still barely 31, he was one of the most prominent representatives of the *PPS* in occupied Poland. Before the war he had been secretary to the Workers' District Committee of the Cracow Area – not a very important post, but he had come to the fore through ambition and because many prominent Socialist leaders had been killed, were abroad or in the Soviet zone, or else, being too well-known, were unable to operate.[6] Immediately on his arrival at Auschwitz, Kuryłowicz lent him a hand and with the help of Dr. Rudolf Diem placed him in the Hospital in Block No. 21 as a night clerk. In a very short time Cyrankiewicz became a member of the secret Fighting Organization of the *PPS* in the camp and, since he was a reserve officer, he also joined the Union of Military Organization. In this capacity he met Pilecki several times and they knew each other well.[7]

On the Right Wing there were also changes, for on March 3rd, 1942, Professor Roman Rybarski died and his place was taken by Jan Mosdorf. The Right Wing also lost men through executions and transports, but there were constantly fresh arrivals to fill up the ranks. Those able to fight were directed to military cadres of Pilecki's organization. Co-operation between the Polish politicians and soldiers still worked faultlessly.

3

In course of time the camp at Auschwitz, originally planned solely for Poles, changed its character. The Germans overran many countries of Europe and penetrated deep into the Soviet Union. Everywhere they carried out mass arrests, and the existing or newly built camps proved to be too small. Auschwitz and its sub-camps, constantly growing, began to receive prisoners from all parts of the continent, in addition to being the largest centre for extermination of the Jews.

On April 25th 1943 the numbers in the camp at Auschwitz were as follows:

Central camp	17,037 prisoners
Birkenau men's	11,671 ,,
Birkenau (Gypsies)	12,000 ,,
Monowice (*Buna-Werke*)	3,301 ,,
Other sub-camps	2,000 ,,
Total	46,009 ,,

To the above should be added about 20,000 women in Birkenau. At least 30 nations were represented in the camp: Americans, Austrians, Belgians, British, Bulgars, Czechs, Croats, Dutch, French, Germans, Greeks, Hungarians, Italians, Latvians, Lithuanians, Norwegians, Poles, Rumanians, Russians, Serbs, Slovaks, Spaniards, Swiss, Turks, Ukrainians, Gypsies and Jews from many countries, including Palestine. There were also one Chinaman, one Egyptian and one Persian.[8]

Among this conglomeration the most numerous from beginning to end were Poles; next came Jews from various countries; later citizens of the Soviet Union representing various nationalities. On January 20th, 1944, in the central camp there were 18,418 prisoners, including 8,649 Poles, 3,830 Jews from different countries, 2,989 Soviet citizens, 742 Germans, 155 French, 66 Serbs and a small number of other nationals, which constantly fluctuated.[9] The smaller a group was in Auschwitz, the less effect it had on life in the camp. This did not apply to the Germans who, although few in numbers and generally criminals, had much influence to the last, since they continued to occupy a number of important positions from which it was not always possible to oust them. They also enjoyed certain privileges by virtue of being *Reichsdeutschen*.

Poles, apart from being the most numerous, differed from the others in that on the whole they were a compact group and, whatever post-war propaganda may say, were not divided by differences of class or political opinions. This unity was brought about by the Germans themselves and their policy of indiscriminate terror against all Poles. In the cities, towns and villages any Pole pursued by the Germans could count on help from his fellow-countrymen, and the situation in Auschwitz was much the same.[10] The common misfortune erased differences and led to great solidarity, and the military underground network, started up by Pilecki and supported by the political movements, reinforced this considerably.

The Jews, also numerous in the central camp, and especially in Birkenau and Monowice, were a much less compact element. Centuries of living in completely different countries, with different customs, language, culture, and even religion, tended to mean that a scholar from Germany or France, or a millionaire diamond-merchant from Amsterdam, although stripped of all his possessions, found it difficult to communicate with a poor Jew from Salonica or Berdichev. The Jews were also a very fluid element, treated with the greatest brutality by the *SS*-men and in every respect the worst off in the whole camp. Thanks to their abilities and knowledge of foreign languages some rose to important positions in the camp, and wore the armbands of *Capos* and Block Chiefs; but in general their chances of survival were considerably lower than those of other nationalities. It was reckoned that Jews survived in Auschwitz on the average no longer than three months,[11] and this at a time when healthy men were no longer murdered because German industry was crying out for hands to work. This state of affairs limited any possibility of clandestine work among Jews and decreased the chances of their forming a strong underground group in the camp.

On earlier pages mention has been made of the contact established with the Czechs by Pilecki, and of the fate of the Czechs in the camp. Mention has also been made of the first contacts with Soviet citizens, established by Col. Karcz in Birkenau. There are very few data concerning these and other nationalities; one can only attempt a fragmentary reproduction of the activities of the Austrian, French and Russian groups as they in turn came into being.

4

Hermann Langbein, a Vienna Communist from his early youth, took part in the Spanish Civil War on the side of the Republic; in February 1939 he crossed the French frontier and found himself in the internment camp at St. Cyprien. In April of the same year he was transferred to a camp at Gurs, near the Pyrenees and in May 1940 to Le Vernet, not far from Toulouse. These were all multi-national camps.

As the war had started and the young men did not wish to be inactive, they began to negotiate with the French authorities. The Austrians proposed the formation of a legion under French command to fight the Germans, but the authorities had other ideas and offered two alternatives: the Foreign Legion or incorporation into the French units which were to fight the Russians in Finland. Both proposals were rejected, and after the fall of France a third emerged. German officers came to the unoccupied part of the country and urged the internees to return to their own countries, promising them freedom and work. After a time the Czechs accepted the proposal,

Józef Mikusz	Henryk Porębski	Juliusz Gilewicz
Stanisław Kłodziński	Karl Lill	Hermann Langbein
Józef Woźniakowski	Edward Gött-Getyński	Czesław Jaworski
Jan Redzej	Józef Cyrankiewicz	Ernst Burger

Leading men in the resistance movement.

and shortly after them the Austrians. They did not trust the Nazis, but they could not stand passive internment any longer. Some of them expected the worst: prison or a concentration camp, but even this did not frighten them. Langbein wrote in his memoirs that '. . . we can carry on political work in the camp'. The pessimists were right. On April 24th, 1941, they all found themselves in Dachau.[12]

From there Langbein was sent to Auschwitz and spent a short time in the Hospital Block No. 21, but when he became the secretary of the senior medical officer he moved to the *Prominents'** Block No. 24 and went to work in the *SS* Hospital, just outside the barbed wire, on the first floor of the barracks in which the Political Department occupied the ground floor. (It was only in the middle of 1943 that the camp *Gestapo* moved to its own barracks, situated near by.) He was a young man of about thirty, with much experience of underground work, having been in the Communist underground in Austria before the Spanish Civil War; he had become acquainted with the camp underground in Dachau, so he had an active approach and expected to organize something in Auschwitz too. His position as Wirths's secretary gave him great opportunities, as he well realized, but to achieve anything he had first to get to know the new camp. He was isolated from it by his special position, but he looked around with a practised eye and at once formed certain opinions. After Dachau he did not like Auschwitz at all. Apart from the cramped conditions and the gas chambers in which people were murdered day and night, he was shocked by the number of German criminal prisoners in positions of importance. He did not yet know that a well-organized Polish underground movement was operating in the camp and had its men in a number of key positions, nor did he suspect that some German trusties worked with this movement, although perhaps not always fully aware of its size and activities.†

In order to get to know the camp and its most important secrets and also to begin any sort of underground work, he had to make preliminary contacts, in the first instance with Austrian Communists. He knew of two even before he left Dachau, having been told about

---

* *Prominent* – slang for a prisoner in a good position in the camp.

† Pilecki in his report (on p. 27) mentions the following Germans: Otto Küsel – the first prisoner in the Labour Assignment Office; Arthur Balke – *Obercapo* of the large Carpenter's Shop; Fritz Biesgen, nicknamed *Meteczka* (little mother) – the Kitchen *Capo*, and from the middle of 1942 *Capo* of the Tannery; Hans Bock – the Senior Prisoner of the Hospital; Johann Lechenich, called Jonny – *Capo* of the very large Agricultural *Kommando*.

them by a fellow-prisoner. They were Ernst Burger, clerk of Block No. 4, and Ludwig Vesely, in the excellent Motor Workshop and garage *Kommando*. He sought them out and later made contact with Hiasl Neumeier (who died soon after of typhus), Rudolf Friemel, Sioma Lachtmann and Dr. Alfred Klahr, a member of the Central Committee of the Austrian Communist Party, who was in the camp under the name of Lokmanis. These two were working in the coal-mines in the sub-camp of Jawiszowice, and Langbein brought them to the central camp.

From them he learnt that there were less than a hundred Austrians in the camp and their situation was not pleasant, for the Poles were understandably hostile to anyone who spoke German. The Poles had to be reckoned with, for they were in a majority in the camp; they had been in it the longest and had taken over many positions; the camp was situated in Polish territory and surrounded by a Polish population, and quite near, in the *General Gouvernement*, a widespread Polish underground movement operated. Even in the very neighbourhood of the camp, in territory incorporated into the *Reich*, Polish underground groups operated and partisan units were beginning to do so, as Langbein soon realized. A similar situation around Dachau would have been absolutely unthinkable.

This situation and also the knowledge that the Communist forces might prove to be much too weak, even if all the nationalities in the camp were brought in, caused Langbein to look for other solutions:

> All those who hate Fascism and are ready to fight, whether Communists or no, must keep together ... It is very important that we maintain contact with comrades of other nationalities ... The most important thing is, however, that we should establish good political contact with the Poles.[13]

He also understood that it would be easier to operate in separate national groups, if only because of language difficulties, and so, although there were only a few of them, he formed the nucleus of an Austrian group. This was towards the end of 1942. He had some loose contact with a few Frenchmen and few Czechs; he had also made closer acquaintance with a few Poles who he thought might be of importance. Langbein, however, cites practically no names and does not define the organizational strength that these contacts represented. Among the French he mentions only the first names of two Communists, Robert and André; among the Poles, Szymon Zajdow, Józef Cyrankiewicz and Tadeusz Hołuj. The last two he simply met on the Hospital Block, where they were night-clerks. He guessed that they must have some connections, for in spite of their high numbers, indicating recent arrival in the camp, they were both in good positions. Although on his own arrival he had immediately got into the Hospital, he says nothing whatever of the underground activities of the Poles, which, when he came to the camp, were already far-reaching and effective.

It is hard to suppose that such an experienced underground worker could fail to notice the Polish groups; perhaps he preferred to close his eyes to them as they were not Communists, and to build up a new network of men of his own or similar convictions? It can also be assumed that Langbein had no knowledge of Polish affairs and characteristics and, basing himself on the situation known to him in Dachau, decided at the outset that since there was no Communist underground, nobody at all was operating there.

At the same time as he was setting up these first underground contacts, which in this phase were little more than symbolic, Langbein was slowly establishing his relationship with Dr. Wirths and deciding on his attitude to the important position of the Senior Medical Officer, which Wirths had only recently taken up.

It was unthinkable that an officer of the *SS* could disobey orders, but the latest directives from Berlin (which ordered that the prisoners' output of work was to be increased) and the selections from the Jewish transports, suggested that by appropriate interpretation of the regulations the prisoners' lot might be improved. In this respect Dr. Wirths might be very useful and Langbein understood this perfectly. He also understood that his own opportunities in such an important position as that of secretary to the head doctor of all Auschwitz might prove more effective than the underground network he was trying to build up. Time proved this calculation to be absolutely right.

Typhus was still raging in the camp, and Wirths received a categorical order from Berlin to stamp it out at any price. The delousing had not helped and the *SS* doctor could not understand why the epidemic was not abating. He had been in Auschwitz too short a time to uncover all its secrets, although he ought to have known what went on in the Hospital. Langbein decided to tell the truth, namely that the prisoners were afraid to go to the Hospital when they were ill, lest instead of treatment there might await them selection for the gas chambers or a phenol injection. Wirths was shocked and indignant, and gave the impression of a man who really had known nothing of these practices. Langbein felt that his risky step might be of advantage to the camp and would give him some influence over the *SS* doctor in the future.

On March 3rd, 1943, there were big changes in the camp Hospital.

The *SS*-men discovered that on Block No. 21 Hans Bock, the Senior Prisoner of the Hospital, had a small camouflaged room in which he met young boys, mostly Polish male nurses. That same day he was made the Block Chief in the Hospital of the sub-camp in Monowice (*Buna-Werke*) and his position in the central Hospital was taken by Ludwig Wörl, brought from the same position there.[14]

At the same time the Political Department noticed that there were a great many Polish male nurses and demanded of Wirths that he should change this. The Senior Medical Officer spoke to Langbein about this problem and accepted his suggestion that male nurses of other nationalities should be brought into the hospital, so that they could more easily talk to their fellow-countrymen. The next day Langbein gave Wirths a list of numbers of Austrian, Czech and French Communists. They were all accepted. At the same time he is said to have pushed through the principle that Jewish doctors should be accepted in the hospital, provided that they treated only Jewish patients.[15]

The new male nurses did not increase the number of the hospital personnel; they only took the places of their fellow-prisoners. Those who had to be dismissed were generally sent to bad *Kommandos* and their chances of survival decreased considerably. This was not a struggle between political and criminal prisoners for influence in the camp, for all the Poles displaced wore red triangles, the mark of a political prisoner. It was a struggle for influence carried on because of a political ideology. In the German concentration camps this was a fairly common phenomenon.

5

French women appeared in Auschwitz with the first female transport on March 26th, 1942, when 999 women of various nationalities were brought from Ravensbrück. The first Frenchmen did not arrive till July 8th of that year, in a transport from Compiègne near Paris with 1,170 men, nearly all French subjects. They were given numbers 45157 to 46326 and were ordered to wear green triangles, although they were all political prisoners.[16] This was probably in order to make contact with other prisoners more difficult, for this whole transport was part of the *Nacht und Nebel* (Night and Fog), the code name for a special operation based on a decree issued by Hitler on December 7th, 1941. When civilians of occupied Belgium, Denmark, France, Holland and Norway committed offences against the German occupation forces, they were taken secretly to Germany and sent to a concentration camp, normally not under their own names but under the initials N.N. They were not allowed to write letters and their families were not told what had happened to them. These precautions were connected with the building of the 'Atlantic Wall'.[17]

The new arrivals were quartered in various blocks of the central camp and divided among various *Kommandos*, usually bad ones. About 600 were sent to Birkenau. Although it was summer, the French began to die like flies. After five months there were barely 200 left, and of those who went to Birkenau, only 20. The *SS*-men must have had instructions to treat them brutally, but apart from that, the French, coming from a rich country with a high standard of living, proved to have less resistance to disease and the adverse physical conditions than those of similar groups from other parts of Europe.

A certain number of the new arrivals were Communists from the French resistance movement and these, having experience of such work, started to make the first underground contacts. In the beginning they were concerned with saving their dying comrades and trying to slow-up the catastrophic death-rate. Georges Varennes, a school-teacher from the Yonne, set about this but his great self-sacrifice in sharing his own minimal rations with others brought about his death from starvation towards the end of 1942. About the same time his colleague Roger Abada met the Austrian Communist Rudolf Friemel, who already had contacts among the handful of his fellow-countrymen in the camp. They came to an agreement fairly easily and began to decide on the principles of co-operation, which related chiefly to an exchange of services and helping each other in the difficulties of camp existence. Abada's comrades Eugène Garnier and Roger Pelissou, who played the part of political leaders of the small group of French Communists, joined in the conversations and co-operation. Abada says that liaison was established with similar groups of Germans, Czechs, Poles and Russians, numerically more or less equal in strength, but he does not cite any names or describe the methods of liaison.

As has been mentioned, the main object of these contacts was, in this phase, the saving of fellow-Communists. This was achieved by scrounging food and necessities from the Stores and getting comrades into good positions in the Kitchens, Laundry, Stores etc. They managed to get three Frenchmen into the Hospital as male nurses, and this enabled them to bring out medicines so that they could directly look after their sick fellow-countrymen. They made efforts to contact the women. One of the Frenchmen (Abada writes only 'Comrade G', probably Garnier) got into the Gardeners' *Kommando*, which went to the sub-camp at Rajsko where the women-prisoners worked. Through this channel contact was established with them and they were sent medicines, news and various directives. Contact was also made with the French Communist Danielle Casanova operating there.

The French group, like the Austrian, was small, so it had to look for support among the other national groups. The most numerous were the Poles, but, as Abada was to find out, the vast majority did not share his political opinions. Abada, as a Communist, calls Poles 'reactionaries'. Nevertheless a pro-French attitude had been rooted in Poles for several centuries, and even the events of the last war did not alter it. Any Frenchmen who proved to be fairly tough were always treated by the Poles as friends and frequently got help from them. Political opinions played hardly any part. After some meetings with the Polish Communists, the French together with them, in 1943, issued one number of a secret newspaper, written out in several copies, and later, in the same year, a political manifesto in several languages.

Later the French, by now with the support of several other national groups, began to spread news collected from the German press, gather intelligence information and organize cautious sabotage in the munitions factories on camp territory. No attempts were made at escape, for without a knowledge of Polish and the country round the camp, they would have had no chance of success. As events developed, the formation of underground military cadres began to be seriously considered.[18]

6

After the unparalleled tragedy of the 12,000 Soviet prisoners-of-war from Łambinowice, who after a short time were practically wiped out, further numerous groups of Soviet citizens began to arrive at the camp. Since the attack on Russia and the occupation of vast areas, the Germans began to deport hundreds of thousands of able-bodied men and women to Germany. They were put into labour camps, in barracks adjoining factories, or on farms, and were generally very badly treated. These people, driven to despair, home-sick for their own country, hating their persecutors, tried to get out of their enemy's hands, changing their jobs and attempting to escape. They were caught and sent to concentration camps. Prisoners-of-war from camps in the heart of Germany also turned up, for although their treatment there was endurable it did not check the impulse to escape. Among the soldiers were hidden many officers, especially political ones, whom the *Gestapo* sought out and murdered without mercy.[19] These men were the most active and the ones who organized escapes, which usually ended in recapture and frequent executions or in transports to Mauthausen, Neuengamme or to Auschwitz.

The Soviet people were generally distinguished by great solidarity. Thanks to discipline and a common political ideology, inculcated in them for many years, they held together and gave complete obedience to their leaders, who tended to be the political officers mentioned above, undetected as such by the Political Department. Years of isolation, and propaganda presenting other nations and countries in a negative light, made the Soviet citizens very mistrustful in their approach to all contacts, but when they did begin to trust anyone, they could be counted on.[20] They were nearly all very tough and coped well with the difficulties of camp life. Their great difficulty was ignorance of German, which made it impossible for them to get into top positions in the camp. They did, however, get into the Kitchen, the Stores and good *Kommandos*, for many of them were skilled workers. Their relations with Poles, in spite of past history, were good, for they had a similar approach to the burdens of camp life and to the basic principles of underground work. As well as assistance to those in need, they considered fighting to be the main end of the camp underground.[21]

The first contacts with the Russians were made by Pilecki's. organization (*ZOW*) in autumn 1941, when nine blocks in the central camp were fenced off as a POW camp and Soviet prisoners-of-war were brought there. Some were murdered cruelly, other isolated from the rest of the camp, driven in their own *Kommandos* to build Birkenau; but they used the same Kitchen, were in the grounds of the same camp and the *SS*-men were unable to cut them off completely from the Polish prisoners. The first contacts were made by Bartosiewicz and also by Ostańkowicz; later they were taken over by Ludwik Rajewski.[22] These were sporadic contacts, hampered by conditions in the camp and by mistrust. Sometimes it was possible to give the unfortunate prisoners-of-war some bread or some extra cauldrons of soup. On their side there were as yet no signs of organized action. They were dying too quickly for there to be any real chance of that.

When they were finally transferred to Birkenau in March 1942 there were under a thousand of them alive. They were still dying every day, but a small number of them got into bearable *Kommandos* and with these Col. Karcz made contact. He did not do this personally, but through Bogdan Gliński. The prisoners-of-war had already started to organize the beginnings of an underground, for they expected to be gassed and meant to defend themselves, not by fighting, which had no chance of success, but by a mass escape. In the autumn of 1942, when the situation was very tense and every night the POWs expected to be sent to the gas chambers, Col. Karcz personally met the leaders of the Soviet group. They were Nikolay Mishin, Alexander Baranow, Aleksey Soroka and an engineer from Leningrad with a Polish name, Siciński. Still earlier Bartosiewicz had brought an order from the central camp[23] that, if the Soviet POWs decided to escape, they should be given help. In the end they were not gassed, but this did not check further huge losses in their ranks.

Systematic underground work started among the citizens of the Soviet Union only when, in 1942 and later, they began to arrive from camps in Germany and the East and were given the same rights as other prisoners, i.e. they were to work in the camp until they dropped, but they were allowed to live.

The best opportunities were, as usual, in the central camp and it was there that the first nucleus of an underground organization came into being. It was started by Major Aleksey Lebedev,* a political officer in the Russian Army, who had escaped from a POW camp in the heart of Germany, was recaptured in Czechoslovakia and sent to Auschwitz in a transport from Brno on January 16th, 1943. Living on Block No. 17 and working in the group at the new railway station (*Neubahnhof*) he met a Yugoslav foreman who had once been in Russia and spoke Russian. This man introduced Lebedev to two Austrian Communists: Ludwig, who spoke Russian, and Ernst, a clerk on Block No. 4. They were Ludwig Vesely and Ernst Burger, and they helped him to change his *Kommando* and get into the Clothing Store, where Bernard Świerczyna was the deputy *Capo*. The Poles held out a helping hand, and in a short time there were about twenty Soviet citizens working in this place. From this time onwards the organization's contact with them was taken over by Świerczyna. There Lebedev met a sixteen-year-old boy from Zaporozhe, Konstantin Sorokin, and enrolled him into the nucleus of his organization. Sorokin proved to be indispensable. From the stores necessities began to filter out to other Russians.[24]

---

* A. Lebedev, *Soldaty* . . ., p. 24. His book, 77 pages of personal memoirs, is devoid of egocentricity and thus gives one confidence in it. Nevertheless it contains many material errors. The author confuses Austrians with Germans and only from other sources is it possible to discover whom he is thinking of. On p. 45 he says that in May 1943 several Russians escaped and that this was the first escape from Auschwitz. In fact up to that time 231 prisoners had already escaped, about 50% successfully. He also writes that Palitzsch, whom he saw often, was a captain in the *SD*, whereas he was an NCO in the *SS*. There are other such mistakes in the book.

Lebedev's Austrian friends acted again and put him in touch with Fyodor Sgiba, a schoolteacher from the Urals and a political officer in the army. After him the small group was joined by Major Vladimir Sokolov (nicknamed *Papasha*); an older political officer, Gricko, who worked in the Laundry; Lieut. Vladimir from Dniepropetrovsk, working in the Bread Stores; an airman named Kola, a cleaner in the *SS* Hospital, from where he brought out medicines; Victor, an engineer from Moscow who had contacts with Polish intellectuals in the camp; and Lieut. Aleksey, whom Polish doctors had saved from death. Further recruitment was slow, for *agents provocateurs* were everywhere. Each new candidate was observed and tested, the circumstances of his being taken prisoner were checked, as were the POW camps in which he had been, and where, how and with whom he had escaped.

In the first months of 1943 the underground group of Soviet officers was already fairly large. Its basic objectives were: co-opera-tion with all anti-Nazi forces in the camp; saving the lives of Soviet citizens, especially officers; organizing diversions and escapes; spreading true information about the international situation and counter-propaganda; and finally, preparations for armed struggle. The best men became the leaders.[25]

Thanks to the help of Poles hundreds of Soviet citizens got into good *Kommandos* such as *Canada*, the Kitchen or the Bread Stores. There they could work in conditions giving them a chance of survival, and also give significant help to their fellows. Fyodor Sgiba came off best, perhaps, for he got into the Hospital as a male nurse. There he saw for himself how hard the Polish doctors worked and how they saved prisoners from selection to the gas-chambers, throwing them out into the camp with feigned brutality just before the arrival of the *SS* commissions. In that way the airmen Valentin Sitnov and Viktor Ivanov, Maj. Piotr Machura and Col. Kuzma Kartsev (code-name *Vasily*) were saved. They all belonged to the Soviet underground group.

Two basic fields of operations were decided on and functions divided. Piotr Machura, the former Commander of the 17th Guards Armoured Brigade, was in charge of escapes. He planned and began to develop three methods: a) bribing the sentries with articles brought out from *Canada*; b) getting into transports to other camps and escaping from them by overpowering the guards; c) getting outside the camp by hiding underneath goods transported in lorries. Machura was also in charge of the contact with the women's camp in Birkenau. He was in the electricians' *Kommando* and thus had freedom of movement around the extensive area under the camp's jurisdiction. He was assisted by airman Nikolay, who worked on a sewer-cleaning machine, and the miraculously-alive prisoner-of-war, Piotr Mishin.

The problem of eventual armed struggle was entrusted to Col. Kuzma Kartsev. He got into the Soviet underground group only in February 1944, as he came to the camp late, but for his tasks this was an appropriate time. He thought in terms of an armed uprising in the camp, and from this point of view he was close to the plans of the Union of Military Organization and, in part, to those of the Austrian Communists, of whom there were very few in the camp, and to some of the Czechs. He enlisted the co-operation of the officers Kuvalin, Lyagushov, Bobkov and Pettilo, together with Prof. Kruglov and two youngsters, Pavel Artemenko and Vladimir Vyazmitinov. They worked out the distances between the watch-towers and the chain of guards, possible ways out of the camp, and the electrical system which supplied the electrified barbed wire surrounding it. With the help of Poles they made contact with Serbs and Russians employed as civilian workers in the town of Auschwitz.

In March 1944, Lebedev, Sitnov, Machura and ten other Soviet officers profited by Ernst Burger's help and transferred to the sub-camp in Monowice to get work in *Buna-Werke*. A large number of civilian workers were employed there, also several hundred British POWs. The Soviet officers counted on a chance to escape and reach the Polish partisan units operating in the Beskids. They made contact with the British, some of whom wished to escape with them and make for the East in the direction of the front. But these plans came to nothing.[26]

7

At the peak of the growth of the Auschwitz camp, i.e. in the second half of 1943 and in 1944, when the influx of transports of various nationalities was at its highest, there must have arisen at least the nuclei of other national underground groups. Some of them have been mentioned above, e.g. the Czechoslovak group and its connections with the Union of Military Organization. Unfortunately the few Czech and Slovak sources[27] do not enlarge on the theme and have not added any details which would allow further elaboration. There certainly existed a Yugoslav group, but there are no sources which discuss it. Thanks to reports from Polish women it is known that the Yugoslav women were active in the women's camp and were divided into two groups: Royalist and Communist.[28] It was probably the same in the men's camp. It must be remembered that the Serbs and Croats were divided during the war by great political differences, which the Germans played on cleverly. There were even Croatian *SS* formations. This did not make it easier to form a common underground group in Auschwitz. According to Langbein the Yugoslav underground movement was stronger in the women's camp than in the men's.

There is no information to allow even the most fragmentary presentation of underground camp activities among the Bulgarians, Belgians, Dutch, Norwegians or Spaniards. No doubt individuals looked for contacts with the underground groups of other nationalities with whom they had either a language or political convictions in common. Membership of an international movement, like Socialism or Communism, could prove to be helpful.

After Poles, Jews from various countries, and Soviet citizens, the Germans were the most numerous group and were in a special situation. They were mostly a criminal element, which at the very beginning had occupied all the most important camp functions, but were slowly and decisively pushed aside by the Union of Military Organization (*ZOW*), by the Polish underground political groups supporting it and by political prisoners from other, incipient clandestine cells. Some of the German trusties turned out to be decent men and these, wittingly or half-wittingly, were drawn into the underground work[29]; the rest, hated by all the prisoners, formed a tightly-knit block of criminals, backing each other up, but naturally they did not build up any underground group. Among the Germans there were a few former Social-Democrats and Communists, but they were only a remnant of the political activists who had been arrested in 1933, immediately after Hitler came to power. They went through the hell of the concentration camps, and the great majority of them died. In Auschwitz very few German Communists (Ludwig Wörl, Karl Lill, Bruno Baum) were active, but they did not form a group of their own, looking rather for ties with Communists of other nationalities. Co-operation with them was very difficult, for they wanted to be leaders and would not serve under representatives of other nationalities. They were especially prejudiced against Poles and Jews.[30] Yet it was unlikely that any Pole, conscious of his own nationality, could have accepted subordination to a German in underground work in Auschwitz. Forced subordination to the *SS*-men was quite enough.

In spite of their not forming a separate group, Germans were necessary in the underground, for they still occupied many key positions. Contact with them was sought and efforts were made to bring them in in one way or another.

8

In the section on politics in occupied Poland it was noted that this had an influence on the pattern of political relations in Auschwitz. As is known, Poland in 1939 found herself under two occupations; later, after the German attack on Soviet Russia in June 1941, the whole country was under German rule. Polish underground political life, in spite of the terror, flourished and the four traditional parties, the Peasant Party, the National Party, the Labour Party and the Polish Socialist Party, not only operated and gave support to the Government Delegacy and the Home Army, but grew in strength throughout the whole country, but especially within the *General Gouvernement.*

During the first phase of the war there were no Communists in the Polish underground. After Hitler's attack on Russia they did not begin to organize at once, not knowing how events would turn out. It was only in January 1942, when the Russians held up the German divisions outside Moscow, that there was started in Warsaw, with the knowledge and help of the Kremlin, The Polish Workers' Party (*PPR*).[31] It was founded by Paweł Finder and Marceli Nowotko, who were dropped by parachute from the USSR, and they became its first leaders.[32]

The development of the war, the strengthening of the Eastern Front, the first German defeats and Soviet victories caused the *PPR* to grow slowly in numbers; the great majority of Poles still backed the Government operating in London and its representatives in Poland, the Government Delegacy and the Home Army. The Polish nation had not forgotten the time when for 127 years the country was divided between Austria, Prussia and Russia, all the more since the Russian rule had been the most brutal and had evoked several national uprisings. The Red Army's victories in the East were bringing nearer the moment of defeat for Germany, but at the same time they were creating new threats for Poland, which was faced with the prospect of exchanging one occupation for another. Class problems played a secondary part here: the Polish nation was fighting for its independence, and in this it was united.

The new set-up in the Polish underground, with the four traditional parties backing the Government in London and the *PPR* looking to Moscow, might have been expected to reflect itself in Auschwitz and the underground movement there. Yet this did not happen. It was already 1943, but in Auschwitz there was no Polish group operating which corresponded to *PPR* nor any Communist group under another name. A great deal has been written in Poland on the Communist underground movement in the country and in the camp of Auschwitz in particular, but the facts are clear.

There were, of course, Polish Communists in the camp, but they did not organize their own group. There could be several reasons for this. There were perhaps too few of them, they may have lacked leaders, or felt themselves too weak, knowing that other Poles had been well-organized for a long time. It may be supposed that all these reasons played their part. In any case, the fact that there was no Polish Communist group is confirmed by the writings of other nationals. Langbein, an experienced underground worker and, at that time an idealistic member of the Communist Party,* writes that he looked unsuccessfully for contact with the Poles through Cyrankiewicz, whom he knew to be a Socialist.[33] Abada speaks of a Polish group, but does not cite any names.[34]

The events of the war, however, had taken such a turn that the Communists in Auschwitz had to act somehow. After Stalingrad came further victories for the Red Army. The Eastern Front began to move westwards; it was evident that the Germans would not win the war against Russia, and clearly this would encourage pro-Soviet elements to action. It would have been logical for the initiative to form an underground Communist network to have come from the Poles, for Auschwitz was a predominantly Polish camp, but it happened otherwise. The initiative was taken by Austrian Communists, although there were only a few dozen Austrians altogether in the camp.[35]

As has been mentioned, Langbein knew that the Communist forces would be too weak if they tried to act alone, and he recognized the necessity of close co-operation with the Poles. Since he could not find any Polish Communist group, he had to approach men of kindred opinions who were in touch with the Polish camp underground. He chose Cyrankiewicz, for he knew him from the Hospital, knew of his left-wing views and guessed at his secret connections. Conversations were begun. From the Austrian side, Ernst Burger, the 28-year-old Communist youth leader from Vienna, also took part in them; from the Polish side Tadeusz Hołuj, who had come to the camp with Cyrankiewicz and attached himself to him, for it made life easier in the camp. He was a young man, quite insignificant[36] and with no political past, although he was considered a Communist. On May 1st, 1943, in Block No. 4, where Burger was a clerk, it was decided to form the nucleus of an international organization, which was given the German name of *Kampfgruppe Auschwitz* ('The Fighting Group of Auschwitz'). Its leaders were Langbein, Burger,

---

* After the Hungarian Uprising in 1956 and Russia's intervention, Langbein left the Communist Party.

Cyrankiewicz and Hołuj.

The name had a brave ring, but this was not borne out by the facts. The organization was confined to a few Austrians and a few Poles, although the Austrians had already made some contact with French, Czechs and Jews. These were Communists and the Austrians came to some sort of international understanding with them.[37] The fact that nobody from these groups joined the leadership of the newly-formed organization suggests that they had very little say in it and that their forces were negligible. Of the four leaders only Langbein, as secretary to the Senior Medical Officer, and Cyrankiewicz, with his established Socialist position behind him, being also one of the leaders of the Polish Socialists in the camp and belonging to the Union of Military Organization (*ZOW*), counted for anything. The position of Burger, Communist youth leader in a single city, was weak, and Hołuj did not count at all.[38]

It is worth considering what induced Cyrankiewicz to accept the Austrian proposals. After all, these were men who spoke the hated German language, numerically few in the camp and holding different political views to his own, although also left-wing. It might be surmised that he was moved by ambition, a desire to get to the top quickly, and a cool-headed appraisal of what might happen when the war was over. The Polish camp underground had been started two years before his arrival in Auschwitz; it was united politically and militarily and already had its leaders. To become one of them would be difficult, especially for someone who had been in the camp a relatively short time, so a new solution had to be sought. Cyrankiewicz was already the head of the underground group of Socialists in the camp (Fighting Organization of the *PPS*), for after Dubois' execution and Barlicki's death there were no other outstanding personalities there.

He conducted the conversations with the Austrians as the camp leader of the Polish Socialists, but he did not seem to take much account of his Socialist colleagues or perhaps did not even inform them of the negotiations, since he took with him into the *Kampfgruppe Auschwitz* only Tadeusz Hołuj, whom he himself regarded as a Communist.[39] Hołuj was a convenient satellite, ready to help in any way. As to the situation likely to prevail in Poland after the war was over, in May 1943 it could already be foreseen that the Red Army would be master of the whole country, that Stalin would arrange matters to suit himself and that he would be looking for Poles who were ready to obey him.*

After the *Kampfgruppe Auschwitz* had been formally inaugurated,

---

* For the subsequent fate of Cyrankiewicz after the war see Appendix I.

the leaders divided the most important positions among them. Burger took over political work and so became the actual head of the group; Langbein was to look after 'legal' members of the group, that is those who occupied important camp positions; Cyrankiewicz, co-ordination of activities and liaison with the outside world; Hołuj organizational work. If the group was to have any effect, it was necessary to look for support quickly from the large numbers of ordinary prisoners scattered among the various *Kommandos*, and to establish contact with other nationalities. Hołuj states that the group had its men in all the *Kommandos* and in the sub-camps, but he does not mention a single name or a single group. No doubt the *Kampfgruppe* found some support from Polish Socialists, influenced by Cyrankiewicz, and from unorganized Polish Communists contacted from time to time, as well as from the small number of Austrian Communists already roped in. These were very modest forces. The group's aim at this stage was political work, so the leaders issued an ideological declaration, of which Hołuj thus presents the most important points:

—The duty of every prisoner is to fight Nazism.
—The fight for democracy can be carried on only by working-class groups.
—The mass left-wing parties are the chief force of this fight.
—National unity should gather round these parties.
—The European left wing is building up real unity, the unity of the fight for freedom and also for social freedom.
—The chief element in the armed struggle against Nazism is the Soviet Union and the Red Army.
—Friendship with the Soviet Union is therefore a guarantee of victory and peace.[40]

This declaration, written by hand and of which there were few copies, reached only a handful of prisoners. Those who read it and had some political awareness recognized it as an attempt at political propaganda of a type familiar in many countries. It had all the signs of a dictatorial and one-sided approach, liable rather to disunite the diverse elements than to unite them. In Auschwitz there were prisoners of many nationalities with their own aims and aspirations, and in each national group there were representatives of various political parties. What would have been the result if each of these groups and each political party had started to issue their own declarations? What chance would there have been of general understanding and co-operation?

As well as looking for contacts in the various *Kommandos*, the

Kampfgruppe Auschwitz tried to widen its opportunities by establishing co-operation with other national groups already active in the camp. Here it received its first surprise. Contact with the citizens of the Soviet Union was completely unsuccessful. It had taken a long time to make any contact at all, for the Russians were cautious and mistrustful, and when at last in the spring of 1944 it was made, their leader, Maj. Lebedev, had no time for ideological declarations and asked: 'What preparations have you made for an armed uprising in co-operation with the partisans and what opportunities have you for organizing escapes, especially mass escapes?' The Communists were so taken aback by this question that Langbein's first reaction was: 'Perhaps they do not appreciate our work in the camp.' But later came reflection and the further sentence: 'The Russians are right, we must get down to practical preparations!'[41]

It was obvious that the newly-inaugurated organization, with its international aspirations, ought to seek for contact with the strong and far-reaching Polish underground, the Union of Military Organization (*ZOW*), backed up by political agreement. Cyrankiewicz was already the leader of the Socialists in the camp and therefore had some chance, but besides the *PPS* there was a strong national and national-radical group, already co-operating closely with the underground. The unification of all the Polish military groups, backed by political unification, proved that agreement was possible even between groups ideologically widely apart from each other, but not on the basis of the declaration put out by the *Kampfgruppe Auschwitz*. The Poles, like the Soviet citizens, realized the need to carry on a common struggle for survival, helping the needy, organizing escapes, sending news outside and all the other activities connected with the existence of a camp underground, and all this they had been doing for nearly three years. They also recognized the necessity of co-operation with other nationals, as they had shown by contacting the Czechs and Soviet citizens as soon as it was possible.

On the other hand they could not be pleased by a one-sided political declaration, which moreover stated that the chief element in the fight against Hitler was the Soviet Union, completely ignoring the Western Allies to whom Poland was bound by a political and military alliance. Poles well remembered 1939, Stalin's friendship with Hitler, the great material help given to the latter and the partition of Poland between them, following the treacherous Soviet attack on a country fighting for its life. They also remembered the attitude of Great Britain, which, though isolated after the fall of France, had gone on fighting Hitler to whom the Soviet Union was still giving every assistance. An additional obstacle was the fact that the head of the *Kampfgruppe Auschwitz* was an Austrian, German-speaking and in the camp as a *Reichsdeutsche.* After the *Anschluss,* when Hitler incorporated Austria into the *Reich,* all Austrians became citizens of the German *Reich.* In the camp those of them who were political prisoners wore red triangles without any letter denoting nationality, just as Germans did. Any chance of negotiations was slender enough at this stage and was definitely made impossible by the fact that they were delegated to Hołuj, responsible for organizational matters. Lack of experience, arrogance and inadequacy for the role assigned to him* made him think that the large Polish camp underground, with its outside contacts and political and military loyalty to the Polish authorities in the occupied country, would consent to place itself under the command of a handful of men who had chosen to form a new organization and give it a brave but unrealistic name. And that was not all: they began to urge men to commit treason, demanding of the Polish Socialists that they should cease to support the Polish Government in London and start to work with the *PPR,* which meant surrendering to Russia. Moreover this same organization, in order to smash Polish unity, sent out from the camp a leaflet calling on the working-class to fight against Fascism, both German and Polish.[42] This lumping together of Nazis and Polish parties fighting for their country's independence was a foretaste of the postwar years, when former soldiers of the Home Army were sentenced to long years of imprisonment on trumped-up charges of collaboration with the German occupiers.†

Naturally the Union of Military Organization demanded that the newly-created body should come under its command.[43] This was a quite correct attitude. In a camp in which Poles were in the majority, situated on Polish soil, with a strong Polish underground movement just outside, in contact with Polish partisans and recognizing the authority of the Home Army, no other arrangement could have been entertained for a moment.

Communist connections permitted the *Kampfgruppe* to approach some Germans who, as *Reichsdeutschen,* held good positions in the camp. Langbein was already in close contact with Ludwig Wörl, the Senior Prisoner of the Hospital, and with two other German

---

* Hołuj, describing the underground activities of Poles in Auschwitz before *Kampfgruppe* was formed, presents them as a group of fools thinking only of their own positions (F. Friedman and T. Hołuj, *Oświęcim* . . . , p. 145).

† After October 1956, when the workers' riots in Poznań led to the post-Stalin 'thaw', many former soldiers of the Home Army were let out of prison and rehabilitation trials took place. These trials afforded plentiful evidence of the methods used in Poland for a decade after the war.

Communists: Karl Lill, who came from Dachau in the same transport as Langbein, and Bruno Baum, who arrived towards the end of April 1943. Emil de Martini, a non-Communist and a Block Chief in the Hospital, was also active.[44] The attitude of the Germans, who considered that only they were entitled to lead, made wider contact difficult. There were only a few Germans in *Kampfgruppe*.

There is no evidence that any groups of Yugoslavs, Greeks, Czechs, Slovaks or Jews belonged to the new organization. Citing a few names without camp numbers and dates is not sufficient proof.[45] In the women's camp things looked a little better for the pro-Soviet underground, but only among the Yugoslavs.

The underground group of Soviet citizens themselves never joined *Kampfgruppe Auschwitz*, although the latter very much wanted them to. This has never been claimed publicly even by Communist sources in post-war Poland. If the Soviet underground had joined the group, as its size certainly entitled it to do, its representatives would have figured among the leaders of the *Kampfgruppe*, as is clear to anyone reading their declaration.

Poles were still represented in the *Kampfgruppe* by Cyrankiewicz and his henchman Hołuj. No-one else of any importance joined. The Union of Military Organization still represented the Polish population of the camp and was still the mainspring of all underground activity, not only Polish. In this phase of its existence *Kampfgruppe Auschwitz* represented a dozen or so Austrian Communists plus Cyrankiewicz and the Austrian contacts with French, German, Czech and Jewish Communists. From time to time a few Polish Communists joined it.

As well as the normal underground tasks such as getting its men into important *Kommandos*, mutual aid, and so on, the new organization tried to make contact with the outside world, in this case with the *PPR* now working in Poland. Three times reports were prepared and three times a vain attempt at contact was made. After that the *Kampfgruppe* came to terms with reality and recognized that the only serviceable contact was that which the Union of Military Organization (*ZOW*) had long since established with the Home Army.[46]

CHAPTER 9

The surveyors' *Kommando*; the morale of
SS-men; conditions in the Hospital; liquidation
of the leaders of the Polish military underground;
the new Commandant and changes in the camp.

1

During the first half of 1943 further German defeats at the front and
a constantly increasing need for industrial labour brought about a
steady improvement in the treatment of prisoners. There was a certain
relaxation of discipline, rest periods were allowed during non-
working hours, food-parcels were distributed honestly; but where
escapes and contact with the outside world were concerned the iron
hand of the *SS* did not loosen its grip for a moment. This was made
very clear in the matter of the surveyors' *Kommando*, which gave such
great service to the Polish camp underground and had long been
under the observation of the Political Department.

On May 20th, 1943, three prisoners from this *Kommando*, Engineer
Kazimierz Jarzębowski, Stanisław Chybiński and Jósef Rotter, all
from the Union of Military Organization, gave an *SS*-man a sleeping
draught and ran from Skidzin-Wilczkowice, where they were carrying out a survey.[1] They had to escape, for the *SS*-men had just
picked up, and put into the bunker, Helena Płotnicka, with whom the
prisoners had maintained contact.

The camp *Gestapo* acted at once, especially as the *Capo* of the
surveyors' *Kommando*, the informer Stanisław Dorosiewicz, reported
that the prisoners under him had contacts in the area surrounding the
camp. The day after the escape three surveyors were sent to the bunker* and with them a member of the gardeners' *Kommando* at Rajsko,
Jan Winogrodzki, who also had been in contact with Płotnicka. On
May 26th another thirteen surveyors were sent to the bunker† and
next day another eleven.‡ They were subjected to cruel interrogation, the *Gestapo* trying to extract the details of their outside contacts. Nearly all of them belonged to the camp military underground

---

* Their names are in Appendix III, item 20.

† Their names are in Appendix III, item 21.

‡ Their names are in Appendix III, item 22.

and knew a lot, but they were able to keep silent. Płotnicka, too, gave nothing away. After a month of interrogation, on June 25th, thirteen men were shot against the wall of death.*

In the bunker there still remained sixteen surveyors and J. Winogrodski. It looked as if they might yet escape with their lives, but the *SS*-men had other plans. On July 17th, on the square in front of the Kitchen, a gallows was erected with twelve nooses and after the evening roll-call all the prisoners were herded to the place of execution. Twelve surveyors were led out from the bunker with their hands tied and were ordered to stand on stools under the nooses.† Höss, the Commandant, began to read out the sentence, in which it was said that the execution was punishment for an escape combined with the poisoning of an *SS*-man. Pogonowski, as a sign of protest, kicked away the stool from under him and dangled in the noose. Immediately the *SS* officers ran forward and knocked the stools from under the other condemned men.[2]

This mass public execution as a reprisal for the escape of fellow-prisoners was a return to the system of collective responsibility. It shook the camp, and unfortunately was not the end of the affair. On the last day of July, Kazimierz Jarzębowski was brought back to the camp. He had been picked up by chance during an ordinary round-up. It would be hard to imagine a worse stroke of luck. Jarzębowski's escape was closely linked to the camp underground's outside contacts, both military and political, for the surveyors were extremely active and served several camp underground groups. The escape was also connected with Helena Płotnicka, who unfortunately was already in the bunker undergoing interrogation. It was extremely difficult to hold out, for Dorosiewicz was informing on them. The Political Department used every method of torture known to it on Jarzębowski. The unfortunate prisoner, unable to stand it and afraid that he would crack and betray his comrades, twice tried to commit suicide, cutting his veins with a piece of glass. In both cases he was brought back to life. This was done by Dr. Diem in the presence of an *SS*-man, who watched him apply the bandages. Jarzębowski managed, however, to whisper to the doctor that he would withstand the torture and that he would not divulge his camp and outside contacts.[3] And so it was. He died on August 20th, 1943, against the wall of death.[4]

The death of the 26 surveyors was a painful loss to the Union of Military Organization, for they, above all, had maintained liaison with the outside world; but in place of the murdered men others came

The gallows in front of the Kitchen at Auschwitz.

---

* Their names are in Appendix III, item 23.

† Their names are in Appendix III, item 24.

forward, equally devoted. The executions had not completely broken up this *Kommando*. Among others, Jósef Barcikowski, Jósef Kret and Edward Padkowski survived in it and went on working for the underground. Padkowski escaped from the camp in August 1944 and joined the Home Army partisan unit *Sosienki* and later *Garbnik*. In spite of the version given in the sentence partly read out by Höss before the hanging of the twelve surveyors, the main reason for the reprisals was not the escape of Jarzębowski and his fellows, but Dorosiewicz's report that almost all the *Kommando* was engaged in maintaining outside contacts.[5]

2

German military reverses were reflected not only in the prisoners' conditions of life, but also in the type of *SS*-men guarding them. At first this was a purely German element, well trained, worthy to be implicitly trusted by the *Reichsführer SS*; but later, as the best men went to the front and the camps swelled in size, things looked different. When the camp Commandant Rudolf Höss complained to his superiors that they were sending him officers with whom it was quite impossible to work, he was told that in the future he would be getting even worse ones. The days were over when an *SS*-man had to prove he was of pure Nordic descent and had other characteristics which gave him the right to be one of the *Führer's* most trusted soldiers. As the war went on various types began to be taken into the *SS*, first *Volksdeutschen* from the occupied countries; later, often by force, men of various nationalities who often could hardly speak German.[6] In Auschwitz, Birkenau and the other sub-camps *SS*-men could frequently be heard singing as they sat at night in the watchtowers. The songs came from various countries and were sung in various languages. In the night of Auschwitz, right beside the barracks, filled with the motley crowd of prisoners of all nations, against the background of the crematoria spouting out flames and smoke, they made a ghastly impression.

The camp command that had to control this multi-national element of the *SS*, further corrupted by the treasures of *Canada*, did its best to make them into an entity and give them some *esprit de corps*, but without much result. Finally a quite exceptional incident occurred.

In 1943 a company of Ukrainian *SS*-men (they differed externally from the others in that they wore black forage-caps) was sent to Auschwitz for guard duty. The time had passed when Ukrainians had believed that Hitler's intentions towards them were honest and that he would help them to build up their own state. Forced to guard the concentration camps and seeing what was happening in them, seeing the crematoria working day and night, they lost the last remnants of trust in their German masters. Apart from disliking their duties they harboured the fear that the day would come when, in order to cover the traces of these crimes, the guards would be liquidated. They, as non-Germans, would die first. Their distrust of the Nazis became so great that, once, when they had to undergo de-lousing and a bath in the military sauna, they refused to go into it, suspecting that it was a camouflaged gas chamber. Only when an SS NCO, a pure-bred German, went in, did they consent to follow him. The atmosphere of suspicion, distrust and hatred deepened more and more until the night of July 3rd–4th 1943, when sixteen Ukrainian SS-men took their weapons and ammunition and slipped out of the barracks. All available units were called out in pursuit. The Germans caught up with them in the neighbourhood of Chełm Wielki near Bieruń. The Ukrainians hid in a quarry and gave battle. Eight were killed; one, wounded, was taken prisoner; the rest preferred suicide to falling into German hands. Two SS-men also fell: Corporal Rainicke and Private Stephan Rachberger. The wounded Ukrainian was executed and the whole company transferred to Buchenwald.[7]

This was the most glaring example of the breakdown of discipline among the SS guards, and not the only one. Working in an extermination camp, watching, every day, the agony of thousands of men, the 'selections' on the railway ramps, helping to drive helpless women and children to the gas chambers, stealing the goods gathered in the *Canada* barracks, weltering in blood day after day, while knowing at the same time that Germany was losing the war – all this was bound to undermine the morale of even the best SS-men, one hundred per cent Germans, believing whole-heartedly in the *Führer* and his star. What, then, must have been the effect on all those others who, at the beginning of the war when the Third *Reich* had gone from victory to victory, had admitted to being of Germanic origin, or who had been forced willy-nilly to join the SS and perform camp duty?

The prisoners knew, of course, how the serried ranks of the SS were wavering and breaking, and they took advantage of it. The camp underground movement also observed the change. In its preparations for an eventual fight the morale of the camp guards had to be taken into account. The Union of Military Organization had among the SS-men, mainly *Volksdeutschen* from Poland, several men who had promised help and access to the munition stores.

The picture would not, however, be complete if it were not stressed that among the ranks of the SS there were a few men who, from the very beginning, independent of successes at the front and other aspects of the war, behaved with dignity and did not disregard the rights of human beings. The years which have passed have veiled these events, but some names have remained in the memories of former prisoners. In the Garage a Bavarian, Corporal Richard Böck, was a lorry driver. He did all he could to help the prisoners. He brought in food and medicines, sent letters outside the camp, passed on radio news. He was suspected and arrested. He was put into the *SS*-men's prison and was lucky to escape with his life.[8] In the prisoners' Deposit Store, from the middle of 1943, the foreman was Corporal Koczy, an elderly man from Rybnik in Silesia. He secretly confessed to some of the prisoners working there that he felt himself to be a Pole, and so he helped them. He sent letters to prisoners' families, visited these families and brought back their answers. *SS*-man Edward Lubusch from Bielsko-Biała, one of the camp guards, also gave help to the prisoners and facilitated illicit correspondence. Several times he provided the papers necessary for escapes. He himself was preparing to leave his unit secretly and join the Polish partisans, operating in the vicinity of Auschwitz. Unfortunately he was caught with false papers just before his escape. He was stripped of his rank and shot.[9]

In Birkenau Corporal Joachim Wolf, who, from the end of October 1943, carried out the duties of *Rapportführer* on Section B II *d*, did much to help the prisoners and indirectly the underground movement. He gave warning of selections for the gas chambers, and in 1944 gave warning that the camp was completely surrounded, at the time when the prisoners, having learnt of plans for liquidating the camp and razing it to the ground, were making ready for a desperate fight. The warning was given to Józef Mikusz, who immediately passed it on to the leaders of the Union of Military Organization in the central camp.[10] Corporal Vladimir Bilan, who worked in the branch of the Political Department in the women's camp in Birkenau, also behaved decently. Of Rumanian origin and with a Polish wife, he did a great deal to relieve the sufferings of the thousands of women around him. After the war he was tried at Cracow and sentenced to eight years in prison for belonging to the *SS*, but was released after three years, as a number of former women prisoners made statements in his favour.[11]

A very rare event took place on April 5th, 1944, when a Czech Jew, Vítězslav Israel Lederer, escaped from Birkenau in the company of an *SS*-man responsible for a barracks, Victor Pestek, a German from Rumania. Lederer reached the ghetto in Theresienstadt and told the Council of Elders of the Jewish community what was happening to Jews in Auschwitz. Pestek returned to the neighbourhood of the camp to help other prisoners to escape, but was caught and shot after cruel interrogation.[12]

Several prisoners, especially women, remember a certain high-ranking officer of the SS as a decent, upright man. This was Lt. Colonel Dr. Joachim Caesar, the Director of Agriculture in Auschwitz from March 12th, 1942. His SS rank being the highest in Auschwitz, he enjoyed certain privileges and great opportunities; but he was not obliged to use these to care for the prisoners under him. Everyone working on his plants and in his laboratories got better clothing, better food and the benefit of his personal intervention in cases where the camp command or the Political Department wished to punish a prisoner. The women especially, among whom were many university graduates, some Jewish, he treated as fellow-workers.[13]

Another SS doctor, Hans Münch, director of the Institute of Hygiene in Auschwitz, also deserves recognition. When his superiors tried to detail him for selections of prisoners for the gas chambers he refused. He was the only one of the accused to be declared wholly innocent when sentences were passed at the trial of forty members of the former SS garrison of Auschwitz in Cracow on December 16th, 1947.[14] His attitude to the prisoners was similar to that of Dr. Caesar.

There were certainly more such examples and it is a great pity that no authentic evidence remains about them, but all these cases were shadowed by the behaviour of one exceptional person, who, although she did not belong to the SS, was counted as belonging to the camp garrison. Maria Stromberger was an Austrian woman of about forty from Tyrol, a professional nurse and a devout Catholic. There is a certain similarity between her behaviour and that of Witold Pilecki. He went to Auschwitz voluntarily as a prisoner, to build up an underground movement there; she, also voluntarily, applied to work in the camp when she heard what was going on there. She wanted to see for herself what she had been told in great secret by two Poles, released from the camp, whom she had nursed in hospital at Królewska Huta.

She applied for a post and on October 1st, 1942, found herself in Auschwitz as sister-in-charge of the SS Hospital on the first floor of a barracks, the ground floor of which was then occupied by the Political Department. (The latter was transferred to its own building in the following year.) Its proximity was a clear enough indication to Sister Maria of what she had come to find, and from the hospital windows she could see Crematorium No. 1 close by. The screams of the tortured, the women and children being driven to the gas chambers, the cruel faces of the young SS-men, the dreadful appearance of the *Kommandos* going to and coming back from work – all this showed her clearly that she really was in a death camp. In the SS Hospital Poles worked as cleaners, and several of them belonged to the military camp underground.

Otto Küsel   Maria Stromberger   Hans Münch

People who helped the prisoners and the underground.

The first to make contact with Sister Maria was Edward Pyś, whom she nursed through typhus. Soon after, Eugeniusz Niedojadło also contacted her. Together they 'organized' food for other prisoners. When they were convinced that they could count on her utterly, they let her into the secret of their underground connections. Zbigniew Raynoch and Czesław Duzel, also soldiers of the Union of Military Organization, took part in this as well. It was a matter of civilian contacts, carrying messages to couriers outside the camp who sent them on to the Home Army District in Cracow and Silesia. Sister Maria undertook these tasks and also brought into the camp illegal correspondence, medicines, arms and explosives. Stanisław Kłodziński collected the medicines from her. She met people on the station in Brzeszcze, Chrzanów, Chorzów and Bielsko. She did not speak Polish, but she managed to learn the necessary passwords. She did not limit her contacts to the Polish military underground and, as often happens in underground work, she also rendered services to other secret groups,[15] mainly to the Austrians through Langbein. Thanks to her he kept up a secret correspondence with his family in Vienna.[16]

Twice she found herself in great danger. Once, in January 1943, she was denounced by an *SS* orderly, a Sudeten German named Kaulfuss, but the Senior Medical Officer, Dr. Wirths, knowing Sister Maria to be an excellent nurse, let her off with a warning. The second time, also probably as the result of a denunciation, she was summoned before the camp Commandant. Only her firmness and rebuttal of all accusations, of which there was no proof, saved her from arrest and the bunker.[17] She was constantly in danger but never ceased in her activities until she was transferred to Berlin in November 1944.*

---

* For the further fortunes of Maria Stromberger see Appendix I.

3

In spite of a certain relaxation of camp discipline and improvement in the prisoners' lot, the struggle between Oswald Pohl, who needed hands to work, and Adolf Eichmann never let up for a moment. Pohl won a victory in selecting able-bodied Jews for work and sending them into the camp instead of straight to the gas chambers, and also in building up industry in the camps[18]; but Eichmann, apart from these concessions, did not yield an inch. So the plan for building four great gas chambers and crematoria in Birkenau was carried out without any hold-ups. On June 28th, 1943, the director of the *SS* central Building Office in Auschwitz duly sent a message to *WVHA** in Berlin, announcing that the ovens were working and could cremate 4,756 bodies a day.† This monstrous figure, which enabled them to reduce to ashes over 140,000 human bodies a month, barely sufficed, and the *Sonderkommando* worked in two shifts, day and night, so that incoming transports did not have to wait on the railway ramp.

In the summer of 1944, when the Jews from Hungary were being exterminated, the increase in transports was so great that the crematoria could not cope and the bodies were also burnt in six big trenches. The work went on day and night. In August of that year the number of bodies burnt during 24 hours reached the total of 24,000. Later burning at night was stopped as the anti-aircraft defence protested.[19]

At the same time, in the camp Hospital, a fight was going on to save the lives of sick prisoners, threatened not only by typhus, chronic lung trouble, malaria, dysentery, various inflammations and septic conditions, but above all by constant selections for the gas chambers and phenol injections. Practically speaking, all the doctors and almost all of the male nurses in the Hospital – ruled by Poles although at the head there stood a new *Lagerältester*, the German Communist Ludwig Wörl – took part in this fight. The Union of Military Organization had, of course, its camp intelligence service and generally knew beforehand when the *SS*-men were coming to carry out selections. Immediately all patients who could stand up were discharged from the Hospital.

These were difficult decisions and prisoner-doctors ran a double risk: on the one hand denunciation for sabotaging the orders of the

---

* Economic and Administrative Head Office.

†	Crematorium No. 1 (old),	Auschwitz, 3 furnaces:	340 bodies
	Crematorium No. 2 (new),	Birkenau, 5 furnaces:	1440 bodies
	Crematorium No. 3 (new),	Birkenau, 5 furnaces:	1440 bodies
	Crematorium No. 4 (new),	Birkenau:	768 bodies
	Crematorium No. 5 (new),	Birkenau:	768 bodies.

Crematorium.

SS, on the other accusations from their fellow-prisoners, who cursed them for throwing them out of the hospital, not knowing that their lives were being saved. The patients' charts were also changed round. When the *SS* had chosen prisoners with a chance of recovery their charts were exchanged for those of men mortally ill, who would have died anyway.[20] Here too, much could be done to help, though the doctors risked their own lives and were open to the accusation of having saved one man at the cost of another. On these grounds, especially just after the war, numerous accusations were made which cannot stand up to an objective appraisal. If a Frenchman saved a Frenchman and not a Czech, it was said that he was anti-Czech; if a Pole saved a Pole and not a Jew, he was called anti-Semitic. Certain people spread this accusation in regard to Dr. Rudolf Diem, one of the most eminent Polish doctors in the hospital, to whom thousands of fellow-prisoners owe their lives.[21] Being a Pole he would sometimes save a fellow-countryman before others. Frenchmen, Russians and Jews acted similarly. The strong political ties which existed among the Communists of various nationalities frequently caused them to save Communists first.

These questions of nationality gave rise to some glaring situations. Ludwig Wörl, the Senior Prisoner of the Hospital, sensing in Dr. Diem an outstanding personality, considering him as a rival and wanting to get him out of the Hospital, denounced him to the Political Department. To his colleagues and those around him Wörl said that Diem must leave the hospital because he was saving Poles first of all and thus was anti-semitic.[22] Diem was sent to the bunker and only got out of it alive by a miracle, being appointed doctor to the gypsy camp. The fact of the denunciation rules out any question of moral principle on Wörl's part. It was a typical expression of the struggle for power within the Hospital, very common in the German camps and showing very clearly to what lengths men could go while still claiming to be actuated by idealism.

Hermann Langbein also joined in the action of saving prisoners from selections for gassing and lethal injections. He had some influence with Dr. Wirths and used it cleverly. After telling Wirths that typhus patients were refusing to go into the Hospital because they were afraid of the selections and injections, Langbein went even further in this direction. Wirths was under pressure from Berlin, who ordered that typhus was to be stamped out and the prisoners' standard of health improved so that they could work better. For this purpose Wirths could act freely without injury to his conscience as a German and *SS*-man. As a result of Langbein's skilful tactics, *SS* Corporal Jozef Klehr, who used to kill prisoners with phenol injections, was transferred to the *SS* Hospital. Moreover, Dr. Wirths, on receiving appropriate information from his secretary, by various directives brought about a considerable fall in the mortality rate. These were considerable achievements on the part of Langbein, by which he rendered service to his fellow-prisoners, his personal achievement, of course, having very little to do with the *Kampfgruppe Auschwitz*.

Suddenly, on August 28th, 1943, his activities were curtailed. *SS* Corporal Gerhard Lachmann from the Political Department took him off to the bunker. There for a moment he saw Ludwig Wörl, also arrested. They had both been denounced by a German Communist named Linhart, who had also been in the International Brigade in Spain, for which reason Wörl had made him the Block Chief on Hospital Block No. 21. The denunciation had mentioned an underground organization in the Hospital and Wörl and Langbein as part of it.[23] Lachmann began his interrogation, but before he

finished it, new dramatic events shook the Auschwitz underground
movement.

4

Witold Pilecki had entered Auschwitz on September 22nd, 1940,
and had almost immediately started to build up the underground
organization, which was the first attempt at starting up a camp
resistance movement. Three years had passed since then – a very long
time in the camp, for almost every day saw a new epic of murder,
struggle, resistance and death.

During these three years the now extensive and strong Polish
underground organization, linked subsequently with groups of other
nationalities (Czechs, Russians), had been under attack from the
Political Department and had sustained losses, but so far the attacks
had affected only a few of the leaders and the camouflaged top men
were almost untouched. This showed that the underground workers
were using adequate security methods. The camp was a multilingual,
international mass of the most varied human types; penetrated by
hundreds of spies and informers; covered by a network of thousands
of trusties, many of whom hung on to their positions only for reasons
of personal advantage; full of wretches dying of starvation and
illness, ready to sell their own brothers for a slice of bread, under the
constant observation and control of the large *SS* garrison. Every
day, every hour, there were threats of denunciation and provocation
and a fresh attack by the Political Department.

On June 25th, 1943, Col. Juliusz Gilewicz, commander of the
Union of Military Organization, was taken to the bunker, but was
released four days later. Suddenly, on September 16th, the colonel's
younger brother, Kazimierz, working in the Labour Assignment
Office in the sub-camp Monowice (*Buna-Werke*), and directing the
military underground there in liaison with the central camp,[24] went
to Block No. 11, the bunker. Between then and September 29th, 74
more prisoners were taken to the bunker,* mainly from the central
camp, but also from Birkenau. Unfortunately this time the blow was
dead on target. Col. Juliusz Gilewicz was taken again, and with him
Lt. Col. Teofil Dziama, Henryk Bartosiewicz, Dr. Rudolf Diem,
Dr. Władysław Fejkiel, Jan Mosdorf, Franciszek Targosz; altogether
38 leading members of *ZOW*.† Many of them occupied high positions
in it; some like Jan Mosdorf, carried out important tasks in the
political groups giving support to the military underground.

---

* For the list of those arrested see Appendix III, item 25.

† For the list of them see Appendix III, item 26.

The arrested men were not taken at once for interrogation to the Political Department,[25] as for some reason the camp *Gestapo* preferred to put this off for some days. Perhaps they were waiting to collect all those whom they meant to interrogate, but nobody knows why the men were brought in over a period of several days and not all at once.

The interrogation, carried out chiefly by Wilhelm Boger and Gerhard Lachmann, was severe, accompanied by beating and extreme physical and psychological pressure. They tried to get from the arrested men further names of prisoners connected with the underground; they were looking for secret links connecting the central camp with the sub-camps, chiefly Birkenau and Monowice (*Buna-Werke*). All the arrested, particularly those who had the most important organizational responsibilities and knew the most, had to resist to the utmost and keep silent, for on their silence depended the fate of their comrades and the whole underground organization, built with such difficulty. It is always easier to resist in interrogation if one is involved alone. Particularly dangerous is the situation in which one's captors confront one with a colleague.

While the interrogation was going on, some of the prisoners were unexpectedly released into the camp. They were: Henryk Bartosiewicz, Franciszek Targosz and Alfred Woycicki, released on September 28th; Jerzy Pozimski, released on September 29th; Xawery Dunikowski, released on October 8th, and Leon Murzyn, released on October· 9th.[26] Two days later a big selection was made in the bunker and 47 prisoners went to the wall of death.[27] Among them were nearly all the leaders of the Union of Military Organization, 28 men altogether. They all died bravely. Dziama and Lisowski demanded that they should be shot not in the back of the neck but in the face, like soldiers. This demand was granted.[28]

Another prisoner, a strong man, chosen from among the cleaners, leads out the first two victims at the run. He holds them by their arms and presses their faces to the wall. 'Prosto' (stand straight), someone orders when they turn their heads to one side. Although tottering skeletons – some of them had existed for months in the stinking cellar in which even an animal could not survive – barely able to stand up, many of them cry out at the last moment 'Long live Poland!' or 'Long live freedom!'[29]

On the same day (October 11th) during this selection and execution, several other members of the Union of Military Organization were saved by being released into the camp. They were Franciszek Balzar, Stefan Chmielewski, Dr. Rudolf Diem, Dr. Władysław Fejkiel, Stanisław Mucha, Józef Otowski and Ignacy Zamojski.[30]

The execution of the leaders of the Polish military underground, combined with the murder of a number of less exposed but equally important military men, as well as a number of eminent politicians, was a shock to the camp underground. It was clear that this time the Political Department had precise information as to where to strike and had directed its blows exclusively at Poles. It is interesting that, although the *Kampfgruppe Auschwitz* already existed, as did underground groups of other nationalities, not one of their members died in the October executions. The conclusion must be that the camp *Gestapo* as yet knew nothing of their activities, which had only just begun and had so far shown no results. Otherwise Langbein and Wörl, who were in the bunker at the same time, would not have got out of it alive.

It was realised that the Political Department could only have dealt this painful blow thanks to its numerous informers or a denunciation by someone who was not a regular informer but wished to deprive the strong Polish camp underground of its leaders and weaken it as much as possible. It was already known that Dr. Diem had gone to the bunker as the result of a denunciation by Wörl, but he had come out again, and moreover this denunciation appeared to be a personal attack. Who then had performed this act of treachery, who had sent to their death men who had tried to help others at such risks to themselves?

An article discussing the *Book of the Bunker*[31] says that the arrests between September 16th and 29th, 1943, were brought about by a denunciation, but this statement is not developed. Following up this suggestion one comes upon Stefan Ołpiński, one of the most dangerous camp spies, who concentrated especially on Poles. He could have betrayed the Polish leaders, for he did not die of typhus until January 1944. Dr. Fejkiel, who came out of the bunker alive in October, is of the opinion that it was Ołpiński[32], but other witnesses think differently. Wojciech Gniatczyński states that his circle of friends in the camp believed that the informer was Leon Markitonn, who was also in the bunker on September 19th but was released 6 days later. In the following months he was severely beaten up by other prisoners, went to the hospital and died there.[33] This accusation of betrayal, the worst that could be brought against a fellow-prisoner, is not supported by evidence or by any other informant, so it is difficult to accept unreservedly that Gniatczyński is right. The fact of having been released from the bunker when others went to the wall of death proves nothing. Other prisoners were also set free, among them several notable members of the Union of Military Organization, like Bartosiewicz, Diem, Fejkiel and Targosz, whom nobody ever suspected in the least.

Another version is put forward by Henryk Bartosiewicz and Józef Otowski, two members of the *ZOW*, who came out of the bunker at that time. They themselves escaped not only death but also interrogation, and Bartosiewicz was let out into the camp three days after his arrest, yet all the same they were able to learn a lot. Both independently consider that the reason for the arrests and liquidation of the leaders of the Polish military underground was that the *SS* got hold of a letter written by Kazimierz Gilewicz, who had tried to send it out of the camp.[34] There are some indications that this might be so, for Gilewicz was the first to go to the bunker, but it is hard to

The 'wall of death'.

accept that his letter was the cause of the further arrests. An experienced underground worker, in the second half of 1943, would not have sent a letter containing information concerning his close camp colleagues and leaders of the underground. It is more likely, on this view, that the letter gave away Gilewicz himself and that he broke down under interrogation and gave away his colleagues. There is no proof of this, however, as narrators state that the Political Department delayed interrogations. Besides, how could Gilewicz, who remained in Monowice, have known so many names of underground workers operating in the central camp and in Birkenau? It would be against all the basic rules of underground work. To sum up, it is most probable that several causes and several denunciations contributed to the October tragedy. Who was the informer? There is no evidence that points to a definite answer. Were the denunciations part of a struggle for power in the camp underground? They may have been, but again we have no proof.

It is also difficult to explain why some of the arrested members of the Union of Military Organization, although they were among its chief representatives, were released from the bunker. The doctors, Rudolf Diem and Władysław Fejkiel, were probably saved by Dr. Wirths,[35] who not only had a certain fellow-feeling for men of his own profession, but also needed them very badly. Franciszek Targosz was probably saved from the bunker by the SS-men from the camp Censorship Office, afraid for their own skins; for if he had begun to talk under interrogation, certain machinations of their own would have come to light. Bartosiewicz is said to have been rescued by his nearest friends paying Boger in gold from *Canada*.[36] Why were the others not bought out? Again one can only guess. It probably depended on what information the Political Department had. Those who were released cannot have been the subjects of such firm denunciations as their less fortunate colleagues.

The leadership of the *ZOW* was seriously weakened, but not completely broken up. Bartosiewicz remained; so did Bernard Świerczyna, now *Capo* of the Clothing Store, and Capt. Stanisław Kazuba, who commanded one of the secret battalions. These two had not been arrested at all. Their cover was so good that no suspicion fell on them, and they now went a long way upwards in the underground hierarchy. Świerczyna especially came to the fore and was designated as the military commander if fighting should break out in the camp.[37] It was true that he was only a reserve Second Lieutenant, but the expected armed uprising would take place under specific conditions, far removed from normal military operations. Świerczyna had an excellent camp position, thanks to which he was in contact with the leaders of the other groups. He came from Silesia, so he knew the terrain very well; he was young, strong and energetic and had a lot of authority among his fellow-prisoners. Dr. Dering, Dr. Jaworski, Stanisław Kłodziński and many other doctors from the central camp, all members of the *ZOW*, had also escaped the bunker. Dr. Fejkiel was back in his old position.[38] Many of the important positions in the Labour Assignment Office, the Tannery, the contacts at the Political Department, the Stores and various other places, were still in the hands of the Polish military underground workers. The men's part of Birkenau had not suffered badly, the women's not at all. The Union of Military Organization, although weakened, was still in existence and operating.

5

Exactly a month after the executions of the Polish leaders, great changes unexpectedly took place at Auschwitz. On November 11th, 1943, Rudolf Höss was transferred to Berlin and replaced by *SS* Lt. Colonel Arthur Liebehenschel, who at once issued an order informing the garrison that he had taken over command. He must have brought clear directives with him, for from the very first days of his stay conditions in the camp changed for the better. Up to this time it was exceptional for an unsuccessful attempt at escape not to be punished by death, but from the moment of the new Commandant's arrival these executions ceased. Prisoners, even Jews, who were caught trying to escape were let out into the camp after a short stay in the bunker. This was not all. On November 23rd the new Commandant carried out an inspection of all the cells in the bunker and something unprecedented in Auschwitz took place: 56 selected prisoners, instead of going to the wall of death, were set free and returned to their blocks.[39]

Big changes also took place among those *SS*-men who had the most influence on life in the camp. Before this, on October 1st, *Rapportführer* Gerhard Palitzsch, his name for ever bound up with the history of Auschwitz, left the camp. He went as Commandant to a small sub-camp in Brno (Czechoslovakia), containing 250 prisoners, but he was not there for long. A few weeks later three *SS* NCOs arrived from the central camp and took him back. His badges were torn off on the spot and he was put into the *SS* prison. Naturally within a few hours the whole camp knew of the fall of the man who for several years had been the terror of all the prisoners, and had been hated by them to the utmost. Only those in the secret knew that he had finally fallen, indirectly, as a result of the camp underground's activities.

As early as 1942 some underground members had thrown typhus-infected lice on Palitzsch, but he himself did not become ill; his wife caught the disease and died. Then the cruel *SS*-man began to visit the women's camp and spend more time there than previously. Despite the strict prohibition on relations with prisoners he began an affair with a Jewess from Slovakia. But little could remain secret in the camp. He was sent to Brno just so that he would not be arrested in Auschwitz itself. After disciplinary proceedings he joined an *SS* unit fighting partisans in the Balkans. He was apparently killed in December 1944 near Budapest.[40]

More or less at the same time, on October 23rd, *SS* Sergeant Josef Schillinger was killed, while occupying the position of *Rapportführer*. A transport of Jews from Bergen-Belsen had just arrived and Schillinger was present on the ramp at the selection. Since the unfortunate people had been told that they were going to Switzerland, but on the ramp they found themselves to be in a death camp, there was confusion and hysteria, and Schillinger, shouting, tried to force the transport to obey orders, At that juncture one of the women seized his revolver and fatally wounded him and shot another *SS*-man. Some of the prisoners were killed by grenades and shot, the rest were gassed.

After Palitzsch's departure the position of *Rapportführer* of the central camp was taken over by *SS* Corporal Oswald Kaduk, a cruel brute, but not as bad as his predecessor. Before the prisoners could accustom themselves to this, a still more dramatic change took place. On December 1st Liebehenschel informed his garrison that the head of the Political Department, Maximilian Grabner, had gone back to the *Gestapo* in Katowice and that *SS* 2nd Lieut. Hans Schurz had taken his place.[41] This was absolutely revolutionary. Grabner, the terror of the prisoners, had made such a position for himself in the camp that although he had only the rank of *SS* Second Lieutenant, even officers were afraid of him.[42] Höss was the Commandant, but he knew much less of what went on than Grabner. The latter held all the threads in his hand and thanks to numberless spies and informers he knew precisely how the land lay. His departure, immediately after Palitzsch had left the camp, was of fundamental importance and changed the whole aspect of life in the camp.*

Only a few days later, on December 8th, a mysterious fire broke out in the camp. A barracks was burnt down in which a Commission, sent specially from Berlin, had collected articles as proof that the *SS*-men from the Political Department had been stealing valuables from *Canada*. The fire was one way of obliterating the traces of their offences.

The new Commandant made certain administrative changes. On November 22nd he issued an order that there would henceforth be three independent camps:

Auschwitz No. 1 (the main camp), with himself as Commandant.
Auschwitz No. 2 (Birkenau, men and women), with *SS* Major Fritz Hartjenstein as Commandant.

---

* Grabner did not go back to Katowice but was taken to Berlin and tried by an *SS* court in Weimar. He was accused of theft and abuse of authority. The trial was never concluded. On December 22nd, 1947, the Supreme National Tribunal in Warsaw sentenced Grabner to death. The sentence was carried out.

Auschwitz No. 3 (the sub-camps: Monowice, Jawiszowice, Sosnowiec, Jaworzno, Świętochłowice, Łagisza, Brno, Goleszów, Ławki and Libiąż Mały), with *SS* Captain Heinrich Schwarz as Commandant.[43]

All three camps still came under Liebehenschel, who was the commander of the whole *SS* garrison in Auschwitz. In this respect the centralization of authority was not affected.

The appointment of Liebehenschel to Auschwitz and the disciplinary proceedings against Palitzsch and Grabner, together with the arrival of a Commission from Berlin, showed that the central authorities were seriously disturbed by the situation in the camp – the more so by reason of its size, connection with important munitions factories and proximity to operational areas of the strong Polish underground movement. The level of discipline among the *SS*-men had fallen off considerably; the constant escapes of prisoners and resulting executions were causing unrest among the huge, multilingual mass of prisoners, who were now very necessary for war production. Germany's military setbacks, and anxiety as to what would happen if the war were lost, may also have had some influence on the change of methods. All the same, it was too soon for a clear decision that it was time to begin to obliterate the traces of the crime. Auschwitz was still a death camp and in this respect its activities were actually intensified. Almost every day transports of Jews arrived from various parts of Europe and after selection they were sent to the gas chambers. Selections were still carried out, mainly in the women's camp in Birkenau, and those unfit for work were killed off in the same way.[44]

6

Before the new Commandant took up office, Langbein had come out of the bunker on November 3rd and returned to his work as Wirths's secretary. From the latter he learnt that the head of the Political Department, Grabner, was ill, and in addition that he was leaving his post. This was closely connected with the arrival of the special Commission from Berlin.

The weakening of the influence of the camp *Gestapo* automatically strengthened the position of the Senior Medical Officer, who had stood up to it, and for this reason he had been able to get Langbein out of the bunker. The new situation also meant that Langbein personally gained greater opportunities for his underground activities.

While he had been away there had been an important change in the Hospital. Since Wörl was also in the bunker, the position of Senior Prisoner of all the Hospital Blocks had been given to Dr. Władysław Dering. This was in September 1943. Dr. Władysław Fejkiel, working as a doctor in the Hospital at that time, who took over this exposed position from Dering and who cannot be reckoned among his friends, gives this opinion of the appointment:

> Dering was appointed *Lagerältester** of the hospital not because he allegedly curried favour with the Germans, but because the head doctor *SS* Dr. Wirths wanted this position to be filled by a doctor and not by a self-taught male nurse. Since there was no prisoner-doctor of German nationality in the camp, the position was entrusted to the senior prisoner-doctor of Polish nationality, W. Dering. Up to 1941 Dering had filled the position of doctor in the out-patients department; later, in difficult conditions, he organized the surgical department and ran it very well ... He was in the camp as a punishment for anti-German activities. He had many complexes ... As *Lagerältester* of the hospital Dering improved the position of doctors in the camp ...[45]

Relations between Langbein and Dering were at first good, but later they deteriorated considerably. Apart from personal dislike and reciprocal accusations, they were separated by a feeling of rivalry. Dering had been active in the Hospital almost from the very beginning; he had survived the worst period, he had been one of those who had built up the Hospital, he had belonged for three years to the Polish camp underground and he was irritated by the Austrian Communist, who had come to the camp in the middle of 1942 and, thanks to his acquaintanceship with Dr. Wirths, was behaving with great assurance. Langbein did not like Dering's rough manners and considered him to be a Polish chauvinist and anti-Semitic on the ground that he saved Polish lives before others. Himself a Communist, Langbein did not tolerate other political opinions. His position as the Senior Medical Officer's secretary enabled him to place his own men in the Hospital against Dering's wishes.

Immediately after his release from the bunker Langbein heard that Józef Cyrankiewicz had been taken there on the previous day. A civilian suit and a wig had been found in his possession and he was accused of attempting to escape. Such a charge meant very severe interrogation and almost certain death, so Langbein set about considering every means of saving him. A fortunate chain of circumstances came to his aid.

---

* Camp Senior Prisoner.

The first event was the arrival of the new Commandant. On Wirths's recommendation, Liebehenschel, who had instructions and perhaps ideas of his own concerning changes at Auschwitz, summoned Langbein to ask him about various camp secrets. He was told that relations in the camp were bad because the Political Department, wanting to grasp full power, had covered the camp with a network of informers and *agents provocateurs*, and that there were still too many criminal prisoners in high positions. It happened that just at this time a *Gestapo* informer, Stanisław Dorosiewicz, escaped from the camp with another spy, the Jew, Hersz Kurcwajg, who worked in *Canada*. With them was an *SS*-man, Corporal Peter Jarosiewitsch from the Political Department, to whom the others promised gold that was supposed to be buried near the camp. On the far bank of the Soła river they killed him and disappeared. This was an excellent opportunity for Langbein to stress that the informers and *provocateurs* were not to be trusted by anyone and were the main reason for unrest in the camp. As Dorosiewicz had previously spoken to Cyrankiewicz and urged him to escape, asking him for a safe address in Cracow, Langbein told the new Commandant of this, representing Cyrankiewicz as an innocent victim of provocation. Before talking to Liebehenschel, Langbein had been in secret contact with Cyrankiewicz and told him of the risky step he was planning to take. Liebehenschel called Cyrankiewicz before him and asked him for details, which naturally confirmed what Langbein had said, and had him and several other prisoners released from the bunker.[46]

There is another version of this episode, given in the *Auschwitz note-books* and later repeated in Poland by some writers. This is that Cyrankiewicz himself asked to see the new Commandant and told him of conditions in the camp. The *Auschwitz note-books* say that this action had beneficial results and increased the importance of the resistance movement in the whole camp. This story, however, must be dismissed as untrue. Liebehenschel, at the suggestion of Dr. Wirths whom he trusted, might have called Langbein, who had the rights of a *Reichsdeutsche*, to report and give his views; but it is unthinkable that he would have agreed to talk to a Pole who was in the bunker for an attempt at escape, and listen to his advice on how to run the camp.

The rider to this version, that Cyrankiewicz's intervention increased the importance of the resistance movement in the camp,[47] is equally unlikely. If any such conversation had taken place, nobody would have been allowed to know about it, except perhaps a very few most trusted men. This was an elementary condition of underground work. It is noteworthy that in the work of Zdzisław Hardt and Stanisław Czerpak, describing chiefly the underground activities of the

Socialists in and around the camp and paying special attention to Cyrankiewicz, there is not a single word of his having had a conversation with Liebehenschel.

Langbein, again with the help of Dr. Wirths, placed Cyrankiewicz as a clerk in the Infectious Hospital Block No. 20, which the *SS*-men hardly ever entered. Selections for gassing and phenol injections had already ended in the Hospital, and it was an excellent place for someone who wanted to keep out of sight.

The new Commandant brought about yet another change which affected conditions in the camp. One of the 56 prisoners let out of the bunker on November 23rd was Ludwig Wörl, the former Senior Prisoner of the Hospital. He could not return to his old position, for it had been given to Dr. Dering, and he was looking round for a good *Kommando* when quite unexpectedly he was given the armband of the Senior Prisoner of the whole central camp. He was the first political prisoner in Auschwitz to be appointed to this position. This was probably in December 1943.

Wörl was a Communist and a friend of Langbein's with whom he had come from Dachau, so he belonged to the *Kampfgruppe Auschwitz*, which was very much strengthened by this appointment. The fact that such a high position had been given to a political prisoner did not automatically mean changes for the better, for criminal prisoners, like Otto Küsel or Hans Bock, could behave magnificently and political prisoners badly, but on the whole it was a sign of improvement. Like Langbein, Wörl personally had great opportunities and it was hoped that he would use them to the prisoners' advantage, unless his political ideas were to lead him into dangerous extremism.

In a further attempt at improving relations in the camp, reducing the number of escapes and increasing war production, Liebehenschel accepted suggestions made to him which coincided with his own ambitions as Commandant, and sent away several of the Political Department's informers.[48] A list of them was given to him by Langbein after he had agreed it with his political friends. Did the new Commandant guess that Langbein was not acting on his own, that behind him there was an organization of some sort? It is difficult to say. Liebehenschel had only once before worked in a concentration camp, for a short time between 1934 and 1936; the rest of his career, until he was sent to Auschwitz, he had spent behind a desk in Berlin.[49] Lack of experience of camps, especially Auschwitz, could have been the reason why he did not see what a professional *SS* eye would have noticed at once. He might also have had his reasons for pretending not to see. At all events, under Liebehenschel's regime neither Langbein, nor any of his underground friends was ever threatened with reprisals on the part of the Political Department or the Commandant's office.

CHAPTER 10

Further activities of the underground; changes at the Hospital; obliterating traces of the crime; the *Book of the Bunker*; liquidation of Hungarian Jews.

1

Langbein's and Cyrankiewicz's release from the bunker was of fundamental importance to the further existence of the agreement to which they had been coming. Langbein had been a member of the Communist Party for years, he had fought in Spain and had many international connections, which helped him to bring together Communists of various nationalities in the camp. Many of these did not belong to any underground group and joined *Kampfgruppe Auschwitz* individually. As secretary to Dr. Wirths and as someone who had influence on him, Langbein was more important as an individual than the group he organized.

Cyrankiewicz's qualities were different, to some extent even opposite to Langbein's. Apart from his personal ambition and abilities, Cyrankiewicz's strength lay in the fact that he was a Socialist and not a Communist. Communists did not have a strong influence amongst the Poles either before the war or during it. This was partly because they were connected with Russia, which had historically been one of Poland's enemies. She had taken part in the partition of Poland, together with Austria and Prussia, at the end of the 18th Century, and her rule was the cruellest. Several of the Polish national uprisings were directed against her.

On the other hand the Polish Socialist Party (*PPS*), with a fine record from the days of fighting for Polish independence, enjoyed great popularity and united in its ranks working-class people, intelligentsia and idealists from every social class. It was enough to know that someone was a member of the Socialist Party for him to be considered trustworthy. Moreover, a very important fact at that time, the Polish Socialist Party was represented in the Polish Government in London and was loyal to it and to its Delegacy in Poland. It also supported the Home Army (*AK*) and had put its fighting units under *AK* command.[1] Thanks to the earlier work of Dubois, Barlicki, Jagiełło, Kuryłowicz and others, the Socialists were already in a strong position in the camp and were connected with the Polish underground there. They also had means of contact with the outside world, partly built up by themselves, Through these channels the camp was linked with the Home Army authorities in Warsaw and Cracow and with the *AK* partisan units, the only outside force that could help the camp if it had to fight. Cyrankiewicz was also a member of the Union of Military Organization so he was able to make use of the contacts already established. All this lay within his reach because he was a Socialist. His official position as a clerk in one of the Hospital Blocks was of no great importance and, unlike Langbein, he had no special influence.

As already explained, the Polish Communists did not create their own group in Auschwitz but joined the *Kampfgruppe* individually.* As the war went on and the Eastern Front came nearer, their numbers were bound to increase. The *Kampfgruppe* also gained members through personal ties. Cyrankiewicz, who came from Cracow, met fellow-Socialists, friends and others who had known him there, and these often joined him in underground work in the camp. One such was Stanisław Kłodziński, who belonged to no party but had been for a long time a member of *ZOW* and as such very active in the Hospital. Some sources[2] give, as members of the *Kampfgruppe Auschwitz*, prisoners who had belonged much earlier to the Union of Military Organization, to the Fighting Organization of the *PPS* that co-operated with it, or even to the right-wing group (the National Party and the National Radical Camp), which was also connected with the military underground. Moreover these same sources give credit to the *Kampfgruppe Auschwitz* for what were actually the achievements of others.

In the *Auschwitz note-books*, which with some reservations must be recognized as an objective source, several times in the footnotes we read: 'Material of the Camp Resistance Movement'. Since the first such footnote appears under the date July 31st, 1942,[3] nine months before the *Kampfgruppe* came into being, it follows that this material must also relate to the activities of the Union of Military Organiza-tion and the political groups working with it. In post-war Poland, when former soldiers of the Home Army (*AK*) were persecuted as enemies of the state, and the military successes of *AK* ascribed to the Communist *Armia Ludowa* (People's Army), the system of obliterat-ing the truth was widespread. The threat hanging over all those who had not declared for the Communists and Soviet Russia in good time precluded a true historical preṡentation, at all events in public, of the wartime reality. Even individual protests could not gain a hearing. This of course applied to the underground in Auschwitz also. Men who had used the underground activities there as a spring-

---

* Their names are in Appendix III, item 27.

board to a post-war career did not scruple to ascribe to themselves the work and achievements of others. Many years passed before voices began to be raised here and there to correct the most obvious falsehoods.[4]

Negotiations for the purpose of co-operation between the *Kampfgruppe* and other groups began in 1943 but had produced no results. The *Kampfgruppe* still consisted only of the Austrian Communists and their connections among French, Czech and Jewish Communists, as well as what Cyrankiewicz stood for. These forces were so weak that plans for military action could not even be thought of. The liquidation of a considerable part of the leadership of the Union of Military Organization had weakened it greatly, but it had not changed the way of thinking of those who remained and still carried on its work. At their head were the young officers Bernard Świerczyna, Henryk Bartosiewicz and Stanisław Kazuba.[5] These were the men with whom a renewed attempt to agree on operations would have to be made, and they stood firm on the position that the military underground cadres in the camp must, as hitherto, be subordinate to the command of the *AK*, represented by the Commandant of the *AK* District of Silesia. The extension of the military underground to other nationalities in no way changed the situation, for the camp could not fight alone and at that time outside help could come only from the *AK*. It might be different if there were any hope of help from the steadily advancing Red Army. Contact with the latter would then have great, perhaps even decisive, significance, and it might well be thought that in this event the *Kampfgruppe Auschwitz* would have a task to fulfil. Later events showed, however, that it was unable to do this.

Having failed to enlist the support of the strong and militant Soviet group, the *Kampfgruppe*'s leaders were forced to draw nearer to the *ZOW*. The latter's lower ranks were almost intact – the gaps made by transports to other camps were filled in by other prisoners and the *ZQW* was still the most important force in the camp. There was always a chance of becoming one of its leaders, and in the meantime co-operation afforded prospects of more effective activity. The idea of the *ZOW* joining the *Kampfgruppe* and coming under its command had fallen through, so another solution was proposed. Cyrankiewicz came forward with it, understanding that using Hołuj for further negotiations was quite senseless. This proposal was for the creation of a common Camp Military Council, composed of representatives of the Union of Military Organization, which would retain the command in its hands, and representatives of the *Kampfgruppe Auschwitz* for the purpose of liaison with elements that belonged to it. This proposal was accepted and the

Council was formed during the first months of 1944. The *ZOW* members were Bernard Świerczyna and Stanisław Kazuba, while the *Kampfgruppe* was represented by Lucjan Motyka, a member of the *PPS* and friend of Cyrankiewicz, and an Austrian Communist, Heinrich Dürmayer,[6] who had arrived from Flossenbürg on January 4th of that year.

In this way a conflict of political ideas was avoided and military agreement reached, although this was still far short of what was necessary. The Soviet nationals again held aloof, although they were an important force in the Auschwitz underground and, along with the Poles, were the element most eager to fight. Meanwhile the Eastern Front was drawing closer. The Red Army had entered Polish soil at the beginning of 1944 in the area of Polesie and the Prypeć river and was swiftly advancing. It was hard to tell how long the Germans would be able to hold out. In this state of affairs it was very important to have a Soviet officer in the underground military coalition. The lack of Soviet representatives on the Camp Military Council only confirmed what had happened a few months earlier, when the efforts of the *Kampfgruppe* to gain the co-operation of the Soviet group ended in complete failure. Of course the nature of underground work required that the number of leaders should be kept to a minimum, but it would have made more sense to have the strong Soviet group represented on the Council rather than the Austrians, of whom there were under a hundred in the camp. The absence of French, Czech, Yugoslav, German or Jewish representatives was of less importance. Fortunately the *ZOW* had had for some time its own contact with the Soviet group, now chiefly maintained by Bernard Świerczyna, so that their participation in any fighting, and the co-ordination of this, was ensured. Nevertheless the international character of the Camp Military Council, as of the *Kampfgruppe Auschwitz*, was problematic.

2

The year of 1944 brought further changes, first of all in the Hospital, which was so important to all the prisoners and the camp underground. On 25th January Dr. Władysław Dering left the camp and Dr. Władisław Fejkiel took his place as the Senior Prisoner of the Hospital.[7] He was the last prisoner to occupy this important position, and remained in it up to the evacuation of the camp. Dering was released from the camp 'on leave', though still a prisoner, thanks to the intervention of a German doctor, Carl Clauberg, who was head of a hospital at Chorzów with a department of gynaecology. There, under the constant supervision of the *Gestapo*, Dr. Dering remained until the Red Army came in, working chiefly as a surgeon.*

Dr. Fejkiel, a valuable and long-standing member of the *ZOW*,[8] proved to be the right man for the difficult hospital job. Apart from his professional qualifications he had great natural tact, unlike Wörl and Dering. He was moderate in his opinions, so he gave no offence; he managed to steer a course between the *SS*-men, the trusties and the underground workers, and to make his way successfully through the dangers and problems which were an everyday part of work in the Hospital Blocks. In particular he prevented a struggle for influence between the military organization (*ZOW*) and the *Kampfgruppe Auschwitz*, which had some of its men in the Hospital and wished to take it over.

The new Commandant, Liebehenschel, continued to relax camp discipline in the interests of productivity: he shortened the time of roll-calls and gave orders that night-shift workers were not to be deprived of rest during the day. As part of the same policy the Germans sometimes made extraordinary propaganda gestures such as the permission to marry granted to the Communist, Rudolf Friemel, a member of the Austrian underground group. Friemel had fought in the Civil War in Spain and there met a French girl, Margarita Ferrer Rey, by whom he had a son. On March 18th, 1944, the camp registry office married them, the photographic laboratory took a wedding portrait and the first floor of Block No. 24 was put at their disposal for 24 hours. The following day Margarita left the camp. This was the only case of this kind in the whole history of the German concentration camps.[9]

After this incident there followed others, much more important, proving that the precise machinery of German terror was beginning to falter and that the breakdown of unlimited Nazi rule was approaching. On April 9th there came to Birkenau the first transport evacuated from the camp at Majdenek near Lublin, and next day the old crematorium in the central camp was turned into an anti-aircraft shelter. Probably on the same day came an order that was both symbolic and significant: the black 'wall of death' in the yard of Block No. 11 was to be razed and the sand beneath it, drenched with blood to a depth of six feet, was to be carted away. Thus the *SS*-men showed for the first time that they were concerned to erase the traces of their crimes.

But these signs of German disquiet and weakness did not alter their attitude towards Jews. At the end of February Adolf Eichmann came to Auschwitz and inspected a camp of Jewish families from Czechoslovakia (Theresienstadt), in Section B II *b* at Birkenau. On

---

* For Dr. Dering's subsequent fate see Appendix II, item 6.

March 9th these families, consisting of 3,791 men, women and children, were taken in lorries to the gas chambers and murdered.[10]
Eichmann's visit, although ostensibly only connected with the family camp, had a wider purpose, for on his return to Berlin he reported to Himmler on the inadequacy of the mass-murder installations. Orders were issued to rectify this state of affairs without delay.

3

The camp bunker in Block No. 11 was a place in which numerous threads of camp life came together. Through it ran the blood-red line of almost all executions; here prisoners who had planned escape or been caught in the attempt were held and tortured; here the terrible camp punishments were meted out, such as the *Stehzelle*, the 'stake' and many others. A *Stehzelle* was a small space measuring 3×3 feet at the base, walled-up to the ceiling in cell No. 22 in the bunker. There were four such spaces. Through small doors at the bottom, four prisoners at a time were pushed into it for the night; they could only stand up inside and by day went to work. There were cases when prisoners sentenced to death by starvation died in these cells. Punishment at the 'stake' meant that the prisoner's arms were bent behind him and he was suspended by the wrists, just above the ground. Sometimes he was beaten in this position or swung to and fro.

In here the members of the camp underground were incarcerated and subjected to cruel interrogation. Sometimes civilians from outside were also imprisoned there. If anyone was able to obtain the evidence of all those who passed through the bunker, he would possess material of exceptional value to a historian.

The *SS*-man responsible for the bunker, a low-ranking soldier, kept the records of the people in it, but these were not available either to the clerk, a trusty who recorded the figures, or another trusty responsible for cleanliness and handing out food. Since the *SS*-man's book, with the records of those imprisoned, was incompetently written up and full of mistakes, for which the clerk was blamed, Franciszek Brol, who held this job, kept his own book, contrary to regulations, and from January 9th, 1941, wrote it up for several months. When in March of that year the number of prisoners was found to be incorrect, Brol brought out his own record and the *SS*-men tacitly accepted it. After Brol the duties of the clerk were carried out by Gerard Włoch, from February 11th, 1942, to December 20th of that year, and then by Jan Pilecki, a long-standing member of the *ZOW*. They both continued the book started by Brol, and on

March 31st, 1943, Pilecki started a new one, since the first was full.

At the beginning of 1944, when the worst years of terror recorded in the *Book of the Bunker* had passed, Jan Pilecki resolved to send both volumes out of the camp as documentary evidence about those times and events. It was impossible to take the existing ones, as they were known to the *SS*-men and constantly in use, so in great secret Pilecki made two copies. The first he put in the place of the earlier volume of the book, up to March 31st, 1943, and took the original, which formed a whole together with the copy of the second volume. The latter was still in use, and the copy was completed up to February 1st, 1944.[11]

Pilecki was in secret contact with Kłodziński and told him what he had done. Kłodziński informed Cyrankiewicz and they agreed that Pilecki's initiative was important and should be put to use. The help of a prisoner, Józef Róg, who worked in a group which went outside the camp was enlisted. He tied both volumes of the *Book of the Bunker* to his legs, left the camp with his group and secretly handed over the volumes to a civilian worker, who belonged to the *PPS*. The latter delivered them to Edward Hałoń, who ensured that they reached Cracow and the Committee for Help for the Prisoners of Concentration Camps. Teresa Lasocka looked after them and hid them until the end of the war. To-day they are to be found in the Auschwitz Museum and they form one of the most important documents on the camp. The exact date of their being smuggled out is unknown, but it must have taken place at the beginning of 1942, for a copy of volume 2 ends on the 1st February. The *Auschwitz note-books*, No. 1, contain a comprehensive account of the *Book of the Bunker*, including the work by the successive clerks, F. Brol, G. Włoch and J. Pilecki and also a statement by J. Cyrankiewicz and S. Kłodziński, but none of these sources give the date or even month in which the two volumes were sent out of the camp.

After this important achievement came another, also early in 1944. Through the *AK* Districts of Silesia and Cracow there existed opportunities for sending news to Warsaw and thence to London. The leaders of the *Kampfgruppe* collected as many names of *SS*-men employed in the camp as they could, with their dates and places of birth. This list reached the West and the BBC broadcast it with the statement that sentence of death had been passed on the persons named. The camp garrison must have learnt of this broadcast, for the behaviour of several *SS*-men changed and there were even some who volunteered for the front.[12] The fact that the *Kampfgruppe*, in spite of its pro-Soviet orientation, sent this list to London and not to Moscow suggests that it had no contact either with the Red Army or with the Polish Workers' Party (*PPR*), which represented Soviet political power in Poland.

Langbein made use of this London broadcast and his influence on Dr. Wirths grew. The latter's wife had a birthday, so in secret a portrait of her with her children was made beforehand from a photograph, flowers were obtained from the hot-houses and sent to her.* The following day Wirths asked Langbein if he knew anything about it. He received the answer that it was not intended to include Wirths and his family in the general sentence passed on the *SS*-men in Auschwitz, and that he, Langbein, was making this statement not only in his own name. Naturally the Chief Medical Officer could have passed this information on to the Political Department, but he did not do so and was impressed by the evidence that Langbein apparently had some secret organization behind him.

4

Eichmann's February visit was in fact a portent of further murders, in spite of the military situation and the intense feelings which might be aroused. On May 8th Liebehenschel was transferred to the position of Commandant of the camp at Majdanek and the labour camps in Warsaw, Radom, Budzyń and Bliżyn, while Rudolf Höss returned to Auschwitz as Commandant of the camp. After this change came others. Auschwitz I (the main camp) was taken over by *SS* Captain Richard Baer, and Auschwitz II (Birkenau) by another *SS* Captain, Jozef Kramer.[13]

Höss's return was by order of Himmler, who had given instructions for the liquidation of Hungarian Jews† as he considered that Liebehenschel would be unequal to the task, lacking Höss's experience. Höss immediately saw to it that crematorium No. V was mended, that five big trenches were dug beside it for burning extra bodies, and that bunker No. 2 (a small, unused gas chamber) was again put into action.

---

* The flowers were taken by a prisoner from a conservatory next to the villa occupied by Höss, who had resumed command of the camp. Höss's wife, invited to the birthday party, recognized her roses and Dr. Wirths found himself in a very unpleasant situation.

† Hungary, although forced to ally herself with Germany and even send some divisions to the Eastern Front, would not agree to hand over Jews to be exterminated. It was only when the German army marched into Hungary in March 1944 that further resistance became impossible.

On May 16th the first wagon-loads of Jews from Hungary arrived at the railway siding in Birkenau. Eichmann also turned up at the camp to see for himself how the operation was going. From this date onwards two to five trains, each of 40–50 trucks, arrived every day. In each truck up to 100 persons were packed with their luggage. Initially these victims were sent straight to the gas chambers without any selection, but later, as industry was still crying out for more

A roll-call in *Mexico*, part of Birkenau.

hands, a transit camp for Jews was opened in Section B III at Birkenau, known in the camp as *Mexico*.[14] There were only a few barracks, so several thousand naked young Jewesses were kept on the bare ground for whole days. From time to time transports of them were made up and they were sent to work in the interior of Germany. The rest went to the gas chambers, but not all at once as the capacity proved to be too small.

The camp underground observed the preparations for mass extermination and sent out warning reports. These reached the governments of the Western Allies and the Soviet Union; they also reached Jewish communities in free countries; but the reports were not believed. What was happening in Auschwitz exceeded normal imagination. It was felt that the reports were exaggerated and that things could not be *that* bad. The threat to the Hungarian Jews was, however, deadly and something had to be done to warn them and to make them believe what they were facing. Reports, however honest and accurate, could not be as convincing as eye-witness accounts and therefore it was decided that an escape had to be organized.

On April 7th two Slovak Jews, Walter Rosenberg and Alfred Wetzler[15] broke out of Birkenau. They were in contact with the camp underground through Paweł Gulba,[16] a member of the Union of Military Organization, and David Szmulewski, a member of the international group. Gulba, with the help of friends in his *Kommando*, concealed the two escapees in the *Mexico* area, in a special hiding-place where they stayed for 3 days and nights. When the outer chain of guards had been called in, they made for the south and with the help of the Polish population reached Slovakia (then a satellite state of Germany), where on April 24th, in the town of Žilina, they met the local Jewish Council. which was still in existence. They handed in a report on Auschwitz, on the extermination of Jews from all over Europe and, above all, on the preparations for the liquidation of Jews from Hungary. The Council, although distrustful and sceptical, promised that the report would be sent to Dr. Rezsö (Rudolf) Kastner, leader of the Hungarian Jews.[17] Rosenberg later saw the Papal Nuncio and gave him a copy of his report on Auschwitz. His task done, he joined the Slovak partisans and fought with them until the end of military operations.

Attempts were made to save the Hungarian Jews, and their fate was the subject of quasi-diplomatic exchanges. Eichmann on the one hand did all he could to send them to the Auschwitz gas chambers as quickly and in as large numbers as possible, while on the other hand he tried to barter the victims' lives for money or goods to be supplied by the Western powers. Nothing came of this attempt, and in the space of a few months more than 400,000 men, women and children were murdered.* The massacre was given the name *Operation Höss*, for he personally directed it until July 29th, 1944, when he handed over his command to Richard Baer and returned to

---

* 437,000 were deported to Auschwitz, but a certain number of young and healthy men and women were picked out and sent to other camps. Some of them survived the war.

Berlin. Almost half of all Hungarian Jews, estimated at 1,100,000, died. The remainder were saved as a result of the resolute stand taken by Admiral Nicholas Horthy, Regent of Hungary, who on June 26th issued an order that the transportation of Jews to Auschwitz was to cease. There were also protests from the Papal Nuncio (Angelo Rotta), the Primate of Hungary (Cardinal Justinian Serédi), the Protestant bishop László Ravasz, and the King of Sweden, as well as President Roosevelt, who threatened reprisals. Horthy was interned on October 17th in the castle of Hirschberg in Bavaria and his son sent to Mauthausen, but the protests, although they did not stop the extermination, delayed it considerably. The deportations were finally stopped by the Soviet advance. On Christmas Eve Eichmann left Budapest, which was surrounded towards the end of December.[18]

While the Hungarian Jews were being murdered, the family camp for Jews from Czechoslovakia (Theresienstadt) was also being wound up. After the mass murder on March 9th, when almost 4,000 people were killed, Section B II *b* at Birkenau began to fill up with new families. At the beginning of July several selections were made and young, healthy men and women were picked out for re-transportation. When this operation had made the others less cautious, lorries were brought up on the night of July 12th–13th and the remaining 4,000 were taken to the gas chambers. On August 2nd, gypsy families living in Section B II *e* at Birkenau met the same fate. On the same day all the Polish doctors and male nurses from the gypsy camp were transferred to the Penal Company.[19]

5

The ceaseless functioning of the four great crematoria did not affect the daily life of the camp. This was getting more and more complicated, for the number of prisoners was rising, on some days reaching the figure of 140,000.[20] This imposed still greater duties on the camp underground organization, which had to be enlarged to cope with the new tasks. To start a fight with the participation of such a mass of people was an extraordinarily complicated matter. It was also difficult to bring help to the sick and needy, who were more and more numerous as rations decreased and the prisoners' state of health grew worse with every day.

For these reasons and because of the obvious signs that the end of the war was coming, much larger numbers of prisoners joined the underground. In Birkenau, apart from the *ZOW*, the most powerful of all groups, there came into being a numerous and strong

Polish organization under Col. Smereczyński.[21] There also arose national and Jewish groups, the latter generally composed of Jews from a single country.[22] It seemed more and more on the cards that a fight might be necessary before the camp was wound up. The inmates of the numerous sub-camps felt the same, though because of the distances it was hard to count on co-operation and help from the main camp. Nevertheless, in the sub-camps too, small groups of prisoners of various nationalities and political opinions emerged. They accepted the risk of underground work and were prepared for a possible fight at the end.[23]

In the central camp at Auschwitz there was the Camp Military Council, under which the most elaborate and strongest operational instrument was the Union of Military Organization. Its numerous Polish members were ready to take up arms against the *SS* garrison, and it was in close contact with the strong Soviet group, the Czechoslovak group and the partisan units operating in the vicinity of the camp. The *Kampfgruppe*, still small in numbers, chiefly depended on Communists and was more political than military; this applied also to the groups of other nationalities that it was linked with. They might combine to distribute leaflets,[24] but in an armed struggle they would be valueless. Accordingly Cyrankiewicz looked round for a means of strengthening his position, which, if dependent solely on what he had created together with the Austrians, would not amount to much.

The approach of the Eastern Front and the greater aggressiveness of the partisan units around the camp, together with the increase in the numbers of prisoners, alarmed the *SS* and gave them the idea of transporting the most dangerous elements into the heart of Germany. From June 1944 transports of Poles and Russians were sent to other concentration camps further west. In one of them, numbering 778 prisoners, which went to Buchenwald on June 26th, was Henryk Bartosiewicz. Before leaving he managed to hand over his functions to Stanisław Kazuba and have a four-hour talk with Cyrankiewicz, whom he made known to Kazuba. In this way, although the organizational side of the Polish military underground still lay in Kazuba's hands, Cyrankiewicz came to know more about it, which he was entitled to do as a member of the *ZOW*. This strengthened his position greatly. As well as being the leader of the Fighting Organization of the *PPS* and belonging to the top four in the *Kampfgruppe Auschwitz* he had now gained direct influence over the activities of the Union of Military Organization, for, besides Kazuba, Bartosiewicz had given a number of other important contacts.[25]

About this time there arrived in the camp Lieut. Wacław Stacherski, from the *AK* at Katowice, who had been arrested on March 20th as the result of a betrayal. He was put into the bunker, but from his earlier contacts outside the camp he already had some secret connections, mainly with Bernard Świerczyna.[26] With the latter's help he was able to send several messages in July and August to his colleagues operating around Auschwitz. In one of these, no doubt at the suggestion of the camp underground – probably Świerczyna himself, he suggested that Cyrankiewicz should be appointed Commander of the underground military cadres in the camp. After the execution of Juliusz Gilewicz nobody had taken over his position, and in the case of a surprise attack and improvised fighting, misunderstandings might arise between the various men wanting to lead. This proposal reached the Commandant of the *AK* District Silesia, Maj. Zygmunt Janke (code-name *Walter*), who approved it, and the appropriate order was sent into the camp via the underground.[27] The date has not been recorded and Janke does not remember it, but it was most probably in August 1944.*

In this way Cyrankiewicz obtained what he had been working towards consistently for two years. In addition to his political position he had taken control of the military command, which was of incomparably greater importance. It was true he was a young man and only a reserve second-lieutenant, but in the conditions of the camp, at this stage of underground work, when the great majority of the higher-ranking officers had been executed, this did not matter. The decision of the Commandant of the *AK* District of Silesia had, at all events, the basic advantage of preventing an eventual struggle for the leadership. The ambitions of the members of the *Kampfgruppe Auschwitz* were far-reaching, and might prove dangerous at a crucial moment.

At the same time as Cyrankiewicz was going up in the hierarchy of the camp underground, the *Kampfgruppe* was weakened considerably, for Hermann Langbein was sent away in a transport. The camp now had a new Commandant, Richard Baer, who had allowed the Political Department to regain some of its influence. Dr. Wirths's enemy Gerhard Lachmann, whom Liebehenschel had moved elsewhere, returned to this Department and it was probably he who put Langbein's name on the transport list. The latter's attempts to evade deportation came to nothing, and he was even beaten up by *Rapportführer* Oswald Kaduk. The transport left on August 25th; it consisted of 750 prisoners, mainly Poles, and was sent to *Borgward-Werken* in Bremen, a sub-camp of Neuengamme. On the very day before the

---

* Stacherski was hanged publicly in Dąbrowa Górnicza, in August 1944 (Z. Walter-Janke, *Armia Krajowa . . .*, p. 238). It may be presumed that the nomination was not sent later than this.

transport left Langbein was to have escaped from the camp to the Polish partisans, and only the lack of up-to-date liaison had prevented this.[28]

CHAPTER 11

Escapes and partisans; 'The Moll Plan'; the revolt
in the *Sonderkommando*; preparations for the
relief of the camp; the final actions of the
underground; evacuation

1

The acute change in the military situation, the approach of a decisive
solution, the uncertainty as to the fate of the camps and the prisoners,
were reasons why, towards the end of 1943 and in 1944, the number
of escapes reached its highest point.* Poles were the chief escapees,
for they were on their own ground and the local population gave
them assistance more willingly than to others. After them the Russians
were the most enterprising, for such was their nature and the Eastern
Front was coming nearer. Next came Jews, equally enterprising and
driven to despair by life in the camp and the nearness of the gas
chambers.

The escapes which took place during the years 1940–1941 and the
beginning of 1942 were purely individual, for the draconian punishments meted out in reprisal were such that the underground movement not only did not organize escapes but even forbade them.
It was only when, early in 1942, directives came from Berlin that
collective responsibility for escapes was to be abolished, that the
ZOW altered its position fundamentally and began to use escapees to
send its reports to Warsaw. The escapee himself still took his life
in his hands, for if caught he underwent cruel interrogation and
died on the gallows. It was only when Liebehenschel took over the
camp that this procedure was mitigated.

Up to 1943 escapees, when they were Poles, as a rule made for
Cracow and then Warsaw, Soviet citizens for the East and Jews for
the country from which they had been deported. Later on things
began to look different. Near the camp and in the Beskid mountains
to the south of Auschwitz, strong partisan units of the *AK* were operat-

---

* Altogether there escaped from Auschwitz and its sub-camps, chiefly Birkenau,
667 prisoners, of whom 16 were women. In 1940 – 2, in 1941 – 6, in 1942 – 120,
in 1943 – 310, in 1944 – 209, in 1945 – 1. Of these 270 were certainly recaptured,
232 Poles escaped, 93 Soviet citizens, 76 Jews, 29 Gypsies, 27 Czechs, 20 Germans,
4 Ukrainians. There are no exact data for others (T. Iwaszko, *Ucieczki* . . . , pp.
45 and 49).

ing and Poles who managed to get outside the barbed wire usually joined them. These Poles were, of course, members of the *ZOW* or affiliated political groups and made use of the secret liaison between the camp underground and the outside world. This type of escape in 1944 grew to such an extent that 21 ex-prisoners of Auschwitz served in a single partisan unit, code-named *Garbnik*, and the first company was commanded by Józef Barcikowski, who escaped from the camp on the night of October 23rd–24th, 1944. This directing of escapees to the *AK* was closely connected with the underground's plans for taking up arms when the camp was about to be wound up or was otherwise threatened.

In June 1944 the numbers of escapes increased and at that time an incident occurred in connection with plans to free Cyrankiewicz. Almost from the beginning of his sojourn in Auschwitz his colleagues from the *PPS* had considered ways and means of getting him out. Adam Rysiewicz had come from Cracow to Brzeszcze to survey the terrain for himself, and had enlisted several new people on the spot. In October 1942 he sent Cyrankiewicz a secret letter suggesting that he should try to escape from a *Kommando* which worked outside the camp putting up new buildings with civilian workers .

Workmen's overalls and personal papers were prepared, while in the Słowacki theatre in Cracow two wigs were made, as the young Socialist Kazimierz Hałoń, known in the camp as Kazimierz Wrona, was to escape with Cyrankiewicz. Just when it appeared that the plan might come off, the Political Department summoned Cyrankiewicz and ordered him to sew on to his striped clothing a badge with the letters 'I.L.' This was short for *Im Lager* and meant that the prisoner was politically dangerous and was forbidden to work outside the barbed-wire enclosure. Thus the idea of Cyrankiewicz escaping by means of an outside *Kommando* had to be given up. On February 10th, 1943, Hałoń escaped alone.[1]

Once again preparations were made and Cyrankiewicz was supplied with a wig and civilian clothes, but this time the *SS*-men discovered what was happening and took him to the bunker, from which he was saved only by great luck. Months passed, and yet once more the attempt was renewed. It is hard to say what Cyrankiewicz's own intentions were. Did he want to stay in the camp and direct underground activities there, or to regain his freedom and join his *PPS* comrades in close association with the *AK*? In the middle of 1944, in the obtaining political situation, this might have been assessed one way or the other. On June 15th news came to Cracow that Cyrankiewicz was going to make another attempt to escape. Immediately three men – Edward Hałoń, Tadeusz Bundzewicz and Ignacy Sękowski – from the *PPS* fighting organization left for Auschwitz to help their comrade when he got outside the camp.

A little later Adam Rysiewicz left Cracow. Together with two other members of the fighting organization – Władysław Denikiewicz and Ryszard Krogulski – he went to the home of the Kornaś family at Spytkowice, where Cyrankiewicz was to come. Once again the escape did not come off: Cyrankiewicz sent a secret letter to say that important affairs kept him in the camp. Rysiewicz, with his companions and young Józef Kornaś, went to the station at Ryczków on June 23rd to catch the train to Cracow. The presence of the four young men on the almost deserted platform caught the attention of the German railway police. Several policemen went up to Rysiewicz and Krogulski and began to search them. At the last second Denikiewicz and Kornaś managed to jump to one side and Denikiewicz used the momentary confusion to leap onto the moving train. Rysiewicz, before raising his hands, managed to fire his pistol through his pocket, without pulling it out, but the shot missed. He fell dead from a burst of a machine-pistol, and next to him fell Krogulski, fatally wounded. Józef Kornaś, who was still on the platform and was unarmed, had to try and escape by flight. He hid in the bushes behind the station building, but the Germans killed him with their grenades. The sole survivor, Denikiewicz, returned to Cracow alone with the bad news.[2] Once again Cyrankiewicz's attempt at escape came to nothing and three men including Adam Rysiewicz, one of the bravest and most valuable members of the fighting organization of the *PPS*, paid for it with their lives.

After this loss it became imperative to strengthen the fighting units of the *PPS* near the camp by adding to their ranks men who knew all the camp secrets, namely new escapees. The choice fell on two veterans of underground work who had been preparing their escape for a long time, the young Socialist Konstanty Jagiełło, and his friend Tomasz Sobański. Having worked for a long time in the Roof-covering *Kommando*, and so having a good deal of freedom of movement around the whole camp, and being soldiers of the *ZOW*, they knew all the secrets of Auschwitz and could not only give valuable information but also play an effective part in operations around the camp. They were to escape in order to give a helping hand to others, who intended to escape in their turn and join the partisans operating in the vicinity.

Sobański, through his organizational contacts in the Labour Assignment Office was made a Foreman of the Roof-covering *Kommando* and made Jagiełło his deputy. They got ready civilian workers' overalls, sewed into them documents and photographs of incidents in the camp and, thanks to their job, moved into the main camp. This was important as the *Kommando* had latterly been working in Birkenau, so when the escape was discovered the search would be concentrated there. During the night of June 28th–29th the prisoners got away from the camp, slipping out from a hiding place in the neighbourhood of the munitions work *DAW*, just outside the barbed wire. They were helped at the final stage by companions from the underground. After sixty hours of hiding by day and marching by night they found themselves in Brzeszcze, in the house of the Pytlik family, which had afforded shelter to many fugitives. After having rested they walked to Cracow, escorted by two members of the fighting organization of the *PPS* near the camp, Władysław Pytlik and Edward Hałoń. In Cracow they handed over all the documentary evidence to the Committee of Help for the Prisoners of Concentration Camps (*PWOK*), were given identity cards, had the camp numbers, tattooed on their left forearms, removed by doctors, and were ready to take up their next duties. Before they could do this they had to stay on in Cracow for a while to supplement the reports they had brought with them. These related to the plans of the central camp and of Birkenau and some of the nearest small sub-camps, and the disposition of the *SS* forces.[3]

Three weeks later, equipped with arms and names of good contacts, they left for the area near Auschwitz. They were accompanied by Jerzy Tabeau, who as Jerzy Wesołowski had also been in Auschwitz and had escaped on October 19th, 1943.[4] Supported by local people, and hiding mainly in the houses of the Nikiel and Kozioł families, they formed a new fighting unit of the *PPS* which, with the help of the *AK* partisans and secret contacts inside the camp, organized assistance to further escapees from Auschwitz, giving them immediate protection, guiding them over dangerous terrain and sending them on to join units fighting near the camp. The unit was commanded by Jagiełło who was directly under the orders of Edward Hałoń, who after Rysiewicz's death had taken over his duties.

The summer and autumn of 1944 saw further escapes by members of the camp military underground who headed for the partisan units of the Home Army. One of these units, commanded by Major Jan Panczakiewicz, carried the code-name *Skala* and reached battalion strength with about 500 men. At this juncture of the war this was quite possible, since the Germans, under pressure from the Eastern Front, no longer were at their former strength, and no longer had the same will to fight. The unit fought against the retreating Germans on the territory of the General Gouvernement in the region of Miechów, Jędrzejów and Kielce, about 40–60 miles to the north-east of the camp,[5] but escapees from Auschwitz managed to reach it even there.*

---

* Their names are in Appendix III, item 28.

The partisan unit *Sosienki,* commanded by Lieutenant Jan Wawrzy-czek, and comprising about 80–100 men, was fighting very much nearer, in the Silesian Beskids, 25 miles to the south of the camp. It was constantly reinforced by escapees, who were among its best soldiers.* In the same direction from the camp, but a few miles further away in the Żywiecki Beskids, operated another partisan unit, *Garbnik,* which consisted of about 200 soldiers, one of whose company commanders, operating independently, was an escaped prisoner, Lieutenant Józef Barcikowski. Naturally other escapees, his recent fellow-inmates, preferred to join him.† Wawrzyczek knew this and when prisoners reached *Sosienki,* had them posted to Barcikowski.[6] There was also a small *PPS* unit in the region of Barania Góra, in the Silesian Beskids.

Partisan units were badly needed near Auschwitz, for, in the event of a fight for the camp, their help would be required. But in the preceding months, when there was no basis for an attack on the *SS* guard and hardly any chance of success, operations in the immediate vicinity of the camp had to be restricted to fighting *Wehrmacht* detachments and attacks on German units, which had no connection with the camp. Every attack on the *SS*-men of the Auschwitz garrison guarding the camp would have produced retaliation against the prisoners. Thus there existed a very strict rule of not firing on *SS*-men in the vicinity of the camp.[7]

2

On August 1st, 1944, an uprising took place in Warsaw organized by the Home Army against the German occupation forces.‡ When fighting broke out the Soviet divisions were on the east side of the Vistula, a few miles away from the city. To the north of the capital, near Modlin, they had already crossed the river, as they had also done much further south, not far from Sandomierz. This town lies about 80 miles north-east of Cracow, the ancient Polish capital, while Auschwitz is 30 miles from Cracow in a westerly direction.

In this situation, when it was hard to say how long the front on the

---

* Their names are in Appendix III, item 29.

† Their names are in Appendix III, item 30.

‡ On August 12th there arrived in Birkenau the first transport of civilians from Warsaw (1,984 men and boys and 3,175 women and girls). They were not tattooed with numbers, but otherwise were treated in the same way as all other prisoners (D. Czech, *Calendar. . . .,* No. 7, p. 76).

Vistula would hold out, the SS authorities, fearing the confusion that had arisen at the evacuation of Majdanek, where the Soviet units caught 5 SS-men, began to make urgent plans for the liquidation of the camp at Auschwitz and its nearest sub-camps. This time it was not a question of finding sufficient trains to carry the prisoners westward. At the beginning of September Rudolf Höss came once more to Auschwitz with an order from Himmler for the complete liquidation of Birkenau together with the prisoners in it, the gas chambers and the crematoria.[8] The whole camp was to be razed to the ground and every trace of the crimes committed there were to be wiped out.

Höss fully understood the difficulties of the task. Birkenau at that time contained nearly 90,000 prisoners, men and women, and covered a large area, to say nothing of the four great gas chambers and crematoria, the *Canada* barracks and many other installations. He inspected the situation personally and asked several experienced SS-men for advice on how to carry out Himmler's order. One of them, SS Sergeant Otto Moll, former *Kommandoführer* of the Penal Company and now in charge of the crematoria, put forward a plan with details of what would have to be done and what would be needed to do it. This plan, known as the *Moll Plan*, called for the use of motorized SS units, artillery to bombard the barracks, six bombers and a large number of people to cart away the ruins, level the ground and give it an innocent appearance. If he were given the means, Moll undertook to carry out his plan.[9]

All this was strictly secret, but there was one SS-man, Corporal Joachim Wolf, who warned the prisoners of what was planned. For some months he had been in contact with Józef Mikusz, one of the leading members of the ZOW at Birkenau. Wolf's warning was in general terms, but Mikusz passed it on at once to the central camp. The underground intelligence service sent an urgent report to Cracow for transmission to London, so that the BBC might broadcast the existence of the plan for total destruction of the camp. The report went off by radio during the first half of September, and soon afterwards was used by the BBC in the guise of a Reuter communiqué.*

---

*H. Wróbel. *Likwidacja* . . ., p. 15. She says that in the evidence for the Nuremberg trial there is a document indicating that the Germans took note of the BBC broadcast. I tried to ascertain the date of the broadcast and wrote to the *Written Archives Centre* (Caversham Park, Reading), but received the answer that in principle the wartime bulletins of the BBC's service had not been preserved. The only extant mention of Birkenau was a bulletin for German women entitled 'News for Women', dated 16.6.1944, on German atrocities in Czechoslovakia and the gassing of Czech Jews at Birkenau in June 1944. (Letter to the author, dated 21.8.1972).

It is hard to say how far the report from the camp underground, sent to London through the signals section of the *AK* and used by the BBC,* contributed to the *SS* giving up their plan, but the fact remains that it was abandoned. Another factor which might have caused delay and finally the dropping of the project was that the *SS*-men who were to carry it out demanded orders in writing, and these Berlin was reluctant to give.

Although the plans for the complete destruction of Birkenau were not realized, the Political Department started in good time to burn the files, which might serve as evidence. This began in July, immediately after the evacuation of Majdanek. The first documents to be burnt, in special stoves built into the crematoria, were the lists of all those prisoners who had been taken straight from the ramp to the gas chambers.[10]

3

The *Sonderkommando* (Special Working-Group) which was forced to carry out the ghastly work at the gas chambers, and the burning of bodies in pyres and in the crematoria, was established in 1942.[11] Initially the corpses were not burnt but buried beside Bunker No. 1, which served as a primitive gas chamber. For this work the *SS*-men chose only Jewish prisoners,† who came from various countries of occupied Europe. There was a practical reason for this, since the authorities wanted the whole procedure to move smoothly and without resistance. The members of the *Sonderkommando*, speaking many languages and dialects, could quieten down those being driven to their death, and this they did in the knowledge that they would gain

* The fact that the report was sent to London and not elsewhere is a further indication that the underground movement in Auschwitz, including the *Kampfgruppe*, had no contact either with the Red Army or with the Communist element in Poland (*PPR*) working with Soviet Russia.

† Only the *Obercapo* and some *Capos* were *Reichsdeutschen*. Also a few Poles were employed at the furnaces: Władysław Biskup, Józef Ilczuk, Jan Agrestowski, and Mieczysław Morawa. On January 5th, 1945, these men were evacuated to Mauthausen, where they were shot on April 3rd (D. Czech, *Calendar, op. cit.*, No. 7, p. 111). There were some other exceptions to the principle that only Jews were to work in the *Sonderkommando*. On April 16th, 1944, nineteen Soviet POWs were brought from the concentration camp at Majdanek and sent to the *Sonderkommando*. It has been impossible to establish whether these POWs were Jews, but they were probably not. (Wśród koszmarnej zbrodni, *Auschwitz notebooks*, special issue [II], 1971, p. 152, f.n. 64).

nothing by behaving differently and that by kindly treatment they could at least mitigate the anguish of the victims' last moments.[12]

The first *Sonderkommando* consisted of eighty prisoners, who were themselves gassed in August 1942. The next *Kommando*, comprising at first 150 and later 300 prisoners, was employed at digging up and burning on pyres the bodies which their predecessors had buried a few months earlier. This second group was also killed by gas on December 3rd, 1942. In its place came a third, also doomed to die within a few months.

At first the *Sonderkommando* lived in one of the barracks in the men's part of Birkenau in Section B I *b*, and when this section was allotted to the women, the *Kommando* took over barracks No. 13 in Section B II *d*.* There they remained until the end of June 1944, to move finally into the extermination area and live in the attics of crematoria Nos. II, III and IV.[13] These were completed in June 1943, and from this date commences the large increase in numbers of the men who worked there. The figures varied, but during about a year and a half they remained 1,000 or so.†

Every prisoner who was sent to work at the gas chambers and the crematoria was doomed, and all the members of the *Sonderkommando* knew this, but it was very hard to revolt. On the one hand the *SS*-men guarded them day and night and any violation of discipline was punished by death; on the other hand they were given a number of privileges which the other prisoners at Auschwitz and Birkenau· never enjoyed. When in June 1944 the whole *Kommando* was moved

---

* The *Sonderkommando's* barracks were separated from barracks No. 11, in which lived the Penal Company, by common wash-rooms divided by a wooden partition. The author, when he was in the Penal Company, talked to members of the *Sonderkommando* through holes in the planks. News from the outside world was passed on, and food was exchanged.

† On August 30th 1944 the strength of the *Sonderkommando* employed in burning bodies in the crematoria was:

Kommando 57–B crematorium II	– day shift	– 111 prisoners
Kommando 57–B crematorium II	– night shift	– 104 ,,
Kommando 58–B crematorium III	– day shift	– 110 ,,
Kommando 58–B crematorium III	– night shift	– 110 ,,
Kommando 59–B crematorium IV	– day shift	– 110 ,,
Kommando 59–B crematorium IV	– night shift	– 109 ,,
Kommando 60–B crematorium V	– day shift	– 110 ,,
Kommando 60–B crematorium V	– night shift	– 110 ,,
	Total =	874 ,,

(D. Czech, *Calendar op. cit.*, No. 7, p. 81).
A further 400 prisoners were employed burning bodies in trenches. They went on living in Section B II *d*.

into the area of the crematoria, everyone in it found good living conditions. Each man had a comfortable bed with a down quilt, slept in pyjamas from *Canada*, could use the showers as often as he wished and in his spare time could read books, of which there were many.[14] They had plenty of alcohol and their food was very different from that served up to other prisoners.

Waiting for us is a table covered with a damask cloth. Fine monogrammed porcelain plates, silver cutlery, china jugs – all this also comes from the transports. The table is laid with all the good things which people deported into the unknown take with them. There are various tinned foods, bacon, salami, fruit juice, cakes and chocolate. [15]

By providing such conditions the camp command hoped to weaken any desire for revolt or attempt to fight, and in fact this is what happened. Nevertheless some attempts by Jews to save themselves or refuse to obey orders did take place at Auschwitz under various circumstances and at various times. In 1942, when 1,500 Polish Jews were being led to the gas chambers, panic broke out among them, for the *Capo* of the Jewish group working nearby, a French Jew by the name of Morris, told them they were going to their death. The transport turned on the *SS*-men escorting them, and about 40 members of the *Kommando* joined the fight on their side. All, of course, were murdered.[16] Another incident took place on October 23rd, 1943, when *Rapportführer* Josef Schillinger was killed by a Jewess with his own pistol. While Jews from Hungary were being murdered, on two occasions large groups tried to escape and hide. On the evening of the 25th May, 1944, as the Hungarian Jews were being led to the crematorium building, they sensed something and scattered into a nearby wood. The *SS*-men switched on the searchlights and shot them all. The same happened three days later. Attempts at unorganized escape at the last minute always ended in a massacre.

The *Sonderkommando* themselves, though doomed to death and aware of their fate, for a long time made no attempt at a break for freedom. It was only when the Hungarian transports began to arrive, when the murder madness had reached a paroxysm, that more concrete plans began to take shape. This was partly due to the Soviet POWs, already mentioned, of whom nineteen were brought from Majdanek and sent to the *Sonderkommando*. They had been forced to do the same sort of work at Majdanek and now, at Birkenau, they began to incite their companions to make secret preparations for a risky fight in the hope of a break for freedom. A group of leaders was formed consisting of Józef Deresiński, Załman Gradowski, Jankiel Handelsman, Ajzyk Kalniak, Lajb Langfus, Załman Lewental,

Lajb Panusz and Józef Warszawski, whose real name was Józef Dorębus.[17] They were all from Poland, although some of them had emigrated to other countries before the war. They had made contact with the Union of Military Organization, mainly through the Poles employed at the furnaces of the crematoria,[18] and a plan was prepared whereby when the *SS*-men set about liquidating the camp and murdering the prisoners, the *Sonderkommando* would start to fight together with the whole camp.

They had a few weapons and hoped to get more from the *SS*-men in a surprise assault. They intended to blow up all the crematoria and cut the wires of the women's camp and other neighbouring sections to facilitate a mass escape.

These plans were to have been carried out in June 1944, while the *Sonderkommando* still inhabited barracks No. 13 on Section B II *d*. Everything was ready; the majority of the members of the *Kommando* had been let into the secret and were ready to fight, the hour of the outbreak had been fixed, a number of the conspirators had almost come into the open, when at the last moment the plan was called off. The revolt in the *Sonderkommando* was to have been synchronized with the taking up of arms by the whole camp underground, and for that it was still too soon. The *SS*-men noticed the peculiar behaviour of several prisoners and killed some of them. The first to be shot was the *Capo* of crematorium No. II, the Jew Kamiński. At that very moment the camp authorities came to the conclusion that the· *Sonderkommando* must be separated from the camp and transferred it to the area of the crematoria. Contacts with other prisoners were made very much more difficult,[19] and plans for an uprising had to be postponed; they had to wait for more favourable conditions.

The leaders of the secret fighting group in the area of the crematoria had luckily survived, so further preparations could go on. Contact was made with Jewish girls in the munitions factory, *Union-Werke*, situated within the camp. From them, through Israel Gutman and Jehuda Laufer, the group's leaders began to receive small quantities of explosives.[20] They maintained contact throughout with the camp underground at Birkenau and through it with the central camp. The aim was to agree upon a common operation, but this was difficult, for the Camp Military Council saw no chance of winning a battle against the *SS* garrison. The *Sonderkommando* leaders grew alarmed by the delay. The gassing of the Hungarian Jews was now nearly completed, and very soon all those who had taken part in it could expect to be liquidated. The atmosphere of anxiety grew from day to day.

On October 7th the camp underground military authorities sent an urgent warning that the *SS* had taken their decision and the liquidation of the *Sonderkommando* was to take place any day now.[21] Its leaders at once met in crematorium No. IV to decide when to begin to fight, but were surprised during their deliberations by the *Capo*, a German criminal. Lest he should betray them to the *SS* he was killed on the spot, and the signal was given to attack the guards. Unfortunately the most important part of the plan, which might have afforded some chance of success, was not put into effect, as fighting broke out during the day instead of by night. Hope also vanished for any help from the partisan units, which had not been informed and could not possibly move in the vicinity of the camp during daylight. The men in *Kommando* 59–B at crematorium No. IV got out the few weapons they had and disarmed the *SS*-men. Using the explosives in their possession they blew up the crematorium, which burst into flames. After cutting the wires, the prisoners got away into the nearby wood. At the sound of the shots and explosions *Kommando* 57–B at crematorium No. II started to fight. The *Reichsdeutsche Obercapo*, and one *SS*-man were thrown into the burning furnace alive; one soldier was beaten to death. The fighters grabbed a few weapons and cut the wires of their own fence and those of the women's camp. They hoped that the mass escape would thus embrace the whole of Birkenau and have a better chance of success. Unfortunately they turned not northeast, in the direction of the Vistula, but south-west, in the direction of the sub-camp Rajsko. They thus remained within the area of the camp's jurisdiction and their chances of escape were minimal.[22] Crematoria Nos. III and V did not join in the fight, for the *SS*-men there were able to take the situation in hand at once.

The camp sirens wailed, and within a few minutes strong units of *SS*-men with machine-guns and dogs drove up in trucks and surrounded the area covered by the revolt. After a skirmish in the wood near crematorium No. IV nearly all the escaping prisoners lay dead. Those who had gone to the south were pursued and surrounded in a barn near Rajsko. Not wishing to take any risks, the *SS*-men set fire to the barn and shot the prisoners as they ran out. A few hours later all was quiet. The bodies of the murdered men were brought in and laid out on the area of crematorium No. IV. There were about 250 of them, including Józef Deresiński, Załman Gradowski, Ajzyk Kalniak, Lajb Langfus, Lajb Panusz and Józef Warszawski, the leader.* When the remainder were counted it was found that twelve were missing. The *SS*-men wanted to go after them at once, but at that

---

* The fact that J. Warszawski was at the head of the whole fighting group is confirmed by Z. Lewental and I. Gutman. Both these men survived the fighting in the *Sonderkommando*, Lewental as one of the prisoners in it, Gutman as a liaison man outside.

very moment the air-raid sirens began to wail. The chances of the twelve who had managed to get away increased. Temporarily unable to pursue them, the *SS*-men shot on the spot about 200 prisoners from the crews of the two crematoria which had revolted. In the evening, when the all clear was sounded, *SS* patrols with dogs set off in search of the twelve who were still missing. It transpired that they had managed to reach the other side of the Vistula, but, being exhausted, they had hidden in an empty building where they were found. They were killed and their bodies were brought back to the camp.[23] Despite the disparity in strength, the prisoners of the *Sonderkommando* managed to kill 3 *SS*-men: Corporals Rudolf Erler, Willi Preeze and Jozef Purke, and wounded a further twelve.[24]

The Political Department had some information about the *Sonderkommando's* outside contacts, for on October 9th three Jewesses in the *Union-Werke*, Ella Gartner, Toszka and Regina, were arrested.* The following day two more Jewesses went to the bunker. One of them was Róża Robota, who had acted as a messanger between Ella Gartner and Wróbel, a member of the *Sonderkommando*, who collected explosives from her.[25] That same day fourteen men who worked at crematoria III and V, but had not taken part in the fighting, were arrested, among them Jankiel Handelsman, one of the leaders. They were sent to the bunker and a cruel interrogation began. The *SS*-men, as usual, tried to find out who had organized the revolt and what were their links with the rest of the camp. The interrogation was fruitless, but none of the arrested men came out alive. A skeleton *Sonderkommando*, now consisting of 198 prisoners, continued to work in two shifts at crematoria Nos. II, III and V.[26]

4

The advance of the Red Army deep into Poland in 1944 made it probable that the camp at Auschwitz would be liberated from that direction. This was a major factor in planning any fight for the camp, for which the underground had been preparing from the very beginning. Witold Pilecki, before he began to build up his secret network, set out the reasons for which it was being founded and had stated clearly that the culminating point would be 'preparing one's own units to take over the camp, if the moment should come in the form of an order to drop either weapons or personnel (parachutists) inside the camp'. Of course when Pilecki had gone voluntarily to Auschwitz in

---

* It has not been possible to ascertain the surnames of the last two women.

order to organize an underground network there, the war situation was very different from that at the end of 1944.

In 1940 the Soviet Union had a pact with Hitler and was supplying him with great amounts of raw materials and food before his attack in the West, and there were no indications that this pact would be discontinued. Pilecki had reason to believe that the Western Front would hold and that Hitler would be defeated there, and that Poland, which had been conquered and divided between the two occupying powers, would be liberated from the west. During five years of war the military and political situation had completely changed; the Western Allies, although now winning, were still very far away, but this did not alter the fact that a fight for the camp would only be possible if it received very strong assistance from outside. By the fortunes of war, the Soviet armies were now nearing the gates and any plans for a fight for freedom would have to be agreed with them.

When on August 1st, 1944, the uprising broke out in Warsaw, it received no help from the Red Army, standing on the other side of the Vistula, and the insurgents had to capitulate to the Germans on October 2nd. Soviet and Communist sources state that the chief reason for this was lack of liaison between the Home Army and the Soviet Command, and the fact that the Poles did not want this liaison, being still orientated towards London and the West. Without going into this controversy here, it must be pointed out that the situation in the camp was different, given the existence of the largely Communist *Kampfgruppe Auschwitz*, which in its proclamation had declared clearly that 'the chief factor in the armed conflict against Hitler is the Soviet Union and the Red Army'. Representatives of the *Kampfgruppe* were in the Camp Military Council and had a say in the decisions of the camp underground. Moreover there existed in the camp a strong Soviet underground group, organized by Soviet officers, so it could not be objected that there were no forces in Auschwitz ready and willing to co-operate with the Red Army.

And yet there was no such co-operation. No sources, whether Soviet, Communist Polish or any other, have claimed even in general terms that there was any liaison between the camp underground and the Red Army.* Nor does any source give details of liaison between this underground and the Polish Communists (*PPR*) in German-

* The lack of liaison is confirmed by H. Langbein (conversation with the author, Paris, June 10th, 1972). It is also maintained by Peter Kalb, a German from Frankfurt-am-Main, who is writing a doctoral thesis on sociological aspects of the underground movement in Auschwitz. He was in Poland in February 1972 and visited the Auschwitz Museum. Mieczysław Kieta told him that the *Kampfgruppe Auschwitz* sent a courier to the Red Army, but he was unable to give the man's name, the date of departure or any other details. (Conversation with the author, London, March 23rd 1972).

occupied territory. On the contrary, Tadeusz Hołuj of the *Kampf-gruppe*, who made every effort to present its activities in the brightest of colours, had to admit that attempts at such liaison were a complete failure.[27]

It is hard to say definitely why the Soviet Command was not interested in freeing the camp at Auschwitz and making contact with the underground there. The liberation of prisoners of so many nationalities would, it might be thought, have been good propaganda for the USSR. It may be presumed that there were two reasons. Firstly, Stalin conducted military operations cold-bloodedly, subordinating them wholly to his political aims, and secondly, the Soviet attitude to prisoners-of-war and all other prisoners was generally hostile. Anyone who fell into the hands of the enemy was worthy of contempt and not help. Many cases are known of Soviet soldiers going to concentration camps after their return from German captivity. Aleksey Lebedev, leader of the Soviet underground group in Auschwitz, met this fate.

The facts being what they were, members of the Auschwitz under-ground had to turn their eyes to the West, whatever their political sympathies. The leaders of the *Kampfgruppe* were well aware of this, although they would have preferred it to be otherwise. This is why the list of *SS*-men drawn up by them went to London and not to Moscow. It also explains why, when the *Kampfgruppe* joined the Camp Military Council, they accepted without reservation its link with the *AK* District of Silesia and so its command.

From the time that Witold Pilecki had reported to the Home Army H.Q. in Warsaw on August 25th, 1943, almost a year had gone by, but the position of its leaders in regard to Auschwitz had not altered. Conditions were still not favourable for a country-wide uprising against the Germans, so only local mobilization of larger units of the Home Army was carried out to attack the retreating divisions of the *Wehrmacht*.[28] This operation was given the code-name *Tempest*. Help from the West by air was still limited by political decisions and technical difficulties, although the air bases had been transferred to southern Italy.[29] Only if at least one of these conditions was realized, i.e. a country-wide uprising or effective Western help, could there be any question of starting a fight in the camp with any chance of success and of saving some of the prisoners.* Nevertheless,

---

* In a U.S. air-raid on September 13th, 1944, on the industrial plants of I.G. Farben, *Buna-Werke*, the central Auschwitz camp and Birkenau were also hit, killing fifteen *SS*-men, forty prisoners and thirty civilian workers and wounding very many (D. Czech, *Calendar, op. cit.*, No. 7, p. 85). This raid, however, was aimed solely at destroying a war production target, and had no connection with any plans for the relief of the camp.

bearing in mind the necessity of helping the prisoners if the *SS* embarked on their plan of liquidation, the H.Q. of the Home Army issued directives approving preparations for an emergency.

Orders regarding the safety and evacuation of the concentration camps were issued at the middle of July of this year. The Commandant of the Silesia District is keeping an eye on the situation. Further possibilities are, however, limited. Nothing can be done within the framework of *Tempest*, since they are being evacuated much sooner than expected.[30]

These preparations, which finally took the form of a detailed plan, were made by Maj. Zygmunt Janke (code-name *Walter*), when, towards the end of 1943, he took over the command of the Silesia District. The plan envisaged the use of *AK* partisan units operating

Aleksey Lebedev   Bruno Baum   Zbigniew Raynoch

Rudolf Vrba   Stefan Jasieński   Władysław Grohs

Leading men in the resistance movement.

in the area and some of the forces of the *AK* Auschwitz Region, suitably armed. Motorized transport was to bring the partisan units to the vicinity of the camp, from where they would take up their positions for an attack to be delivered in complete surprise between midnight and 1 a.m. The *SS* barracks were to be cut off by machine-gun fire. It was reckoned that the camp could be kept open for half an hour only. By that time German troops stationed near the camp would have come on the scene, so that the partisans retreating after the attack would be able to take with them at the most 200–300 prisoners. The rest would have to save themselves as best they could. The retreat would be southward towards the Beskids.

This plan was drawn up in the spring of 1944, when the camp contained nearly 100,000 prisoners. Any attempt at liberating them would thus have ended in the massacre of several thousands, while at best freeing a few hundred only. Since even this degree of success was doubtful, the *AK* decided that the operation would not be carried out unless it became necessary to give immediate help in the case of mass-murder of the prisoners. The *AK* commander in Warsaw, Gen. Tadeusz Komorowski (code-name *Bór*), accepted this situation.[31]

Apart from preparations for an emergency, the H.Q. of *AK* wished also to have a general and unbiased picture of the situation, and therefore, in full agreement with the command of the Silesia District, it sent its own man to the area near the camp. The choice fell on. 2nd Lieut. Stefan Jasieński, a parachutist from Britain, specially trained for intelligence work.[32] He was sent from Warsaw just before the Uprising, at the end of July 1944. Under the code-name *Urban* he reported to the commander of the District, Maj. Janke. Jasieński at that time was probably using the name Janusz Kręcki.[33]

Maj. Janke personally took charge of Jasieński, conveyed him to Kańczuga on the Soła river and put him into the care of the inspector of the *AK* Region Bielsko, Capt. Antoni Morawski; Jasieński lived in the home of J. Chlebus. He was provided with necessary contacts in the area and means of secret liaison with the Camp Military Council. Janke also told him the details of the emergency plan described above, for an attack on the camp and also plan 'W', which covered the operations of the whole District in the event of a country-wide uprising.

Plan 'W' had now been changed. Since it was to be carried out at a time when the German resistance was completely broken, it would be necessary first to acquire more arms, then mobilize a large number of men as quickly as possible. Arms were expected from parachute drops, carried out from southern Italy, and the District had made ready a number of dropping zones. It was also anticipated that before the fighting was over, arms would be dropped straight into the camp for the use of the military underground there. Men were to come in the first instance from the partisan units, the Silesian Legion and the military camp underground, and only then from local mobilization.[34] During a general uprising the chances of saving a large number of prisoners and absorbing them into the neighbouring villages and towns would be considerably greater.

Jasieński began a careful reconnaissance of the district and thanks to the contacts provided by Maj. Janke met many people who had been operating there for a long time. He also established secret liaison with the Camp Military Council, in particular with Bernard Świerczyna.[35] Widening his contacts, he also met the men who organized the partisan units round the camp and the patrols that helped in escapes. He gave them the impression of a man wholly devoted to his tasks, but inexperienced in operating on such different terrain as that near the camp. This was probably why he fell into an ambush towards the end of September, when hiding in Kęty with the Paw family. He was on his way with Kazimierz Paw to meet the surveyor Kazimierz Petkowski, when at night, in a gorge near the rendezvous, they were surprised by two armed Germans. Paw escaped by running away; Jasieński, wounded in the hip and stomach, ran to the nearby manor house at Malec, but was caught. That night, or early next morning, he was brought to the camp at Auschwitz.[36]

Jasieński's wounds were severe, and the Political Department ordered him to be put into Hospital Block No. 21 for an operation. This was performed by the prisoner doctor Tadeusz Orzeszko, who had the patient put into the room of male nurse Jan Wolny, knowing the latter to be a member of the camp underground.[37] The wounded man was given various sedatives to keep him in a semi-conscious state so that he could not be taken for interrogation. By thus gaining time it was possible to warn the appropriate men in the underground and avoid further consequences. A prisoner, Tadeusz Szymański, was sent from the Prisoners' Registration Office to take down his personal details. Jasieński confided in him and said that the news of his arrest must be sent outside the camp at once, while inside the camp '*Benek*' must be informed.[38] The news was passed on without delay to Kazimierz Smoleń and Tadeusz Wąsowicz, who worked in the Registration Office, and through them was conveyed further. An emergency report went to Cracow and to Konstanty Jagiełło, who after his escape from the camp had joined a fighting group close by. *Benek* was Bernard Świerczyna, at this time *Capo* of the Clothing Store and a member of the Camp Military Council. Jan Wolny also immediately informed his underground contacts about Jasieński. For a few days the wounded man was left in peace, then he was

The wooden door of the death cell in the bunker, with the pictures carved by Stefan Jasieński. At the front, a chalice; higher to the left, a missal (Jasieński was very religious); beside the missal a sabre, the end of a cavalry lance and a pennant (he served in the cavalry); beneath the sabre, a motor-cycle and a tank; beneath the motor-cycle, a greyhound (he used to go to the dog races in Glasgow); to the right of the sabre, the parachute corps emblem, a plane and a parachutist; to the left of the chalice, a drawing board (he was an architect); to the right, the Jasieński family crest.

The words *Kołodziej* . . ., above the parachutist, were written by somebody else.

taken to the Political Department for interrogation. Luckily he was prepared for questioning. From one of these sessions he never returned to the Hospital.[39]

We do not know the substance of the interrogation, or what the camp *Gestapo* learnt from *Urban*. He probably stood up to the cruel pressure, for nobody whom he knew or with whom he had taken refuge outside the camp was arrested. Inside the camp, too, none of his contacts was touched. It was said that photographic copies of the Camp Military Council's plans for military action were found on him, but this is unlikely, for there would have been obvious consequences. He lived for some time in the bunker in Block No. 11; on the wooden door of cell No. 21 there are drawings which could only have been done by him. There is the Jasieński family crest, the badge of the *Arkonia* student corps to which he belonged, the outline of an English bomber, a descending parachutist, a tank, a sabre and lance (he was a reserve officer of cavalry) and a small letter 's'.[40] It is known that he was still alive on December 3rd, since on that day he met Father Władysław Grohs, also brought from the bunker and awaiting interrogation in the corridor of the Political Department. This happened at a moment when some *AK* soldiers who had been arrested near the camp were led into the corridor. The *SS*-men busied themselves with the *AK* soldiers at once, and Father Grohs and Jasieński managed to exchange a few sentences. Jasieński learnt that the other was a priest and was aware who Jasieński was. He asked if he could make a quick confession, and did so in these extraordinary conditions.[41] He was a deeply religious man. Nothing more is known of his fate. Some say that he perished at Auschwitz in January 1945, just before the evacuation, others that he was transported to Germany about December 10th, apparently to Dachau.[42]

There never was any fight to liberate the camp. The country-wide uprising against the Germans never took place, for they retreated in good order, giving no chances to the poorly armed units of the *AK*. Help from the West proved too small even to save Warsaw. Both strategic and political considerations prevailed here, for Poland, by decision of the Western Allies, found herself in the Soviet sphere of influence.[43] The Red Army was not interested in freeing the camp and the *SS* luckily did not carry out the mass-murder of many thousands of prisoners there. The *Moll Plan* was abandoned. Only the *Sonder-kommando* took up arms, in very unfavourable conditions and without aid of any sort. There was good reason for it to fight, for all its members were threatened by death.

The fact that the camp military underground did not have an opportunity to carry out one of its basic aims does not mean that the organization was not necessary. It fulfilled its role during the years that the camp existed, giving physical and moral support to many prisoners. It was ready to fight for life if this became necessary and its existence was one reason why the *SS* decided not to murder the prisoners and raze the camp to the ground. If they had started to put this plan into operation they would have met with resistance. Perhaps then a small number of prisoners would have been saved, but the huge majority would have been put to death by the *SS*-men.[44] All the same, there would have been good reason to take up arms in a desperate, hopeless situation. But not otherwise.*

5

In the autumn of 1944 optimists in the camp were at last right when they maintained that Christmas would be the last one behind the wires. The Eastern Front was closing in and Soviet reconnaissance planes (*Kukuruzniki*) were often seen near the camp, though it was never the object of their flights. Several Soviet parachutists who joined the Home Army partisan units did not even know of the existence of the camp at Auschwitz. The *SS* command, unloading the camp of the most active elements, was still sending transports of Poles and Soviet citizens into Germany. In September and October 1944, twelve transports of men, consisting almost wholly of Polish and Soviet prisoners and comprising more than 10,000, left the camp for Buchenwald, Flossenbürg, Karlsruhe, Mauthausen and Stutthof.[45]

The *Kampfgruppe Auschwitz* had previously considered sending one of its leaders outside the camp to establish close co-operation with the partisans and assure itself of their help in case of need. Later this was transformed into the idea of sending out all the group's leaders. At this period, when escapes had become easier and more frequent, the plan was quite feasible, but before it could be realized, Langbein was removed from the camp. The plan was altered and taken over by the Camp Military Council, which was better able to put it into practice.

It was decided that five prisoners should escape: the Austrians,

---

* On August 22nd, 1944, the camp at Auschwitz, together with Birkenau and Monowice (Auschwitz I, II and III), contained 135,000 prisoners and was guarded by 3,250 *SS*-men. The mass transports into the heart of Germany reduced the numbers of prisoners from day to day, but they were still very large.

Ernst Burger and Rudolf Friemel, and the Poles, Czesław Duzel, Zbigniew Raynoch and Bernard Świerczyna.[46] The fact that among the leaders of the international military underground only Austrians and Poles escaped is a further indication that the Soviet group never joined it and the other groups were weak. Świerczyna was the most prominent among the escapees and had been longest in the camp and in the underground. This attempt to get away from the camp, as part of the plan for the final armed struggle, had to succeed if possible and was very carefully planned. As the end of the war was clearly approaching and some *SS*-men, especially *Volksdeutschen*, had shown their inclination to take sides with the prisoners, it was decided to use two of them who seemed to be quite trustworthy. One of them was *SS* Private Frank from Łódz, who had already worked with the camp underground for some time, the other was *SS* Corporal Johann Roth from Rumania. They were to drive out a big lorry with dirty linen for a laundry in Bielsko, with the escapees hidden inside it. At the same time the leader of the *PPS* fighting group near the camp, Konstanty Jagiełło, was warned to be ready to pick up and protect the five men and ensure that the latter phase of the escape went off smoothly.

Very early in the morning of October 27th, a lorry powered by wood-gas, driven by Johann Roth with Frank sitting beside him, started out from the central camp. On the platform, in the box containing wood used to make the gas, were hidden Ernst Burger and Bernard Świerczyna. The lorry went through the main gate without being halted and stopped by the *SS* Motor Workshops. There, unseen, the other three climbed on to it and crawled into the box: Rudolf Friemel, working in the local *Kommando*, and Czesław Duzel and Zbigniew Raynoch, employed in the nearby *SS* Hospital. The whole operation of loading, made easier by the morning mist, was covered by Ludwig Vesely, also from the *SS* Motor Workshops. From a short distance away it was observed by yet another prisoner who was in the secret, Karl Lill, who had taken Langbein's place as secretary to Dr. Wirths and worked in the *SS* Hospital. He saw the lorry leave the area of the workshops and make for the barrier and the control hut. Suddenly several uniformed men appeared around the vehicle, which had come to a stop. The *SS*-men began to climb up on to the platform. Unfortunately they were from the Political Department.[47]

Johann Roth had proved to be an unreliable contact. He had betrayed the escape and, instead of driving to Bielsko, he had driven up to the barracks occupied by the *SS*-men (*Blockführerstube*), at the gate of the main camp. There Frank was ordered to get down and the lorry was driven to Block No. 11. The prisoners were ordered to come out of the box, but only three could do so and that with great difficulty. Two, Duzel and Raynoch, had to be carried out, as they were unconscious. They had all taken cyanide, but the doses had not been strong enough. All five were shut in the bunker.

At the same time, in an inn belonging to Julian Dusik, about half a mile to the south of the cross-roads at Łęskie Zasole, the *PPS* local fighting group under Konstanty Jagiełło, with Franciszek Dusik, Kazimierz Ptasiński and Tomasz Sobański to help him, was lying in wait. They had ready five suits of civilian clothes and were looking out for the lorry from the camp. It drove up, but instead of their escaping companions armed *SS*-men jumped out of it, ran for such natural cover as they could find and made ready to fight. It was strictly forbidden to open fire on *SS*-men near the camp for fear of provoking reprisals on the prisoners and the civilian population, so the surrounded men could only try to get away quickly. Sobański alone was successful. Jagiełło was killed by a burst from a machine-gun; the others were caught and taken not to the camp but to the *Gestapo* in the town of Auschwitz. They were Franciszek Dusik, his uncle Julian Dusik, his daughter Wanda and Kazimierz Ptasiński. The latter managed to escape during the first night, for the *Gestapo* quarters, in an old rectory, were poorly guarded.

The interrogation which followed was carried out partly in the Political Department and partly in the town *Gestapo*. It may seem strange that the underground workers caught outside the camp were not brought at once to the camp bunker. This was probably in order to keep the matter secret and to surprise those arrested by means of a confrontation. If the *SS*-men reckoned on this, they underestimated the secret liaison between the camp and the outside world. Duzel and Raynoch had died without regaining consciousness, so in the bunker only Burger, Friemel and Świerczyna were interrogated, together with Piotr Piąty and Ludwig Vesely, arrested the following day as accomplices. In the old rectory, the Dusik family were questioned.*

By physical and psychological pressure every attempt was made to trace the secret links between the camp, the outside world and the partisans. The interrogation brought no results; nobody else was incriminated. There were attempts to get Dr. Wirths to intervene and save the imprisoned men; the leaders of the camp underground tried to play on differences between the camp command and the Political Department. There was a slight hope that the approaching

---

* Ten days later Franciszek and Julian Dusik were taken to the camp bunker and Wanda was sent to Ravensbrück. Franciszek and Wanda survived the war, Julian perished in the camp.

end of the war might influence the final decision, but all was in vain. Berlin upheld the camp *Gestapo's* demand for the death sentence.

On December 30th, 1944, after the evening roll-call, on the square in front of the Kitchen of the central camp, Ernst Burger, Rudolf Friemel, Piotr Piąty, Bernard Świerczyna and Ludwig Vesely were hanged from a single beam. They died bravely, and despite their maltreated bodies they managed to utter shouts proving that the interrogation had been unable to break them.

These were the last executions in the men's camp at Auschwitz.[48]

6

Less than two weeks later, on January 12th, 1945, the Red Army started its unexpected winter offensive. Its objective was the river Oder and Berlin, not Auschwitz; but it was bound to take in the camp as well, so the *SS*-men had to evacuate it speedily. It was also important to erase all traces of the crimes committed there. On November 26th, 1944, Himmler had given orders to destroy the crematoria. This concerned only three large installations, as crematorium No. IV had been destroyed during the *Sonderkommando* revolt. A *Kommando* was formed, composed of men and women prisoners, which set about taking down the fittings, to be sent to Gross Rosen and Mauthausen, and blowing up the walls and concrete with dynamite. This work went on all through December. Crematorium No. V was the last to be dismantled and destroyed, for in the middle of January 1945 the bodies of dead men and women prisoners were cremated there, although the gassing had ceased.

Documents were also destroyed. The first to be burnt were the transport lists of all those who had gone straight to the gas chambers; then came the files of the Political Department. At this time the camp doctor, *SS* Lieutenant Horst Fischer, gave the order for the records of the Hospital in the central camp to be burnt. The same happened to the records of the men's and women's Hospital in Birkenau.[49] The barracks of *Canada* were not left alone either. During December and half of January more than 500,000 articles of clothing were removed and the rest were burnt in the barracks on January 19th. Six barracks remained undestroyed.[50]

The transports which for months had been taking thousands of prisoners to the west had unloaded the camp very considerably, but it was still a huge multi-lingual conglomeration of men and women. At the final evening roll-call, on January 17th, the whole complex, comprising the central camp, Birkenau and Monowice with a number of sub-camps, contained 48,340 men and 18,672 women. By this time

The first Russian soldiers at the gates of Auschwitz on the 27th January 1945.

there was no rail transport available, for it was given up wholly to the *Wehrmacht*, which was retreating all along the vast front. The enormous mass of prisoners had to set out westwards on foot.

On January 18th a huge column of about 20,000 prisoners left the central camp. They were divided into groups of five hundred, given a few dry rations, surrounded by *SS*-men and marched off to the south-west. Similar columns left Birkenau, Monowice and many other sub-camps. The general direction was towards Gross Rosen.

It was frosty and snowing and most of the prisoners were in miserable physical condition. Anyone who lagged behind was shot by the road-side. Some tried to run away, and these, when they were noticed, were also killed out of hand. It was a real death march.

In the camp there remained only those who were absolutely unable to walk, and a few doctors and nurses. In the central camp there were about 1,200 of such sick prisoners; in Birkenau about 5,800, of whom 4,000 were women.[51]

At 3 p.m. on January 27th some small reconnaissance groups of the First Ukrainian Front appeared in the large area that had been under the jurisdiction of the camp. They were close on the heels of the retreating Germans.[52]

The 1,688 days of the history of the camp at Auschwitz had come to an end.

CONCLUSION

Several years of work on this subject and the knowledge gained from a large number of sources, as well as conversations and correspondence with many witnesses, have convinced me thàt the existence of the underground movement in the camp of Auschwitz is, as I have shown in this book, an unquestionable fact. This statement is important, since many ex-prisoners of Auschwitz, including men who were in the camp for several years, have declared and still declare that there was no such movement.

There are various reasons for this. Some really had no idea of its existence, for it was naturally kept secret and within close groups; others prefer to say that nothing was done because they themselves took no part in it; but the most numerous are those who have been made sceptical by post-war propaganda, especially in Poland. Various memoirs and narratives have tried to persuade former prisoners that the underground movement controlled all the *Kommandos* and sub-camps; that its achievements made the Germans quake with fear and forced Berlin to change its decisions; that its representative, a Pole, instructed the Commandant how to run the camp; that it put out manifestos and leaflets which were sent beyond the camp and were of considerable influence; and, finally, that it united and subordinated to itself numerous international groups, who unreservedly accepted a one-sided political ideology. Confronted with these claims, anyone who knew Auschwitz must declare that there was no such underground movement.

This propaganda, intended above all to provide a springboard for political and social ambition, has overshadowed the true story of the activities of the camp underground, which nevertheless existed and certainly accomplished something.

The greatest achievement of the underground was to restore men's faith in themselves and their abilities, a desperate necessity to the down-trodden prisoners. The whole camp system was aimed at intimidating and degrading thousands of men and women, so that they would be easy to control, like mindless cattle. This process was checked by those brave men and women who unhesitatingly stood up to the most frightful terror. These people came from various countries and from different social classes; they professed various religions and held many political opinions.

In this book it is Poles who appear the most frequently and Polish underground achievements are presented as the most outstanding; but this is not because of any desire to set Poles above others. It is simply by reason of the factual situation at the time. The camp at Auschwitz was set up by the Germans on Polish soil, and to the end Poles were the predominant element in it. Just outside the camp a strong Polish underground movement was operating, and its site was barely thirty miles from Cracow, the historic capital of Poland's earliest kings. If a similar camp had been set in France the French would have predominated, if in Holland the Dutch. Naturally at the beginning people of the same nationality, speaking the same language, got together; but later, as time passed, these differences lessened, and when men began to trust each other the closest ties were between those of similar character and attitude. The reason for different national groups coming together in underground work was that they had a similar understanding of the objectives of a camp underground organization. This is why the strong groups of Soviet citizens never joined the pro-Communist *Kampfgruppe Auschwitz* but co-operated with the Polish military underground, which the Communists stigmatized as a Fascist organization. Naturally common political opinions brought people together, but it was not conducive to unity of action when attempts were made to assert that these opinions were the only ones admissible. On the other hand it was important for the underground military cadres, like any other army, not to remain suspended in an ideological vacuum, and therefore *ZOW*, the Union of Military Organization, found support in both political wings, left and right. The underground groups of other nationals sought similar political reinforcement.

The second achievement of the camp underground was to establish contact with the outside world and send out information concerning all that was happening in the camp. Such contacts were mainly possible through Poles, as has been shown earlier.

A further achievement was to obtain medicines and food from outside and assist fellow-prisoners. These advantages were only available to a small number of people. But news from the outside world and the battle fronts, spread round the camp as widely as possible, was of great significance and was available to all. The news, often grossly exaggerated and crudely optimistic, raised people's hopes and helped them to survive the darkest of days. Those who passed the information on were aware of this, and therefore made it their business to embellish the truth.

Worthy of note also was the help afforded, with aid from the partisan units, to prisoners attempting to escape. This help was initiated in the second half of 1942, when the *SS* ceased to apply collective responsibility. However, it could only concern a few, and the general mass of prisoners received no direct benefit from it.

The underground workers devoted much of their effort to preparing to fight, if it should become necessary, when the camp was liquidated and an attempt made by the *SS* to murder all the prisoners. Such preparations were in hand from the very beginning, in the hope that help from outside would permit its success. There never was any fighting, for no mass-murder of prisoners took place before evacuation, and the help from outside proved to be illusory. The Western Allies were too far away, the Polish Underground Movement, with insufficient help from the West, was too weak for a general uprising, and the Red Army was not interested in this problem. Apart from revolts in the Penal Companies and sporadic, individual acts of physical resistance, the only fighting on a larger scale was the revolt of the *Sonderkommando* in October 1944. This was a failure; no-one who took part in it survived, but the struggle was fully justified, for it was embarked on in the face of certain annihilation. It has gone down in the history of the camp as an heroic act of resistance.

The underground movement in the camp suffered losses throughout its existence, and many of its members and leaders fell to the *SS*-men's bullets or dangled from the gallows. This was a hard way to die, not with weapon in hand but naked and defenceless, against the wall of death or at the end of a cruel rope knotted by the hand of the executioner. In the camp, however, there could be no other death for the soldiers of the underground, who met it like men of valour. Women perished too, and equally courageously. These sacrifices were unavoidable; they had to be accepted as a consequence of the struggle.

The chronicles of Auschwitz record two cases of the voluntary sacrifice by an individual, acting alone, of his own life to save another. The first of these was Marian Batko, the second was Father Maksymilian Maria Kolbe. Witnesses say that there were more such examples of self-sacrifice and that men of other nationalities were involved. There is no evidence to enable us to name them.

These acts of sacrifice had no connection with underground activity, they were made spontaneously; but they testify to the indomitable spirit of opposition to what was happening in the camp. Besides these people, who were moved by love the their fellow-men to give their own lives, we must record the name of Witold Pilecki. He went into the camp of his own free will; he got out of it to continue his work; and he died a few years later fighting for the same ideals.

Without the men and women who had the courage to stand up to violence and oppression, and those who deliberately sacrificed their own lives for others, there would have been no resistance in Auschwitz and there would have been no underground movement.

SUPPLEMENT

A newly discovered report of Witold Pilecki was published in 1991. In the report he details the members of the first four 'upper' fives of the camp's underground organisation.

First 'upper' five (October 1940): Władysław Surmacki, Władysław Dering, Jerzy de Virion, Eugeniusz Obojski, Roman Zagner.

Second 'upper' five (March 1941): Witold Szymkowiak, Antoni Rosa, Tadeusz Słowiaczek, Mikołaj Skornowicz, Tadeusz Pietrzykowski, Władysław Kupiec, Bolesław Kupiec (exceptionally there were seven of them).

Third 'upper' five (May 1941): Eugeniusz Triebling, Włodzimierz Makaliński, Stanisław Gutkiewicz, Wincenty Gawron, Stanisław Stawiszyński.

Fourth 'upper' five (October 1941): Henryk Bartosiewicz, Stanisław Kazuba, Konstanty Piekarski, Stefan Bielecki, Tadeusz Lach.

(Raport Witolda, edited by Adam Cyra, Towarzystwo Opieki nad Oświęcimien. Bulletin No. 12, Warsaw, September 1991.
p. 79.)

APPENDIX I

Subsequent fate of the more important persons mentioned in the text.

Witold Pilecki, the organizer of the underground movement in the camp at Auschwitz, took part in the Warsaw Uprising in August and September 1944 as a company commander in the *Chrobry II* battalion.[1] After the surrender he became a prisoner-of-war in the *Oflag* (POW camp) in Łambinowice and later in Murnau.[2] There, for the first time, talking to his fellow-officers, he revealed that he had been at Auschwitz, built up an underground military organization and escaped from the camp.

After the war he found himself in Italy in the Polish Second Corps. In the summer of 1945 he began to write his report, covering especially his time in the camp and the building up of the underground organization. He dictated the text to Maria Szelągowska, his closest fellow-worker, who had accompanied him to Italy. As his report was being written he read passages to his friend Jan Mierzanowski.

During his short time of service with the Second Corps Pilecki could not adapt himself to post-war reality, nor could he reconcile himself to the fact that Poland had lost the war and was now under a new occupation. His active nature looked for something to do. He went voluntarily to the command of the Corps, was entrusted with a mission and returned to Poland towards the end of 1945.[3] Nothing is known of his activity there, which ended in his arrest.

He was tried on March 3rd, 1948 before the Regional Military Court in Warsaw, together with Maria Szelągowska, Makary Sieradzki, Tadeusz Płużański, Witold Różycki, Maksymilian Kaucki, Ryszard Jamontt-Krzywicki and Jerzy Nowakowski. On March 15th Pilecki, Szelągowska and Płużański were sentenced to death and the others to long terms of imprisonment.[4] The Court found *inter alia* that:

> As a paid agent of Anders's[5] intelligence service he organized on the territory of Poland an intelligence network, gathering and sending abroad information concerning state, military and economic secrets.[6]

Szelągowska and Płużański had their sentences commuted to life imprisonment. They were released after the events of October 1956, when many former soldiers of the *AK* were also released and afterwards rehabilitated. Pilecki was executed in 1948 in the Mokotów prison in Warsaw,[7] the exact date is not known. The Prime Minister of the Polish Government at that time was Józef Cyrankiewicz.

Pilecki's body was not handed over to his family and nobody knows where he was buried. A symbolic grave has been erected in the cemetery at Ostrów Mazowiecka.[8]

Col. Władysław Surmacki, almost immediately after his release, was arrested in Warsaw and sent to the *Pawiak* prison. He was killed in the ruins of the Warsaw Ghetto in July 1942.[9]

Col. Kazimierz Rawicz was sent from Auschwitz to Mauthausen, where he remained until the end of the war. He returned to Poland and died there on December 12th, 1969.

Józef Cyrankiewicz returned to Poland after the war from the camp at Mauthausen, offered his services to Władysław Bierut, who was then ruling Poland on Stalin's behalf, promising his co-operation as well as the support of the Polish Socialist Party (*PPS*). He remained in power for over twenty years. During his stay in office former Home Army members were jailed under the fabricated accusation of collaboration with the Germans; he was Prime Minister when the workers of Poznań were massacred during the riots in 1956; he gave the order to shoot when over 1000 people were killed in December 1970, because they demanded tolerable living conditions. After this he was removed from office, for a short time became the Head of State, a post without political influence, and ended as chairman of the Committee of Freedom Fighters.

Henryk Bartosiewicz, Stanisław Kazuba, Józef Mikusz and the doctors **Rudolf Diem, Władysław Fejkiel** and **Stanisław Kłodziński** also survived the war and live in Poland. **Edward Ciesielski,** who escaped from the camp with Pilecki, took part in the Warsaw Uprising, in which he was severely wounded. He was one of the youngest members of the camp military underground, but his health was ruined by his wartime experiences and years of imprisonment after the war as an ex-soldier of the *AK*. He died in 1961, barely 39 years old. **Kazimierz Gosk** also survived the war and now lives in the United States. **Dr. Dering's** fate is discussed on pages 273–75.

Among prisoners of other nationalities **Roger Abada, Bruno Baum, Hermann Langbein, Aleksey Lebedev, Karl Lill** and **Jan Stranski** survived. Lebedev, like thousands of other Soviet prisoners-of-war and ex-inmates of German camps, spent many years in a Soviet concentration camp after the war. Bruno Baum died in East Germany on December 13th, 1971. Hermann Langbein was for years secretary of the International Auschwitz Committee, but was deprived of this post after he resigned from the Communist Party in protest at the Soviet action in crushing the Hungarian uprising in 1956. He now concentrates on writing about Auschwitz. Jan Stranski returned to Czechoslovakia after the war. A former Auschwitz prisoner who escaped from Poland to the West in 1945 visited him in Prague and received cordial hospitality.

Otto Küsel, after his escape, went to Warsaw and joined the Polish underground movement. Recaptured and sent back to Auschwitz on September 25th, 1943, he spent several weeks in the bunker. During the rest of the war he was in Flossenbürg, from where he was liberated. He now lives in a small village in Bavaria.

Among the women there were fewer executions than among the men and the underground work in the women's camp was not discovered by the Political Department. Consequently the majority of the women underground workers, if they did not die of typhus or some other disease, survived the camp and for the most part returned to their own countries.

Maria Stromberger was interned after the war in the French occupation zone of Germany on suspicion of having worked for the *SS.* She was released thanks to the intervention of Poles, who were former Auschwitz prisoners. She was a witness at Rudolf Höss's trial in Poland and was made an honorary member of the Austrian Union of Former Prisoners of Concentration Camps. She died in the Tyrol in 1957.[10]

Of the *SS*-men who played important parts in the history of Auschwitz, **Rudolf Höss, Arthur Liebehenschel, Hans Aumeier** and **Maximilian Grabner** were tried, with many other members of the garrison, by the Supreme National Tribunal in Poland, and in December 1947 were sentenced to death by hanging. Höss was hanged in the camp at Auschwitz, the rest within prison walls. Of a total of 40 accused, 23 received death sentences, including two women: **Maria Mandl,** Commandant of the women's camp at Birkenau, and **Therese Brandl,** an *SS* wardress. **Dr. Hans Münch** alone was acquitted.[11] The last Commandant of the camp at Auschwitz and commander of the garrison, **Richard Baer,** remained in hiding until 1960. He was arrested and imprisoned at Frankfurt-am-Main, and died suddenly in July 1963.[12]

APPENDIX II

Item 1 (see pp. 37 and 52)

Leon Głogowski (No. 1281), a Pole from Wrocław, came to the camp in a transport from Rybnik on 26th June, 1940, and very soon afterwards got into the Hospital, at first as a male nurse. Later he got into the bad books of the Senior Medical Officer, Dr. Siegfried Schwella, who decided to get rid of him. He ordered Głogowski to take a group of 250 tubercular patients to Block No. 11, who were gassed there together with 600 Soviet POWs (this took place on September 3rd, 1941, and was the first time that people were gassed in Auschwitz). Dr. Dering hid Głogowski for several days in the Hospital and managed to convince the *SS*-men that he was indispensable. Głogowski was set free in December 1942 (verbal statement to the author, London, November 1st, 1969. Also: S. Kłodziński, 'Dr. Leon Głogowski', *Medical Review*, No. 1, Cracow, 1971).

Item 2 (see p. 37)

Pilecki in his report used only numbers instead of names. He was to have made a list of the names corresponding to the numbers, and, as some informers say, is supposed to have left it with the Polish Ambassador to the Vatican, Kazimierz Papée. The latter, however, in answer to a query by the author, says that he had no such list and cannot recollect ever receiving it. For several years I have checked Pilecki's report against many other sources and publications, with former members of the camp underground movement who are now scattered all over the world, and talked to witnesses; but I have only been able to identify the holders of numbers in cases where Pilecki gave further details (e.g. a Christian name, block, *Kommando*, date of arrival in the camp, function in the organization, some important exploit etc.). Some of them were identified in 1946 by Konstanty Piekarski, a member of Pilecki's camp organization, and some by Dr. Dering, also in 1946, but both these witnesses made mistakes. The cavalry Captain whom Pilecki calls No. 3 and who belonged to the first 'five' has been identified as Jerzy de Virion (known to his friends as 'Orcio'), from the 10th regiment of Uhlans, who was in the camp as Jerzy Hlebowicz. This is the recollection of Karol Świętorzecki in a letter to the author dated January 7th, 1972. Świętorzecki was a member of Pilecki's organization from October 1940 (W. Pilecki, *op cit.*, p. 32) and was sworn in by Pilecki and de Virion. He was released from the camp in May 1941. He is not absolutely sure that No. 3 was de Virion; his second guess is cavalry Captain Woźniak, who arrived in the same transport.

Item 3 (see p. 103)

In 1968 a book was published in Poland by Aleksander Kunicki *Cichy Front (The Silent Front)*, with a chapter entitled 'The Traitor'. This alleges that Jaster was an agent of the *Gestapo*, recruited while in Auschwitz, that the whole escape was prearranged, that Jaster, when in Warsaw, betrayed to the Germans soldiers of the Home Army (*AK*), and that he was sentenced to death by the underground court and the sentence carried out. Kunicki offered no serious proof to support his statements. In 1971 the weekly *Za Wolność i Lud*, the organ of the official ex-combatants' organization in Poland (*Zbowid*), published a series of articles by Jerzy Ambroziewicz entitled 'Traitor or Hero?', criticising Kunicki's accusations and pointing out that they are not supported by any hard evidence.

After much research I have come to the conclusion that Kunicki's accusations are unfounded. I reached this conclusion before Ambroziewicz's articles appeared and quite independently of them. Having access to Pilecki's report, I knew that Jaster, when he escaped, was already a soldier of the camp underground and Pilecki's courier to Warsaw. If he had been an agent working for the Germans, the Political Department would never have let such a valuable man escape.

Kunicki's charge is also rebutted by Wincenty Gawron, who escaped from Auschwitz five weeks before Jaster and was hiding in the village of Zasadne, not far from the camp. After the escape of Jaster and his companions the Germans carried out an extensive man-hunt which lasted for several days. They could not have done so if the escape was a put-up job by the Political Department. Gawron ends his article with the words: 'I reject the accusations of Kunicki from Bielsko that the *Gestapo* organized Jaster's escape'. (*Dziennik Związkowy Zgoda – The Union Daily*, USA, November 3rd, 1971). In my opinion, two men have been mixed up here, and to Jaster have been ascribed the deeds of another. For probable explanation of the conflicting evidence see Appendix II, item 5.

Item 4 (see p. 149)

After the war a number of prisoners (W. Fejkiel, W. Kosztowny, S. Kłodziński, H. Langbein and others) accused Stössel of having given lethal injections of phenol in his Hospital Block. I have collected many statements on this subject and have come to the conclusion that these charges cannot be accepted as completely just. There are no details of this matter in Pilecki's report.

Aleksander Giermański, who was a cleaner on Stössel's Block, says that he was a decent man, although tough and sometimes brutal. If he gave injections, it was only to informers and men who had to be got rid of. He saved a lot of prisoners' lives.

Czesław Jaworski, *op. cit.*, mentions Stössel several times, although he mis-spells his surname and gives him the wrong Christian name (Zygmunt). Jaworski was a doctor on Stössel's Block and stresses his brutality and bad relations with the doctors, but also says that he saved prisoners from selection to the gas chambers. Jaworski never once even suggests that Stössel gave lethal injections.

Wiesław Kielar in his book *Anus Mundi*, Cracow, 1972, also mentions Stössel several times, as he worked in his Block as a male nurse. In his opinion Stössel was brutal but worked for the underground and his brutality was a kind of camouflage. Kielar like Jaworski never suggests that Stössel gave lethal injections.

Czesław Ostańkowicz, *op. cit.*, p. 118, who was in the central camp at the same time, states:

Where Stössel is concerned it was otherwise. The undeniable fact that he administered lethal injections excludes him from the list of political prisoners worthy of respect . . . All the same, many cases are known of the saving of Polish, French and Jewish prisoners by this man. There are men living to-day who owe him their lives. Moreover, Stössel also killed informers, henchmen of the Political Department, German prisoners, who were also executioners. He warned us of their denunciations . . . Stössel was put into the bunker as the result of a denunciation to Grabner by a German prisoner-informer. He was interrogated a number of

times and severely beaten, but did not betray any of the colleagues
known to him from the underground.

Item 5 (see p. 165)

The Kuczbara affair probably explains A. Kunicki's mistake (see
Appendix II, item 3) in accusing another escapee, S. Jaster, of
working for the *Gestapo*. Both escapes, Jaster's and Kuczbara's, took
place in 1942 and in *SS* uniforms; both involved four prisoners.
Kuczbara, who broke down under interrogation, did in fact agree
to work for the Germans and was shot by *AK* soldiers in Warsaw
(W. Pilecki, *op. cit.*, p, 102). The similarity of the two escapes may
have caused Kunicki to think that it was Jaster who was used by the
Gestapo.

Unfortunately, the three men who escaped with Kuczbara, were
also picked up by the Germans. After the escape Baraś and Januszewski went to Cracow and got forged identity-cards from *AK*. Unluckily
they ran into a round-up in Cracow and were put into prison. There
it was discovered that their identity cards were forged and they were
sent back to Auschwitz. Januszewski committed suicide during
transport; Baraś, back at Auschwitz, was saved by friends who got
him into a transport for Buchenwald. He now lives in the USA.
Otto Küsel was also caught and sent back to the camp on September
25th, 1943. He was put into the bunker but, as he was a *Reichsdeutsche*,
was not hanged and after two months was sent to Flossenbürg
(conversation with Otto Küsel on September 26th, 1972. Also: D.
Czech, *Calendar, op. cit.*, No. 4, p. 136).

Item 6 (see p. 228)

In 1947 the Polish Government in Warsaw, whose Premier was
Józef Cyrankiewicz, asked the British Government to extradite Dr.
Dering, then in the British Isles, on charges of carrying out experimental operations at Auschwitz. The accusations were based in part
on evidence given by Dr. Alina Brewda to a United Nations commission.

Dr. Brewda, who from September 1943 to January 1945 worked as a
prisoner-doctor in Block No. 10, where experiments were carried out,
testified that Dr. Dering had performed about 16,000 experimental
operations in the camp. The British Government ordered him to be
put into Brixton Gaol and carried out a thorough investigation,
scrutinizing all the charges and hearing witnesses. After 19 months

Dr. Dering was released and on August 30th, 1948, he received a document from the Home Office stating that he had been released as there was not sufficient proof of his guilt.

In 1965 Dr. Dering brought an action for libel against the American writer Leon Uris, author of the novel *Exodus*. On p. 155 of this novel Uris stated that 'Dr. Dering had performed 17,000 experimental operations without anaesthetics'. The libel suit revealed that Dr. Dering had performed some 80 operations for the removal of sexual glands which had been burnt by X-rays during previous experiments by *SS* doctors. It also revealed that the numbers of experiments cited by Uris and Dr. Brewda were false. The jury brought in a verdict that the charge of libel against L. Uris was proved, but awarded Dr. Dering the nominal sum of one halfpenny in damages (Mavis M. Hill and L. Norman Williams, *Auschwitz in England*, London, 1965, pp. 16, 22, 268). Dr. Dering died the following year of lung cancer.

Many witnesses state that Dr. Dering saved their lives in the camp. The opinions of the hospital staff are important. Dr. Fejkiel, quoted on p. 220, goes on to say: 'The camp owes him a lot as a surgeon, he also saved many prisoners from ill-treatment in the camp'. ('O służbie zdrowia w obozie koncentracyjnym w˙ Oświęcimiu' – 'The health service in the camp at Auschwitz', *Medical Review*, 1961, p. 49). Father Konrad Szweda, a male nurse in the hospital, wrote: 'On another occasion I saw Dr. Dering sewing up a wound on the upper thigh. He was covered with sweat and tired, but was doing his best to snatch a victim of terror out of the jaws of death. He performed gall-bladder operations, re-setting of broken bones and even trepanning' ('Pierwszy okres oddziału chorób zakaźnych w obozie oświęcimskim' – 'The first period of the infectious department in the camp at Auschwitz', *Medical Review*, 1972, p. 98). For Dr. Głogowski's opinion see Appendix II, item 1. C. W. Jaworski, op. cit., pp. 90–91, noted: 'Suddenly Dr. Dering appeared at the door of Block No. 28. I went up to him and told him of my misfortune. He told me to wait a moment, and in a few minutes came back with medicines, telling me to say nothing, as it was forbidden to give medicines outside the hospital.' For other opinions from people who received help from him under difficult circumstances, see: Maria Maniakówna, 'W oświęcimskim bloku nr. 11' ('In the Auschwitz Block No. 11'), *Medical Review*, 1970, p. 211; Tadeusz Orzeszko, 'Relacja chirurga z obozu oświęcimskiego' ('The statement of a surgeon from the camp at Auschwitz'), *Medical Review*, 1971, p. 43; Tadeusz Paczuła, 'Organizacja i administracja szpitala obozowego w KL Auschwitz I' ('Organization and administration of the camp Hospital in the concentration camp Auschwitz I'), *Medical Review*, 1962, p. 65; W. Kielar, *op. cit.*, pp.

187–190. I have also in my possession a number of statements on this subject by former Auschwitz prisoners that have not appeared in print.

Those who attack Dr. Dering accuse him of saving Poles first and foremost and of doing this at the expense of Jews. These accusations are also made by H. Langbein in *Menschen in Auschwitz*, Vienna, 1972, pp. 255–257, where he describes Dr. Dering's behaviour in Auschwitz and his post-war fortunes. It is a pity that Langbein, while writing at length about Dr. Dering and quoting people who speak ill of him, says nothing of the British Government investigation as a result of which Dering was released from Brixton Gaol.

APPENDIX III

Item 1 (see p. 50)

Władysław Dering, Marian Dupont (released in 1941), Rudolf Diem, Stanisław Dziurski (died in the camp on 16.7.1942), Władysław Fejkiel, Józef Gałka, Mieczysław Garbowiecki (killed on 25.1.1943), Czesław Gawarecki (killed on 23.4.1942), Tadeusz Gąsiorowski, Leon Głogowski (released at the end of 1942), Kazimierz Hałgas (transferred to Gross Rosen on 19.12.1941), Eugeniusz Jabłoński (died on 15.6.1942), Dr. Kencer, Julian Kozioł (killed on 16.6.1942), Edward Nowak (transferred to Majdanek, died of typhus on 24.12.1942), Jan Pakowski, Stefan Pizło (died of typhus on 7.7.1942), Jan Rogacki (committed suicide before execution in 1942), Stanisław Suliborski (released in 1942), Romuald Sztaba (transferred to Majdanek on 18.2.1942), Tadeusz Szymański, Wilhelm Türschmidt (killed on 16.6.1942), Leon Wasilewski, Ludwik Witkowski (killed on 15.10.1941), Nicet Włodarski.

These names are cited from:
– W. Dering, *op. cit.*, pp. 63, 72–75.
– W. Fejkiel, 'O służbie zdrowia w obozie koncentracyjnym w Oświęcimiu I – oboz główny', *Medical Review*, Cracow, 1961, pp. 44–51.
– L. Głogowski, 'Moje pierwsze dni w obozie oświęcimskim', *Medical Review*, Cracow, 1968, pp. 191–194.
– S.Kłodziński, 'Pierwsza oświęcimska selekcja do gazu', *Medical Review*, Cracow, 1971, pp. 156–159.

– Tadeusz Paczuła, (a) 'Obóz i szpital obozowy w Oświęcimiu we wczesnych okresach istnienia', *Medical Review*, Cracow, 1963, pp. 50–53. (b) 'Organizacja i administracja szpitala obozowego K.L. Auschwitz', *Medical Review*, Cracow, 1962, pp. 61–68.

– Kazimierz Szczerbowski, 'Wspomnienia pierwszego pisarza rewiru oświęcimskiego', *Medical Review*, Cracow, 1970, pp. 198–201.

Item 2 (see p. 52)

Wojciech Barcz, Józef Horodyński, Ryszard Kwoka, Roman Sediwy, Henryk Sieniawski, Czesław Sowul, Feliks Walentynowicz.

Soon after them: Teofil Banasiuk (in charge of the mortuary; died of typhus), Marian Batkowski, Tadeusz Burski, the brothers Adam and Mieczysław Dembowski, Marian Dybus, Stefan Frolik, the brothers Roman and Tadeusz Gabryszewski, Czesław Głowacki, Kazimierz Gosk, Zdzisław Gutowski, Jan Hrebenda, Krzysztof Hoffman, Jerzy Jackowski, Marian Kieliszek, Julian Kiwała, Roman Klimczyk, Tadeusz Kośmider, Czesław Kozłowski (released from the camp on 11.12.1941), Edward Kulik, Czesław Lachowicz, Bolesław Leśniak, Marian Mikołajczyk, Jan Musioł, Eugeniusz Obojski, Mieczysław Pańszczyk (afterwards guilty of the mass killing of prisoners by injections of phenol), Tadeusz Parys, Jan Pierzchała, Zygmunt Pociecha, Zbigniew Rybka, Sieniawski, Zdzisław Stańda, Alfred Stössel, a young priest Konrad Szweda, Zygmunt Wanicki, Marian Wesołowski, Tadeusz Wójcicki, Adam Wysocki, Stanisław Zelle. In the *SS* Hospital: Ludwik Bas, Eugeniusz Niedojadło, Edward Pyś.

These names are cited from:

– K. Szczerbowski, *op. cit.*, pp. 198–201.
– S. Kłodziński, *op. cit.*, pp. 39–50.
– W. Fejkiel, *op. cit.*, pp. 44–51.

Item 3 (see p. 54)

Doctors: Rudolf Diem, Marian Dupont, Władysław Fejkiel, Józef Gałka, Mieczysław Garbowiecki, Czesław Gawarecki, Leon Głogowski, Tadeusz Gąsiorowski, Julian Kozioł, Edward Nowak, Jan Pakowski, Stefan Pizło, Wilhelm Türschmidt, Ludwik Witkowski, Nicet Włodarski.

Male nurses and laboratory assistants: Teofil Banasiuk, Tadeusz Burski, Kazimierz Gosk, Krzysztof Hoffman, Józef Horodyński, Jan Hrebenda, Antoni Jakubski, Witold Kosztowny, Tadeusz

Kośmider, Czesław Lachowicz, Włodzimierz Lachowicz, Eugeniusz Niedojadło, Eugeniusz Obojski, Jan Pierzchała, Tadeusz Paczuła, Czesław Sowul, Alfred Stössel, Kazimierz Szczerbowski, Marian Toliński, Zygmunt Turzański, Zbigniew Rybka.
These names are cited from:
– W. Pilecki, *op. cit.*, pp. 24–26.
– W. Dering, *op. cit.*, pp., 12–13 and 163–164.
– L. Głogowski, *op. cit.*, pp. 191–194.
– Confidential verbal statements to the author, 1970–1972.

Item 4 (see p. 106)

Julian Dębiec, Mieczysław Jaworski, Mieczysław Kawecki, Henryk Lachowicz, Stanisław Maringe, Jerzy Neymann, Adam Palluch, Bolesław Pejsik, Władysław Pruszyński, Edward Rogaliński, Władysław Skurczyński, Bogusław Szubarga, Antoni Urban.
These names are cited from:
– D. Czech, *Calendar, op. cit.*, No. 3, p. 76.

Item 5 (see p. 106)

Aleksander Buczyński, Tadeusz Chruścicki, August Kowalczyk, Jan Laskowski, Jerzy Łachecki, Józef Pamrow, Zenon Piernikowski, Eugeniusz Stoczewski, Józef Traczyk. Buczyński and Stoczewski were recaptured two days later and shot on June 14th.
These names are cited from:
– D. Czech, *Calendar, op. cit.*, No. 3, p. 77.

Item 6 (see p. 119)

Doctors: Kotulski, Janusz Mąkowski, Jerzy Reichman, Rożkowski, Nicet Włodarski, Bolesław Zbozień.
Male nurses and laboratory assistants: Wojciech Barcz, Stefan Czubak, Mieczysław Dembowski, Marian Dybus, Wiesław Kielar, Julian Kiwała, Witold Kosztowny, Luba (from Czechoslovakia), Zenon Ławski, Marian Mikołajczyk, Eugeniusz Obojski, Stanisław Paduch, Zbigniew Rybka, Czesław Sowul, Jan Szary, Marian Toliński, Zygmunt Turzański, Jan Wolny.
These names are cited from:
– Julian Kiwała, 'Szpital w obozie żeńskim w Brzezince na przełomie lat 1942–1943', *Medical Review*, Cracow, 1965, p. 114.

– Maria Nowakowska (in the camp as Anna Żelińska), 'The women's hospital at Auschwitz-Birkenau', *Medical Review* (special English issue), Cracow, 1962, p. 33.

Item 7 (see p. 120)

Jiři Beranowsky (a Czech electrician), Edward Galiński, Michał Kula, Czesław Łachecki, Józef Plaskura, Andrzej Rablin, Zbigniew Zasadzki.
These names are cited from:
– J. Kiwała, *op. cit.*, p. 115.
– A. Piątkowska, *op. cit.*, p. 3–4.

Item 8 (see p. 121)

Women doctors: Irena Białówna, Zofia Garlicka, Janina Głąbkowska, Adelaide Hautval (French), Izabela Jarnicka, Jadwiga Jasielska, Jadwiga Kobielska, (died on 27th May, 1943), Stefania Kościuszkowa (died on 11th January, 1943), Janina Kościuszkowa, Janina Kowalczykowa, Ella Lingens (Austrian), Ernestyna Michalikowa (died in 1943), Zdena Nedvedová (Czech), Halina Sobolewska, Stabrowska, Wanda Tarkowska, Janina Węgierska.
Nurses: Janina Komenda, Halina Kinalska, Wanda Mende, Irena Miłaszewska, Anna Patoczkówna, Jadwiga Patocza (Anna's mother, died on 15th February, 1943), Jadwiga Prażmowska, Maria Schneiderska, Halina Skonieczna, Zdzisława Sosnowska, Anna Żelińska, Zofia Żelewska.
Hospital Clerks: Monika Galica, Helena Matheisel.
Outside the Hospital: Zofia Palmowa and Zofia Szukalska helped by supplying underclothes, food and medicines.
These names are cited from:
– Jadwiga Apostoł-Staniszewska, *Echa okupacyjnych lat*, Warsaw, 1970, p. 268.
– M. E. Jezierska, *op. cit.*
– J. Kiwała, *op. cit.*
– Ella Lingens, 'Dr. Adelaide Hautval', *Medical Review*, Cracow, 1964, pp. 119–121.
– A. Piątkowska, *op. cit.*
– Wanda Marossányi, *op. cit.*
– A. Tytoniak, *op. cit.*
– H. Włodarska, 'Ze szpitala kobiecego obozu w Brzezince', *Medical Review*, Cracow, 1970, p. 215.

Item 9 (see p. 122)

Women doctors: Irena Białówna, Zofia Garlicka, Adelaide Hautval, Janina Kościuszkowa, Stefania Kościuszkowa, Janina Kowalczykowa, Ella Lingens, Ernestyna Michalikowa, Zdena Nedvedová, Janina Węgierska.
Nurses: Wanda Mende, Irena Miłaszewska, Anna Patoczkówna, Jadwiga Patoczka, Jadwiga Prażmowska, Zdzisława Sosnowska, Anna Żelińska.
Hospital clerks: Monika Galica, Helena Matheisal.
These names are cited from:
– A. Piątkowska, *op. cit.*
– W. Marossányi, *op. cit.*
– Confidential verbal statements to the author in 1970–1972.

Item 10 (see p. 122)

Celina Chojnacka, Jadwiga Havelka, Irena Konieczna, Katarzyna Łaniewska, Stefania Perzanowska, Alina Przerwa Tetmajer, Maria Werkenthin (committed suicide on 22nd January, 1944).
These names are cited from:
– Helena Włodarska, *op. cit.*, p. 215.
– Confidential verbal statement to the author in 1971.

Item 11 (see p. 123)

Irena Bereziuk, Krystyna Cyankiewicz, Jadwiga Dylówna, Stefania Hercok, Antonina Kopycińska, Celina Mikołajczyk (the wife of Stanisław Mikołajczyk, who in July 1943, after the death of Gen. Sikorski, became Prime Minister of the Polish Government in London), Barbara Stefańska (now Anna Tytoniak), Henryka Stockmüller, Barbara Wiśniewska.
These names are cited from:
– J. Kiwała, *op. cit.*
– A. Piątkowska, *op. cit.*

Item 12 (see p. 123)

Doctors: Władysław Dering, Leon Głogowski, Janusz Mąkowski, Nicet Włodarski, Bolesław Zbozień.
Male nurses: Julian Kiwala, Czesław Sowól, Marian Toliński.

280   *Fighting Auschwitz*

These names are cited from:
- W. Dering, *op. cit.*, p. 163.
- L. Głogowski, *op. cit.*

Item 13 (see p. 135)

Doctors:
Belgian: André Ewerling, Jean Royer.
Czech and Slovak: Otto Rubicek, Johann Weiss, Hubert Wolf, Paul Wurzel.
Dutch: Hendricus Akkerman, Johann Bosk, Michael Steynes, Elizar de Wind.
French: Albert Flechner, Prof. Klein, Moritz Spitzer, Jozef Stoffer.
Hungarian: Max Hayes, Janö Korach, Laszlo Reichenfeld, Istwan Wittman.
Jews from many countries: Ernö Alexander (Czechoslovakia), Sigismund Block (France), Alfred Boris (Hungary), Leon Cohen (France), Adalbert Fekete (Hungary), Prof. Bruno Fischer (Czechoslovakia), Wilhelm Freisinger (Czechoslovakia), Jakub Gordon (Poland), Leon Greif (France), Mikulas Herz (Czechoslovakia, a dentist), Jacobs Jonas (Holland), Otakar Kalensky (Czechoslovakia), Samuel Kropveld (France), Henryk Krauze (Poland), Jakub Landau (France), Baruch Maisel (Belgium), Salomon Maissa (Greece), Michael Marunczak (Czechoslovakia), Lejzor Moszkowicz (France), Mieczysław Monderer (Poland), David Mossel (Holland), Arpad Schwarz (Hungary), Samuel Stenberg (France), Josef Weissenstein (Czechoslovakia), Samuel Veissi (Greece), Abraham Weichsman (Hungary), Salomon Wolf, Jakub Wollman.
Poles: Bronisław Augustyn, Jan Brzeski, Jerzy Budny (a dentist), Przemysław Duś-Dobrzański, Czesław Gaca, Roman Gęźba, Teomir Gajewski, Zenon Hoffman, Stanisław Kapuściński, Prof. Janusz Krzywicki, Ignacy Kwarta, Witold Kulesza, Jan Malinowski, (died May 14th, 1942), Janusz Mąkowski, Tadeusz Orzeszko, Józef Panasewicz, Witold Preiss, Adam Przybylski, Aleksander Smerek, Janusz Okła, Tadeusz Śnieszko, Michał Szewczuk, Roman Szuszkiewicz, Władysław Tondos, Jan Zielina, Adam Zacharski.
Russian: Franz Stiefel.
Ukrainian: Oleg Witoszynsky.
Yugoslav: Hermann Singer.

Male nurses: It is difficult to enumerate all the male nurses and other trusties in Hospital, like laboratory workers, clerks and others, for there were about 300 of them and it was a very mobile element. Besides about 200 Poles there were over 20 Jews from various countries, over 20 Germans and some Austrians, French, Belgians, Dutch, Czechs, Slovaks, Ukrainians and Yugoslavs. A few names of representatives of these nationalities, less numerous in Auschwitz, have been preserved: Heinrich Haak (Dutch), Georg Herman (Czechoslovakia), Milorad Lukić (Yugoslavia), Oleksa Łatyszewski and Leon Mostowycz (Ukrainians), Fyodor Sgiba (Russia).

These names are cited from:
- W. Fejkiel, *Medycyna za drutami*, Warsaw, 1964, pp. 525–6.
- W. Dering, *op. cit.*
- S. Kłodziński, several articles already mentioned.
- Czesław W. Jaworski, *Wspomnienia z Oświęcimia*, Warsaw, 1962.
- H. Langbein, *op. cit.*

Item 14 (see p. 136)

Henryk Czuperski (killed in the camp in 1942), Jerzy Bujalski (died in the camp 19.6.1944), Jan Gadomski (died in the camp 27.2.1943), Jósef Gałka (died in the camp), Prof. Marian Gieszczykiewicz, Jan Grabczyński, Franciszek Gralla, Czesław W. Jaworski, Stanisław Kłodziński, Józef Mężyk, Prof. Jan Olbrycht, Jan Rogacki (a suicide before execution in 1942), Jan Suchnicki (killed in the camp in 1942), Zbigniew Sobieszczański, Edward Witkowski, Stefan Żabicki.

These names are cited from:
- W. Pilecki, *op. cit.*, p. 65.
- W. Dering, *op. cit.*, p. 72.
- C. W. Jaworski, *op. cit.*, pp. 147, 153.

Item 15 (see p. 140)

Wierusz-Kowalski (Pole), Stanisław Dorosiewicz (he called himself a Georgian), Ernst Malorny (German), Rudolf Kauer (German), Hersz Kurcwaig (Jew), Jozef Rusin (Czech), Zolotov (Russian).

These names are cited from:
- Józef Kret, 'Więźniowie miernicy w obozie oświęcimskim', *Medical Review*, Cracow, 1971, p. 56.
- Jerzy Rawicz, *Karjera Szambelana*, Warsaw, 1971, pp. 341–2.
- C. Ostańkowicz, *op. cit.*, p. 136.

Item 16 (see p. 149)

Stanisław Adamczyk, Manfred Bock, Stefan Grywacz, Władysław

Grywacz, Jerzy Janicki, Mieczysław Kaniewski, Stefan Kluska, Wincenty Konieczny, Bernard Koschentka, Stefan Kowalow, Jan Kozuk, Józef Krall, Juliusz Kutzner, Kazimierz Kwaśniewski, Kazimierz Poprawski, Czesław Przeor, Zygmunt Nosek, Jósef Raczkowski, Kazimierz Superson, Jan Stuczeń, Jan Sworzeń, Bronisław Własło, Mieczysław Wojciechowski, Zdzisław Wróblewski. They were taken from Blocks No. 4, 5, 6, 7, 9, 16, 16a, 17, 17a, 21a, 22, 22a, 24.
These names are cited from:
– The *Book of the Bunker, Auschwitz note-books*, No. 1. Auschwitz, 1957, pp. I/94–97.

Item 17 (see p. 151)

Tadeusz Biliński, Eugeniusz Eberle, Mieczysław Garbowiecki, Edward Gött-Getyński, Mieczysław Koliński, Włodzimierz Koliński, Karol Korotyński, Karol Kumuniecki, Wiktor Kurzawa, Józef Lichtenberg, Bronisław Motyka, Paweł Nierada, Henryk Suligórski, Wilhelm Szyma, Jan Wróblewski.
These names are cited from:
– D. Czech, *Calendar, op. cit.*, No. 4, p. 64.

Item 18 (see p. 151)

Antoni Cebularz, Józef Drążek, Stefan Konosewicz, Franciszek Kübasch, Henryk Lurie, Roman Łokieć, Franciszek Motyka, Czesław Nowak, Artur Poeplan, Franciszek Pisarek, Władysław Polaczek, Tadeusz Radwański, Zbigniew Ruszczyński, Paweł Sobczak, Michał Sroka, Henryk Stirer, Marian Studencki, Wilhelm Walda, Henryk Weber, Józef Wiendlocha, Jan Wrotniak, Heliodor Zaleśny.
These names are cited from:
– The *Book of the Bunker, op. cit.*, pp. I/107–113.

Item 19 (see p. 157)

Wiktor Bilczewski, Antoni Bobek, Rozalia Bolkowa and her husband, Głuszek, Jan Ilisiński, Kazimierz Jędrzejowski, Piotr Jarzyna, Adam Jedrzejowski, Wawrzyniec Kulig and his sister Magierowa, Jan Nosal and his wife, Henryk Siuta, Edward Szczerbowski, Franciszek Żurek.
These names are cited from:
– Jan Jaźwiec, *Pomnik dowódcy*, Cracow, 1971, pp. 120 and 142.

– Janina Kajtoch, 'Znałam ludzi dobrej woli', a chapter from the book *Kominy*, Warsaw, 1962, pp. 259–342.

Item 20 (see p. 201)

Edmund Hakaszewski, Czesław Marcisz, Stanisław Stawiński.
These names are cited from:
– D. Czech, *Calendar*, No. 4, p. 102.

Item 21 (see p. 201)

Władysław Ćwikliński, Józef Dziuba, Wacław Jamiołkowski, Tadeusz Kokesz, Romuald Krzywosiński, Władysław Krzyżagórski, Witold Lendzion, Jan Lisiak, Edmund Sikorski, Janusz Pogonowski (Skrzetuski), Leon Wardaszko, Jerzy Woźniak, Bogdan Zaręba-Zarębiński,
These names are cited from:
– The *Book of the Bunker*, *op. cit.*, p. II, 11/12.

Item 22 (see p. 201)

Leon Czerski, Zbigniew Foltański, Józef Gancarz, Mieczysław Kulikowski, Marian Moskalski, Bogusław Ohrt, Władysław Pierzyński, Leon Rajzer, Tadeusz Rapacz, Stanisław Tokarski, Józef Wojtyga.
These names are cited from:
– The *Book of the Bunker*, *op. cit.*, II, 11/12/13.
– J. Kret, *op. cit.*, p. 57.

Item 23 (see p. 202)

Władysław Ćwikliński, Leon Czerski, Józef Dziuba, Wacław Jemiołkowski, Tadeusz Kokesz, Romuald Krzywosiński, Władysław Krzyżagórski, Jan Lisiak, Marian Moskalski, Władysław Pierzyński, Stanisław Tokarski, Leon Wardaszko, Bogdan Zaręba-Zarębiński.
These names are cited from:
– The *Book of the Bunker*, p. II. 11/12/13.

Item 24 (see p. 202)

Zbigniew Foltański, Józef Gancarz, Mieczysław Kulikowski,

284 *Fighting Auschwitz*

Czesław Marcisz, Bogusław Ohrt, Tadeusz Rapacz, Janusz Pogonowski (Skrzetuski), Leon Rajzer, Edmund Sikorski, Stanisław Stawiński, Józef Wojtyga, Jerzy Woźniak.
These names are cited from:
– D. Czech, *Calendar*, No. 4, p. 119.

Item 25 (see p. 212)

On 16.9.43 Kazimierz Gilewicz was arrested; on 17.9.43 Teofil Dziama, Juliusz Gilewicz, Tadeusz Lisowski; on 19.9.43 Edward Skorupa, Jan Chmielewski, Leon Markitonn, Jerzy Skibiński, Wacław Skibiński, Rudolf Homa, Franciszek Karbowiak, Zygmunt Bończa (Bohdanowski), Stanisław Cyga; on 20.9.43 Stanisław Wnorowski; on 21.9.43 Józef Domaniewski (Domaniecki), Stanisław Mucha, Kazimierz Stamirowski, Jan Mosdorf; on 24.9.43 Kazimierz Kowalczyk, Władysław Fejkiel, Władysław Węgielek, Władysław Zatorski, Józef Augustyniak, Stefan Frolik, Rudolf Diem, Edward Hallek; on 25.9.43 Franciszek Targosz, Józef Gabis, Franciszek Wieczorkowski, Henryk Bartosiewicz, Alfred Woycicki, Kazimierz Spiechowicz, Norbert Kurzędkowski, Zygmunt Stawarz, Julian Zgłobisz, Stanisław Jelonek, Mieczysław Dobrzański, Karol Karp, Xawery Dunikowski, Leon Murzyn, Franciszek Balzar, Władysław Patrzałek, Michał Kołodziej, Stefan Chmielewski, Zbigniew Koelner, Henryk Kalinowski, Wacław Weschke, Józef Otowski, Julian Drozda, Jan Chmiel, Ignacy Zamojski, Jan Fangrat, Zbigniew Mossakowski, Józef Piotr Zalewski, Zbigniew Emmerling, Michał Kubiak, Eugeniusz Łukawiecki, Karol Holler, Heronim Kurczewski, Zdzisław Del Ponti, Kazimierz Szelest, Józef Somper, Antoni Szczudlik, Wacław Szumański, Ignacy Malicki, Aleksander Szumielewicz, Maurycy Potocki, Roman Knida, Józef Leroch, Józef Poklewski-Koziełł, Henryk Sokołowski; on 27.9.43 Jerzy Pozimski, Kazimierz Szafański; on 29.9.43 Józef Woźniakowski.
These names are cited from:
– The *Book of the Bunker*, *op. cit.*, pp. II/42–II/49.

Item 26 (see p. 212)

Names in order of arrest: Tadeusz Lisowski, Teofil Dziama, Jan Chmielewski, Zygmunt Bończa (Bohdanowski), Kazimierz Stamirowski, Jan Mosdorf, Stanisław Mucha, Kazimierz Kowalczyk, Władysław Fejkiel, Rudolf Diem, Mieczysław Dobrzański, Karol Karp, Władysław Patrzałek, Michał Kołodziej, Zbigniew Koellner,

Henryk Kalinowski, Julian Drozda, Heronim Kurczewski, Franciszek
Targosz, Henryk Bartosiewicz, Alfred Woycicki, Xavery Dunikowski,
Leon Murzyn, Franciszek Balzar, Stefan Chmielewski, Józef Otowski,
Ignacy Zamojski, Jerzy Pozimski, Zdzisław Del Ponti, Józef Somper,
Antoni Szczudlik, Wacław Szumański, Aleksander Szumielewicz,
Maurycy Potocki, Józef Poklewski-Koziełł, Henryk Sokołowski,
Kazimierz Szafrański, Józef Woźniakowski.
The names and the fact that they belonged to *ZOW* have either
been mentioned earlier in the text or have been verified by other
sources, viz.: 'Jot' (Józef Otowski), 'Wspomnienie z Oświęcimia',
Na antenie, Munich, 11.7.1965, p. 3; Wojciech Gniatczyński, 'Proces
oświęcimski', *Na antanie*, Munich, 2.3.1965, p. 2; Alfred Woycicki,
'Zeznanie dla prokuratury we Frankfurcie nad Menem', a report,
Cracow, 25.11.1959; H. Bartosiewicz, *op. cit.* It is possible that
among the 74 arrested men there were more members of the *ZOW*,
but there is no proof.

Item 27 (see p. 225)

Stefan Bratkowski, Marian Łaptaś, Julian Rydiger, Józef Szpilski,
Julian Wieczorek, Kazimierz Wojnar, Wojciech Ziemba.
These names are cited from:
– B. Dziubińska, 'Ruch..' p. 140.
– Z. Hardt and S. Czerpak, *op. cit.*, p. 56.

Item 28 (see p. 241)

Kazimierz Andrysiak, Ryszard Kordek, Zdzisław Michalak and
Józef Papuga, all of whom escaped on 17th July, and Henryk Dzięgie-
lewski, who escaped by himself.
These names are cited from:
– T. Sobański, *op. cit.*, pp. 119–130.

Item 29 (see p. 242)

Tadeusz Donimirski, Wacław Maliszewski, Jan Prejzner, Alfons
Szumiński, Leonard Zawadzki, Tadeusz Żaboklicki.
These names are cited from:
– T. Sobański, *op. cit.*, p. 188.

Item 30 (see p. 242)

Stanisław Furdyna, Stanisław Maliński, Marian Szajer, Antoni Wykręt, Stanisław Zyguła.
These names are cited from:
– T. Sobański, *op. cit.*, pp. 199–203.
– Antoni Andrzejewski, 'Ucieczka z Oświęcimia', statement, *Polish Underground Movement (1939–1945) Study Trust.*
– Henryk Świebocki, 'Obwód oświęcimski *ZWZ/AK* w akcji niesienia pomocy więźniom *KL* Auschwitz', *Studia Historyczne*, Cracow, 1972, No. 4, pp. 599–622.

APPENDIX IV

SS Ranks

SS	*British Army*
Reichsführer	Field-Marshal
Oberstgruppenführer	General
Obergruppenführer	Lieutenant-General
Gruppenführer	Major-General
Brigadeführer	Brigadier
Oberführer	no equivalent
Standartenführer	Colonel
Obersturmbannführer	Lieutenant-Colonel
Sturmbannführer	Major
Hauptsturmführer	Captain
Obersturmführer	Lieutenant
Untersturmführer	Second-Lieutenant
Hauptscharführer	Warrant Officer
Oberscharführer	Staff-Sergeant
Scharführer	Sergeant
Unterscharführer	Corporal
Rottenführer	Lance-Corporal

NOTES

Part One

Chapter One

1 Witold Pilecki, report, pp. 1–2; Stefan Korboński, *Fighting Warsaw*, pp. 48–50.
2 Ibid, p. 102.
3 Ibid, p. 1. Władysław Dering, report; Zofia Pilecka (Witold's daughter), report.
4 Jan Sehn, *Obóz*..., pp. 11–14; Friedrich K. Kaul, *Ärzte in Auschwitz*, pp. 47–48
5 Ibid.
6 Danuta Czech *Kalendarz*..., No. 2, p. 82.
7 Ibid.
8 Czesław Madajczyk, *Polityka*..., pp. 483–493.
9 Czech, No. 2, p. 83.
10 Sehn, p. 16.
11 Czech, No. 2, p. 85; Karol Świętorzecki, 'Stille Nacht...,'
12 Dering, pp. 19–20.
13 Pilecki, p. 2.
14 Sehn, p. 57
15 Rudolf Höss, *Wspomnienia*..., p. 287.
16 Ibid.
17 Sehn, p. 114.
18 Andrzej Kamiński, *Hitlerowskie*..., pp. 231–233.
19 Czech, No. 2, p. 92.
20 Ibid, p. 91.
21 Höss, *Kommandant*..., p. 175.
22 Ibid.
23 Ibid.
24 Czech, No. 2, p. 96.
25 Höss (German version), p. 153.

Chapter Two

1 Pilecki, p. 8.
2 Edward Ciesielski, *Wspomnienia*..., p. 151.
3 Pilecki, p. 8.
4 Hermann Langbein, *Der Auschwitz-Prozess*, pp. 587–588.
5 Leon Głogowski, statement.
6 Ibid.
7 Pilecki, p. 8.
8 *Armia Krajowa w Dokumentach*, p. 139.
9 Lucjan Dobroszycki, *Centralny*..., p. 168.
10 Tadeusz Bór-Komorowski, *The Secret Army*, p. 50.
11 Leon Wanat, *Apel*..., pp. 73–74.
12 Tomasz Sobański, *Ucieczki*..., pp. 142–143.
13 Barbara Dziubińska, 'Ruch oporu...,' pp. 140–141.

14 Kazimierz Moczarski, 'Czy można było...'
15 Kazimierz Rawicz, 'Oświęcimskie podziemie'.
16 Jan Zaborowski, przedmowa..., p. 33.
17 Zygmunt Pawłowicz, 'Jeszcze o planach...
18 Zygmunt Walter-Janke (from 1943 District Commander of the Home Army in Silesia), *Armia Krajowa*..., p. 242.
19 Pilecki, p. 30.

Chapter Three

1 Wojciech Jekiełek-'Żmija', *W pobliżu*..., pp. 25–32.
2 Ibid, pp. 24, 28, 29–32; Zygmunt Urbańczyk, 'Wspomnienia...,' p. 1; Jan Danuta-Wawrzyczek (a former Commander of *ZWZ-AK* District Auschwitz), 'Ziemia...', p. 2.
3 Danuta-Wawrzyczek, pp. 1–2.
4 Pawłowicz.
5 Jekiełek, pp. 33–42 and 63.
6 Czech, No. 2, pp. 89–91.
7 Pilecki, pp. 24–26.
8 Dering, pp. 22 and 103–104. Also: Głogowski.
9 Stanisław Kłodziński, 'Dr. Stefan Pizło...,' pp. 258–260.
10 Dering, pp. 11 and 55–61.
11 Kazimierz Szczerbowski, 'Wspomnienia...,' pp. 198–201.
12 Dering, pp. 30–31.
13 Ibid, p. 89.
14 Henryk Bartosiewicz, statement.
15 *Armia Krajowa*..., pp. 431–433.
16 Pilecki, pp. 26–27 and 33.
17 Głogowski. Oral evidence.
18 Pilecki, p. 41; Otto Küsel, statement.
19 Bartosiewicz, oral evidence.
20 Józef Garliński, *Poland*..., pp. 78–81.
21 Bartosiewicz, oral evidence.
22 Pilecki, pp. 30–35; Lech Życki, 'Ucieczka...,'; Ryszard Zieliński, 'Historia...'
23 Świętorzecki, letter to author.
24 Pilecki, p. 55.
25 Świętorzecki, letter; Pilecki, p. 32.
26 Czesław Ostańkowicz, *Ziemia*..., p. 73.
27 Dering, pp. 146–148.
28 Pilecki, p. 30.
29 Czech, No. 2, p. 90.
30 Franciszek Brol, Gerard Włoch, Jan Pilecki, 'Książka bunkra' (later the *Book of the Bunker*), p. 30.
31 Jan Dobraczyński, 'Dał życie...'
32 Tadeusz Iwaszko, 'Ucieczki...,' p. 50.
33 Pilecki, p. 37.
34 Dering, p. 83.

Part Two

Chapter Four

1 Bartosiewicz, oral evidence.

2 Jerzy Brandhuber, 'Jeńcy . . .,' p. 13.
3 Kłodziński, 'Pierwsza . . .,' pp. 39–50.
4 Höss (English version), p. 146.
5 Pilecki, pp. 38 and 41–42.
6 Bartosiewicz, written statement.
7 Pilecki, p. 41.
8 Jekiełek, pp. 63–64.
9 Marian Malinowski, *Polski Ruch* . . ., pp. 155–156.
10 Pilecki, p. 41.
11 Jerzy Ptakowski, '25 rocznica . . .'; Pilecki, p. 41; Bartosiewicz.
12 'Wiciak . . .', letter.
13 Pilecki p. 45; Bartosiewicz, written and oral evidence; 'Wiciak", letter to author.
14 Sehn, p. 20.
15 Czech, No. 2, p. 103.
16 Brandhuber, p. 36. Also: author's own observations.
17 Czech, No. 3, p. 69.
18 Sehn, p. 18.
19 Author's own observations.
20 Brandhuber, p. 13.
21 Höss (Polish version), p. 111.
22 Czech, No. 2, p. 90.
23 Sehn, p. 72.
24 Czech, 'The Auschwitz Sub-Camps', pp. 45–47.
25 Anna Ziemba, 'Farma . . .,' pp. 37–67.
26 Ziemba, 'Podobóz Rajsko', pp. 71–89.
27 Czech, 'The Auschwitz Sub-Camps', p. 39.
28 Höss (English version), p. 184.
29 Kaul, pp. 56–57.
30 Otto Wolken, 'On the problem . . .,' p. 88.
31 Czech, No. 3, p. 72.
32 Höss (English version), pp. 149–150 and 189.
33 Höss (Polish version),p. 189.
34 Sehn, pp. 124 and 133.
35 Höss (Polish version), p. 194.
36 Author's own observation.
37 Julian Kiwała, 'Kuchnia . . .,' p. 81.
38 Höss (Polish version), pp. 195–196.
39 Pilecki, p. 58.

Chapter Five

1 Pilecki, p. 58.
2 Czech, No. 2, p. 99.
3 Pilecki, p. 49. (He had a high opinion of the Colonel, for on the same page he wrote: 'Col. Karcz was a brave man').
4 Bartosiewicz, *op. cit.*
5 Author's own observation.
6 Bartosiewicz, *op. cit.*
7 Pilecki, p. 49; 'Wiciak', *op. cit.*
8 Czech, No. 3, p. 72.
9 Pilecki, p. 51; Ciesielski, p. 154; Rawicz, *op. cit.*
10 Ibid.
11 'Wiciak', *op. cit.*

12 Sobański, p. 60.
13 Pilecki, p. 59.
14 Czech, No. 3, p. 78.
15 Pilecki, p. 59.
16 Zaborowski, p. 37.
17 Czech, No. 3, p. 94.
18 Zenon Różański, *Mützen ab*, p. 59.
19 Pilecki, p. 62.
20 Czech, No. 3, p. 62.
21 Pilecki, p. 62.
22 Karl Langenhage, *Capo* of the Penal Company at that time.
23 Różański, pp. 64–65.
24 Czech, No. 3, p. 76.
25 Ibid, p. 75.
26 Höss (Polish version), pp. 123–124.
27 Czech, No. 3, p. 94.
28 Pilecki, p. 51.
29 Cass Stankiewicz-Wiśniewski, letter.
30 Pilecki, p. 55.
31 Pilecki in his report does not specify these tasks.
32 Pilecki, p. 55.
33 Ciesielski, p. 154; Pilecki, p. 55; Ostańkowicz, p. 68.
34 Pilecki, p. 56.
35 Bartosiewicz, *op. cit.*
36 Pilecki, pp. 55–56.
37 Archives of the International Tracing Service, Chief Records.
38 Czech, No. 3, p. 96.

Chapter Six

1 Wanda Marossányi, statement; Pilecki, p. 53.
2 Jerzy Rawicz, *Dzień* . . ., pp. 66–74.
3 Stanisława Leszczyńska, 'Raport . . .', p. 105.
4 One couple, Albin and Maryla Ossowski live now in London.
5 Czech, No. 3, p. 70.
6 Antonina Piątkowska, 'O pracy . . .', p. 1.
7 Maria Elżbieta Jezierska, 'Chorować nie wolno', p. 197.
8 Czech, No. 3, p. 94.
9 Anna Tytoniak (in the camp as Barbara Stefańska), 'Jesień 1942 . . .', p. 195.
   Her description is confirmed by Höss (Polish version), p. 123.
10 Kiwała, 'Szpital . . .', p. 114; Maria Nowakowska (in the camp as Anna
   Żelińska), 'The women's hospital . . .', p. 33.
11 Janina Kościuszkowa, 'Brief biographies . . .', p. 48.
12 Jan Wolny, 'O organizowaniu . . .', p. 118.
13 Kiwała, 'Szpital . . .', p. 115.
14 Nowakowska, p. 33.
15 Ibid, p. 35.
16 Ella Lingens, 'Nationale Fragen . . .', pp. 111–113.
17 Nina Guseva, 'O tym zapomnieć . . .', p. 133–140.
18 Piątkowska, pp. 3 and 6.
19 Dering, p. 163. Piątkowska, pp. 4–5.
20 Piątkowska, p. 5.
21 Marossányi, letter, Sept. 1971.

22 Piątkowska, pp. 5 and 7.
23 Maria Kozakiewicz, letter.
24 Bartosiewicz, *op. cit.*; Marossányi, letter.
25 Zdzisław Hardt and Stanisław Czerpak, *W cieniu krematorium*, p. 80.
26 Langbein, *Die Stärkeren*, pp. 122–124; Czech, No. 4, p. 70.
27 Dziubińska, pp. 165–166.
28 Bruno Baum, *Widerstand in Auschwitz*, pp. 80–81.
29 Guseva, pp. 133–140.
30 Dorota Lorska, 'Z pobytu w Oświęcimiu', pp. 2–7; Kozakiewicz, *op. cit.*
31 Czech, No. 7, p. 111.
32 Stanisława Rachwałowa, letter, Aug. 1971.
33 Lorska, 'Blok X . . .', pp. 99–104.
34 Kozakiewicz, Marossányi, Piątkowska. Letters. (Some details in the chapter about the women's camp and the resistance there have been taken from a work by Dziubińska and the book by Baum. Unfortunately both are very imprecise and superficial. They give none of the prisoners' numbers, dates are lacking and all the names are mixed up. Dziubińska gives the names of a number of women in a row without any explanation, as if they worked together. Among others she cites the names of the Frenchwoman Danielle Casanova and the Russian Nina Guseva. But Casanova died on May 10th, 1943, and Guseva came to the camp in October of that year. They never met each other.)
35 Władysław Fejkiel, 'Medycyna . . .', p. 475.
36 Kłodziński, 'Dur wysypkowy . . .', p. 50; Langbein, *Die Stärkeren*, pp. 83–84; Baum, p. 66.
37 Dering, p. 24.
38 Głogowski, *op. cit.*
39 Pilecki, p. 67.
40 Fejkiel, 'The Health Service . . .', p. 49.
41 Tadeusz Paczuła, 'Organizacja . . .', pp. 163–164.
42 Langbein, *Die Stärkeren*, pp. 62, 72, 75.
43 Fejkiel, 'Ethical and Legal . . .', pp. 97–117.
44 Höss (Polish version), pp. 345–348; Langbein, *Die Stärkeren*, pp. 84–85.
45 Pilecki, p. 48.
46 Bartosiewicz, *op. cit.*
47 Jerzy Rawicz, *Karjera . . .*, pp. 341–342. Also: Dering, p. 175.
48 Pilecki, p. 48.
49 Adelaide Hautval, 'Adelaide speaks . . .'.
50 Pilecki, p. 67. (The name 'Trzęsimiech' is given in inverted commas, as it has been impossible to determine whether this was a code-name or a real name.)
51 Jaworski, p. 204.
52 Pilecki, p. 73.
53 Ibid. pp. 67, 69, 72 and 82.
54 *Polskie Siły Zbrojne . . .*, p. 26; Madajczyk, pp. 324–333.
55 Pilecki, p. 69. Also: Czech, No. 4, pp. 77, 79. (These murders were carried out on February 23rd and March 1st, 1943.)
56 Höss (Polish version), p. 229.
57 Pilecki, p. 74.

Chapter Seven

1 Pilecki, p. 72.
2 The *Book of the Bunker*, p. I/81.
3 Pilecki, p. 73.

4 The *Book of the Bunker*, p. I/120.
5 Pilecki, p. 75.
6 Różański, pp. 83–88.
7 Brol, Włoch, J. Pilecki, p. 32.
8 Adam Ciołkosz, 'Zgon Teodora'.
9 Garliński, pp. 141–142.
10 Janina Kajtoch, 'Znałam ludzi . . .', pp. 259–342.
11 Jekiełek, pp. 82–83, 85–86, 102, 160–163.
12 Ibid; Czech, No. 3, p. 89.
13 Bartosiewicz, *op. cit.*
14 Pilecki, p. 51; Jekiełek, p. 63.
15 Czech, No. 4, pp. 102 and 142.
16 Danuta-Wawrzyczek, pp. 3–5; Tadeusz Bielewicz, letter. (Bielewicz, born in Auschwitz, knowing the district very well and having operated there in *ZWZ* and *AK*, gave a number of details and accurate appraisals of the people and operation near the camp.)
17 Sobański, pp. 106–107; Jekiełek, p. 292.
18 Edward Padkowski, 'Dlaczego nie . . .'.
19 Walter-Janke, p. 151.
20 Ibid; Ludwik Kubik, 'Jeszcze o sprawie . . .'.
21 Pilecki, p. 84.
22 Czech, No. 3, p. 125.
23 Pilecki, p. 85; *Muzea Walki*, p. 116.
24 Author's own experience. Before his arrest he was at the head of this intelligence service.
25 Pilecki, p. 74; Dering, p. 186.
26 Ibid, p. 85.
27 Bartosiewicz, *op cit.*
28 Pilecki, p. 85. Also: Ciesielski, pp. 99 and 103.
29 Ciesielski, pp. 104–105.
30 Langbein, statement.
31 Ciesielski, pp. 108, 112–114, 124–150.
32 Pilecki, pp. 100–102.
33 Ibid.
34 Czech, No. 7, p. 79.
35 Ibid, No. 4, p. 95.
36 *Polskie Siły Zbrojne* . . .. pp. 169–203.
37 Garliński, pp. 167–233.
38 Ciesielski, p. 178.

Part Three

Chapter Eight

1 Küsel, *op. cit.*
2 Bartosiewicz, Dering, Świętorzecki and others.
3 Pilecki, p. 48.
4 Confidential statement.
5 Hardt and Czerpak, p. 45.
6 Ciołkosz, statement.
7 Jan M. Mierzanowski, letter 1971.
8 Czech, No. 4, p. 95; Sehn, p. 39.
9 Report of the Government Delegacy . . .

10 Bartosiewicz, Świętorzecki and author's own observations.
11 Langbein, *Menschen* ..., pp. 197–206.
12 Langbein, *Die Stärkeren*, pp. 7–39.
13 Ibid, pp. 90–91.
14 Ibid, p. 100. (The author also obtained from Langbein supplementary verbal evidence on this subject in Vienna, July 1970.)
15 Ibid, p. 101.
16 Roger Abada, *Témoignages sur Auschwitz*, p. 169; Czech, No. 3, p. 82.
17 Höss (Polish version), p. 291.
18 Abada, pp. 170–176.
19 Brandhuber, pp. 9–12; Höss (Polish version), p. 183.
20 Author's own observations.
21 Langbein, *Die Stärkeren*, pp. 157–158.
22 Bartosiewicz, *op. cit.*
23 Ostańkowicz, p. 245; Bartosiewicz, *op. cit.*
24 Aleksey Lebedev, '*Soldaty* ...', pp. 31, 36, 37.
25 Ibid, p. 35. (Lebedev does not give the names of these leaders, nor does he mention that he was head of the whole organization, but this was so, for other sources mention it: Langbein, Baum, Bartosiewicz.)
26 Ibid, pp. 36–64. (Among the leaders Fyodor Sgiba escaped on 16th January, 1944. He was then working in Birkenau.)
27 Erich Kulka, *Útěk z tábora smrti*, Jozef Lánik, *Co Dante neviděl*, Manca Švalbová, *Vyhasnuté Oči*, Júlia Škodová, *Tri Roky bez Mena*, Rudolf Vrba and Alan Bestic, *Factory of Death*, Jožica Veble, *Přežívela sem Taborišče Smrti*.
28 Veble, *op. cit.*
29 Küsel, *op. cit.*
30 Langbein, *Die Stärkeren*, p. 170; Baum, pp. 74–78 and 258.
31 Malinowski, pp. 155–156.
32 Jan M. Ciechanowski, *The Warsaw Rising of 1944*, p. 87.
33 Langbein, *Die Stärkeren*, pp. 66 and 117.
34 Abada, pp. 170–171.
35 Filip Friedman and Tadeusz Hołuj, *Oświęcim*, p. 124.
36 Langbein, conversation.
37 Langbein, *Die Stärkeren*, p. 113.
38 Langbein, conversation.
39 Friedman and Hołuj, p. 130.
40 Ibid, p. 131.
41 Langbein, *Die Stärkeren*, p. 157.
42 Friedman and Hołuj, p. 132.
43 Ibid, p. 147.
44 Langbein, statement.
45 Dziubińska, p. 142. (She says that in the Czechoslovak group in the central camp the following Communists were active: Aleksy Cepicka, Igor Bistry, Feber, Emil Panevič, Karol Beren and Dr. Dora Kleinová, and in Birkenau O. Krauss and E. Schoen.)
46 Friedman and Hołuj, p. 136.

Chapter Nine

1 Czech, No. 4, p. 102; Józef Kret, 'Więźniowie-miernicy ...', p. 56.
2 Ibid, p. 119.
3 Rudolf Diem, 'Śp. Kazimierz ...', p. 47.
4 Czech, No. 4, p. 121.

5 Edward Padkowski, 'Jeszcze . . .'.
6 Author's own observations.
7 Pery Broad. (He was an *SS*-man working in the Political Department. While a POW in British hands he wrote the above statement. In the Auschwitz trial at Frankfurt-am-Main in 1965 he was sentenced to 5 years imprisonment.) 'KZ Auschwitz', p. 37.
8 Stanisław Kocyan, statement. (Böck survived the war and now lives in West Germany.)
9 Stanisław Okęcki, 'Przejawy . . .', p. 106.
10 Confidential statement.
11 Marossányi. Langbein, *Der Auschwitz-Prozess*, p. 997.
12 Kulka, p. 142.
13 Höss (Polish version), pp. 335–338; Ziemba, 'Geflügelfarm . . .', pp. 42, 63.
14 *Biuletyn Informacyjny*, p. 3.
15 Kłodziński, 'Maria Stromberger', p. 104.
16 Langbein, *Die Stärkeren*, pp. 120 and 162.
17 Kłodziński, 'Maria . . .', p. 104.
18 In 1943 the firm of Krupp took over a large hall in the Auschwitz area, which was equipped with machines to make fuses for grenades. Next to it the firm Union also began to manufacture fuses. Munition works were also built in the sub-camps: Eintrachthütte, Neue Dachs, Lagischa, Fürstengrube and Janinagrube.
19 Höss (Polish version), p. 190.
20 Jaworski, p. 131.
21 Fejkiel, 'Medycyna . . .', p. 487.
22 Langbein, *Menschen* . . ., p. 254.
23 Langbein, *Die Stärkeren*, p. 133.
24 Cass Stankiewicz, letter to author.
25 Alfred Woycicki, 'Zeznanie . . .', p. 8.
26 The *Book of the Bunker*, pp. II/45, II/46, II/48.
27 Czech, No. 4, p. 140. (She says that 54 prisoners were chosen and shot then, but a careful examination of the *Book of the Bunker* shows that only 47 were shot that day.)
28 Ludwik Rajewski, *Oświęcim* . . ., p. 112; Stefan Jellenta, 'Podpułkownik Dziama'.
29 Broad, p. 13.
30 The *Book of the Bunker*, pp. II/44–46.
31 Brol, Włoch, J. Pilecki, p. 30.
32 Fejkiel, 'Medycyna . . .', p. 505.
33 Gniatczyński, p. 2.
34 Bartosiewicz, *op. cit.*; 'Jot' (Józef Otowski), 'Wspomnienie . . .' (Bartosiewicz made his statement in London in 1970 and Otowski wrote his article in Stockholm in 1965.)
35 Langbein, *Prozess* . . ., p. 383 (Fejkiel's evidence).
36 Bartosiewicz, *op. cit.*
37 Ibid.
38 Fejkiel, 'Medycyna . . .', p. 487.
39 Czech, No. 4, pp. 146–149.
40 Eugeniusz Niedojadło, 'Podobóz Brno', pp. 109–110; Józef Ścisło, *Świat musi osądzić*, p. 170.
41 Czech, No. 4, p. 151.
42 Höss (Polish version), p. 303.
43 Czech, No. 4, pp. 149–152.
44 Ibid.

45 Fejkiel, 'Medycyna ...', p. 511.
46 Langbein, *Die Stärkeren*, pp. 147–151.
47 Brol, Włoch, J. Pilecki, p. 34.
48 Langbein, *Die Stärkeren*, p. 153.
49 Höss (Polish version), p. 273.

Chapter Ten

1 *Polskie Siły Zbrojne* ..., p. 140.
2 Friedman and Hołuj; Dziubińska; Adam Lutnik, 'Front Oświęcimia'.
3 *Auschwitz note-books*, No. 3, p. 89.
4 The first voice raised in Poland to draw attention to the tendentious information concerning the underground movement in Auschwitz, was an article by Kazimierz Rawicz, 'Oświęcimskie podziemie', published in the *Tygodnik Powszechny*, only in 1957. It was in answer to an article by T. Hołuj published in the same weekly a few weeks earlier.
5 Zaborowski, p. 36; Bartosiewicz, *op. cit.*
6 Ibid.
7 Fejkiel, 'Medycyna ...', p. 512; Dering, p. 109.
8 e.g. he helped Pilecki to escape from the camp in April 1943 (Pilecki, p. 88; Fejkiel, 'Medycyna ...', p. 506–507).
9 Czech, No. 6, p. 62.
10 Ibid, p. 61.
11 Brol, Włoch, J. Pilecki, pp. 10–13.
12 Langbein, *Die Stärkeren*, p. 154. (It has not been possible to establish the date of this broadcast.)
13 Czech, No. 6, p. 70.
14 Ibid, p. 79.
15 Vrba and Bestic, p. 208.
16 Sobański, p. 228.
17 Vrba and Bestic, p. 228.
18 Robert M. W. Kempner, *Eichmann* ..., pp. 427–430.
19 Czech, No. 7, p. 74.
20 On August 22nd, 1944, Auschwitz I, II and III together contained 135,000 prisoners, men and women. (Czech, No. 7, p. 79.)
21 Zaborowski, p. 28. (There is no further information about this group.)
22 Ota Kraus and Erich Kulka, *The Death Factory*, p. 174.
23 Henry Bulawko, *Les Jeux* ..., pp. 123, 128, 146 and 182.
24 Friedman and Hołuj, p. 131.
25 Bartosiewicz, *op. cit.*
26 Walter-Janke, pp. 236–238.
27 Bielewicz, letter, 1972. Also: Henri Michel, *La Guerre* ..., p. 188. (Michel says that the appointment was made by the Polish Government in London, but this is not so.)
28 Langbein, *Die Stärkeren*, pp. 189–194.

Chapter Eleven

1 Sobański, pp. 68–73.
2 Ibid, p. 75; Hardt and Czerpak, p. 99; Ciołkosz, 'Zgon Teodora'.
3 Ibid, p. 100.
4 Czech, No. 4, p. 149.
5 Sobański, pp. 119–130.

6 Danuta-Wawrzyczek, written report.
7 Sobański, pp. 247–248.
8 Halina Wróbel, 'Likwidacja . . .', pp. 13–14.
9 Such levelling works were carried out by a special 'Team 1005', subordinate to Eichmann and led by *SS* Colonel Paul Blobl (Gerard Reitlinger, *Die Endlösung*, pp. 160 and 264); Wróbel, p. 15.
10 Wróbel, 'Likwidacja . . .', pp. 15–17.
11 *Wśród koszmarnej zbrodni*, p. 136, footnote 27.
12 Höss (Polish version), pp. 138–139.
13 *Wśród koszmarnej* . . . p. 152.
14 Miklos Nyiszli, *Pracownia Doktora Mengele*, p. 175, f.n. 31.
15 Ibid, pp. 31–32.
16 Yad Vashem, microfilm, sign. 03/2616.
17 *Wśród koszmarnej* . . ., pp. 143–171.
18 Confidential report.
19 *Wśród koszmarnej* . . ., pp. 152–155.
20 Israel Gutman, 'Der Aufstand . . .', pp. 273–275.
21 Czech, No. 7, p. 91; Gutman, p. 275.
22 Ibid, p. 92.
23 Nyiszli, pp. 127–128.
24 Czech, No. 7, p. 92.
25 Raya Kagan, 'Die letzten . . .', p. 284.
26 Czech, No. 7, pp. 93–94.
27 Friedman and Hołuj, p. 136.
28 *Polskie Siły Zbrojne* . . ., pp. 169–203.
29 Garliński, pp. 141–142.
30 Despatch from the commander of the Home Army in Warsaw to the Commander-in-Chief in London, ref. no. 7524, sent on 29th August, 1944 – i.e. after the outbreak of the Warsaw Uprising (Polish Underground Movement Study Trust, file 3.16.)
31 Walter-Janke, pp. 244–246.
32 Garliński, pp. 260–261.
33 Świętorzecki, 'Życiorys . . .', p. 3.
34 Walter-Janke, p. 243.
35 B. więzień 20034, 'Kilka uwag . . .'.
36 Sobański, *Ucieczki*, pp. 114–117.
37 Tadeusz Orzeszko, 'Relacja chirurga . . .', p. 46.
38 B. więzień, *op. cit.*
39 Orzeszko, p. 47.
40 Sobański, 'Żył jeszcze . . .' (see photographs).
41 Ibid.
42 Świętorzecki, letter.
43 Garliński, pp. 176–177.
44 Padkowski, 'Dalczego nie . . .'.
45 Czech, No. 7, pp. 83–100.
46 Sobański, *Ucieczki* . . ., pp. 241–242; Czech, No. 7, pp. 99.
47 Ibid, p. 244.
48 Ibid, pp. 245–251; Czech, No. 7, p. 110. (Sobański and Czech says that Johann Roth received in reward a photograph of Oswald Pohl, the head of *WVHA*, with a personal inscription).
49 Czech, No. 7, p. 114.
50 Wróbel, p. 16.
51 Ibid, p. 16.
52 Czech, No. 7, p. 123.

Appendix 1

1 Z. Pilecka, *op. cit.*, p. 11.
2 Jan Mierzanowski, letter to the author, May 12th, 1971.
3 Jan Mierzanowski, letter to the author, July 27th, 1971.
4 Z. Pilecka, *op. cit.*, p. 12. *Życie Warszawy* (*The Life of Warsaw*), March 16th, 1948.
5 Gen. Władysław Anders, the commander of the Polish Second Corps in Italy.
6 *Życie Warszawy, op. cit.*
7 'Wiciak', letter to the author, February 21st, 1970.
8 Z. Pilecka, *op. cit.*, p. 13.
9 Władysław Bartoszewski, *Warsaw Death Ring*, Warsaw, 1968, p. 136.
10 S. Kłodziński, 'Maria Stromberger', *op. cit.*
11 Janusz Gumkowski, Tadeusz Kułakowski, *Zbrodniarze hitlerowscy przed Najwyższym Trybunałem Narodowym* ('Nazi Criminals before the Supreme National Tribunal'), Warsaw, 1961, p. 171.
12 *Oświęcim w oczach SS* (*Auschwitz in the eyes of the SS*), Auschwitz, 1972, p. 284.

SELECT BIBLIOGRAPHY

The archives contain few documents on the underground movement in Auschwitz, and I have had to supplement these by seeking out living witnesses, thanks to whom I have been able to piece together a picture of the events of that time. That is why the list of short reports, letters and verbal statements takes up a large amount of space among my sources. First-hand evidence obtained in conversation often gave me much more than publications or written statements. Each conversation has been annotated with the exact date on which it took place.

The bibliography of secondary works on Auschwitz comprises more than 7,000 items in various languages. I have selected those which give essential information about the camp itself and, of course, at least some information about the underground movement there. Above all I have used Danuta Czech's basic 'Kalendarz wydarzeń w obozie koncentracyjnym Oświęcim-Brzezinka' (*Calendar* of events in the concentration camp Auschwitz-Birkenau), to be found in the *Zeszyty Oświęcimskie* (*Auschwitz note-books*). Equally important are numerous works published in the *Przegląd Lekarski* (*Medical Review*). Each year the January issue of this monthly carries the sub-title *Oświęcim* (Auschwitz) and is devoted to questions concerning the camps.

When in the case of an unpublished report I do not state where it is to be found, this means that the original or a copy of it is in my possession. In the list of publications I have omitted works on Nazism in general which are not directly connected with my subject.

I. ARCHIVAL SOURCES
  A. Unpublished documents, reports and statements
    1. Archives

     —**Stadium Polski Podziemnej** (Polish Underground Movement [1939–45] Study Trust), London:
     Files of the VIth Bureau of the Polish General Staff,
     Files of the Polish Ministry of the Interior,
     Files of the department of reports.

     —**Państwowe Muzeum w Oświęcimiu** (State Museum at Auschwitz):
     Central records,
     Department of reports,
     Photographic department.

—**International Tracing Service,** Arolsen, W. Germany:
Central records,
Archives of the Auschwitz concentration camp,
Archives of the Buchenwald concentration camp,
Archives of the Mauthausen concentration camp,
Archives of the Ravensbrück concentration camp,
Photographic department.

—**Wiener Library,** London:
Reports on the fate of Jews in Auschwitz-Birkenau concentration camp.

—**Rijksinstituut voor Oorlogsdocumentatie,** Amsterdam,
Department of reports.

—**Yad Vashem,** Jerusalem:
Reports on the *Sonderkommando*.

—**BBC Written Archives Centre,** Reading:
File: *Sonderbericht* programme.

2. Unpublished reports

—Antoni Andrzejewski, *Ucieczka z Oświęcimia*, Polish Underground
Movement Study Trust, File: II competition of the Home Army Circle.

—Henryk Bartosiewicz, written account of his activities in the Auschwitz
concentration camp.

—Tadeusz Bielewicz, *Ocena relacji J. Danuty-Wawrzyczka i jego list*,
Warsaw, 12.11.1971.

—Tadeusz Bielewicz, *Uwagi do książki Wojciecha Jekiełka 'W pobliżu
Oświęcimia'*, Warsaw, 20.7.1971.

—Leopold Czekalski, written account of his arrest and imprisonment in
the Auschwitz concentration camp, Auschwitz, 21.10.70.

—Jan Danuta-Wawrzyczek, *Ziemia Oświęcimska w walce*.

—Władysław Dering, *T.A.P. (Tajna Armia Polska)*.

—Władysław Grohs, *Uwagi odnośnie relacji Zygmunta Urbańczyka*,
15.2.1966.

—Zofia Krasińska-Lesniak, a written account of her arrest and stay in the
Auschwitz concentration camp, Auschwitz, 25.5.1970.

—Anna Pawełczyńska, a written account of her arrest and stay in the
Auschwitz concentration camp, Auschwitz, 28.5.1969.

—Antonina Piątkowska, *O pracy i działalności Polek – więźniarek
politycznych w obozie Oświęcim-Brzezinka w latach 1942–1945*
Oświęcim, Brzezinka, Ravensbrück, Neustadt-Glewe.
Z Oświęcimia na wolność.

—Zofia Pilecka, written account of the fate of her father, Witold Pilecki.

—Witold Pilecki, written account of his underground activity in the
Auschwitz concentration camp, Italy, 1946. Polish Underground Movement (1939–45) Study Trust. File: Witold Pilecki.

—Józef Putek, *Ponura rzeczywistość i mity oświęcimskie*, Poznań, 1963.
State Museum at Auschwitz, Syg. Wsp. (Putek, 267).

—Karol Świętorzecki, *Życiorys Stefana Jasieńskiego*.

—Zygmunt Urbańczyk, *Wspomnienie okupacyjne.*
Jakie mam zastrzeżenia do książki 'W pobliżu Oświęcimia', 13.12.1965.
—A. F. van Velsen, written account (in Dutch) of his experiences in the German concentration camp Auschwitz-Birkenau, 5.2.1948. Netherlands State Institute for War Documentation, Amsterdam. (Copy in author's hands).

—Alfred Woycicki, *Zeznanie dla prokuratury we Frankfurcie nad Menem*, Cracow, 25.11.1959. Polish Underground Movement (1939–45) Study Trust, File: 2.33.

—Unknown author, written report (in German) about the fate of the *Sonderkommando*, Yad Vashem, Jerusalem, Sign. 03/2616. (Microfilm in author's hands).

3. Unpublished short statements and letters

—Tadeusz Bielewicz, letters to the author: Dec. 8th, 1970, June 6th, 1971, June 21st, 1971, Oct 18th, 1971, June 6th, 1972.

—Bolesław Burski, letter to the author, Apr. 10th, 1972.

—Zbigniew Bogdan Drecki, written report, July 3rd, 1972.

—Stefan Buthner (in the camp as Stefan Budziaszek), letter to the author, Sept. 15th, 1972.

—Barbara Dubiel, letter to the author, Aug. 23rd, 1971.

—Zbigniew Stanisław Emmerling, written statement, Aug. 17th, 1971.

—Stanisław Kocyan, written statement, Aug. 11th, 1970.

—Maria Kozakiewicz, letter to the author, Sept, 13th, 1971.

—Mikołaj Kurlit, letter to the author, Feb. 26th, 1972.

—Wanda Marossányi, letters to the author: Sept. 9th, 1971, Oct. 3rd, 1971, Oct. 30th, 1972.

—Jan M. Mierzanowski, letters to the author: May 12th, 1971, July 27th, 1971.

—Kazimierz Nowicki, letter to the author, Aug. 19th, 1970.

—Kazimierz Papée, letter to the author, Dec. 19th, 1972.

—Stanisława Rachwałowa, letters to the author: Aug. 23rd, 1971, July 3rd, 1972.

—Janusz Nel Siedlecki, letter to the author, May, 1972.

—Cass Stankiewicz-Wiśniewski, written statement, Nov. 19th, 1970 and letters to the author: Oct. 27th, 1970, Nov. 5th, 1970, Nov. 19th, 1970.

—Michał Stempkowski, letter from Warsaw, March 7th, 1972.

—Karol Świętorzecki, written statement, April 1971 and letters to the author: Apr. 1971, Nov. 5th, 1971, Jan. 7th, 1972, March 6th, 1972, Apr. 12th, 1972, May 9th, 1972, June 19th, 1972.

—Stefan Świszczowski, written answers to the author's questions, Jan. 19th, 1973.

—Rudolf Vrba (in the camp as Walter Rosenberg), letter to the author, August, 11th, 1972.

—'Wiciak', written statement, Jan, 1970, and 12 letters, 1969–1971.
Plus 26 other letters and statements the authors of which prefer to remain anonymous.

4. Unpublished verbal statements to the author.

—Henryk Bartosiewicz, 18th September, 1970.

—Marian Bohusz-Szyszko, September, 1970.

—Jerzy Budkiewicz, October, 1971.

—Adam Ciołkosz, 3rd October, 1970.

—Jerzy Cynk, 13th February, 1971.

—Halina Czarnocka, May, 1971.

—Leon Głogowski, 5th November, 1969.

—Peter Kalb, 3rd March, 1972.

—Otto Küsel, 26th September, 1972.

—Hermann Langbein, 10th July, 1970, in the presence of Jerzy Budkiewicz, 2nd June, 1972.

—Wanda Marossányi, 19th October, 1972.

—Henryk Sienkiewicz, 18th September, 1970.

—Stefan Świszczowski, 23rd January, 1972.

Plus 36 other statements by former Auschwitz prisoners who prefer to remain anonymous.

B. Published documents

—*Armia Krajowa w Dokumentach 1939–1945, Tom I, Wrzesień 1939 – Czerwiec 1941.* Polish Underground Movement (1939–45) Study Trust, London, 1970.

—T. Bernstein, A. Eisenbach, A. Rotkowski, *Eksterminacja Żydów na Ziemiach Polskich w Okresie Okupacji Hitlerowskiej,* Zbiór Dokumentow, Warsaw, 1957.

—Mgr. N. Blumental, *Dokumenty i Materiały, Tom I, Obozy,* Łódź, 1946.

—*Dokumenty i materiały do dziejów okupacji niemieckiej w Polsce, Tom II, Akcje i wysiedlenia, Cześć I,* Opr. Dr. Józef Kiermisz, Warsaw, 1946.

—Dr. Filip Friedman i Tadeusz Hołuj, *Oświęcim,* Warsaw, 1946. The part comprising documents, pp. 163–262.

—Joe J. Heydecker und Johannes Leeb, *Der Nürnberger Prozess,* Köln-Berlin, 1962.

—Hermann Langbein, *Der Auschwitz-Prozess, Eine Dokumentation,* Vol. I, II. Wien, 1965.

—*NS-Juristen Auschwitz Massenmord,* Dokumentation zum Auschwitz-Prozess, Berlin, 1965.

—*Obóz koncentracyjny Oświęcim w świetle akt Delegatury Rządu na Kraj,* a special issue (I) of the *Auschwitz note-books,* Auschwitz, 1968.

—*Okupacja i Ruch Oporu w Dzienniku Hansa Franka, 1939–1945,* Vol. I, II, Warsaw, 1970.

—Stanisław Piotrowski, *Hans Frank's Diary,* Warsaw, 1961.

—*Przegląd Lekarski* (Medical Review), Auschwitz issue, Nos. from 1961 to 1972, Cracow.

—*Wśród koszmarnej zbrodni, notatki więźniów Sonderkommando odnalezione w Oświęcimiu,* special (II) issue of the *Auschwitz note-books,* Auschwitz, 1971.

—*Zeszyty Oświęcimskie* (Auschwitz note-books), Nos. 1–4, 5–7, 9–13. Auschwitz Museum.

II. BOOKS AND ARTICLES

—Roger Abada, 'Organisation de la Résistance au Camp d'Auschwitz', *Témoignages sur Auschwitz*, Paris, 1946.

—H. G. Adler, *Theresienstadt 1941 bis 1945*, Tübingen, 1960.

—H. G. Adler, Hermann Langbein, Ella Lingens-Reiner, *Auschwitz, Zeuginsse und Berichte*, Frankfurt-am-Main, 1962.

—Jadwiga Apostoł-Staniszewska, *Echa okupacyjnych lat*, Warsaw, 1970.

—O. Augustyn, *Za drutami obozu koncentracyjnego w Oświęcimiu*, Cracow, 1945.

—Wojciech Barcz, 'Die erste Vergasung', *Auschwitz, Zeugnisse und Berichte*, Frankfurt-am-Main, 1962.

—Lesław M. Bartelski, *Walcząca Warszawa*, Warsaw, 1968.

—Władysław Bartoszewski, Bogdan Brzeziński, Leszek Moczulski, *Kronika wydarzeń w Warszawie 1939–1945*, Warsaw, 1970.

—Władysław Bartoszewski, *Palmiry*, Warsaw, 1969.
Prawda o von dem Bachu, Warsaw, 1961.
Warsaw Death Ring, 1939–44, Warsaw, 1968.

—Bruno Baum, *Widerstand in Auschwitz*, II Ed., Berlin, 1962.

—Paul Blobl, *Die Endlösung*, Berlin, 1956.

—Józef Bogusz, 'Słowa wstępu', *Medical Review*, Cracow, 1968.

—Tadeusz Borowski, Janusz Nel Siedlecki, Krystyn Olszewski, *Byliśmy w Oświęcimiu*, Germany, 1946.

—Tadeusz Bór-Komorowski, *The Secret Army*, London, 1950.

—Franciszek Brol, Gerard Włoch Jan Pilecki, 'Książka Bunkra', *Auschwitz note-books*, No. 1, Auschwitz, 1957.

—Jerzy Brandhuber, 'Jeńcy radzieccy w obozie koncentracyjnym w Oświęcimiu', *Auschwitz note-books*, No. 4, Auschwitz, 1960.
'Ziemia zapomniana', *Auschwitz note-books*, No. 5, Auschwitz, 1961.

—Pery Broad, 'KZ Auschwitz', *Auschwitz note-books*, No. 9, Auschwitz, 1965.

—Hans Buchheim, *Totalitäre Herrschaft*, III ed., München, 1964.

—Henry Bulawko, *Les Jeux de la Mort et de l'Espoir*, Auschwitz-Jaworzno, Paris, 1954.

—Irena Bundzewicz, 'Kostek', *Auschwitz note-books*, No. 11, Auschwitz, 1969.

—Tadeusz Chowaniec, 'Epilog', *Auschwitz note-books*, No. 7, Auschwitz, 1963.

—Tadeusz Chruścicki, 'Ojciec Maksymilian Kolbe', *Życie Warszawy*, No. 237, Warsaw, 1971.

– Jan M. Ciechanowski, *The Warsaw Rising of 1944*, London, 1974.

– Edward Ciesielski, *Wspomnienia Oświęcimskie*, Cracow, 1968.

– Adam Ciołkosz, 'Tajemnice Oswięcimia', *Na antenie*, No. 5, Munich, 1964.
'Zgon Teodora' *Na antenie, No. 7*, Munich, 1964.

– T. Cyprian, J. Sawicki, M. Siewierski, *Głos ma prokurator*, Warsaw, 1966.

—Danuta Czech, 'The Auschwitz sub-camps', *From the History of KL-Auschwitz*, Vol. I, Auschwitz, 1967.

'Deportacja i zagłada Żydów greckich w KL Auschwitz', *Auschwitz note-books*, No. 11, Auschwitz, 1969.
'Kalendarz wydarzeń w obozie koncentracyjnym Oświęcim-Brzezinka', *Auschwitz note-books*, Nos. 2–7, Auschwitz, 1959–1964.
—Anna Czuperska-Śliwicka, *Cztery lata ostrego dyżuru*, II Ed., Warsaw, 1968.
—*Camps de Concentration en Allemagne (1939–1945)*, 3me ed., Genève, 1947.
—Rudolf Diem, 'Śp. Kazimierz Jarzębowski', *Przeglad Geodezyjny*, Warsaw, 1947.
—Jan Dobraczyński, 'Dał życie w ofierze', *Wrocławski Tygodnik Katolicki*, No. 33, Wrocław, 1971.
—Lucjan Dobroszycki, *Centralny Katalog Polskiej Prasy Konspiracyjnej 1939–1945*, Warsaw, 1962.
—*Drogi Cichociemnych* (collective work), London, 1961.
—Barbara Dziubińska, 'Ruch oporu w obozie masowej zagłady w Oświęcimiu' *Wojskowy Przegląd Historyczny*, Vol. 3, Warsaw, 1965.
—*Dynamit*, Vol. I, II, Cracow, 1964, 1967.
—'Eichmann erinnert sich', *Auschwitz, Zeugnisse und Berichte*, Frankfurt-am-Main, 1962.
—Władysław Fejkiel, 'Medycyna za drutami', *Pamiętniki lekarzy*, Warsaw, 1964.
'Ethical and Legal Limits of Experimentation in Medicine in connection with Professor Clauberg's Affair', *From the History of KL-Auschwitz*, Vol. I, 1967.
'The health service in the Auschwitz concentration camp', *Medical Review* (special English edition), Cracow, 1962.
'Starvation in Auschwitz', *From the History of KL-Auschwitz*, Vol. I, 1967.
—Alfred Fiederkiewicz, *Brzezinka-Birkenau*, Warsaw, 1965.
—Gracjan Fijałkowski, 'Nie trzeba umierać', *Auschwitz note-books*, No. 5, 1961.
'Odwszenie w Birkenau', *Auschwitz note-books*, No. 8, 1964.
—Viktor E. Frankl, *Psycholog w obozie koncentracyjnym*, (translated from German), Warsaw, 1962.
—Filip Friedman and Tadeusz Hołuj, *Oświęcim*, Warsaw, 1946.
—Józef Garliński, *Poland, SOE and the Allies*, London, 1969.
—Adolf Gawalewicz, *Refleksje z poczekalni do gazu*, Cracow, 1968.
—Wincenty Gawron, 'Losy niektórych oficerów kawalerii w Oświęcimiu', *Przegląd Kawalerii i Broni Pancernej*, No. 55, London, 1969.
'Nasz kalejdoskop – Dalsze szczegóły o ucieczce Jastra', *Dziennik Związkowy (Zgoda)*, USA, Nov. 3rd, 1971.
—*German Crimes in Poland*, Warsaw, 1946.
—Leon Głogowski, 'Moje pierwsze dni w obozie oswięcimskim', *Medical Review*, Cracow, 1968.
'Szpital w Brzezince', *Medical Review*, Cracow, 1965.
—Wojciech Gniatczyński, 'Proces Oświęcimski', *Na antenie*, Munich, Apr. 2nd, 1965.
—Tadeusz Gędziorowski, *Widma*, Warsaw, 1966.
—Kurt, R. Grossmann, *Die unbesungenen Helden*, II, Ed., Berlin, 1961.

—Robert A. Graham, *Pope Pius XII and the Jews of Hungary in 1944*, New York, 1964.

—Janusz Gumkowski, Tadeusz Kułakowski, *Zbrodniarze hitlerowscy przed Najwyższym Trybunałem Narodowym*, Warsaw, 1961.

—Israel Gutman, 'Der Aufstand des Sonderkommandos', *Auschwitz, Zeugnisse und Berichte*, Frankfurt-am-Main, 1962.

—Nina Gusiewa, 'O tym zapomnieć nie wolno', *Auschwitz note-books*, No. 5, Auschwitz, 1961.

—Kazimierz Hałgas, 'Oddział chirurgiczny szpitala obozowego w Oświęcimiu w latach 1940–1941', *Medical Review*, Cracow, 1971.

—Zdzisław Hardt i Stanisław Czerpak, *W cieniu krematorium*, Warsaw, 1969.

—Kitty Hart, 'Kanada', *Auschwitz, Zeugnisse und Berichte*, Frankfurt-am-Main, 1962.

'Das Frauenlager', *Auschwitz, Zeugnisse und Berichte*, Frankfurt-am-Main, 1962.

—Adelaide Hautval, 'Adelaide Hautval speaks about Auschwitz and the Dering trial', reported by Hallam Tennyson, *The Listener*, Vol. 86, No. 2221, London, 1971.

—Paul Heller, 'Das Aussenlager Jaworzno,' *Auschwitz, Zeugnisse und Berichte*, Frankfurt-am-Main, 1962.

—Mavis Hill and Norman L. Williams, *Auschwitz in England*, London, 1965.

—Tadeusz Hołuj, 'Czy można było uwolnić więźniów Oświęcimia', *Tygodnik Demokratyczny*, No. 48, Cracow, 1957.
Koniec naszego świata, III Ed., Cracow, 1965.
'Nieznana rocznica', *Polityka*, No. 21, Warsaw, 1968.
'Marian Toliński', *Medical Review*, Cracow, 1964.

—Rudolf Höss, *Kommandant in Auschwitz*, Stuttgart, 1958.
Commandant of Auschwitz, London, 1959.
Wspomnienia komendanta obozu oświęcimskiego (Polish version), Warsaw, 1956.

—Kazimierz Iranek-Osmecki, *Pierwsze półrocze Armii Krajowej (S.Z.P. – Z.W.Z.)*, London, 1948.

—'Imprisonments Cell of the Government Delegacy', materials sent to London and published by the Ministry of Interior as Report No. 14/44, on Oct. 21st, 1944, *Najnowsze Dzieje Polski*, Vol. XII, Warsaw, 1968.

—Tadeusz Iwaszko, 'Ucieczki więźniów z obozu koncentracyjnego Oświęcim', *Auschwitz note-books*, No. 7, Auschwitz, 1963.
'Podobóz Günthergrube', *Auschwitz note-books*, No. 12, 1970.
'Podobóz Laurahütte', *Auschwitz note-books*, No. 10, 1967.

—Emeryka Iwaszko, 'Podobóz Janinagrube', *Auschwitz note-books*, No. 10, 1967.

—Stanisław Jagielski, 'Psychiczne galwanizowanie muzułmana', *Medical Review*, Cracow, 1968.

—Antoni Jakubski, *Organizacja niemieckich obozów koncentracyjnych*, London, 1948.

—Stanisław Jasiński, 'Moja ucieczka z Oświęcimia' *Auschwitz note-books*, No. 5, 1961.

—Czesław Wincenty Jaworski, *Wspomnienia z Oświęcimia*, Warsaw, 1962.

—Jan Jaźwiec, *Pomnik dowódcy*, Cracow, 1971.

—Franciszek Jaźwiecki, 'Wspomnienia', *Auschwitz note-books*, No. 5, 1961.

—Wojciech Jekiełek, 'Żmija', *W pobliżu Oświęcimia*, II Ed., Warsaw, 1963.

—Stefan Jellenta, 'Podpułkownik Dziama', *Wrocławski Tygodnik Katolicki'* Wrocław, Feb. 8th, 1970.

—Maria Elżbieta Jezierska, 'Biały efekt', *Auschwitz note-books*, No. 8, 1964.
'Chorować nie wolno', *Medical Review*, Cracow, 1966.

—'Jot', 'Wspomnienie z Oświęcimia', *Na antenie*, Munich, July 11th, 1965.

—Tadeusz Joachimowski, 'To było przed blokiem 14a, *Wrocławski Tygodnik Katolicki*, No. 42, Wrocław, 1971.

—Raya Kagan, 'Die letzten Opfer des Widerstands' *Auschwitz, Zeugnisse und Berichte*, Frankfurt-am-Main, 1962.

—Janina Kajtoch, 'Znałam ludzi dobrej woli', *Kominy*, Warsaw, 1962.

—Andrzej Jósef Kamiński, *Hitlerowskie obozy koncentracyjne i środki masowej zagłady w polityce imperializmu niemieckiego*, Poznań, 1964.

—Yitzhak Katznelson, *Vittel Diary*, Tel-Aviv, 1964.

—Friedrich K. Kaul, *Ärzte in Auschwitz*, Berlin, 1962.

—Zbigniew Kączkowski, 'Próba ucieczki z obozu oświęcimskiego', *Medical Review*, Cracow, 1967.

—Robert M. W. Kempner, *Eichmann und Komplizen*, Zürich, 1961.
SS im Kreuzverhör, Munich, 1964.

—Antoni Kępiński, 'Anus mundi', *Medical Review*, Cracow, 1965.
'Oświęcimskie refleksje psychiatry', *Medical Review*, Cracow, 1964.
'Refleksje oświęcimskie; psychopatia władzy', *Medical Review*, Cracow, 1967.'
'Refleksje oświęcimskie; rampa; psychopatia decyzji', *Medical Review*, Cracow, 1968.
Rytm życia, Cracow, 1972.

Maria Orwid, 'Z psychopatii nadludzi', *Medical Review*, Cracow, 1962.

—Wiesław Kielar, *Anus Mundi*, Cracow, 1972,.
'Edek i Mala', *Auschwitz note-books*, No. 5, 1961.

—Mieczysław Kieta, 'Prof. dr. Jan Sehn', *Medical Review*, Cracow, 1966.

—Julian Kiwała, 'Kuchnia dietetyczna w szpitalu obozu koncentracyjnego w Oświęcimiu', *Medical Review*, Cracow,1964.
'Szpital w obozie żeńskim w Brzezince na przełomie lat 1942–1943', *Medical Review*, Cracow, 1965.

—Alfons Klafkowski, *Obozy koncentracyjne hitlerowskie jako zagadnienie prawa międzynarodowego*, Warsaw, 1968.

—Stanisław Kłodziński, (all articles in the *Medical Review*).
'Dur wysypkowy w obozie Oświęcim I', 1965.
'Dr. Dorota Lorska', 1967.
'Dr. Edward Nowak', 1971.
'Dr. Leon Głogowski', 1971.
'Dr. Ludwik Witkowski', 1971.
'Dr. Stefan Pizło', 1970.
'Dr. Wilhelm Türschmidt', 1970.
'Dr. Władysława Jasińska', 1969.

'Esesmani w oświęcimskiej służbie zdrowia', 1966.
'Fenol w KL Auschwitz-Birkenau', 1963.
'Laboratorium Instytutu Hygieny w Oświęcimiu', 1969.
'Maria Stromberger,' 1962.
'Paczki Międzynarodowego Czerwonego Krzyża dla więźniów Oświęcimia', 1967.
'Pierwsza oświęcimska selekcja do gazu', 1970.
'Wkład polskiej służby zdrowia w ratowanie życia wieźniów w obozie koncentracyjnym Oświęcim,' 1961.
'Zbrodnicze doświadczenia farmakologiczne na więźniach obozu koncentracyjnego w Oświęcimiu', 1965.
'Z zagadnień ludobójstwa', 1964'.
—Franciszek Kobielski, 'Kontakty z obozem', Auschwitz note-books, No. 5, 1961.
—Alfred Konieczny, 'Uwagi o początkach obozu koncentracyjnego w Oświęcimiu,' Auschwitz note-books, No. 12, 1970.
—Wanda Koprowska, 'Odwszenie', Auschwitz note-books, No. 5, 1961.
—Stefan Korboński, Fighting Warsaw, London, 1956.
—Henryk Korotyński i Adam Wysocki, Przez druty Oświęcimia, Warsaw, 1961.
—Janina Kościuszkowa, 'Brief biographies of deceased Polish physicans and health service workers who distinguished themselves helping prisoners of the Auschwitz concentration camp.' Medical Review (English issue), Cracow, 1962.
—Janina Kowalczykowa, as above.
'Choroba głodowa w obozie koncentracyjnym w Oświęcimiu', Medical Review, Cracow, 1961.
—Johann Kremer, Pamiętnik, Auschwitz note-books, No. 13, 1971.
—Józef Kret, 'Dzień w karnej kompanii', Auschwitz note-books, No. 1, 1957.
'Lekarze znaleźli wyjście', Medical Review, Cracow, 1966.
'Przyczynek do historii zagłady inteligentów polskich w obozie oświęcimskim', Medical Review, Cracow, 1969.
'Więźniowie-miernicy w obozie oświęcimskim', Medical Review, Cracow, 1971.
'Ze wspomnień oświęcimskich', Medical Review, Cracow, 1968.
—Ludwik Kubik, 'Jeszcze o sprawie Jasieńskiego', a letter to the editor, Tygodnik Powszechny, No. 5, Cracow, 1972.
'Oświęcimski gryps', Tygodnik Powszechny, Cracow, Jan. 2nd, 1972.
—Erich Kulka, The Death Factory (translation from Czech), London, 1966.
Útěk z tábora smrti, Praha, 1966.
—Aleksander Kunicki, Cichy Front, Warsaw, 1968.
—Simon Laks et René Coudy, Musiques d'un autre monde, Paris, 1948.
—Hermann Langbein, Auschwitz, Zeugnisse und Berichte (together with H. G. Adler and Ella Lingens), Frankfurt-am-Main, 1962.
Der Auschwitz-Prozess, Vol. I, II, Wien, 1965.
Menschen in Auschwitz, Wien,1972.
Die Stärkeren, Wien, 1949.
—Jozef Lánik, Co Dante neviděl, Bratislava, 1964.
—Aleksey Lebedev, Soldaty Maloy Voyny, Moscow, 1957.
—André Lettich, Trente-quatre mois dans les camps de concentration, Tours, 1946.
—Ella Lingens, 'Dr. Adelaide Hautval', Medical Review, Cracow, 1964.

Auschwitz, Zeugnisse und Berichte, (together with H. G. Adler and H. Langbein), Frankfurt-am-Main, 1962.

'Nationale Fragen im Revier', *Medical Review*, Cracow, 1966.

Prisoners of Fear, London, 1958.

—*Lista strat kultury polskiej*, Warsaw, 1947.

—Dorota Lorska, 'Blok X w Oświęcimiu', *Medical Review*, Cracow, 1965.

'Z pobytu w Oświęcimiu', *Medical Review*, Cracow, 1967.

—Jerzy Lukowski, 'Ruch oporu w obozie koncentracyjnym Oświęcim-Brzezinka', *Przeglad Historyczny*, Tom LVIII, Zeszyt 3, Warsaw, 1967.

—Adam Lutnik, 'Front Oświęcimia', *Za wolność i lud*, No. 1, Warsaw, 1952.

—Czesław Madajczyk, *Generalna Gubernia w planach hitlerowskich*, Warsaw, 1961.

Polityka III Rzeszy w okupowanej Polsce, Vol. I, II, Warsaw, 1970.

—Marian Malinowski and others, *Polski Ruch Robotniczy w okresie wojny i okupacji hitlerowskiej, wrzesień 1939 – styczen 1945*, Warsaw, 1965.

—Maria Maniakówna, 'W oświęcimskim bloku nr. 11', *Medical Review*, Cracow, 1970.

—Roger Manvell, 'The Camps', *History of the Second World War*, Vol. 5, No. 13, London.

—Emil de Martini, *Vier Millionen Tote klagen an!*, Munich, 1948.

—Tadeusz Mazurkiewicz, *Moja wojna z Niemcami*, Warsaw, 1969.

—Henri Michel, *La guerre de l'ombre*, Paris, 1970.

—Leon Mitkiewicz, *W najwyższym sztabie zachodnich Aliantów, 1943–1945*, London, 1971.

—R. J. Minney, *I shall fear no evil*, The story of Dr. Alina Brewda, London, 1966.

—Kazimierz Moczarski, 'Czy można było uwolnić więźniów Oświęcimia', *Tygodnik Powszechny*, No. 43, Cracow, 1957.

—Gustaw Morcinek, 'Wartość ofiary', *Wrocławski Tygodnik Katolicki*, No. 33, Wrocław, 1971.

—Jerzy Mostowski, 'Dwie ampułki', *Auschwitz note-books*, No. 5, 1961.

—Hans Münch, 'Głód i czas przeżycia w obozie oświęcimskim', (translation from German), *Medical Review*, Cracow, 1967.

—Eugeniusz Niedojadło, 'Podobóz Brno', *Medical Review*, Cracow, 1966.

—Maria Nowakowska, 'The women's hospital at Auschwitz-Birkenau', *Medical Review*, (English issue), Cracow, 1962.

—Miklós Nyiszli, *Pracownia doktora Mengele* (translation from Hungarian), Warsaw, 1966.

—Stanisław Okęcki, 'Przejawy internacjonalizmu, możliwości zrzutów broni i udział GOPR w walce z okupantem w Beskidzie Śląskim', *Resistance Movement in the Silesian Beskids during the years 1939–1945*, Katowice, 1968.

—*Okupacja i medycyna* (collective work), Warsaw, 1971.

—*Okupacja i ruch oporu w dzienniku Hansa Franka, 1939–1945*, Warsaw, 1970.

—Jan S. Olbrycht, 'Sprawy zdrowotne w obozie koncentracyjnym w Oświęcimiu' *Medical Review*, Cracow, 1962.

—Tadeusz Orzeszko, 'Relacja chirurga z obozu oświęcimskiego', *Medical Review*, Cracow, 1971.

—Czesław Ostańkowicz, *Ziemia parująca cyklonem*, Łódź, 1969.

—*Oświęcim w oczach SS*, Auschwitz, 1972.

—Tadeusz Paczuła, 'Die ersten Opfer sind die Polen' *Auschwitz, Zeugnisse und Berichte*, Frankfurt-am-Main, 1962.
'Obóz i szpital obozowy w Oświęcimiu we wczesnych okresach istnienia', *Medical Review*, Cracow, 1963.
'Organizacja i administracja szpitala obozowego KL Auschwitz', *Medical Review*, Cracow, 1962.
'Szpital obozowy', *Auschwitz note-books*, No. 5, 1961.

—Yvonne Pagniez, 'Niedziela w obozie' (translation from French), *Medical Review*, Cracow, 1969.

—Zacheusz Pawlak, *Przeżyłem*, Warsaw, 1964.

—Edward Padkowski, 'Dlaczego nie zaatakowano Oświęcimia', *Tygodnik Powszechny*, No. 6, Cracow, 1972.
'Jeszcze o tragedii pomiarowców', *Tygodnik Powszechny*, No. 19, Cracow, 1972.

—Zygmunt Pawłowicz, 'Jeszcze o planach odbicia więźniów Oświęcimia', *Wrocławski Tygodnik Katolicki*, No. 30, Wrocław, 1967.

—Zofia Posmysz, 'Sängerin', *Auschwitz note-books*, No. 9, 1964.

—'Polish women in German concentration camps', *Polish Fortnightly Review*, London, May 1st, 1945.

—Antonina Piątkowska, 'Z przeżyć oświęcimskich', *Medical Review*, Cracow 1968.

—Franciszek Piper, 'Podobóz Althammer', *Auschwitz note-books*, No. 13, 1971.
'Podobóz Blechhammer', *Auschwitz note-books*, No. 10, 1967.
'Podobóz Neu-Dachs', *Auschwitz note-books*, No. 12, 1970.
'Podobóz Sosnowitz (I, II)', *Auschwitz note-books*, No. 11, 1969.

—*Polskie Siły Zbrojne w II-giej wojnie światowej, Tom III, Armia Krajowa*, London, 1950.

—Jerzy Ptakowski, '25 rocznica uwolnienia więźniów hitlerowskich obozów koncentracyjnych', *Nowy Świat*, USA, May 20th, 1970.

—Ludwik Rajewski, *Oświęcim w systemie RSHA*, Warsaw, 1946.
Ruch oporu w polskiej literaturze obozowej, Olsztyn, 1971.

—Jerzy Rawicz, 'Dokument hańby', *Auschwitz note-books*, No. 13, 1971.
Karjera szambelana, Warsaw, 1971.

—Kazimierz Rawicz, 'Oświęcimskie podziemie', *Tygodnik Demokratyczny*, No. 53, Cracow, 1957.

—Henryk Rechowicz, *Ruch oporu na Śląsku i w Zagłębiu Dąbrowskim w latach okupacji hitlerowskiej*, Śląski Instytut Naukowy, Katowice, *Zeszyty Naukowe*, No. 30, 1970.

—Gerald Reitlinger, *Die Endlösung*, Berlin, 1950.

—*De la Résistance à la Déportation*, France, 1965.

—Zenon Różański, *Mützen ab*, Hannover, 1948.

—*Ruch oporu w Beskidzie Śląskim w latach 1939–1945*, Katowice, 1968.

—Zbigniew Rybak, 'Ziemia naznaczona krwią', *Gazeta Krakowska*, No. 149, Cracow, 1972.

—Czesław Rychlik, 'To była decyzja niezwykła', *Wrocławski Tygodnik Katolicki*, No. 42, Wrocław, 1971.

—Julian Rykała, *Więźniowie, Heftlingi, Emigranci*, Warsaw, 1972.

—Zdzisław Ryn, 'Błękitny Krzyż podczas okupacji hitlerowskiej', *Medical Review*, Cracow, 1970.

—Grete Salus, 'Frauen in Auschwitz', *Auschwitz, Zeugnisse und Berichte*, Frankfurt-am-Main, 1962.

—Jan Sehn, *Obóz koncentracyjny Oświęcim-Brzezinka*, Warsaw, 1964.
'Sprawa oświęcimskiego lekarza *SS* J. P. Kremera', *Medical Review*, Cracow, 1962.

—Júlia Škodová, *Tri Roky bez Mena*, Bratislava, 1962.

—Mieczysław Słowikowski, *Oświęcim*, Warsaw, 1945.

—Kazimierz Smoleń, *Auschwitz 1940–1945*, Auschwitz, 1965.
'The concentration camp Auschwitz', *From the history of KL Auschwitz*, Vol. I, 1967.
'Karjera', *Auschwitz note-books*, No. 5, 1961.

—Jenny Spritzner, *Ich war Nr. 10291*, Zürich.

—Tomasz Sobański, *Ucieczki Oświęcimskie*, II Ed., Warsaw, 1969.
'Żył jeszcze w grudniu 1944', *Za wolność i lud*, No. 38, Warsaw, 1972.

—Cass Stankiewicz-Wiśniewski, 'W strzępach na posterunku', *Związkowiec*, USA, August 7th, 1970.

—Judith Sternberg-Newman, *In the hell of Auschwitz*, New York, 1963.

—Irena Strzelecka, 'Podobóz Bismarckhütte', *Auschwitz note-books*, No. 12, 1970.
'Podobóz Hindenburg', *Auschwitz note-books*, No. 12, 1970.
'Podobóz Hubertushütte', *Auschwitz note-books*, No. 12, 1970.
'Podobóz Neustadt', *Auschwitz note-books*, No. 13, 1971.

—Manca Švalbová, *Vyhasnuté Oči*, Bratislava, 1964.

—Kazimierz Szczerbowski, 'Wspomnienia pierwszego pisarza rewiru oświęcimskiego', *Medical Review*, Cracow, 1970.

—Seweryna Szmaglewska, *Dymy nad Birkenau*, Warsaw, 1945.
'Sylwetki lekarzy – więźniów Oświęcimia', *Medical Review*, Cracow, 1964.
'Warszawskie dzieci w Oświęcimiu', *Głos Nauczycielski*, No. 3, Warsaw, 1961.
'Wybuchnie krzyk buntu', *Auschwitz note-books*, No. 8, 1964.

—*Szukajcie w popiołach*, papiery znalezione w Oświęcimiu, Łódź, 1965.

—Roman Szuszkiewicz, 'Dentystyka w obozie koncentracyjnym w Oświęcimiu', *Medical Review*, Cracow, 1964.

—Tadeusz Szymański, 'Nase', *Auschwitz note-books*, No. 5. 1961,
'Dr. Franciszek Gralla', *Medical Review*, Cracow, 1961.
'Przypadki *noma* w obozie cygańskim', *Medical Review*, Cracow, 1962.

—Józef Ścisło, *Świat musi osądzić*, Warsaw, 1969.

—Tadeusz Śnieszko, 'Dr. Tadeusz Szymański', *Medical Review*, Cracow, 1971.

—Henryk Świebocki, 'Obwód oświęcimski ZWZ/AK w akcji niesienia pomocy więźniom KL Auschwitz', *Studia Historyczne*, No. 4, Cracow, 1972.

—Michał Tokarzewski-Karaszewicz, 'Jak powstała Armia Krajowa', *Zeszyty Historyczne*, No. 6, Paris, 1964.

—Jan Trombaczewski, 'Ostatnia droga', *Auschwitz note-books*, No. 5, 1961.

—Anna Tytoniak, 'Jesień 1942 roku w szpitalu kobiecym w Brzezince', *Medical Review*, Cracow, 1968.

—Jožica Veble, *Preživela sem Taborišče Smrti*, Ljubljana, 1960.

—Rudolf Vrba and Alan Bestic, *Factory of Death*, London, 1964.

—Zygmunt Walter-Janke, *Podziemny Śląsk*, Warsaw, 1968.

W Armii Krajowej w Łodzi i na Śląsku, Warsaw, 1969.

—Leon Wanat, *Apel więźniów Pawiaka*, Warsaw, 1969. *Za murami Pawiaka*, V Ed., Warsaw, 1972.

—*Warszawa lat wojny i okupacji*, Zeszyt 1, Warsaw, 1971.

—Georges Wellers, *De Drancy à Auschwitz*, Paris, 1946.

—Leon W. Wells, *Ein Sohn Hiobs*, Munich, 1963.

—Jacek Wilczur, *Krzyż Skandynawów*, Poznań, 1968.

—Otto Wolken, 'Komentarz do statystyki chorych i zmarłych w obozie–"kwarantannie" w Brzezince za okres od 20.9.1943 do 1.11.1944' (translation from German), *Medical Review*, Cracow, 1965.
'Oswobodzenie obozu koncentracyjnego Oświęcim-Brzezinka' (translation from German), *Medical Review*, Cracow, 1966.
'Z zagadnień losu Żydów w Oświęcimiu' (translation from German), *Medical Review*, Cracow, 1964.

—Jan Wolny, 'O organizowaniu pomocy lekarsko-sanitarnej w obozie kobiecym w Brzezince', *Medical Review*, Cracow, 1965.

—Halina Wróbel, 'Likwidacja obozu koncentracyjnego Oświęcim-Brzezinka', *Auschwitz note-books*, No. 6, 1962.

—*Wspomnienia więźniów Pawiaka*, Warsaw, 1964.

—*Wśród koszmarnej zbrodni*, manuscripts of members of the *Sonderkommando*, *Auschwitz note-books*, (special issue II), 1971.

—Jan Zaborowski, preface to the book by T. Sobański, *Ucieczki Oświęcimskie*, 2nd ed., Warsaw, 1969.

—Ryszard Zieliński, 'Historia napisana przez życie', *Za i przeciw*, No. 15, Poland, 1972.

—Anna Ziemba, 'Geflügelfarm Harmense', *Auschwitz note-books*, No. 11, 1969.
'Podobóz Rajsko', *Auschwitz note-books*, No. 9, 1965.

—Lech Życki, 'Ucieczka skazanych', *Chłopska Droga*, No. 18–27, Poland, 1959.

III. PERIODICALS AND RESEARCH AIDS

1. Periodicals

—*Archeion* (occasional), periodical devoted to archival questions, Warsaw.

—*Biuletyn Głównej Komisji Badania Zbrodni Hitlerowskich w Polsce* (monthly), Warsaw.

—*Biuletyn Informacyjny* (weekly), underground newspaper, Warsaw.

—*Biuletyn Informacyjny* (monthly), Comité International d'Auschwitz, Warsaw.

—*Chłopska Droga* (weekly), Warsaw.

—*Dziennik Związkowy (Zgoda)* (daily), Chicago.

—*Gazeta Krakowska* (daily), Cracow.

—*Głos Nauczycielski* (weekly), Warsaw.

—*History of the Second World War* (weekly), London.

—*Kierunki* (weekly), Warsaw-Cracow.

—*Kultura* (monthly), Paris.

—*The Listener* (weekly), London.

—*Muzea Walki* (annual), Warsaw.

—*Na antenie* (monthly), Munich.

—*Najnowsze Dzieje Polski* (quarterly), Warsaw.

—*Nowy Świat* (daily), New York.

—*Piechota* (quarterly), London.

—*Polish Fortnightly Review*, Polish Ministry of Information, London.

—*Polityka* (weekly), Warsaw.

—*Polska Żyje* (fortnightly), underground newspaper, Warsaw.

—*Prosto z Mostu* (weekly), Warsaw.

—*Przegląd Geodezyjny* (monthly), Warsaw.

—*Przegląd Historyczny* (monthly), Warsaw.

—*Przegląd Kawalerii i Broni Pancernej* (quarterly), London.

—*Przegląd Lekarski* (monthly), Cracow.

—*Studia Historyczne* (quarterly), Cracow.

—*Tygodnik Demokratyczny* (weekly), Cracow.

—*Tygodnik Powszechny* (weekly), Cracow.

—*Wiadomości* (weekly), London.

—*Więź* (monthly), Warsaw.

—*Wojskowy Przegląd Historyczny* (quarterly), Warsaw.

—*Wrocławski Tygodnik Katolicki* (weekly), Wrocław.

—*Za i przeciw* (monthly), Warsaw.

—*Za woność i lud* (weekly), Warsaw.

—*Zeszyty, Historyczne* (annual), Paris.

—*Zeszyty Majdanka* (occasional), Lublin.

—*Zeszyty Naukowe* (quarterly), Katowice.

—*Zeszyty Oświęcimskie* (annual), Auschwitz.

—*Znak* (monthly), Cracow.

—*Życie Warszawy* (daily), Warsaw.

2. Research aids

—*International Tracing Service*, Arolsen, Operations Report, 1970.

—Adam Kaczkowski, *Auschwitz-Birkenau* (album of photographs), Auschwitz.

—Jerzy Lukowski, *Bibliografia obozu koncentracyjnego Oświęcim-Brzezinka*, Vol. I-V, Warsaw, 1968–70.

—*Oświęcim-Birkenau* (album of photographs), Warsaw, 1964.

—*Zbrodnie hitlerowskie w Polsce* (album of photographs), Warsaw.

Place and Name Index

The camp numbers of prisoners of Auschwitz or its sub-camps are given after their names. Empty brackets indicate that the person was a prisoner but that it has not been possible to establish his or her number.

Abada, Roger (45157) 187, 188, 195, 269
Adamczyk, Stanisław (14095) 281
Agrestowski, Jan (74545) 244
Akkerman, Hendricus (   ) 280
Aleksander, Ernö (A13642) 280
Aleksey (   ) 191
Alsace 154
Alwernia 171
Ambros, Otto 83
Ambroziewicz, Jerzy 271
Amsterdam 5, 181
Anders, Władysław 267
André (   ) 184
Andrzejewski, Antoni (   ) 286
Andrysiak, Kazimierz (89) 285
Apostoł-Staniszewska, Jadwiga 278
Arolsen 4, 7
Artemenko, Pavel 192
Augustyn, Bronisław (87440) 280
Augustyniak, Józef (150161) 284
Aumeier, Hans 102, 106, 141, 150, 152, 269
Austria 183, 194, 199, 224

Babice 45
Bach-Żelewski, Erich von dem 12, 17, 43
Baer, Richard 150, 231, 233, 236, 270
Balkans 217
Balke, Arthur (3) 59, 60, 70, 193
Baltic 67
Balzar, Franciszek (969) 213, 284, 285
Baltosiński (   ) 63
Banasiuk, Teofil (   ) 276
Baranov, Alexander (   ) 190
Barania Góra 242
Baraś, Józef (564) 163, 164, 273
Barcz, Wojciech (754) 276, 277
Barlicki, Norbert (   ) 40, 41, 62, 75, 76, 196, 224
Barcikowski, Józef (66750) 161, 202, 239, 242
Bartosiewicz, Henryk (9406) 41, 42, 72, 73, 75, 76, 96, 97, 109, 116, 117, 120, 123, 128, 140, 144, 157, 165, 166, 178, 189, 190, 212, 213, 214, 215,

216, 226, 235, 268, 284, 285
Bas, Ludwik (3468) 276
Batko, Marian (11785) 65, 265
Batkowski, Marian (   ) 276
Baum, Bruno (118359) 193, 200, 252, 269
Bavaria 92, 234, 269
Beerová, Vlasta (   ) 131
Belgium 36, 84, 129, 186, 280
Bełżec 32
Bendera, Eugeniusz (8502) 102
Benek, see Świerczyna 254
Beranowski, Jiři (20940) 278
Berdichev 181
Bereziuk, Irena (6894) 279
Bergen-Belsen 218
Berlin 4, 31, 86, 92, 101, 106, 109, 177, 185, 208, 209, 211, 217, 218, 219, 229, 234, 238, 244, 260, 263
Beskid Mountains 159, 192, 238, 253
Białówna, Irena (43117) 278, 279
Bielecki, Stefan (12692) 64, 76, 101, 102, 172, 174
Bielsko (Bielsko-Biała) 45, 206, 208, 253, 258, 272
Bieruń 205
Bierut, Władysław 268
Biesgen, Fritz (Mateczka) (4) 183
Bilan, Vladimir 206
Bilczewski, Wiktor (   ) 282
Biliński, Tadeusz (420) 282
Binder, Anne (   ) 129
Birkenau, passim
Biskup, Władysław (74501) 244
Black Sea 67
Blech, Ivonne (   ) 129
Bliżyn 231
Block, Sigismund (B3691) 280
'Bloody Alojs' (   ) 20
Bobek, Antoni (   ) 282
Bobkov (   ) 192
Bobrzecka, Maria (Marta) 155, 156
Bochnia 172
Bock, Hans (5) 37, 49, 51, 56, 66, 119, 135, 167, 183, 186, 222
Bock, Karol (   ) 62
Bock, Manfred (32861) 149, 281

Subject Index

OSLO

Norway

STOCKHOLM

NORTH SEA

Denmark

COPENHAGEN

BALTIC SEA

SWEDEN

L

Li

Gdansk

I.

G. BRITAIN

LONDON

AMSTERDAM

Neuengamme   Ravensbrück

Sachsenhausen   Oranienburg

BERLIN

Wannsee

Poznań

WARS

2.

Brussels

3

Rhine

Weimar

Buchenwald

Dresden

Sonnenstein

Gross-Rosen

Cracow

Auschwitz

Compiègne

4

PARIS

Loire

Seine

Yonne

Flossenburg

PRAGUE

P O L

L

Oder

Vistula

G E R M A N Y

5

Brno

Slovakia

F R A N C E

Dachau

Mauthausen

BERN

6

Murnau

VIENNA

Klagenfurt

BUDAPEST

H U N G

Danube

Toulouse

St. Cyprien

Spain

Po

I

t

a

l

y

Yugoslavia

BELGRADE

ROME

ADRIATIC SEA

TIRANA

7.

M E D I T E R R A N E A

LEGEND

1. Eire
2. Holland
3. Belgium
4. Luxemburg
5. German Protectorate

6. Switzerland
7. Albania
8. Lebanon
9. Palestine
10. Transjordan

..... Ribbentrop–Molotov Line &
Demarcation Line in France

SCALE

0   100   200   30

Designed by S. Gruca

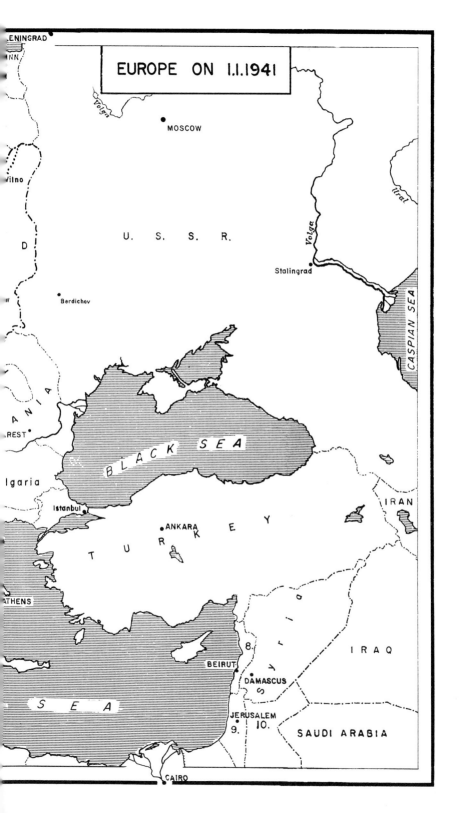

EUROPE ON 1.1.1941